Jim Jarvie's forty-year career began as a Commissioned Officer for HM Customs and Excise in 1973. Within a short time, he was promoted to the front- line operational and intelligence team, the Deltas, who investigated and prosecuted major drug trafficking crime groups.

His job, his "targets", were cannabis smugglers. He covered UK ports and airports, carrying out surveillance, collecting evidence and making arrests. He worked closely with overseas Drug Enforcement Agencies including Germany, Italy, the USA and Canada. The pursuit of drug suppliers took him to Kenya seeking evidence of the Mafia's illegal acquisitions and Thailand, to track the source of cannabis.

Howard Marks, the infamous "Mr Nice" was a target. A mafia man, Francesco Di Carlo, aka "Frankie the Strangler", was another. Di Carlo was part of the Italian "family"; "The Bankers of the Costra Nova."

The self-titled "Godfather of British Crime", Freddie Forman, (a fixer for the notorious Richardson gang) went on the run after a colleague of Jim's was shot dead on a London street. Jim was part of the murderer's arrest team, pinning the armed assailant to the floor until help arrived. For this act Jim received a Queen's Bravery Award.

A secondment to Scotland Yard was followed by posting in Portugal then Brazil as a Drugs Liaison Officer, tracking, intercepting and seizing drug shipments.

Jim spent three years in Brussels co-ordinating the setting up of Custom's locations and logistics throughout the EU.

Back in the UK he was promoted to become Head of Operations for the UK Border Force (Central England) with a £20 million plus budget. He headed teams tasked with the investigation and prosecution of major drug and firearms importations, money laundering, counterfeit offences, immigration crime and the growing diversity of frontier fraud.

Jim's career had its quieter moments but apathy played no part. Staying ahead of the game was paramount no more so than when villains would risk all for profit, giving no mercy to tenacious Customs Officers. Jim was awarded an OBE in 2012.

JIM JARVIE

"TRAPPER"

My Life in UK Customs

Written with Michael Sellers

ACKNOWLEDGEMENTS:
Throughout my forty-year career as an investigator, I have been privileged to have worked with so many professional and dedicated colleagues. I would particularly like to thank Terry Byrne, Nick Baker, Chris Hardwick, George Atkinson and Peter Finch who have helped jog my memory about the numerous cases we worked on.
My wife and soulmate, Pauline, has been at my side for almost all of my working life. My sons Alex, Alistair, Jimmy and my stepson Robert, never complained when work prevented me from attending so many of their school activities. I cannot thank them enough.   JJ.

MY LIFE IN UK CUSTOMS

CHAPTERS:

CHAPTER 1
WELCOME TO DRUGS D

'You're too tall, Jarvie,' my boss barked. 'They're looking for nondescript persons who can blend into the background.'

Three inches over six feet was tall in those days and the suggestion that my appearance was above standard issue was, perhaps, a sort of compliment.

I wasn't put off, I applied, and weeks later arrived at Custom's Investigation Division Headquarters in New Fetter Lane, London, for a vetting process.

Nondescript I must have been. I got the job.

On January 17th 1977, I was told by my new bosses, Roy Brisley, a Customs Senior Investigation Officer and Nick Baker, a Higher Investigation Officer, to climb into the back of a blue, unmarked, security van, used mostly for transporting illegal drugs to and from Court.

I did so willingly. It was my first day as an Investigation Officer. I was part of "Drugs D" team with a call sign of India Delta 8.

We were heading from our offices in New Fetter Lane to Willesden Crown Court in North London where drug couriers were being tried for importing Thai sticks through Heathrow Airport.

Thai sticks are the flowering tops and leaves of a very potent type of cannabis. The THC (tetrahydrocannabinol) level is very high and therefore worth a lot more money than just herbal cannabis.

The eight-mile journey seemed to take forever. There were no seats so I sat bouncing up and down at every pothole we drove over. The pong of herbal cannabis was quite mellow as I climbed in, grew in intensity with each passing mile.

I started feeling heady, the first sign, I thought, of experiencing a "high". If so, it would my first "high" at least my first on illegal drugs.

Loud squeaks, bangs and thuds blotted out all other sounds. The metal barrier that separated me from my colleagues in the front seats prevented any conversation and my only clue to a world going on outside was through fleeting images that flashed across the barred rear windows.,

We came to a stop. Roy and Nick got out, locked their doors and shouted to me, 'This is your first job as an investigator. Try and get out of the security van.'

'What?' I yelled.

And they walked away.

What am I doing here I thought? One minute a cosy VAT Customs job in Norwich and the next locked in a cramped van stinking of drugs.

It took only seconds for me to realise that without the type of equipment the Fire Brigade uses for cutting injured people out of crashed cars there was no way I could break out of the van. I might have made a few twists and dents with a wrench and sledge hammer but not much more. It was not called a security van for nothing. It was tricky to get in and just as tricky to get out.

I heard the laughter before I heard the footsteps.

A fist hit the body work, a key was inserted, a handle turned and the back door sprung open.

Two faces wide with laughter bore down on me.

'Welcome to Drugs D, Jarvie.'

It was a packed day.

That morning I had turned up in the staff selection office with three of my colleagues from the Norwich Customs and Excise office. Tim Manhire, Peter Finch and John Holton. Tim went on to be a drugs liaison officer in New York and Jamaica. He sadly died in 2015 from a heart attack after successfully battling against a protracted kidney illness.

Peter Finch and I are still friends, meeting up on a regular basis. Our careers ran in parallel and we worked together many times over the years.

We sat in the staff selection and eventually a lady with a clipboard told me I would be going on a VAT investigation team because of my experience as a salesman.

'I've never been a salesman,' I said.

She looked closely at her paperwork and said,' Oh, no, that's not you. It's Peter Finch. Jim Jarvie. Here we are. Jarvie. You're on Drugs D.'

When I arrived at the Delta Team office on the first floor I was welcomed by Roy Brisley (Delta1) who introduced me to Nick Baker, who would be a close friend for forty years.

I shook hands with the rest of the team. John Dickerson was Delta 2 and Mike Chester Delta 3. Bruce Letheren was Delta 4, Mike Farrand Delta 5, Mike Stevenson Delta 6, Ray Smith was Delta 7. Last one in was Delta 8; me.

Delta was an Investigation Division with a brief to track cannabis imports from Asia, identify the smugglers, arrest them and instigate Court proceedings.

There were other divisions that covered drugs; Bravo/ Charlie (Cannabis Targets), Kilo (Cannabis from Morocco), Romero and Sierras (Cocaine), Lima (Heroin), Foxtrot and Golf (Heroin) and November (Cocaine). Other teams embraced areas that included Intelligence, Postal smuggling, VAT and Maritime.

There was a total of two hundred or so staff, male and female, working across the teams,

Our office was just off Fleet Street fairly close to the old Daily Mirror building. It was a six-storey building with about 120 staff spread over the six floors.

The building was owned by Robert Maxwell, the British media tycoon and one-time Member of Parliament. He built an extensive publishing empire including the Daily Mirror, ending up misappropriating the Mirror Group pension fund. It was one of the three buildings in London used by the Investigation division.

Senior Management, the Drugs Teams and two non-VAT teams were based there. There was also a Custom House at 6-8 Bouverie Street opposite the old Daily Mail building and in Atlantic House in Holborn opposite Smithfield Market. There were Investigation Offices in Manchester, Leeds, Bristol and Glasgow and Birmingham.

Our office had no notice on the door, nothing in view that suggested what went on inside. All staff were managed by the Chief Investigation Officer, Douglas Jordan who was to retire at the end of 1977 to become The Customs Commissioner in Hong Kong. Peter Cutting took over.

On paper, my job was an Executive Officer. My immediate boss was Bruce Letheren, a Higher Executive Officer, who had come from the uniformed side of Customs and had worked at Heathrow Airport, Harwich and the land boundary between the North and the South of Ireland. There was a physical boundary in those days. Roy Brisley was the Team Leader.

There was a sharp learning curve on my day at Willesden Court. It was the first time I had been into a "Crown" court so everything was new. I sat with the prosecution team watching my new colleagues giving evidence. At the end of the trial the two smugglers were found guilty and were sentenced to six years in prison.

I have never smoked so when the "herbal" cigarettes were passed around at a party I always declined and bought myself another pint of beer. So, cannabis in all its forms was new to me. Pot, dope, marijuana, hashish, reefers and other variations were simply names of illegal drugs.

Thai sticks were a variation. Made from high quality marijuana buds, the flowering part of the plant, it is wrapped around a stick of bamboo. Packed this way a large number could be carried in a suitcase, hidden in enclosed secret compartments at the top and bottom. Thai cannabis was readily available in the 70's but later replaced by cheaper sources.

The drug couriers flew from Bangkok to Paris and then on to Geneva before flying on to London. There were very few checks at Geneva Airport. In those days the Swiss authorities saw little risk of illegal imports on a flight from Paris.

A lot of couriers had discovered this route and presumably had some success even though UK customs were constantly watching out for them. At Heathrow, Immigration teams would scan passports for a Thai visa. Once spotted the details were passed to uniformed Customs officer and the passport owner was shadowed through to the Green Channel (Nothing to Declare). As they walked through, they would be stopped. (The Red Channel was used when something had to be declared).

When someone enters the "Nothing to Declare" Channel it provides evidence that states no contraband is being carried. So, if they are carrying something illegal, they have already committed an offence by entering the Green Channel. That is why we usually wait for the suspect to recover their luggage from the carousel and claim ownership.

Some would argue that they were heading for the Red Channel or they were carrying a suitcase for another person, suggesting that they were far from happy about the arrangement.

Those early days were long. A six o'clock start, getting home at 8 or 9 in the evening was the norm. I just wanted to have a quick pint, grab something to eat then sleep. I had very little social life and had difficulty planning leisure activities.

For some reason I wasn't sent on a year's training course. Although the tasks I carried out were limited to house searches, being second officer on an interview and transporting evidence, it was training on the job. I listened and observed. Hints from colleagues were plentiful as were stories of past cases. My three years in Norwich as a Customs and Excise Executive Officer helped only in relation to detail. You had to get it right. If you didn't, your assignment, small or large, would fall apart.

Having moved from Norfolk I stayed with a cousin Annie from Scotland who had a house in West Wickham in Kent for a few days and then a few days with a colleague who had also transferred from Norwich. Eventually I rented a spare room in one of our colleague's houses in South Croydon.

I went back home to Stamford on the odd occasion, playing football when I could but any thoughts of a foot-balling career diminished every time I ran on to the pitch. I blamed lack of training time!

CHAPTER 2
COLLECTING TAXES; NORWICH

Geoffrey Chaucer's job as "Comptroller of the customs for the port of London" in 1374 did not influence my decision to apply for a job at Customs and Excise in Norwich. Neither was it the fact that King Edward III granted him "a gallon of wine daily for the rest of his life" for his efforts. Nor was it that I was poetically moved by his opening line of The Canterbury Tales; "Whan that Aprill with his shoures soote. The droghte of March hath perced to the roote,".

It was the result of my mother's insistence that I filled my newly acquired "unemployed days" with useful endeavour.

'You're not sitting around the house all day.'

My three years as a labourer turned tunneller for a company building and laying giant concrete rings to feed a dam in nearby Rutland had come to an end. My mother, a forceful and energetic lady who had never been without work since leaving school aged 14, could not stand by and watch one of her two son's fritter away days without application. Certainly not a fit and able son in his early twenties. I was detailed to paint my grandmother's kitchen.

My grandmother lived in a small council house six miles from us in Empingham and she needed to brighten up her kitchen. I duly arrived in my pride and joy, a "B" registered white MGB Roadster, 1964, paid for by my earnings as a tunneller. It was not, I admit, your average painter and decorator work vehicle.

I prepared the room and myself for the task. A brush was selected and paint tin opened. As I lifted the tin a newspaper page came with it, stuck to the bottom from a recent spill. As I pulled the paper (The Daily Mail) away I spotted an advert in Situations Vacant. The wording was large and clear; "Would you like to be a Customs Officer?"

I kept the advert aside and as I painted the prospect seemed more and more interesting. I knew nobody who had worked for Customs and Excise (I didn't really know what they were all about) it interested me enough to put in an application to join the Civil Service stating that my preference would be to join Customs followed by Immigration.

A few months later, long after my short-lived painting career was over, I was summoned to a Civil Service Recruitment Office in Nottingham, less than 30 miles from Stamford. I had to sit in front of a panel of 3 Civil Servants who questioned me on my work history and asked hypothetical scenarios and projects to see how I would respond and which projects I would prefer to continue with. The choices were the Channel Tunnel, Concorde and London's third airport.

I had to explain what I chose and why I chose it. I think they were looking for the ability to present a structured argument.

In 1973 I had a letter of appointment. I was to start in an office known as the "Harwich Collection", a term that goes back 700 years or more as does a lot of terminology used in the department. (Perhaps Chaucer had something to do with it). The work "Collection" means a "Region". Harwich Collection covered Port Harwich, Great Yarmouth, Norwich Airport and the VAT Offices in Ipswich and Norwich.

No one in my family was quite sure what Customs and Excise did so, although my parents were pleased about my appointment, they were perplexed at what I would be doing. At the time, so was I. I'm certain though that they were relieved I had a proper job with security and a pension rather than cashing in on another "tunnel" job.

Value Added Tax was a consumption tax levied in the United Kingdom by the national government. It was the third-largest source of government revenue, after income tax and National Insurance. It was administered and collected by HM Revenue and Customs. It replaced Purchase Tax.

With others I joined the VAT Office in Norwich. We were part of a recruitment drive to process the new and additional demands of the new taxation system.

It was an eye-opener for me. I had previously thought that "Customs" was limited to checking in duties at an airport.

The Customs and Excise Department operated under the Her Majesty's Treasury, sometimes referred to as the Exchequer, or more informally the Treasury. (It is the British government department responsible for developing and executing the government's public finance policy and economic policy.)

The Customs and Excise was managed by a Board.

In the Harwich Collection where I worked there was a Collector, two Deputy Collectors. Six Assistant Collectors and each office would have Surveyors who were team leaders. There were Higher Executive Officers and Executive Officers.

My Commission that I received on 26th September 1974 on completion of my probation period in Norwich. *"To all whom these presents shall come greeting We the Commissioners of Her Majesty's Customs and Excise pursuant to the powers in that behalf invested in us do hereby appoint James Frederick Jarvie to be an Officer of Customs and Excise and to be employed on any duty or service which we may, from time to time, direct and approve with full power and authority to do and perform all such matters and things as are by any Act of Parliament enforced relating to the Revenues of Customs and Excise or any other matter assigned to the Commissioners of Customs and Excise directed or authorised to be done and performed by an officer of Customs and Excise and to enforce all laws, regulations, penalties and forfeitures as directed by the Commissioners of Her Majesty's Customs and Excise in all which premises he is to proceed in such manner as the law directs hereby praying and requiring all and every constable and members of Her Majesty's armed forces or coast guard and all others it may concern to be aiding and assisting him in all things that becometh said, James Frederick Jarvie to observe and obey all orders, instructions and directions that he hath received and shall from time to time receive from the said Commissioners and to hold the office to which he is hereby appointed during the pleasure of the said Commissioners. In witness thereof I the undersigned being one of the Commissioners of Her Majesty's Customs and Excise have here unto set my hand and seal at Kingsbeam House London this 26th day of September 1974. Signed by Commissioner."*
I was appointed as an Executive Officer to The Harwich Collection based in Norwich.

CHAPTER 3
CHILDHOOD

Twenty-two years before committing myself to "observe and obey all orders, instructions and directions" I was born in a small market town in Lincolnshire, a county in the east of England a hundred miles north of London with a population of three quarters of a million, with my town making up 15 thousand.
My father was born in Kilsyth, a small mining town in Scotland, roughly halfway between Glasgow and Stirling. He was one of seven brothers and sisters. His father, who died young, was a coal miner. He died when my father was 14, the age he left school to work and provide money for the family. He was an apprentice iron-moulder, pouring molten iron into moulds - a difficult and dangerous environment to work in handling products over 1500 degrees centigrade.

Towards the end of WW2, he was conscripted into the Army and sent to North Africa and Gibraltar guarding prisoners of war.

After the war he carried on his apprenticeship.

At one point he was approached by a Henry McNair who was going to open a foundry in Stamford in Lincolnshire. McNair wanted my father and others to move down country to get the foundry started.

Initially not enthusiastic, the prospect of higher wages seduced him. So, he and twenty others moved South, some single, some with families. In Stamford they created their own Scottish community.

They all started working in the factory in Ryhall two miles north of Stamford making iron grates and fire baskets using the same methods as the Scottish foundry.

My father took lodgings along with other single men. At a dance in Stamford Hospital, he met my mum. She was the daughter of a farm worker near Cromer in Norfolk. Although as a farm worker, my mum's father, would not have been called up for the war but he volunteered for the RAF and was sent to Burma to fight behind the lines of the Japanese invasion force. He wasn't captured but he returned home suffering from Malaria and a troubled mind. He became withdrawn, refusing to take part in family events. In 1966 he died aged 52 when I was 13. My great regret was that I was too young to ask him questions about his fighting time.

Mum had a sister and two brothers.

My mum started work as an auxiliary nurse before marrying my father in 1952. Mum was 18, Dad 22. They were married for over 60 years.

I was born in Nov 1952 and my brother Ian, 2 years later.

Childhood for my brother and I was what we called normal; discipline at school a real chore, your mind focused on break-time and playing football at every opportunity. Like the friends I had, we drifted through the years ending up as teenagers with no direction in life. There was no real view of the outside world.

There appeared to be only two choices; more schooling or get an apprenticeship at the local engineering company, Blackstones, who made diesel engines which had been operating for a century or more.

I attended a secondary modern school although we had a grammar school in the town which attracted the 25% of those who passed the 11 plus. There were other schools, all fee paying, beyond the pocket of the Jarvie family.

There was a youth club associated with the church but most of my time was playing football with my mates in the winter and cricket in the summer. In the holidays and weekends, we would play non-stop football on our local sports field. We also had cycles and sometimes, in late summer, I helped a farmer to stack bales of straw. We didn't get paid for it but it was fun.

I played for the local adult's football team when I was 14 and had trials for Leicester City and Peterborough United. Unfortunately, I was not destined to be the next George Best.

The exams I was taking were CSEs, the forerunner of GCSEs, and were probably not deemed important in the academic world. I left Exeter Secondary Modern School in Stamford at fifteen. The school was named after the Marquis of Exeter, Lord Burghley of Burghley House near Stamford. Most of my mates had joined the local engineering company or worked on a building site.

My mum, who was a very resilient and hard-working lady, had left school at fourteen, starting her working life as a nurse. When we were born, she worked at night as a care assistant in an old people's home with 70 residents. Through hard work and dedication, she ended up as a well thought of Matron. She was the driving force of our family. It was she who decided to buy a house in 1962 as opposed to renting or living in a tied cottage belonging to the foundry where my father worked.

Both my mother and father worked incredibly hard but we were not well off. My mum was never out of work, for a year doing night-shifts in Blackstone's factory working on the assembly line that handled electrical components. It was obviously light work compared to other departments but it ensured she was at home when we went to bed and was there when we woke up for school.

She never failed to give us breakfast in the morning and supper at night.

Although my father was well paid my mother's income allowed them a few extras such as the motorcar. I have great memories of our first car an Austin 1100 and Ian and I would eagerly be passengers on even the shortest journey.

She was not happy I was leaving school without any qualifications and when she learned about a GCSE O level course at Grantham Technical College, she decided that was a good approach for me. She drove me there and accompanied me at a meeting with the Principal, Mr Dack. She did most of the talking explaining that it was my wish to enrol on a GCSE Course.

'I'm sorry, Mrs Jarvie, the course has already been signed up for. There are no spaces.'

My mum sat back in her chair. 'I'm sorry, Mr Dack, but I'm not leaving this office until my son has been accepted on the course.'

I was totally crimson at this stage but give my mum her due, she stuck to her guns and got me on the course. This lasted two years and it was a good time for me. There was a great atmosphere, no uniform and relaxed teachers. On Wednesdays we had a lesson called liberal studies. A broad term as it turned out for having some skills as a footballer, I was chosen for the College team managed by one of the teachers, Mr Noon.

The team would travel around other colleges and RAF stations. As a sixteen-year-old I played against RAF Cranwell recruits and at the end of the game instead of being given water and oranges the stewards, wearing white jackets, arrived with pies and chips and cups of tea. It had all the style of a silver service. Our mouths were wide open having that sort of reception. We won 4-3. By then I was 6'3 and quite lanky, playing on the left wing which was not a natural position for me. The following years I was picked as centre-half, part of the defence.

After I had taken my O-Levels I had to decide what my next move would be. The most obvious thing for me to do was to stay at the college and do A levels. This I did and signed up for another two years, helped by a grant from the local authorities (about £180 a year) which helped with living costs. I was then approaching 19 years old and still living at home.

At 7.30am a bus picked a few of us from Stamford, taking us the twenty miles to Grantham. We arrived back at 5pm.

I got 2 A levels in 1972 when I was 20.

I was uncertain if I should try to get a place at university or look around in the job market. I was offered places to study geography at Strathclyde University and at Queens in Belfast but failed to follow up.

During the summer holidays with my best friend Paul Warrington, who I had known since I was nine, we saw a factory being built on the outskirts of Stamford. When finished, it would build concrete rings for tunnels designed to take water from three rivers to dam a valley in nearby Rutland. This would provide a reservoir for the West and East Midlands.

Paul and I approached the manager of the factory site and asked for jobs. (We did not mention it would only be for the summer).

We were taken on. The factory was well-advanced when they started manufacturing the pre-stressed concrete segments. A large drill-like machine called a "mole" would remove a meter of soil and rock and a concrete segment would be wedged in to make it water-tight.

We were there for three or four weeks making the concrete segments. The money was quite a spike in income from a school grant.

At that age having money in your pocket was a fantastic feeling. My first wage was £60 in cash. I thought I'd died and gone to heaven having that amount of money.

As the summer grew to a close, Paul and I were approached to work on the tunnel project near Tinwell, close to where I was living and close to the factory. It had its attractions, more money and outside of a factory environment. We both said yes, putting further education on hold.

We started off doing general labour work around the site. The shaft they were digging was deep and 35 meters across. As the concrete rings were put in place liquid concrete was poured around the sides to make it secure.

Any promotion on a tunnelling project takes you down, not up. After working in the factory, I became a "tea boy" whose responsibility went beyond tea. A group of Irish labourers would come up for the week bringing with them steaks and onions which I would cook for lunch. As the work progressed to night as well as day-shifts the "lunch" break stayed the same. There is nothing like steak and onions cooked fresh at three o'clock in the morning.

I used to slice a little off each steak to supplement my cheese sandwiches. My explanation to the questioning foreman on the average size was the steaks shrank a little while being cooked, even more if it hung around waiting for the diners to arrive.

A "banksman" is someone who stands at the top of the shaft guiding the crane down to scoop up all the fallen soil. I did this for 6 months before my 4 months as a "pit bottom man", someone at the bottom of the shaft. I would hook up the container that would be lifted from the bottom of the dig.

I was at the bottom of the 120ft deep shaft as they broke through to start the tunnel a JCB digger had to be lifted by a crane out of the shaft. It was such a precarious lift that I was told to put my safety helmet on. How that would have helped if a few ton of machinery came crashing down I don't know.

We then moved on to other shafts at Wansford on the River Nene and Empingham on the edge of the reservoir.

I spent about nine months working on the shaft project.

There were some funny moments. A crane driver, Tommy Long, a big lad who lived on site in a caravan that was small and round with stabilising legs. One day we lifted up the legs. The laughs came when Tommy got into it and it started to roll down a gentle slope. It did grind to a halt before damage was done.

We chose the wrong day to be cheeky to Tommy. We were in the large bucket hanging from Tommy's crane as we carried out work at the top of the shaft.

As we dangled over the shaft, Tommy's crane lifted us up to the top of the jib where he released the brake sending us hurtling down 130 feet before he stopped it. He knew exactly what he was doing by gauging the distance from the crane cable. By the time he brought us up we were both ashen faced. It was funny afterwards but we knew that a lesson was learned. Don't take the mickey out of someone who has your life in their hands.

I did about two years tunnelling and ended up working 4 and a half miles underground at the face of the tunnel itself. We would go down at 7 in the morning and come back up at half five in the evening. It was summer and everyone on terra firma had been enjoying the sunshine. It was about that time I decided I had better get a real job with a future.

I still had no clear idea of a career direction. I had put aside the idea of going to university.

Paul became an antiques dealer with a shop in Stamford for many years. He married Ann with a daughter Charlotte but much later got divorced and remarried. He is still involved in antiques.

17

It was at this time I was dragooned into painting my grand-mother's kitchen.

CHAPTER 4
"WE WILL DISTRAIN ON YOUR GOODS AND CHATTELS."

When I first moved to Norwich, I stayed at The Arrow Guest House, run by a Mr and Mrs Arrow in Britannia Road, close to Norwich Prison. There were three other Customs and Excise employees staying there. I booked in on the Sunday, spending the evening speculating on what the next twenty-four hours would bring.

Bright and early on my first day I turned up at the office in Surrey Street and unknowingly parked in the Assistant Collector's parking place.

I was introduced to everyone, put on a team and set to work trying to understand the workings of what was, for most, a new way of being taxed and the seemingly endless amount of paperwork that went with it.

At the end of the day, I went to collect my car which had sticky paper stuck to the windscreen with the instructions; "Don't Park Here."

Alas, my flashy car lasted only a few months before the costs exhausted my Civil Service salary of £30 per week. Accommodation and living expenses had to be found. Fun and indulgencies were at weekends when I drove home to my parent's house, played football and went out with mates. It was then I discovered the real meaning of "skint". I waved goodbye to my beloved two-seater and replaced it with a four door, four-seater, run of the mill, bottom of the range, green Hillman Minx. Any street cred I had disappeared that day.

I spent 3 years in Norwich, mainly on VAT matters including educational visits to individuals and companies who had been captured by the VAT net. We would explain procedures, how to keep correct records and method and time of VAT payments.

After a year I was transferred to a job in the enforcement section which dealt with people who had failed to pay their VAT. There was less talking, less paperwork and would sometimes have an edge to proceedings which backed up the position of "Enforcement" Officer.

Most people did pay up but there was still a lot of confusion about VAT records and payment. If payment was not paid on time, I had to chase it.

My first move was a telephone call to the defaulter encouraging them to settle. If that failed, I would hand deliver demand letters. A knock on the door, an official standing on a door-step, often added weight to the process.

Refusals to pay would often lead to bailiffs being appointed. I would accompany a bailiff and enter the company premises telling them what they owed and failure to pay up would result in the seizure of goods and chattels. Items of value were listed with the view that should the VAT payment not be made these goods would be taken from the premises.

We had problems with a particular farmer. Farmers were allowed to claim back the VAT on all the business goods they had purchased such as tractors, planters, harvesters and so on. Some farmer's businesses ended up not paying any VAT at all. Some did end their financial year owing tax.

I had to drive into deepest Norfolk, find the narrow lane leading to the farm and turned into a courtyard to find the farmer holding a shotgun.

I told him that he owed Customs and Excise money and I was there to collect it.

'Pay us the money now,' I said. 'If not, we will distrain on your goods and chattels.'

'What does that mean?' he asked.

'We make a list of items you have on your premises and if you don't pay the bailiffs are entitled to come along and remove those items to be sold at a later date to pay off the debt.'

'You can put my wife on the list,' he joked.

With difficulty I resisted laughing and had to inform him his wife could not be on the list.

The farmer, like many in the early days of VAT hadn't grasped the detail and responsibilities attached to the new Tax. We were all on a learning curve. Although we never admitted it, my department did exercise a certain amount of leniency in the early days.

I did make one visit to chase up payment and was met by a chap who didn't look very well. It was a small printing company who owed a few hundred pounds. He apologised by saying he was ill with terminal cancer and he only had a few weeks to live. He produced letters from doctors and consultants.

I wasn't sure if I had the clout but I took the decision to file the case away and not take any action. It was a sobering encounter.

Our office was open plan on the second floor. The Surveyors (Team Leaders) had their own offices but the ten of us on the enforcement team worked in and around each other. This was made up of two Higher Executive Officers, four Executive Officers and four Assistant Officers.

There were never any risk assessments to any given job - no questions as to whether the people we were chasing might be dodgy or dangerous or even if they were known criminals. We would simply look up what records we had on the individual or company and act accordingly.

There were people who resented the new Tax and were disparaging about having to keep extra paperwork and being a de facto "collector" of tax for the government.

The vast majority did pay their VAT. Some were given the opportunity to pay by instalments and to discuss the matter with one of our officers.

On one occasion I had to take a demand letter to Lotus Cars in Hethel, Norwich. When Colin Chapman was owner of Lotus he was very close to Harold Wilson, the Prime Minister and it was thought that he was able to extend his credit in a way outside normal circumstances.

But the time came when I had to hand deliver the demand to Lotus Cars by placing in the safe keeping of one of the company directors. I was still driving my Hillman Minx. It was no Lotus Elan or Lotus Elite.

An impressive shingle drive and lovely limed avenue led to their imposing offices. Parked outside were a number of gleaming new and nearly new Lotus cars, presumably owned by employees. I brazenly parked my Hillman amongst them.

I went into reception and announced that I needed to see the Financial Director.

'Could you make an appointment,' she suggested. 'He's busy at the moment.'

'I'm from Customs and Excise,' I replied. 'I'm charged to deliver this letter so please ask him to come down and see me.'

I was shown into a beautiful oak panelled office with a fantastic antique table at one end. I recall the echo of my heavy footsteps across the wooden floor. The Financial Director then appeared.

I introduced myself and showed him my ID card saying, 'I've got a letter for your company from Her Majesty's Customs and Excise in relation to non-payment of VAT.'

He took the letter, opened it up and read it. 'We'll deal with this immediately,' he said.

And they did. It was probably an oversight by someone within the company.

Satisfied, I said goodbye hiding a smile as I climbed into my Hillman and holding my emotions back as I drove off. By the time I reached the end of the drive I was freely chuckling.

I reflected on being a normal lad from Lincolnshire delivering a letter to one of the most iconic companies in the UK.

Team Lotus competed in Formula One between 1958 and 1994, winning seven constructors' titles and six drivers' titles between 1963 and 1978. In 1960 Stirling Moss won the marque's first Grand Prix in Monaco driving a Lotus 18.

Most of my time was in enforcement but occasionally we were given an insight into the Excise operation which was the collection of taxes on wines, spirits and the like. I went to Reckitt and Colman's bonded warehouse in Norwich with a senior OCX (an officer of Customs and Excise). His name was George Butler, very long in the tooth and we were tasked to inspect casks of Sherry coming from Jerez in Spain.

'You've got to take the cork out of each cask,' said George, 'take a dip sample and have a taste to make sure its sherry and not water.'

'Why would it be water?' I asked.

'If they filled it with water, they could claim tax back as if it was sherry.'

I duly started dipping and tasting. After an hour and a half of dipping and sipping I realised I was getting rather tiddly.

I said to George, 'I'm getting a bit tiddly.'

'Ah, what you should do is when you dip and taste you spit it straight out.'

He just smiled as I told him he should have explained before I started. Another lesson learned. I was not really the worse for wear but George did drop me home when our working day had finished.

Although we were a VAT office, we did have a close relationship with the Investigation Unit that was based in Harwich. They investigated VAT fraud and prosecuted small illegal importations of drugs and tobacco into the Port of Harwich and Felixstowe. They would do this when specific importations or VAT cases were not taken on by the Investigation Division of Customs and Excise.

I was able to help our local investigation unit on a few of their cases and I got a good feel about that line of work. It was interesting and challenging. A bit cops and robbers but with real villains rather than those who had made genuine tax mistakes.

Departmental Weekly Orders was issued from our Headquarters in London identifying changes in legislation along with announcements on people retiring and any vacancy arising. In one they advertised posts in the Investigation Divisions based in London, Manchester, Bristol, Leeds and Glasgow. They dealt nationally and internationally with the importation of drugs, high levels of VAT fraud, tobacco smuggling, misrepresentation of goods and other frontier matters.

I applied even though I lacked (according to my boss) two essentials; being short and inconspicuous.

I was interviewed at HQ in New Fetter Lane.

Three people interviewed me, a Senior Chief Investigations Officer and two were Senior Investigation Officers.

They asked about my past and gave me a few "What if" scenarios. "What if you went on a VAT visit and a drawer was open and you can see an "off-record" VAT book. What would you do about it? Would you ignore it or try to get hold of it?"

I answered in the best way I could. 'As we had no powers of arrest or seizure, I would try to talk my way into grabbing hold of the record. If talking didn't work I would just grab it. I wouldn't let that one past me.'

They also asked about my willingness to do long hours in uncomfortable circumstances and about my ability and temperament in dealing with difficult people. How would I handle stroppy people? I think I answered that you had to be diplomatic, strong but reasonable and making clear you had the law behind you. I recalled my time as a youth working on the tunnel where you had to get on with all sorts of people with all sorts of temperament, some reasonable, even kind, others bolshie and aggressive.

I did well enough. I got the job.

CHAPTER 5
THROWN INTO THE DEEP END. THE JUJU MAN.

I had just got over the trauma of being locked in the security van on my first day and things were about to get even more exciting. My first boss was Senior Investigation Officer, Roy Brisley, was a tall, gangly man in his mid-fifties. A real character, an ex-high jumper at English County level. A very distinctive looking guy.

The first thing he did when we met for the first time was to try and sell me an Investigation Division tie and book a seat for me at the ID Annual Dinner in the March of 1977.

'You won't fit in unless you've got one of these ties,' he said.

He succeeded. I still have that tie with the colours of the Crown, Treasury, the Waterguard (the uniform side of Customs).

There are occasions, funerals and retirement parties where we all wear our ties.

In 1977 there had been an increase in the number of officers appointed to the Investigation Division and there was a backlog for those waiting for the three-week Basic Investigation Techniques (BITs). I didn't receive my training until 1978. Much of my skills were acquired, not in a classroom but out on the ground, learning from others. Roy Brisley, my SIO thought it would be good for me to visit Hull Docks to look at the arrivals of cargo vessels from West Africa, a source country for herbal cannabis.

A ferry from Holland, a transit country for drugs, arrived daily. One of our sniffer dogs and his handler were due to make a routine visit to the port. In those days Customs had only two sniffer dogs trained to sniff out cannabis. Years later dogs were trained to detect heroin, cocaine, tobacco and even bush meat (although I thought every dog would react to the smell of meat).

I stayed in a cheap hotel near the docks and the next day, at 05.30 met up with Jim and his golden Labrador, Brumbie. Jim was an ex-police dog handler who had transferred when the Customs started to use sniffer dogs. It was in February and there was a freezing cold north wind so I had to wear a departmental, lined anorak.

Despite the fact we had no specific objective we planned to look at vehicles coming off the ferries that had sailed the 12 hours or so from Holland to Hull. Hull is a passenger port on the Humber Estuary handling over 1 million passengers and over 10 million tonnes of traffic a year.

The first ferries from Rotterdam or Zeebrugge arrived at 06.00 in the morning.

As the vehicles disembarked and headed for the open road they slowed at Customs Control. We would walk past the queue of traffic waiting to go through Custom's Control relying on Brumbie to smell any give away odours of cannabis to indicate if there was anything untoward in a consignment.

When Brumbie reacted (by becoming more agitated) to a smell the vehicle was pulled out of the queue into a special Custom's channel where Customs Officers would have an in-depth look.

After the first ferry unloaded Jim and I discussed what to do until the next one arrived.

There was a Green Line Nigerian cargo ship in port called the Ahmadu Tijani. This ship was not on our suspect radar but over the years there had been many drugs seizures from ships arriving from Africa, Morocco and South Africa being deemed countries of risk for cannabis shipments.

The Ahmadu Tijani happened to be the first one we came across. We went around different sections, the crew's sleeping quarters on one deck, the bridge and looked at the various lockers around the ship. It was a medium sized cargo ship with a cargo of beans crewed by twenty.

As we passed a locker room, Brumbie reacted by scraping at the door, tail wagging excitedly. Inside the room, which was the size of a small garden shed, we found 300 kilos of cannabis in 10 hessian sacks, which in the 1970s, was a large seizure of drugs. It was worth at least half a million pounds.

As with many of the previous detections in cargo ships a member of the crew (the only people with access to these areas) would be involved. The drugs were often taken off a few kilos at a time and handed over to local dealers or those from nearby cities. We had no information whether they were planning to hand it over either at the Port of Hull or another port on its voyage. This type of vessel would call into other UK and European ports to offload and pick up cargo.

From the Docks Customs office, staffed by uniformed Customs staff, I rang my office in London and spoke to Roy Brisley on a land-line., our radio telephone had a limited range, 25 miles from London and only a few miles from the Hull office.

He told me to initiate a curfew on the boat using the available uniformed Customs staff. We would allow the officers off and on but the general crew's movements were restricted. Local customs staff and uniformed offices manned the scene, sealing off the gangplank.

Roy contacted our Leeds office and they were dispatched immediately to Hull. Six officers who I had never met before turned up. Mike Simms was the senior officer and he and his team took on the investigation.

It was very tense. The rest of the crew were unhappy having been at sea for a month. They just wanted to visit the local pubs and brothels and we were stopping them.

I stayed on in Hull to assist. Three of the crew that had access to the locker room were arrested and taken to Hull police station. Two seamen were arrested, one called Makindi and the other, Odine. The bosun was called Apappa. All three were Nigerians.

During the search of one of the cabins the uniformed Customs found something written in Yoruba, a Nigerian dialect and the translation by a Customs Officer, originally from Nigeria revealed it was a juju curse.

I conducted my very first interview under caution. Mike Simms and I interviewed Odine, one of the three suspects. I opened my very first notebook that had nothing of importance written in it. Until that day!

I took down name, date of birth, address, his position on the ship. He stated he was one of the deck hands.

Half way through the interview, Mike Simms asked Odine, 'Do you believe in God?'

He said, 'Yes, I believe in God.'

'Do you believe in the juju man?'

Odine's face dropped.

Mike pressed. 'Who's more important? God or the juju man?'

Odine then started to shake and roll his eyes as he lay prostrate on the cell floor.

Mike read out the juju verse. After he finished, he whispered to me, 'I'll go and get a doll and some pins.'

I said to Mike, 'I know I have only been in the job a short time but this tactic didn't seem right.'

Mike just shrugged.

Odine was still rolling about on the floor. We left him to it and others interviewing got a confession from Makinde. With no firm evidence or an admission from the bosun, he was released without charge.

Odine and Makinde were both charged with importing cannabis. They were held in custody until their trial six months later in the very impressive York Crown Court. They pleaded not guilty but were found otherwise by the jury and went to prison for 8 years. I gave evidence at the court about the initial find of the cannabis and the interviews.

If suspected drug couriers were identified on arrival at Heathrow Airport, we would follow them through to "Nothing to Declare", pull them over, and whisk them out of sight of other passengers. If drugs were found a gentle approach was made, designed to calm them down and feel less threatened. We hoped that conversing in this way would lead to the smugglers co-operating with us. We would try to "turn" them. We wanted them to identify the next onward stage of the drugs, the people who would receive them.

The first break-through would come when they agreed to telephone their contact and receive instructions. (Couriers were rarely given the whole plan in one go, the next step revealed only after the previous one had been successfully completed. This gave the mastermind the option to proceed or cut and run if suspicions were aroused).

If we thought they really had been "turned", we would book a hotel room for them and an adjacent room for ourselves.

We stayed as close as we could, trying to maintain control and covering every possible angle that the courier might take to get away from us.

If we failed to book an adjacent room two of my colleagues went up to the courier's room and concealed themselves in a wardrobe. We always preferred to plan ahead but often it was a seat of your pants job.

On one such case a team member suffered severe cramp and as soon as the suspects entered the room, he burst out of the wardrobe screaming with pain. The courier was arrested along with the person who turned up at the hotel. Other arrests followed.

Our small Investigation Unit at Heathrow prosecuted. In court the courier, Norman Williams, and the person meeting him, Winston Smith, received prison sentences of four and six years.

Being on "Squad" meant being on call for a week assisting teams from London and the provinces. If often entailed house searches and you never knew what was going to happen one day to the next.

Forced entry into properties using a sledge hammer was never the first option. Wielding a 20lb weight requires two strong hands and a torso swinging motion to achieve maximum impact. It also demands a certain composure not usually present in a body surging with adrenalin.

On one assist a police officer insisted he had the perfect sledge hammer technique so we stood back as he took aim.

To our surprise he struck the door in the middle rather than near the lock, smashing a small hole in the timber door. The sledge hammer slipped out of his hands and disappeared inside the house.

He then resorted to shouting through the letter box asking the occupant if he could have his hammer back. Not sure who was laughing more, us or the suspect.

"Station 25," the freight terminal at Heathrow airport referred a suspect discovery to The Deltas who found cannabis resin in a freight consignment from India. An address in Forest Gate, East London appeared on the packages and the import paperwork.

It was a clever concealment within film cannisters, requiring the unwinding of 20 metres of film before you came across a semi-circle of cannabis resin. Being malleable the resin had been wound around the film spool. So, if the film was examined by only unwinding a few metres the drugs would not have been detected.

The resin was removed and we discussed how the cannabis could be removed and substituted. We wanted the consignment to be reconstructed for a controlled delivery. To do this we needed a jig saw to make a replacement for the resin, to cut out semi-circle shaped pieces of timber to the exact dimensions. Once painted up the packages would look like cannabis resin.

One of the freight team officers, Doug, said he had a golfing mate who had a senior position in Black and Decker in Maidenhead fifteen miles west of Heathrow. I drove with Doug to their office and met the Training Director who, after seeing the cardboard template we had roughly made, said he would find a suitable tool for the job.

He set about the task by clamping some wood to a rather nice oak desk in a very plush office and started to cut around the shape with a jig saw.

My colleague Doug and I looked at each other as we both noticed the saw biting into the desk top as well as the piece of wood. We both got a fit of giggles. As the Director finished guiding the jig saw around the shape, the wood fell off but so did a piece of his oak table.

Embarrassment spread across his face when the damage become fully revealed.

Try as we may we could not stop laughing with tears rolling down our cheeks.

How we said our thanks and our goodbyes I don't know as we were still laughing when we got back to Heathrow.

The wooden shape did fit on the spool so we painted it black and wound on the film. It was not perfect but to all intents and purposes it looked like the original. The recipient would not have seen the reels of film or the cannisters before it left India.

The consignment was reconstructed and delivered to a lock up garage in Forest Gate.

At that time, we were working with a group of policemen called The Special Patrol Group. This group were normally brought in when there were street demonstrations, troublesome football crowds and where there could be a serious threat of public disturbance.

They were hard men, mostly over six foot three, 17 stone or more, cauliflower ears, twisted noses. They looked like a rugby team front row recovering after a brutal game. You sensed that whatever they had been doing - they won!

They loved working with us. Live drug trafficking cases was something different for them to be involved in.

Six of them, led by Dave, the Inspector and Ashley the Sergeant, came into our office. They were casually dressed but still looked like sportsman on a tour! We trusted them 100 percent and they were just the people to have with you when the going got tough.

Audio machines and light sensitive equipment had been installed in the packaging. An alarm would set off if one of the film canisters were opened.

I spotted a potential observation flat with one of the SPG officers, Terry. We approached the lady tenant of the flat that would give us the best vantage point and asked if we could look out of her kitchen window for a short while. She was quite happy for us to do that.

We expected the "baddies" to turn up to collect the drugs that day. We would have been in and out of the flat in a matter of hours. Our best laid plans rarely worked out as we hoped they might. As dusk arrived, we knew we would be spending the night there.

Two officers at a time occupied the flat changing over every 12 hours. We also had four cars and eight officers parked up nearby.

As it turned out we were there for three days, twenty-four hours a day in shifts.

The lady was more than tolerant. There was plenty of banter. We thought she was probably enjoying the company. After a day she started cooking us breakfast. We volunteered to wash and dry the dishes.

All humour, all conversation stopped as a group of people entered the premises. We readied ourselves for action. Within minutes the alarm went off and we ran from the flat and stormed the building. Inside the lockup three smugglers, all Asians in their late twenties, were standing behind a table with the consignment opened and one of the reels of film partly unwound spread out before them providing all the evidence we needed. They were all charged, arrested and carted off to await trial.

After we left the flat, we had a whip round and bought the lady a bunch of flowers. She did say she enjoyed us being in the flat and she hadn't felt so safe with the officers in her kitchen whilst she slept through the night.

The three defendants later pleaded guilty and were each sentenced to 7 years in prison.

Another operation with the Special Patrol Group was when drugs were flown into Heathrow and were being transported to a Kenyan Airways depot on the airport's perimeter track. A colleague, Nigel and I and two SPG officers were in a car tracking the consignment as it left in a Kenyan Airways van. The van needed to be stopped and we left this to the SPG. I drove the car past the vehicle and we pulled in 50 yards ahead of it ready to challenge.

I knew some of the SPG carried firearms. As the vehicle drove towards us, one of the SPG officers jumped out into the middle of the road, pulling out his Magnum pistol, aimed it at the driver and shouted, 'Stop! Police!'

(The .44 Magnum delivers a large, heavy bullet with high velocity for a handgun. In its full-powered form, it produces so much recoil and muzzle blast that it is generally considered to be unsuitable for use as a police weapon.)

The van stopped. The driver and passenger were arrested and the drugs were found in the back of the vehicle.

I did ask the SPG officer what would have happened had the vehicle not stopped.

'This gun,' he said, 'is so powerful that a bullet into the engine block would knock it out.'

They were great people to work with.

They were disbanded in the 80's after a few controversies including the death of anti-fascist protester Blair Peach who was almost certainly was killed by a blow to the head, possibly caused by a police truncheon, at a demonstration in 1979.

Sir Paul Stephenson, the Metropolitan police commissioner at the time, said that the case reports made "uncomfortable reading" but unequivocally accepted the finding that a Met officer was likely to be responsible for the death and expressed his "regret".

Often suitcases would travel through airports as unaccompanied baggage. It happens less today as there are rigorous restrictions in place to hopefully forestall any terrorist activity. One such suitcase was inspected by Customs and found to contain about 20 kilos of cannabis. The suitcase was addressed to a house near Earl's Court. We took on the operation and we established that the address was a rented flat. Within a few hours we had contacted the owner who surprisingly gave us the key to the property.

The suitcase was delivered and left in the hallway. Five of us hid in a small bedroom of the flat, myself, Nick Baker, Mike Stephenson John Dickerson and Bruce Letheren. We were all packed into a tiny box room for a couple of hours and waited for someone to take ownership of the suitcase.

We heard someone enter the flat and seemed to stop in the hallway as John stood on a squeaky floorboard.

John whispered, 'Quiet! They'll hear us.'

'I hope they do,' said Mike. 'I'm fed up in here.'

For some reason we started giggling and couldn't stop. John and Nick were standing over the sink crying with laughter. We abandoned our "cover" and found a young girl holding the unopened suitcase.

As we arrested her, we asked if she knew what was in the case. She simply shook her head.

The next day she was granted bail by Snowhill Police due to lack of evidence. A few weeks later she voluntarily came into our office to collect her Australian passport that we had seized. Stevo and I took this opportunity to re-interview her.

After the case against her was explained and the evidence of her wrongdoing was laid out, she eventually admitted she had imported the cannabis (she obviously thought our case was stronger than it was). At her trial at Guildhall Crown Court, she pleaded guilty and was sentenced to 3 years in prison.

One of Roy Brisley's children was a competent cellist. Roy was in the office one day when he said to me, 'Would you drive me over London Bridge. I've got to take a cello to a shop that sells musical instruments.'

The cello went into the back of the official car and we drove over London Bridge and parked outside the shop. We both went in and Roy stood at the counter holding the cello.

An attendant arrived and Roy said, 'This is not right. It's definitely not right. For example, the "F" doesn't sound correct.'

The attendant took the cello, did an "F".

'You're right, Roy. We'll have it in and look after it and resolve the problem.'

As Roy and I drove back to New Fetter Lane I said, 'I didn't know you were a cellist.'

'No, I'm not but they don't know that.'

It was a small and important lesson for me. If you are convincing enough, you can convince most people about anything.

Whenever you had your private car with you on surveillance or go to a location you could claim back expenses through a rate of mileage arrangement. This helped with my cash flow and it was a welcomed addition to the monthly salary. It was a few pence a mile and an extra two pence for having a communications radio fitted into your car. Also, two pence for the first passenger and one-pence for additional passengers. So, the ideal scenario was that you would drive your own car with the radio in with three passengers.

Roy rang me up while I was at home and asked if I would drive to his home in Sutton in Surrey saying, 'We're going up to Hull.'

I immediately thought that this would be a good way of earning a few extra pounds on top of my salary.

I filled the car up with petrol, checked the oil, water and tyres and cleaned it out. (My car has a habit of accumulating old wrapping for fish and chips).

I drove around to Roy's house and parked on his drive and knocked on his door. Roy opened it.

'Ready to go, Roy,' I said. 'All ready for Hull.'

'Good,' he said. 'Would you squeeze your car to the side of the drive. We're taking my private car.'

I turned away to hide the look that must have spread across my face.

I spent a year on the Deltas learning the ropes, starting with the basics of investigation. Recognising what drugs looked like, smuggling methods, how you substitute drugs, correct and lawful arresting procedures and investigation methods, tricks of the trade picked up by others over the years.

Other colleagues joining Investigation went on the "Juliet's" Team which was a "Parcel Post" importation team. They dealt with all parcels arriving at Royal Mail's Mount Pleasant Sorting Office in Farringdon Road, East London which was opened in 1889.

Every day small drug parcels would be identified coming from drug source countries across the world. Once intercepted the officers would substitute the drugs for lookalike material and, kitted up as a postman, would carry out the delivery, interview the recipients, make arrests and institute court proceedings. I was often called on to assist them with their cases.

When drugs were found they were replaced by suitable looking substitute and gentian violet was painted on them. When in contact with sweat the lotion would turn purple.

After one delivery we gained entry to a house where a man denied all knowledge of a parcel. He was obviously under pressure and as he sweated more the violet stain became more evident. He had rubbed his face as he had opened the package and the skin was covered with violet smears. He of course could not see what was happening and I took great delight taking him to a mirror. The look on his face as he stared at a Smurf was priceless.

Although I hadn't been on the Investigation Training Course, I undertook all the roles of an Investigator and was trusted to liaise with police officers, particularly from the Drugs Squads throughout the UK.

In September 1977 I went with one of the other Deltas, Nigel Holland, to Blackburn. Although in his early twenties Nigel had gone prematurely bald. He had decided to wear a wig which wasn't the best made or the most expensive and he was very conscious of having it. We met up with the Drug Squad Officers to discuss the search of the premises in Blackburn the next day in a local pub. We got on really well with the team and enjoyed a couple of beers. Nigel didn't drink and he got some strange looks when he ordered an orange juice.

After I had drunk a few beers I decided to ring the office in London to update them on the meeting.

There was a pay phone in the bar, which in those days took ten and two pence coins. I didn't have any change and in a loud voice I asked Nigel 'Do you have a two 'p'?' (Meaning a two pence piece.)

He looked at me in horror, his face crimson. 'What do you mean?' 'a two p?'

'A two pence coin for the phone,' I replied before realising what I had said.

Nigel thought I was asking him if he had a toupee.

The police officers were trying to stifle giggles behind their pint glasses.

I finally went on the three-week, Basic Investigation Techniques course, on 17 October to the 4 November. The office still got their pound of flesh as I had to work on Deltas cases at weekends throughout the course.

A week after I had finished (and passed) the course I had my first case as a Reporting Officer for a detection of cannabis resin and cannabis oil smuggled through Heathrow Airport. I had to collect all the evidence, prepare all the witness statements, photographs of the seizures and other relevant material.

In those days Customs had their own solicitor housed on the 17th floor of the building mostly occupied by London Weekend Television who were the ITV network franchise holder for Greater London and the Home Counties at weekends.

Visiting our solicitors was often a real treat as we used the same canteen as TV stars. Bruce Forsyth dined there as did Jimmy Tarbuck, Michael Aspel, Frank Bough and Nick Owen.

When we had arrested someone and the case was going to Court the Solicitors Office would nominate a Case Solicitor who would deal with the case initially by going through the "bundle" of Court evidence, the witness statements and exhibits. Accompanied by a report from the Case Officer this would be passed to a barrister, or, if an important case, a Queen's Counsel or a lesser case, a junior.

The solicitors had a list of barristers and Standing Counsel who would appear for the prosecution on Customs cases. Barristers sought to be on this list as it provided a continual flow of cases (and fees for them). Many of the cases were for large amounts of drugs and high profile with media attention.

Often our prosecution barrister would appear weeks later for the defence of another case in which he or she would be cross-examining you. This happened to me on a number of occasions and to this day I cannot understand why a barrister would leave no stone unturned to secure a guilty verdict on one case and the same a few weeks later for a not guilty verdict.

It was a strange situation after a rapport had been developed on prosecution cases and see it completely evaporate in the heady atmosphere of a courtroom. Mostly we would liaise with the solicitors but as the case got close, we would often have a conference with Counsel. With our solicitor we would go through the case in detail. These meetings would often take place around 5pm after the Counsel had been in Court on another case. Key points of our prosecution case would be spelled out - they may ask for more evidence to be made available. In these meeting the actual plan for prosecution was set out.

In 2005 the solicitor's office was taken over by the Crown Prosecution Service who would take on all of H.M Customs related cases as well as the Serious Fraud Office, The National Crime Agency. They all go through the CPS.

My first case in Court involved a relatively small import; about 3kilos of cannabis oil, a high concentration of THC (tetrahydrocannabinol). This is the active element in the drug found in the flowering part of the plant. This was discovered by uniformed officers on two couriers at Heathrow Airport carrying this oil in condoms hidden in their underpants.

It was a fairly straightforward case. One of the couriers, Baur, had the drugs concealed in his underwear. Henneck had accompanied Baur on the journey. Seahausen and Wein met them at the airport.

The drugs were seized but Baur and Henneck were allowed to go out onto the concourse so we could observe who was meeting them. Seahausen and Wein were then arrested.

You always remember your first case and the two German nationals, Mr Wein and Mr Baur pleaded guilty and were sentenced to 4 and 6 years at Middlesex Crown Court a building which now houses the UK's Supreme Court. (The Supreme Court is the final court of appeal in the UK for civil cases, and for criminal cases from England, Wales and Northern Ireland.)

Seahausen fought the case in front of a jury who were shown paperwork that linked him with the importation. The jury was out for two hours and found him guilty. He got 8 years.

Henneck was not prosecuted as there was insufficient evidence of his involvement.

Arrested suspects were initially appeared at Magistrate's Court for a lay or stipendiary magistrate to hear the evidence and ensure there was a prima facie against then. The magistrates would then decide to hold suspects in custody or allow bail - dependant on the seriousness of the accusations and if they are foreign nationals. (And those likely to interfere with witnesses or not turn up for their trial). It would then go through a committal process to decide if it should go to a Crown Court. Given the "value" and weight of drug importations we dealt with, invariably the cases were committed to Crown Court to be heard in front of a Judge. A Crown Court, unlike the magistrates' courts, is a single entity which sits in 77 court centres across England and Wales dealing with serious criminal cases. In this case it went to Middlesex Crown Court.

There are a number of factors that determine sentences. At that time there was 14 years maximum for the importation of controlled drugs, cannabis, heroin, cocaine, any drugs. There could be mitigating circumstances - someone pleading guilty could get a third off their sentence having saved the cost of going to Court. So, if the evidence was stacked against them, it could be in their interest to plead guilty at the earliest opportunity. If there was a leader of the criminal group who organised the operation and put up the money, he would receive a longer sentence than his accomplices.

Sentences varied depending on the judge, court and location. For example, a judge in London would rarely give the maximum, tending to be more lenient than others in the provinces. It's suggested that there are still places, primarily in rural locations, that would hang drug traffickers if Capital Punishment hadn't been abolished in 1965.

At the end of December 1977, a mixture of drugs; methedrine, cannabis and amphetamines were found at the cargo section of Heathrow Airport. We substituted the drugs with similar but legal substances and observed it being picked up by a van. We followed the vehicle into a lorry park in London E16.

It was two days before Christmas and we knew the park would be closed on the Xmas Day and Boxing Day but we kept a watching brief. It was a fairly secure lorry park spread out and had good cover for us.

On Boxing Day, Nigel Toulman and I were dispatched to keep an eye on the lorry park which we did with a twenty-four- hour cover. It went on for days, taking in New Year.

I actually spent New Year's Eve sitting in a car with a colleague watching a rain soaked, motionless lorry park.

In the evening I rang home from a call-box nearby and listened in to everybody enjoying the New Year celebrations. I spoke to my parents at home with friends celebrating Hogmanay.

At midnight two police officers (who were aware of our stake-out) pulled alongside in a Panda car and handed over a can of lager each wishing us Happy New Year.

We usually had sleeping bags with us for warmth. We had picked up sandwiches and drinks from a local petrol station before the stakeout began. To relieve ourselves we would find hedgerows for a pee or stroll along to the garage.

Thankfully, at 10am on the 2nd January two people collected the vehicle and they were arrested.

We robustly questioned them often raising our voices, pressing for answers. We spelt out (probably exaggerated a little) the reasons they should co-operate and the dire consequences if they didn't.

Eventually one of them agreed to make a phone call to the people he was due to meet. We marched to a telephone box to make the call.

Not many words were spoken. When the phone was put down, I asked, 'Do they know who you are? Have they met you?'

'No,' he said. 'They don't know who we are. They've never met us. We were paid 50 quid each for providing transport.'

On the 3rd of January Nigel and I took control of the van. We were going to drive it to a prearranged destination, pretending to be the couriers. We telephoned the dealers, arranging for a meeting to be as close to our office as possible at a place off the main road that could be easily observed. We decided on Temple Place, a semicircle road near Temple Tube Station. There would be lots of people milling around reducing the chance of things going wrong.

I drove to Temple Place and parked the van opposite to the tube station. I rang the number from a nearby telephone box and said I was the driver and the van had broken down.

'Okay,' said the voice. 'We'll send someone along.'

I took off the cable to the starter motor in case someone tried to start it then stood by the van with the bonnet up.

As I was looking into the engine one of our Deputy Chief Investigation Officers, Sam Charles walked by. Sam was an iconic figure and instrumental in establishing the Customs Investigations role in tackling drug smuggling. He was a driving force who built up the strength and capabilities of our investigation teams, resisting the desire of the Police Force taking over our role as prime prosecutors for drugs importation. He grew the investigation drugs capability from a handful of officers to 300 when I joined in 1977.

He strolled past with all the bearing of a city worker, briefcase in hand.

Out of the corner of his mouth he audibly whispered 'It's very good, son,' he said and walked on.

On returning to the office, he rang Roy Brisley to tell him the scenario looked genuine.

After two hours a van pulled in front of my position.

The driver got out and said, 'Have you got any problems?'

I said, 'Yes, my van has broken down.'

'I don't mind taking the load for you.'

'Why is that then?'

'I'm just trying to help you out.'

'Then how do you know I've got a load on board.'

'Just passing,' he said. 'Thought you might need some help. I could move your stuff on.'

To me that proved he had knowledge of the haul.

I nodded in agreement and he walked around to the back of our van and started carrying packages to his vehicle.

At that point my colleagues on the Deltas arrived on foot and in vehicles and promptly arrested him and took him away to New Fetter Lane to interview.

A colleague drove his vehicle away.

When I was waiting with the bonnet of the van up, I had seen a large grey Vauxhall car drive past three or four times driving along the Embankment into Temple Place and slowing down to take a look. There were two people inside the car.

After the arrest Nigel arrived in his car.

'There's a car,' I said. 'The occupants looked shifty and they have driven past a few times, slowing down and looking at me. I think we should try and find it.'

Nigel and I drove off and along the Embankment we could see the car with two guys aboard heading east. We were heading west.

'There's the car,' I said.

With that Nigel mounted the central reservation, cut across to the other side of the road and pulled in front of the target car. I ran to the driver's side and pulled the male out and arrested him. Nigel arrested the passenger.

They were identified as Mr Malik and Mr Yasheem. Malik had taken our phone call earlier. They were both charged with the importation. The original delivery driver turned out to be an innocent party and was sent on his way after being interviewed. Malik and Yasheem were found guilty at their trial and received eight years in prison.

That was my final parting shot on Drugs D.

CHAPTER 6
BRAVOS AND CHARLIES.

I joined Bravos with a call sign of Bravo 6 with Mike Knox (Bravo 1) as
my SIO (team leader). Although this wasn't a promotion it seemed like
it. I sat in his office in New Fetter Lane.

'We've been very quiet of late,' he said. 'We have a few targets that
we're looking but not many.'

These words turned out to be both restrained and inaccurate. Over the
next week our "to-do" list grew and kept growing. Our work days
changed dramatically and stayed dramatic. It was a carousal of job after
job.

The "Bravos" were half of the double headed cannabis target team, the
"Charlies" making up the other half.

The two teams operated as one, investigating some of the largest
importations of drugs into the UK. They were well respected within the
Investigation Division and with law enforcement agencies across the
world. These teams worked differently to the Deltas who investigated
drugs that had intercepted at ports and airports. Bs and Cs targeted
known smugglers to identify other members of the gang and their
method of smuggling.

Mike headed up the "Bravos." He was a long serving investigator and
fully understood the working of his department, the Solicitors Office and
the administration.

Heading up the "Charlies" was senior officer, Terry Byrne (Charlie 1).
He was in his mid- thirties and had only recently been promoted to the
post. He was supremely confident. It was obvious he was very keen to
make his mark in Investigation. He was the one who made the big call
on the operations. When deciding to make an arrest or perform a
"Knock", Junior officers deferred to Terry. He would give the go ahead,
back you up when you made the right decision and importantly,
understand that front-line decisions can be difficult to make when lots of
unexpected things are happening.

When adrenaline is flowing you can make a bad call and make a
"Knock" too soon. Ideally it is better to be too soon than too late. Terry
would not abide fools but would always give support to the junior
officers as they made their way.

Under Mike Knox were 3 Higher Investigation Officers (HIO); George
Atkinson (Bravo 2), Chris Hardwick (Bravo 3) and Bruce Letheren (Bravo
4). Bruce was my immediate line manager.

Junior Officers (including me) were Len Watson (Bravo 5) and Alan Griffiths (Bravo 7).

Higher Investigation Officers under Nick Baker (Charlie 2), were Gordon Hall (Charlie 3), Dave Thomas (Charlie 4)

It turned out to be the most enjoyable and interesting period of my career. On occasions it was Roy of the Rovers stuff but it is where I learnt the true meaning of camaraderie. I was fortunate to work with the group of colleagues all of who remained great friends throughout my career.

Alan Griffiths was from Liverpool. He had worked in his home city, at Luton Airport and had joined the investigation division a few months before me. He was on a team that investigated cannabis smuggling from Morocco, Nigeria and South Africa. Known as Griff, he became a very close friend.

Junior officers in "Charlies" included Mike Fannon, an East Londoner with a hang dog look on his face. He taught me a lot about target work particularly regarding interviewing and surveillance. The other two junior officers were Ray Smith (Charlie 6), "Smudger" and Mike Stephenson (Charlie 7), who we called "Stevo". He was a real character from Heathrow Airport whose father had been a Waterguard Superintendent, a top position in the uniform side of Customs and Excise.

Stevo was a difficult man to work with. He would completely blank anyone he didn't rate no matter what level they were at. And he gave junior officers, including me, a bit of a hard time. If Smudger left at 5.30 in the evening Stevo would say,' I suppose you've got your paper round tonight.'

The fact that Smudger had arrived at 6.30 in the morning and Stevo had rolled up at 11 o'clock was lost to Stevo.

There were team meetings. Mike and Terry Mike would chair the meeting of minds as the tasks in hand were discussed.

Often Mike would say something and be immediately followed by an exaggerated theatrical "tut" from Stevo as he shook his head. There wasn't much that Mike said that wasn't poo-pooed by Stevo. However, as soon as Terry spoke, Stevo would state loudly, 'Great idea, Terry. Fantastic idea. Really, really good. A good thing to do.'

During one meeting Stevo went too far. It was the final straw for Mike. 'Stephenson,' he barked. 'In my office.'

All of us inched toward the door so we could hear the conversation.

'Look,' Mike said, 'what do you think of me?'

'To be honest,' said Stevo, 'I see you as the thinking man's Mickey Mouse.'

Mike's fuse blew. The blast lasted only a few seconds but Stevo would hear it for hours and days after. Laughter echoed around the office for weeks.

Today, when management skills include getting on with people, would not have suited Stevo so I suspect he wouldn't have lasted long. He did consider himself above the rest of us.

But Mike and Terry made sure we all gelled together.

When suspected drug smugglers were identified they were they became our "target". Attempts would be made to establish locations they visited, people they met, what transport they used, their houses and boats, their visits to airports. Surveillance was mounted wherever possible and a detailed dossier was compiled.

Under the Interception and Communication Act 1985, Customs and Excise as a law enforcement agency along with police and security services were allowed to tap telephones. This could only be done at the behest and authority of the Home Secretary. If we applied for an intercept our designated office would apply in writing and, if approved, a warrant would be signed by the Home Secretary. This approval would be reviewed every six months to ensure the legality of our practice.

As this area of interception became more sophisticated so did the response of the criminal. Customs Investigation were at the top of the league as regards the use of intercept. Throughout my career it was deemed to be the "Crown Jewels", due to the rates of success.

Operational officers like me were not officially aware if a telephone intercept was being used on a job being investigated. We would be instructed by interception colleagues to go to observe a meeting between suspects. We had no idea where the source of the information came from: human source, an informant or surveillance or information from the police. It was a safeguard for us that when we undertook the observation and would have to write a witness statement for a court case. If required, you would give your evidence in court from the notebook you wrote in at the time or a summary statement. If you are called in to give evidence a defence barrister could ask you if there was a telephone intercept in this operation. Bearing in mind we were then under oath we could honestly say we had no knowledge of such matters. So, we were not embroiled into legal arguments about our knowledge of the information source.

After a weekend visiting my parents, I walked into the office early on the Monday morning. It was already full of my colleagues, drinking coffee.

As it was winter, I was wearing a heavy "poacher" type Parker jacket made from waterproof and breathable fabric. It was lined with many inner and outer zipped pockets, had adjustable cuffs and roll-up hood.

Mike Fannon and Stevo took one look at me and said, 'What have you been using that jacket for. Poaching rabbits? ….. TRAPPER!'

With that everyone burst out laughing.

From that day to this I am known, particularly to my former Bs and Cs colleagues as "TRAPPER". I think I bought the jacket for about £3 off a market stall in Stamford. I was never known for my sartorial elegance. In fact, one morning I walked into the office to be met by Nick Baker looking at my clothes and saying, 'Did you get dressed in the dark Trapper?'

The only time we wore a suit was when we went to Court. There was a standing joke in the office if you walked in wearing a suit.

'Are you going to a funeral, a wedding or Court?'

The "uniform" for investigators was leather jacket, jeans and trainers. It was always casual wear.

We kept our suits on hangers in the office in case a meeting with Counsel or an appearance in Court was called for. A smart shirt and tie were waiting along with recently polished shoes.

On occasions the team were caught in the cross fire of the friction between Terry Byrne and Mike Knox. This was a rare occurrence.

We all had to go down to the Hereford to investigate an operation that featured a van intercepted at Southampton docks and found to contain a large quantity of cannabis. The van was to be delivered to a remote property in the Ross on Wye area.

This friction resulted in Mike Knox's Bravos team being sent back to London before the operation was concluded. Terry's decision was not just as a result of this spat with Mike but because of information received on a quantity of drugs in London. I kept my mouth shut but Len Watson (Bravo 5) was a bit more up front and complained to Terry that he had bought a new pair of wellington boots for the (potentially muddy) operation.

Len got short shrift from Terry which confirmed I was right not to say anything.

When we got back to London, we were sent to the Fulham area where we observed and searched a house looking for a consignment of heroin. No drugs were found but we did find links to another house in the Acton area where we conducted a further house search. In one of the bedrooms, I lifted the mattress to reveal a large pair of padded underpants. These pants contained two kilos of heroin sewn into the garment that would or could have been used as a concealment when travelling through an airport.

The underpants would become Exhibit "Jarvie A".

A few people were arrested, one having a close relationship with a female hairdresser in the Fulham area.

Alan Griffiths and I visited the hairdressers and found the girl, an Italian, with her head under a hairdryer.

I pointed out that she was under arrest and we would have to take her away.

Although her English was not great, she was adamant that she wanted her hair done first but ungallantly we insisted she came with us straight away, her hair still wet and un-styled.

After questioning she volunteered some information, enough for us to decide we would use her as a witness rather than as a suspect.

We booked her in the Y Hotel (YMCA Hotel) just off Euston area. She wasn't technically under arrest but was helping us with our enquiries. She had been booked into the hotel to avoid her being contacted by the crime group.

Our intelligence team were there including Frank Jones, an Italian speaker, who translated for us. So, Alan and I "baby-sat" her overnight so she would be ready to face our interviewers. The only room available to Alan and myself was one with a double bed which I had to share with Alan. The girl had a room next to ours.

As part of our intelligence gathering with the Italians, we quickly found out that this lady was not all she seemed to be. It turned out that she was a prostitute so she had to be treated at arm's length.

At one point our telephone rang. It was our witness asking me to go to her room saying that her radio was not working.

I said to Alan, 'I'm not going in there on my own. You'll have to come with me.'

We both went in and low and behold the radio wasn't working. There was no sign that she had intended to seduce me away from my professional duties.

The next day we took her to New Fetter Lane where she was interviewed again.

The "owner" of the heroin, Tekbali, was also interviewed and charged with importing two kilos of heroin.

Several months later Tekbali's trial was held at the Central Criminal Court, the Old Bailey. I was the one who found the heroin so I gave evidence for the prosecution.

During examination I held up the exhibit bag containing the underpants. The Judge ordered the underpants be removed from the bag and held high so the jury could see them clearly.

At one point it was suggested that the underpants were passed around the jury member so I hastily appealed to my barrister telling him that the exhibit still contained traces of heroin that would give off dangerous fumes. Prior to the trial it had been inspected by a Government Chemist, confirming that heroin was present. The Judge requested that the garment be placed back into the see-through bag and securely sealed. This could then be shown to the jury.

Most of our operations depended on intelligence received but every now and again an incredible piece of luck came our way. Shortly afterwards on the 18th January I was in the office with the rest of my colleagues when we had a phone call from the Dutch Police giving us the information that there was a courier, a Dutch male, who had travelled in a car from Amsterdam and he was staying in a 20th floor hotel room in London. They could add no more than that.

We spoke to an Intelligence team at Scotland Yard who were able to confirm to us that (at the time) there were only two hotels in London with 20 floors or more., One was the Penta Hotel in West London that opened in 1973 and had 27 floors.

Mike Fannon and I drove to the Penta Hotel and spoke to the head of security there. Many of the hotel security officers were ex police or ex-military who were really keen to help law enforcement if required.

We explained that there was someone we were interested in. He checked the hotel register. The name Noce Santori, a Dutch national was entered. Room 2022.

The Security Head whispered, 'He has been here but is checking out right now. He's at the other end of reception. His car is in the basement car-park.'

We took a brief look at the suspect then moved quickly outside to my car. Mike and I watched the car-park exit until a Dutch registered Ford Taunus, a car based on the UK Cortina, came up the ramp and drove off down the road.

I radioed my office in London asking if they would speak to Mike Knox and ask what he wants us to do. Message came back immediately; follow him as best you can.

Unlike fictional stories on television surveillance is very difficult with one vehicle. Even with co-ordinated multiple vehicles it can go wrong. But on this occasion, we had no choice. We followed in our lone car.

We travelled along the Cromwell Road when he started to head north. It was tricky keeping the right distance, far away so we were not spotted but close enough not to lose him. We knew that other Division cars were on their way but they were miles behind us.

We ended up in the Wembley area and instructions came through that we should try to intercept the car.

As he pulled up at a junction I swept around to the front of his car and stopped. We dashed out and tried to open the car doors. They were all locked. He obviously realised what was happening and started to reverse his car and drove rapidly off. Thankfully, neither of us were hurt as he sped away.

By the time we got back into our car he was long gone. We lost him.

We decided to scour the local streets in the hope of spotting the unusual car. We did find it parked up a side road and empty. The driver had disappeared.

We summoned a traffic police officer who broke into the car and after a search we found 50 kilos of cannabis resin hidden in the door frames.

We looked around the Wembley area, the railway and underground stations, in coffee shops and other places. We had seen the driver very briefly but hoped we would recognise him if he came into view.

After a couple of hours, we thought we had exhausted every avenue. We decided we would go into central Wembley and get something to eat. There were many restaurants there. For some reason we chose one called The Golden Egg. We sat at a table placed our order for sausage and chips. As we sat there eating the door opened and a man came in and sat at one of the tables.

'I think that's him,' I whispered. 'That's the driver.'

'It can't be,' said Mike. 'Of all the restaurants around, he chose the same one as we did!'

I pressed. 'I'm sure that's him.'

We gestured for the waitress to come over.

'Does that fellow speak English?' I asked.

'He speaks English,' she said, 'but he's got a foreign accent.'

With that Mike and I picked up our half-eaten plates of sausages and chips and sat next to this fellow.

'Where are you from,' I asked.

'I'm from Holland.'

'Are you here on business or holiday?

'I'm on holiday.'

'Where are you staying?' Mike asked.

'I'm staying at the Penta Hotel in the Cromwell Road.'

'You're under arrest,' I barked, 'for knowingly importing a quantity of cannabis resin.'

I then cautioned him with the words we then used, "You are not obliged to say anything unless you do so and anything you do say will be taken down and may be used as evidence."

(Today an arresting officer must state clearly; "You do not have to say anything. But it may harm your defence if you do not mention when questioned something which you later rely on in Court. Anything you do say may be given in evidence." The officer must follow up by asking: "Do you understand?")

He was then arrested, taken back to our office and interviewed.

His hotel room was searched. He was charged and as a foreign national with no family links to the UK was remanded in custody to appear at his trial a few months later.

I was nominated as the case officer and it was my first visit to The Old Bailey.

My, I was impressed.

I had to appear in front of a very famous Judge called Lord Melford Stephenson. He was a renowned and outspoken Judge.

(His reference to the Sexual Offences Act 1967 as a "buggers' charter" earned him a reprimand from the then Lord Chancellor).

As a defence lawyer he defended the last woman to be hung in the UK, Ruth Ellis for murdering her lover. Public disgust at the case is thought to have played a part in the abolition of capital punishment in the UK in 1969.

In 1969 Judge Stephenson sentenced the Kray twins, Reggie and Ronnie, to a minimum of 30 years in jail each, saying, "In my view, society has earned a rest from your activities."

It is intimidating enough to be in The Old Bailey. Normally guilty pleas or "Remand in Custody" are cases that are dealt with first. So, I was there at 10am and Judge Stephenson was dealing with a nondescript lady in the dock. When the indictment was read out it was for murder. My ears pricked up and when she pleaded guilty in such a matter-of-fact way that it knocked me back a bit. She was sentenced to life imprisonment.

My case was the next one up in front of the same Judge.

Noce Santori was brought up from the cells and the Clerk read out the indictment.

'How do you plead?'

'Guilty' he replied.

He was sentenced to five years in prison which didn't seem a lot of time but he had spent a lot of time on remand in custody. His guilty plea would have been taken into consideration. The quantity of drugs, although not small, was not in the tonnage league of importations.

I had to read out Santori's antecedents, the details of any previous convictions. I was also asked to confirm he had not caused any problems when he was arrested which I again confirmed he hadn't.

It was such a relief to get a successful prosecution under my belt. More importantly, I could get back to the work I enjoyed most. Following suspects around and watching them as they progress their drug smuggling ventures and the frustrating wait before making our planned move.

The Bravos and Charlies had investigations in in Cardiff, Liverpool and Scotland. I loved every minute of this work and didn't want to miss any of it.

Trapper was on the road again!

CHAPTER 7
EXPOSED NEEDING A PEE.

Observation is a key part of investigation work. Days and weeks of planning, days and weeks with little happening. Everything slows down as if in a trance, concentration wavers, sleep beckons. Then, an unexpected sudden movement, the shadow of a half-hidden person comes into view. Hands jerk as if giving instruction, heads switch left to right, walking pace increases almost to running speed. Something is happening. Lethargy is immediately replaced by verve, loose becomes tight. Then more waiting until that vital piece of incrimination is clearly observed.

If you have a target premises suspected of housing an illegal operation, receiving, storing or distributing drugs, a convenient and useful observation post must be found. It must be close enough for a clear view of entrances but distanced enough to avoid personnel being spotted. You have to assume that the people you are observing are observers themselves. They could well know the area intimately, know the comings and goings of neighbours, the cars they drive and the pattern of everyday activity.

Sometimes we had advance notice of the importation i.e. sea or airfreight and we were able to recci at potential delivery addresses days in advance. With air passengers we didn't have that luxury and had to quickly set up an observation point. Along with other investigators, we would park at least half a mile away, creep in unspotted, negotiate with the occupants of a building which had a clear view of the target premises. We would show the occupants our warrant cards and tell them we were interested in the area. We would be as vague as possible in case the occupant inadvertently compromised our operation by speaking to neighbours. As we said in the office 'careless talk can cost an operation'.

An office or flat are ideal. There, old or known faces come and go mingling with unfamiliar visitors and, (our dearest and longed for hope) a good chance of occupying a heated room.

One winter I was with Nick Baker in an empty house in London where we could observe from an upstairs bedroom. Electricity had been turned off and it was freezing. Nick brought along his golfing hand-warmer (burning charcoal in a sealed container). He placed this under his shirt hoping his heart would benefit. It didn't work. At least, it didn't stop him complaining.

We were able to take photographs of people entering or leaving the suspect building, noting time spent there and frequency of visits. Car and van registration numbers were logged on all vehicles that turned up. These would be checked through our vehicle data base to see if their owners were of interest.

Notes were taken. Times logged. A dossier was built up for future use. A seemingly trivial detail could, at a later stage of the investigation, prove a vital link.

All the Customs Investigation teams had access to an observation vehicle but drugs operations generally took priority. The observation vans had no heating or air conditioning so it wouldn't be the first choice for most of us. Too hot in the summer and always too cold in the winter. Being too hot was worse and on a number of occasions I was stripped down to my underpants whilst holding a camera, clicking away at any movement in and out of the target premises.

On one operation, an address linked to drugs couriers was identified in north London. We secured an observation place in a school in the area. I was with Mike Stephenson (Stevo), an officer who had a lot of experience working at Heathrow Airport. He joined the Investigation division only a year before me but annoyingly he never stopped trying to give the impression he was a seasoned operative who knew it all.

We were looking at a house that had appeared in a number of address books of couriers arrested at Heathrow with Thai sticks of cannabis. We didn't know the significance of the address at the time but wanted to identify the owner of the premises, what vehicles they were using and who visited them.

With the permission of the school's Head of Science we were able to use a back room in the lab where the laboratory assistant used to store material. Through the window we were able to look at the premises we were interested in. We arrived before the children came and left after they had gone. We were able to arrange lunch and visits to the toilet without being seen as when the classroom was not being used, we were able to go in and out. From our window we could see part of the school playground and could hear banging below. We could just see a group of boys acting out martial arts. One was armed with a kung fu star, a martial arts weapon that years later was banned, which was being thrown at the back door of the school embedding itself in the woodwork.

We could hear a teacher shouting, 'Don't do that. Stop throwing that star.' He wisely remained the other side of the door.

It was disturbing for us seeing a potentially dangerous weapon in the hands of children but we couldn't do anything about it and, it also seemed, no one else was doing anything about it. We reported the event to the Science teacher who, to our surprise, gave a shrug of acceptance - this obviously went on and it was school policy to let it go on.

The photographs I took were hit and miss - I had received no training. It was like taking holiday snaps without thought of focus or positioning. And in those days, constantly worried if you had attached the film reel correctly.

I did, however, have to work out the best field of vision - usually a few steps back into the room so I could not be seen from outside through a narrow gap in curtains or blinds.

We were there for two days and obtained a lot of intelligence that fed back to our intelligence teams to research further.

Mike Stephenson had worked for years at Heathrow airport and stories filtered through that he hadn't got on with any of his colleagues. I soon found he was quite difficult to work with but since his arrival at Investigations Division I had sorted out how to achieve a practical relationship. I would never take any truck off him whatsoever. He was one of the few people I came close to punching.

We carried out a long and exhausting surveillance following two Turks from London to Liverpool. Although on the surface driving from London to Liverpool seemed a bit of a breeze, the driver and navigator had to concentrate all the time giving a commentary, swopping 'eyeball' and looking for other suspects vehicles that may be looking out a surveillance team. We had a debrief led by Dave Thomas, the Senior Officer at the hotel. In the bar we chatted about what we thought what was going to happen, what our tactics would be.

I said, 'We'll have to be up early in the morning.'

Stevo, in his usual undiplomatic style said, 'I don't know what you've got to say about it. You're new in the job. You don't know anything.'

Enraged, I said, 'Steve, one of these days I'm going to punch your lights out.'

He said, 'I'm fast. I'm faster than you.'

'You might be faster than me but I'll still catch you.'

To stop my anger getting the better of me I got up from my seat and made my way to the hotel toilet.

Within seconds Stephenson arrived at my side saying, 'We're the best of mates, Jim. We've got through so much together.'

'Look, Stevo,' I said, 'you really are going to get the wrong end of my temper.'

'No, Jim. We're mates. Always have been.'

Stevo was one of those men who, if you didn't front up to him, would try to put you down. If he was fronted up, he was okay.

In fairness it can be quite intimidating being restrained for hours in a small room with nothing to do but wait. You talked, but in hushed tones. You must not be overheard by anyone. Even in empty premises the voices were kept low to prevent any echoing. All jokes and yarns had been used up in past operations so our conversation focused on topics of the day – sometimes interesting and controversial – sometimes deadly dull.

Friendships were often tested during a lengthy stake-out. We could be hours together in a car and often I tried to choose a colleague to partner up with. Often it didn't work and you we stuck with someone with a problem with flatulence or were messy eaters.

On one observation I was found out but not by any suspect. I was parked in a side street in an official car in East London watching a potential smugglers car. After a few hours I needed to have a pee. I asked over the radio if another surveillance car could take over watching the vehicle for a short while. As we were talking a door opened in a house next to where I was parked. A guy rushed out and stuck a message against the car window. On it was written in large letters, "Would you like to use the toilet?"

I got out of the car and I was a bit worried but I had to sort out the situation and I knew colleagues were nearby. He was in his sixties and appeared to be a genuine member of the public.

'I've got a CB radio,' he said. 'I've been listening in to your messages. Much more interesting than what's on television.'

He came across as a genuine person as a criminal would not have invited the "opposition" into their home. He thought we were the police and I did use his toilet. When I left, I thanked him and he gave me packet of digestive biscuits. This sort of thing didn't happen very often.

I then had to reposition the car calculating that my messages could not be received by the good Samaritan or anyone else.

Some stake-outs took place from a non-descript observation van which contained a purpose-built hide. It was far from sophisticated. It appeared as though it been made from bits found in a domestic shed assembled by someone who had failed a do-it-yourself course.

Someone would drive the van with you inside, park the van, lock it up and leave you in the back to observe the target. The van was boiling hot in the summer, freezing cold in the winter. And, of course, there were no toilet facilities apart from a much used (sometimes unemptied) jerry can.

You could sit in there for hours on end with your camera taking shots of anyone turning up at the premises hopefully building up the evidential chain. I spent many hours in an observation van watching premises but also what else was happening in the street. You would often see people talking to themselves or looking at themselves in car mirrors. It certainly relieved the boredom. In the back of the van there were switches to operate the washers and wipers so you can get a clear view. On one occasion a group of teenagers were passing as I was using the washers. They were sprayed a bit and kept looking up to see where the water had come from. It wasn't very professional but it made me chuckle and relieved the boredom.

On one occasion, a recently arrived colleague Cedric Woodhall, was in an observation van when the driver's side was broken into and a man began hot-wiring the vehicle intending to steal it. Before he got the engine going Cedric opened the back window and shouted, 'What the fuck do you think you're doing?'

The intruder panicked and fled and I am not sure who was most shocked, Cedric or the car thief.

It took new investigators a while to get used to using the phonetic alphabet. Cedric had only been in a few weeks when he was out on the ground. He passed details of a suspected vehicle's registration which included Delta Yankee Tango. When he came on the radio he said "Delta Yankee Tankee". We all fell about laughing and kept asking him to repeat it. Cedric saw the funny side and we still laugh about it, years later.

In 1977 there had been an increase in the number of officers appointed to the Investigation Division and there was a backlog for those waiting for the three-week Basic Investigation Techniques (BITs). I didn't receive my training until 1978. Much of my skills were acquired, not in a classroom but out on the ground, learning from others.

If suspected drug couriers were identified on arrival at Heathrow Airport, we would follow them through to "Nothing to Declare", pull them over, and whisk them out of sight of other passengers. If drugs were found a gentle approach was made, designed to calm them down and feel less threatened. We hoped that conversing in this way would lead to the smugglers co-operating with us. We would try to "turn" them. We wanted them to identify the next onward stage of the drugs, who would receive them.

The first break-through would come when they agreed to telephone their contact and receive instructions. (Couriers were rarely given the whole plan in one go, the next step revealed only after the previous one had been successfully completed. This gave the mastermind the option to proceed or cut and run if suspicions were aroused).

Often, the couriers were told to book a room at a hotel near the airport.

If we thought they really had been "turned", we would book the room for them and an adjacent room for ourselves.

We stayed as close as we could, trying to maintain control and covering every possible angle that the courier might take to get away from us.

We tried but failed to book an adjacent room so two of my colleagues went up to the courier's room and concealed themselves in a wardrobe. We always preferred to plan ahead but this was a seat of your pants job.

One of the team was suffering from severe cramp so as soon as the suspects entered the room he burst out of the wardrobe screaming with pain. The courier was arrested along with the person who turned up at the hotel. Other arrests followed.

Although we assisted on this operation the case itself was fairly routine and was often left with our small Investigation Unit at Heathrow to prosecute. On this case the courier Norman Williams and the person meeting him, Winston Smith received prison sentences of four and six years.

In August 1977 I was asked to help the Bravos and Charlies, the IDs cannabis target teams on an operation at Stansted Airport. Bravos and Charlies led by Terry Byrne and Mike Knox were considered the elite teams and to be able to work with them was a real feather in my cap. Little did I know that I would join them in a few months. A cargo jet had arrived for repair work but intelligence told us that there were drugs onboard and would be picked up by people based in the Battersea area.

The plane was outside of the engineering section off the main runway some distance from the passenger terminal. All airports have engineering hangers used to repair and service both passenger and cargo aircraft. Mike Knox decided the best location to watch the aircraft was in a cornfield. It was during the day and the corn was high so Mike could conceal himself.

Along with five other cars we managed to park in laybys. I was with Mike Fannon (Charlie 5) and we managed to park up in the service station just off the Stansted airport spur of the M11.

That morning we had been to look at an address in Battersea which was suspected as being linked to the importation. A West Indian male in his early fifties who I later found out to be called Moses Winston came out wearing a white suit and trilby hat and drove off towards the South Circular. We followed him for a short distance before dropping the surveillance but passed the information by radio to our colleagues waiting at Stansted that he was on the move.

The drugs were loaded into the car which drove off heading for the slip road of the M11. Terry and the team were following the car.

Terry called the "Knock" and our cars went in front, at the side and behind the car. It was brought to a "rolling stop" and we all piled out of our cars and arrested the two occupants. Mike and I took Moses back to our office in New Fetter Lane.

I was asked to interview Moses with Mike and after issuing the caution Mike asked him to account for his movements earlier in the day. He was fairly vague and I said to him, 'I saw you leave your house at 7.30. You had a white suit on and a trilby hat.'

'Yeah.'

As a joke I said, 'I even know your hat size is six and seven-eighths.' (The vast majority of males who wear hats have that size.)

'How do you know that?' he asked.

He was convinced I knew more about him than I actually did.

In the end he admitted he had travelled to Stansted to pick up a quantity of drugs and at Middlesex Crown Court he pleaded guilty and when to prison for six years.

CHAPTER 8
LIVERPOOL

Between 1830 and 1930 Liverpool Docks was in its heyday, a gateway for mass emigration. Nine million people sailed from Liverpool, bound for North America, Australia and New Zealand. However, trade began to suffer after World War One when Cunard's liner services, that first sailed from Liverpool in July 1840, moved their operation to Southampton. The gradual decline of the docks continued as cargo shipping moved to Felixstowe in the South of England.

Dramatic changes took place in the late 1970's, early 1980's amongst the work force following Prime Minister, Margaret Thatcher's determination to break the Trade Union influence by passing restrictive legislation.

As people left the UK others arrived. By far the largest wave was from Ireland followed by Afro-Caribbean immigrants. (In the 1940s and 1950s the British Government encouraged people move to the UK to take up job vacancies).

Historically, Liverpool had always been a conduit for drugs entering the UK, particularly cannabis. Jamaica was a major source.

The cosmopolitan nature of the city added colour and diversity, particularly along the waterfront. Alongside the law-abiding majority came the delinquents, the villains, the drug smugglers.

In October 1978 the Bravos and Charlies, under the leadership of Terry Byrne the SIO, began targeting five people that were part of a Liverpool based crime group.

Investigations in Liverpool were generally conducted by HM Customs Investigation office in Manchester. Being a small office most of the Manchester investigators had, over the years, been identified by the criminal groups in the North West. Names were known, addresses, rank, family members and out of hours haunts.

The Manchester office and the Liverpool Police Drug Squad knew much of their industry had been compromised.

The situation called for a team of unknown investigators to take on the operation. Fresh faces were needed.

Despite having operational commitments in other parts of the UK, Terry saw this as a challenge and agreed to take the case on.

On the 14th October myself and Gordon Hall (Charlie 3) were dispatched to Liverpool. Our brief was to watch any premises used by Tommy "Tacker" Commerford and others who had been previously identified.

Commerford had been a thorn in the side of law enforcement for a number of years. Crimes had been committed with all the hall-marks of Commerford's involvement but credible evidence was always just out of reach. It was thought that if we identified and tracked his accomplices a way could be found to implicate Commerford himself.

This resulted in a lot of time being spent watching Commerford's pub, The Dale, in the centre of Liverpool and other regular haunts.

He would meet up with his cronies at the pub and in the Adelphi Hotel. It was impossible for us to go into the pub without being spotted. Strangers stuck out like sore thumbs. The hotel was easier as it was used by the many visitors to Liverpool, arriving one day, leaving a few days later to be replaced by more new and unknown faces.

We would often drive past the home addresses of the suspects to see what cars were outside, using a Dictaphone to record the number plates which were checked out later by HQ.

Over a number of years investigations by the local Customs and the Police had been further compromised by the fact that criminals had "insiders" in the force who would readily inform them if they were being investigated. The right amount of cash would easily turn heads.

Although a large city, Liverpool operated like a small village resulting in them knowing if any outsiders are around. I thought this was an exaggeration until I drove into Liverpool for the first time. It seemed everybody was clocking our car and watching us until we drove out of sight. It was a long way from my previous fond impressions of this famous City which mainly was in relation to the Beatles, Gerry and the Pacemakers and of course the two successful football teams, Liverpool and Everton.

I had already experienced the Scouse humour working with my close friend and colleague Alan Griffiths. We joined the Bravos and Charlies within a few weeks of each other at the start of 1978.

Gordon had booked a hotel, The Lord Nelson, where he had previously stayed when working in Liverpool. It was the norm to share a room as we were on a fixed rate of subsistence. If we could save on the cost of the room more money was left over. The hotel was in the city centre just behind Lime Street Station.

At 8 o'clock on the Sunday morning 15 October 1978 I was woken up by a marching band outside. It was an Orange Lodge Band. There were flutists, ten or so of them and eight drummers with marchers behind carrying flags showing a cross of St George and a purple star and Orange Lodge banners.

The Lodge, more commonly known as the Orange Order, is a Protestant fraternal organisation based primarily in Northern Ireland. Its name is a tribute to the Dutch-born Protestant king William of Orange, who defeated the army of Catholic king James II in the Williamite–Jacobite War (1688–1691).

I was brought up in a household of Rangers Football Club fanatics and my father gave us a good insight into the Orange Order. He was not a bigot at all but would happily play the "Sash" and other tunes on the record player. (The Sash is a ballad from Ulster commemorating the victory of King William, often called, "The Anthem". The tune is used by Liverpool F.C. fans in their song "Poor Scouser Tommy").

It was the first Orange Lodge Parade I had actually witnessed.

In the next few days Gordon and I drove past the target addresses, taking notes and photographs when we could. We would respond to any intelligence generated by the police or Customs Intelligence Teams. The police on routine patrols would often report when known criminals were seen, where they were, what they were doing and who they were with.

Our "head office" had other pressing commitments in north Lincolnshire, the Torquay area and London but it was decided to have a couple of officers in Liverpool all the time. If the full surveillance team was needed, they would all go up. Generally, two of us would be there for about a week to be replaced by others to ensure our faces did not become known. Gordon was running his own operation in London and spent most of his time in the south visiting Liverpool infrequently.

Criminals tend not be early risers and often surfaced at lunchtime. We were on duty the same hours as them, often worked into the early hours. We would watch them in the pubs and nightclubs meeting other members of the gang. Often when they have been arrested, suspects deny knowledge of knowing others so these observations were vital. Previously unknown members would be observed, followed on foot to a vehicle which hopefully would be registered to them.

Liverpool was probably one of the most difficult areas we could work in. We had taken on board two senior Liverpool Drug Squad members, Superintendent Bill Griffiths and Chief Inspector Derek O'Connell. They had a small trusted group under them who were aware of some of the details of our operation on a "need to know" basis.

Over the years the local police drug squad, totalling no more than 10 officers, had experienced an exhausting time trying to get evidence that they could take to Court. Rumours of nobbled juries abounded. Once the list of jury members became known they would be approached, offered money or received threats to ensure the verdict went the way of the accused. Acquittals were regular, convictions rare.

Tommy 'Tacker' Anthony Comerford who was born in 1932, was a well-known Liverpool organised crime figure involved in narcotics and drug trafficking, one of the first criminals to establish an international drug trafficking network in England. Along with Pat Hart and Brian Mogan, he dominated criminal activity in the Merseyside area spending over 34 years in prison during the course of his criminal career.

The three of them were suspected by the Chief Superintendent and Inspector of the Liverpool Drugs Squad of importing cannabis through Liverpool Docks. This force gave us the background to the suspects.

The Liverpool Dock system has quite a history, its enclosed commercial dock was the world's first, built in 1715, eventually covering a coastline seven and a half miles long. Bulk Grain, timber, oil and millions of tons of other cargo were shipped through the port along-side containers, ships and ferries.

To the outsider it was a small city with its own boundaries, rules and laws. There were plenty of gates, fences and signs but you knew that before you entered you would be monitored. There was no way I or a colleague could enter without an alarm bell going off. We would be seen, sniffed or sensed by informants with highly tuned whiskers that instantly recognised an alien presence. Within minutes, anyone who needed to know you were there, knew you were there.

With the right sort of clothes, mixing with other people around going about their business, we could get away with surveillance at a distance but get up close and even the pallor of a Southerner's skin would tell a tale. And, of course, as soon as you spoke, your accent echoed like an out of tune bell.

The Scouse accent, like much else in the city, owes its roots to Liverpool's position as a port. The melting pot created by the influx of people from far and wide was the foundation of the distinctive Scouse sound.

Speaking with a Scouse accent is a fairly recent trend, up until the mid-19th century Liverpudlians spoke pretty much the same as their Lancastrian neighbours, and traces of the warm Lancashire sound can still be heard in the accent of older residents.

There are areas of Liverpool that have their own impenetrable language, "backslang", a linguistic ploy that splits words, rendering them incomprehensible to the uninitiated.

An example was, 'Got these jarg shades off this wool, they're a bit antwacky but I was skint, like.'

Something to do with old fashioned sun glasses being reluctantly bought off a dodgy character due to lack of funds, I think.

Years later when the Dutch police tapped the phone of Liverpool drug baron Curtis Warren, officers from Merseyside Police conversant in backslang were called in to help translate the recorded phone conversations.

It was a very tight community around the docks. Strangers would immediately be challenged by the dockers and trade union people.

In those days there was an AA Members handbook that listed regional number plates for cars so if you spotted an unusual set, you would look it up it and tick it off. So, as we entered a "restrictive" area there would be children with their books ticking us off. I was told later that criminals would slip the children a pound or two if they reported a car with a London registration plate driving around.

We later overcame this problem by putting Liverpool or Lancashire number plates on our cars.

In those days we were naive. We did not understand how a small knit community works in spite of being a large city. It seemed, at times, everyone knew everyone else.

We did dress down. Our hair was long, tatty jeans, donkey jackets. In the port area we wore the jackets. In the City we wore smarter jeans and a leather jacket. Although it was fashionable at the time, I resisted getting my hair permed. A lot of men did probably because they were fans of the TV series The Professionals in which a curly permed Martin Shaw played Ray Doyle, a MI5 man.

When driving into Liverpool on the same operation with Bruce Letheran who had a mop of naturally curly hair we stopped for petrol and as Bruce went up to pay the girl behind the counter started giggling. She thought Bruce was a local comedian called Bobby Knutt who had later appeared in the soap shows, Emmerdale and Coronation Street. Echoes of laughter could be heard as we drove away.

Bruce and I stayed in the centre of the city at the Merchant Navy Hotel, in Parliament Street. We did get an accommodation allowance which sometimes exceeded the hotel bill. The overnight rate was about £13.30 plus a daily rate of £2.11. It seemed a fortune at that time. Occasionally we would squeeze 3 or 4 men into a room to save money.

On this type of trip there was no way of knowing how long we going to stay at the hotel. Each week we paid the bill and claimed it back later on a subsistence claim form. We often desperately waited for the reimbursement to arrive (in those days by a cheque).

In the city and the area around the docks we were often asked what we were doing in Liverpool and we spotted people inspecting our cars and asking questions of hotel staff. It was always our hope that we would be following suspects but it was often turned around by various people tailing us.

I was close to Bruce and remain good friends. In 1983 he moved from Bs and Cs to a Customs Fraud team.

Most days seemed a waste of time. We would drive around the known suspect addresses or park up outside pubs waiting for them to arrive. They rarely did.

Alan Griffiths was originally from Birkenhead and 'spoke the language'. He was often called on to go to Liverpool and I was with him on numerous occasions. Alan became a close friend as well as a colleague. We were the junior members of Bs and Cs and we spent a lot of time working together. Invariably we worked long hours and it was even worse for Alan who was married with two young children.

Whilst away we would eat and drink together but he lived near Luton (he was a uniformed officer at the airport before he joined Investigation) and I lived in Biggin Hill, Kent so we did not socialise outside of work. If we were in London we would often wind down over a pint.

On the Commerford case I was alone in my car driving around the known premises. Alan Griffiths was doing the same in another car. Alan had driven past a target address just as a suspect came out of the house. Within seconds Alan realised that Pat Hart and Brian Mogan were in the car behind him. Both were key members of Commerford's smuggling group and knew they were people not to be crossed. Alan came on the radio to tell me he was being followed by a car.

'Do you need help?' I asked.

'No, no. I'll try to lose them.'

This went on for half an hour. I was about three miles away but I desperately tried to get closer to where Alan was. The longer it went on the higher Alan's voice became. He said he was driving towards the city centre but was still being followed. I was about a mile away from where Alan was driving and he came on the radio to say he had pulled into the car park of St Anne's Police station and his "tail" had driven off.

Over the previous few weeks, we had got to know the areas and roads of Liverpool and it is not a large city. However, the criminals knew the streets and "rat runs" a lot better.

Usually, you would have two people in the car, one to drive, one to read maps but two males in one car made it look even more suspicious, particularly in Liverpool.

The safety of our colleagues was always on our minds knowing that steps must be taken immediately if a threat was serious.

Having back up, ready and equipped, was paramount.

Surveillance in a car had its limitations so we did try to avoid that as much as possible. Ideally, we would find a convenient lookout. I would walk past a known address and look around to see premises that would make a good observation post.

A member of Commerford's group, Norman Bancroft-Thompson, lived in a house next door to a mortuary. The obvious place to watch the coming and goings was from inside the mortuary itself. As you can imagine, there wasn't a mad rush of volunteers to man this position.

Three officers were persuaded, parking their cars nearby.

Investigators from our Manchester office were helping us out with our operation and were watching from a distance.

To relieve the spooky atmosphere one of officers inside the mortuary, expecting the arrival of a colleague, lay on a trolley and pulled a sheet over himself. As the newly arrived officer passed the trolley the other sat up, bellowing a ghostly moan. The victim didn't see the joke. He ran out of the mortuary and refused to return.

The investigation into Commerford, Hart, Mogan and the Malloy Brothers ran from the middle of 1978 to May 1979. I would spend at least ten days a month in Liverpool. Some days the weather would be fantastic but most of the time it was grey and rainy. One weekend at the end of February 1979 I was with Terry Byrne and Mike Stephenson and it was one of the coldest days for years. Well below freezing. Even drug smugglers stay indoors when it is that cold. We did venture out of the hotel but the roads were deadly and we spent most of the weekend shivering in the hotel whose heating system failed to live up to its name. Condensation froze on the inside of the windows.

It didn't help the already frosty atmosphere. Stevo was his usual obnoxious self and we nearly came to blows. He thought he knew everything and I knew nothing, a junior upstart. Words became louder and angrier. It almost got to a chest thumping stage when, thankfully, Terry stepped in to keep the peace.

Every day we would patiently watch the docks, houses or commercial premises, mostly just parking up for an hour or so or just driving past registering the movements of individuals and vehicle numbers.

In those days the computer system was very slow and limited. The Police National Computer via our Control Office in New Fetter Lane was available for vehicle checks, establishing the legal owner and address. Also, each Police Station had a collator who registered all incidents in a given area. This was entered manually on an alphabetical card system. We had a similar system in New Fetter Lane which almost filled a whole room.

The observations and surveillance on Commerford and the other gang members would all help to build up our intelligence picture. When on surveillance I would enter all of my observations into my notebook. The film for any photographs taken would be sent to our official photographer Dick Palmer and, if relevant, would be produced in court as an exhibit labelled for example as "Jarvie A". The nominated case officer would collect the observations and produce a running log as to what occurred.

If we had a full surveillance team (normally five cars) and were heading towards Toxteth, permission had to be obtained from the local Chief Constable. Our drug squad contacts would facilitate this. We did go in on a couple of occasions but at this time tensions were high and any law enforcement activity had to be low key.

Toxteth is an inner-city area to the south, bordering Liverpool City Centre.

The Toxteth riots of July 1981 were a civil disturbance in inner-city Liverpool, which arose in part from long-standing tensions between the local police and the black community. They followed the Brixton riots earlier that year.

Target work in Liverpool was taking up a lot of our time. Long stints and frequent weekend work, often up to 10 days at a time. The days were long and often we did not finish until the early hours.

I was single at the time so it wasn't too bad for me. In 1978 I had bought a maisonette in Biggin Hill in Kent for £13,000 which seemed a huge amount of money. I remember saying to my parents how will I be able to pay off a £12,600 mortgage.

Unsocial hours could be a strain on the relationships for married colleagues who had families. So, weekends and Bank holidays were mostly covered by those of us who were single. Most of Bs and Cs were married, including my close friend Alan and most of them had children. Long term relationships were difficult as I couldn't guarantee being around from one day to the next. We had to be careful when working away in case you were being targeted by the crime groups using a 'honey trap'. Any relationship away from London was short lived.

So, we were in Liverpool until the end of 1978 but this year, unlike 1977, I had Christmas off and returned home to my parents in Lincolnshire. The Bravos and Charlies team members changed little in the late 70s and early 80s. We were like a family and we got to know each other's strengths (and weaknesses).

The Liverpool case was still ongoing. Routine enquiries with airlines came up trumps. Kenyan Airways records showed that Comerford and others were flying out to Kenya.

Officers (called Outward Intelligence teams) at main airports including Heathrow had access to all computers used by airline companies. Kenyan Airways would have all records of departing and arriving passengers which thankfully narrowed down our search area. The Heathrow officers looked at the airline computer and they would feed back to us any and all information they could gather. Flight details, destinations and length of stay gave us connections to other travelling habits as well as anyone accompanying the suspect. Where and how they paid for tickets provided more intelligence in the UK. The drugs were coming from Kenya, a source of relatively, poor quality cannabis that was grown in the country. Some came from South Africa.

I was in Liverpool with a colleague Len Watson (Bravo 5) when Tommy Commerford and another male were returning from Kenya. They were observed arriving at Heathrow Airport, boarding the train to Euston Station for onward transport to Liverpool. Len and I were waiting at Liverpool's Lime Street railway station when the Euston train arrived.

It was there I first used a covert camera bag. It was similar to a sports shoulder bag with a still camera inside, a lens at one end and a small button control. From a distance the lens looked like a design feature of the bag. You held the bag so the lens pointed at the suspect and at the bottom of the bag was the release button that you pressed to take the photo. If the view was good, you simply pressed away. I was able to take photos of Commerford and another male. They were dressed in tropical clothing (short sleeve shirts and slacks) and both were pink from being in the sun. I thought I'd been careful and discreet but as the two of them got off the train and climbed into a taxi Commerford looked over at me and stuck two fingers up. I was mortified at the thought of my action blowing out an operation. I spoke to Phil Byrne in our intelligence office and told him what happened.

'Look,' he said, 'it won't be a problem, keep a lid on it. Commerford probably does that out of habit to everyone he thinks might be watching him. In any case it might not have registered with him what you were doing.'

One morning back in my office in London, Terry Byrne (Charlie 1) our team leader, bowled into the room and threw a batch of black and white photographs on to the table.

'Who is the tosser who took these photographs in Liverpool?' He barked.

'It was me, Terry', I replied defensively.

'They're rubbish. Absolute crap, Trapper! I am going to put you on a photographic course. All you've got is Lime Street Station roof and Commerford's feet.'

I looked at the photos and to my dismay, Terry was right. Just the station roof and some feet.

What I didn't know then was Terry had taken all the good photos out. It was a wind up but I went on to explain.

'It's the first time I've used the camera. The light was bad and I kept being jostled around by people rushing for trains. I had to keep moving as I followed. I couldn't stand in front and click away.'

I wanted the ground to open and swallow me up. Terry went back to his office and I sheepishly followed. He couldn't keep the pretence for too long and eventually a grin swept over his face. Nick Baker was hiding outside Terry's office laughing his head off. and Nick, hidden around the corner, started laughing. Terry joined in the hilarity and my relief that my efforts were not a total cock-up was heightened by the quality photos I had taken.

For days I had been distraught, convinced that my cover was blown, trying to think what I did, what I didn't do that gave me away. I'd been on Bs and Cs for a year and still the junior man and to "show out" (do something that alerts the bad guys they are being watched) like that and compromise the operation.

On the 17th May all 12 Bs and Cs supported by officers from London and Manchester were at work in the Liverpool docks when a suspect consignment arrived by ship from Kenya. Customs at the docks had checked the ships manifest and identified the likely consignment. Ray Smith (Charlie 7) and Dave Thomas (Charlie 4) managed to board the ship and find the drugs which were enclosed in a bag of mothballs and concealed in a crate in one of the ship's holds. For the first time ever, we employed a tracking device which was put into the crate containing the cannabis by Ray and Dave overnight. It was an early version, the size of a house brick which gave off a signal that could be picked up with a correctly aligned receiver. The receiver had a screen containing green, orange and red lights in a vertical row. Green was a very good signal, orange to red could be tricky. If the tracker was moved the audio warning would change from a constant to a warbling sound. The lights gave us a direction and the audio a distance.

This device would tell us if it was moving and in what direction it was going and more importantly if the concealment had been opened.

Everything was going swimmingly well. The cargo box came off the ship and put in a secure custom's shed in a fenced area within Hutcheson Dock. This area is where all high value goods such as cigarettes were placed.

An indication from the tracker came through that the box was being moved. The orange indicator deepened in colour. We got closer hoping that the signal would swing to red.

What had transpired was that one of the gang had broken into the secure customs shed at the docks, had opened the crate and picked out the bag of cannabis, thrown the crate away and put the bag into a Toyota car and driven out of the docks. We were able to follow the car's movements but we were now not in control of live drugs. The seriousness of this could not be under-estimated. One moment we had secured a large quantity of illegal drugs, the next allowing it to roam free onto public streets in the hands of ruthless criminals.

We were also concerned about getting the tracker back as it was the first time it had been used. The case officer, Nick Baker (Charlie 2) was tasked by Terry to retrieve the tracker.

The rest of the surveillance team were told by Terry to follow the car containing the drugs as it drove away from the docks. The car stopped after a few miles outside a pub. We watched as the driver went in and I quickly followed. I didn't have to be told the next few minutes would be crucial as the drugs could be handed over at anytime. I was dressed as a docker, wearing a donkey jacket and jeans and went up to the bar, and in my best mumbling Liverpool accent ordered a pint (an orange juice would have raised suspicion) and a plate of scouse. (Scouse is a type of lamb or beef stew. The word comes from "Lobscouse", a stew commonly eaten by sailors throughout Northern Europe, which became popular in seaports such as Liverpool. Hence Scouser).

Next to me on the bar was a public telephone. As I stood there the driver of the car, who was mid- thirties, tall and wearing jeans and an anorak made a phone call. He stood right next me as I supped my pint and ate my plate of "scouse". I could hear the conversation.

'Everything is fine,' he said. 'I've got it here.'

I was mentally jotting down as best I could and he mentioned 'Tommy' a few times.

After about 20 minutes he left the bar and returned to his car. I returned to my surveillance car which was being driven by Mike Ratcliffe (Delta 2) with a passenger from the Drug Squad a policeman called Elmore (Elly) Davies. The Toyota then stopped behind a white Opel car. Terry Byrne went out on foot and confirmed Tommy Commerford had opened the boot of the Toyota where the drugs were located and had put his thumb up to the driver. He also confirmed two other males were in the Opel.

Both cars went away in convoy and as they did so Terry Byrne decided that we had enough evidence to enact a "knock". The drugs were still in the first car which was stopped and blocked off by the other surveillance cars containing Bs and Cs officers. I was in the surveillance car still being driven by Mike whose eyesight was not that good. I shouted to Mike to drive past the car containing the drugs which had been stopped by my colleagues and pull in front of the white Opel. He did this and we quickly ran to the car to arrest the suspects. I went one side of the suspect car and arrested Tony, one of the Molloy brothers.

Mike arrested Tommy Commerford and Jimmy Molloy was pulled out of the car by Elly Davies.

Jimmy shouted out to a gathering crowd, 'Phone Maybone, my brief.'

In the car was a large baseball bat and a knuckle duster on the back seat

'Whose bat is that?' I asked Tony Molloy.

'My daughter plays baseball,' he replied.

'Does she use a knuckle duster with it?'

Gang members usually carried such weapons in case they were being ripped off by another criminal group.

The driver of the Toyota was arrested at the scene and Pat Hart and Brian Mogan were arrested at their home addresses and a total of nine suspects were interviewed and charged with importing drugs. All eventually were granted bail and appeared at Liverpool Crown Court in September 1980.

Giving evidence at Liverpool Crown Court was something else. There were nine defendants in the box in two rows all smartly dressed in suits, shirts and ties, unlike their usual "working" clothes.

Friends and family filled the public gallery. Their wives, partners and "hangers on" gave us the evil eye.

Liverpool Crown Court was an intimidating place to give evidence. With nine defendants all with their lead barristers and juniors and the prosecuting team it was a sea of wigs and gowns. Our lead barrister was John Kay who went on to become a QC and following his Knighthood, Lord Justice of the Appeal Court. He was the father of Ben Kay who became a rugby second row forward for England.

I had to give evidence on my observations in Liverpool and the arrest of Tony Malloy and I formally produced the drugs as an exhibit. In the witness box the barrister took my notebook and stared at it with a very large magnifying glass.

He looked like a Cyclops. He was looking for any mistakes, crossings out, margin notes, anything untoward. He gave me a hard time looking for any mistakes I had made.

He said, 'These notes were not made at the time and they contained pencil notations.'

I clarified the position, 'The additions in pencil were added by me when the original note required clarification. For example, when a hand-written word could not be read easily.'

This was a tense time when the slightest error, was seized upon in any attempt to find one glaring inaccuracy or omission that could be used to throw doubt on all the evidence you were submitting.

Because I had been in the pub and overheard the driver calling 'Tommy' and the other defendants it was suggested that I couldn't possibly hear what was going on because there was a juke-box playing in the pub.

'Was there a juke-box in the pub?' he asked me.

'I can't tell you if there was a juke-box in the pub.'

'You must be able to tell me that.'

'There may have been one there but it certainly wasn't playing at the time I was listening to the conversation.'

I was in court for a day and as with any such trial I was not allowed to make contact with any of my fellow officers. If an officer is part heard in court, they are not allowed to receive any guidance or clarification from any of their colleagues. It prevents officers being coached and is a cornerstone of our justice system.

So, at lunchtime I went to St Anne's Police Station in Liverpool.

I was eating my lunch and Nick Baker (Charlie 2), the case officer, walked past me saying, 'You've dug yourself a few holes there, Trapper.' Then he walked off.

Suddenly my throat seized, my mouth went dry and I had to abandon the food. What have I done, I thought? What have I said?

I continued giving evidence after lunch for about another hour which passed really quickly. I was happy I hadn't scored any own goals and the defence team could not get me to admit I did things wrong.

Sometime later when I went back to the hotel that evening, I asked Nick why he had made the off the cuff comment at the police station.

'I did it to keep you on your toes,' was his reply.

As the prosecution case progressed there were a number of legal arguments, one of which related to mothballs discovered on the operation. It was thought that when Commerford went out to Kenya he took a quantity of mothballs with him. We assumed he hoped these would disguise the smell of the drugs. When the drugs came into the UK they were surrounded by mothballs.

Alan had exhibited the mothballs that went out as exhibit "Griffiths A" and exhibit "Griffiths B". These were the actual mothballs surrounding the imported drugs. So, the records showed there were two exhibit bags both containing mothballs. Alan was told to produce both exhibits and show to the Court.

Alan was devastated. He discovered that mothballs start breaking down and virtually disappear after a few weeks, so when he held the exhibit bags aloft - they were empty. The defendants and the gallery all burst into laughter.

The jury was asked to retire whilst the case officer Nick Baker was asked to look for an expert on mothballs. He contacted the company that manufactured them in the UK.

A senior executive from the company that made mothballs. ("Mothax" were the only company at that time producing mothballs) was called to give evidence. He confirmed that if mothballs were left for a period of time they would evaporate into the atmosphere.

Terry Byrne the SIO who ran the operation along with Nick was to give evidence next so I thought I would wait in the Court and find out what evidence Terry would give.

After I had given my evidence, I sat behind the prosecution barristers listening to Terry in the witness box. Terry's evidence should have been short and sweet but it didn't work out that way. His observations were limited to what happened on the day of the arrests when he saw Tommy Commerford at the boot of the car that contained the drugs.

When Tommy Comerford had turned up, he looked inside the boot and put his thumb up to the driver.

A policeman from the Drug squad who was watching the same activity stated that the thumb gesture was to the passenger. This was sorted out well before the trial but for some reason the defence solicitors had got hold of a copy of the original incorrect paperwork. So, some of the barristers had the wrong witness statement. Confusion as one barrister was saying the driver's side and another barrister saying the passenger side.

The jurors had to be absent when a legal argument had to be settled so they were sent out, Terry, the judge and barristers were still there. Members of the public were allowed to stay. So was I.

Terry got a grilling from Commerford's barrister as to how his version of events became a witness statement.

Terry explained that after looking at his notebook, he would write out the account which would then be typed out in the office typing pool. He would then look at the typed version and compare that with his notebook.

The barrister was trying to suggest that there was unfair play as regards to recording the statement. He wanted to know what Terry did with the original hand-written notes.

Terry said that version no longer existed. That caused uproar in the Court when Tommy Comerford shouted out, 'A bit like the mothballs, Terry.'

The public gallery all started to laugh and cheer at this comment.

Terry's evidence was concluded but only after the few minutes he thought he would spend in the witness box had turned into a few hours.

Len Watson gave evidence the following day and as the officer who conducted the interviews was asked by the defence barrister to point out Mr Commerford to him.

Now Len didn't have the best of eyesight so he, quite rightly, took his time. The defendants had different clothes, some different hairstyles and they all looked different to the day they were arrested.

Len looked along the line then took a second look.

Tommy shouted out,' This is me, Len, if you're having problems.'

The Court fell about laughing.

The whole trial was like that, serious matter interjected by funny comment. There was banter between the defendants themselves and with Court officers. The defendants would crack jokes to each other and make witty comments about the suits they were wearing. Commerford in particular relished the theatre of the court proceedings. When talking to a local newspaper reporter he quipped that he had, 'spoken to the judge and told him he would not accept a community service order'.

That Autumn the country was experiencing power cuts as a result of the miner's strike. Liverpool was no exception. Nor was a Court of Law. The judge insisted the court would sit until the close of play arranging for a court usher to light candles.

As darkness fell outside the judge announced that if anyone could not conduct their business in poor light (the stenographer was one) please let him know. One of the barristers shouted out, 'Who said that?'

The judge tutted theatrically and decided to finish and retire for the night to resume the next day.

Thankfully, after several weeks they were all found guilty. The judge in his sentencing after the guilty verdict said that even a small amount of cannabis (about 17kilos) this had been one of the most important prosecutions in the Liverpool area. The main reason being was the influence that Commerford and his like had over law enforcement, the police and the public. They thought they were bomb proof, that they could get away with almost anything in Liverpool and that no-one would get close to arresting them and successfully prosecuting them. The gang received prison sentences between six and nine years.

We all thought our work in Liverpool was over but as the saying goes 'the King is dead, long live the King'.

Almost immediately after that case information filtered through from our police contacts in the Drug Squad that a new crime group was moving in to takeover. Intelligence from the drug squad confirmed the gang including Joey Evans, Jerry Bennett, Joe Murphy and John Kennedy had access to Seaforth container docks and a number of corrupt officials working there. They were suspected of using planted dockers to get containers out of the docks by forging release notes (the documents given to security staff at the port gates) and just driving the suspect container out without going through security and Customs controls. We had learned lessons from our previous work in Liverpool and we moved hotels from the city centre to the outskirts of Liverpool.

The Investigation Division had started to give cases operational names. Normally the names started with the letter of the team investigating it and although Bravos and Charlies were the lead team, this operation was called "Woodpile" (it started as a police operation with this name). The Bravos and Charlies had changed. Terry Byrne, Mike Knox, Nick Baker had transferred to other investigation teams. Peter Corgan and Alan Huish became the team leaders (Bravo 1 and Charlie 1). George Atkinson (Charlie 4) remained my line manager and I looked to him for guidance and mentoring. He, along with Chris Hardwick, Bruce Letheren, Ray Smith, Alan Griffiths and Len Watson were the link between the successful Bs and Cs of the mid 70s and early 80s and the new set up.

We encountered the same difficulties when operating in all parts of Liverpool. Whilst we had learned a lot about the methods used by smuggling groups they also learnt about our tactics, particularly those given in evidence at the trial of Commerford. We often commented that crime groups have a better intelligence and communication network than law enforcement. Smuggling and crime are not hobbies to them. It is a 365 x, 24 - 7 commitment. They didn't have to fill in forms, make notes and live away from home. And, they had access to unlimited funds to source their illegal activity.

I spent the majority of January and February 1981 alternating between working in Cardiff and Liverpool. Mike Ratcliffe (Ratters – Charlie 2) had taken over from Nick Baker and having originated from West Houghton near Bolton was the case officer.

As before, we kept observation on the home addresses for the main suspects, Evans, Bennett and Murphy and would follow them when we could. By car for short distances, identifying the routes they drove. Rather than follow them from home we would pick them up in traffic on their usual route. Similar tactics were used on foot, walking close to other pedestrians, mingling where we could, trying to blend in, never being in a position where we stood out. This was so important in the dock area.

It was necessary to obtain evidence of the main suspects meeting with dock workers and transport companies. The suspects regularly visited Seaforth container port and we saw them meeting with Kennedy who, we discovered, was the link to corrupt workers.

One of the target addresses was near the protestant cathedral in Liverpool and myself and Mike Ratcliffe approached the senior verger to see if we could use one of the rooms to watch the premises. He was a bit apprehensive but eventually agreed. The archbishop's changing area was ideal, particularly during the week. Everything was working well until Sunday when Pete Lovelock (Charlie six), armed with a camera and binoculars was confronted by the then Archbishop, the ex- England cricket player, David Shepherd who was dressing for his morning service. Pete tried to hide the empty beer cans and fish and chip paper whilst saying to the Archbishop, 'Your verger knows all about this joint police and customs operation'.

Pete always maintained he didn't know what to say to him but came out with a comment, 'Sunday. I suppose this is your busy day'.

Not surprisingly he received no reply and we still laugh about this today.

We were at heightened security level when Mike's car was stolen from outside the Customs office in Liverpool's Coburg dock. It was later found torched with the words "bizzies" and "pigs", scratched into the bodywork. After that we certainly looked over our shoulders more than usual.

I was with Steve Frodsham watching a flat in an area called Cantrell Farm, a high-rise block of flats on the outskirts of Liverpool. It sounds rural but it was a high- rise block and had experienced social disorder over the years. As we sat in a car it started to bounce up and down. I got out to be confronted by four boys, no older than twelve, standing on the bumper.

'Are you the fucking bizzies?' One of them shouted.

I told them to clear off so myself and Steve "Frodders" decided to leave the area. Didn't live it down with the team when they found out we had been hounded out by schoolboys.

During one of the deployments to Liverpool in July, I was with Ratters, Alan Griffiths, Dave Thomas, Chris Caton and Frodders at the Crest Motel on the East Lancs Road. It was a Bank Holiday to celebrate Charles and Diana's wedding. Although we were on standby, the whole country, including drug smugglers, were tuned in to the television. The Crest Motel had organised a fun day which was attended by a local social club, St Josephs. We participated in the tug of war and five a side football and other games. I was leading in the yard of ale drinking competition, downing about two and a half pints in under a minute, only to be beaten by a lady from St Josephs who drank it 30 seconds faster than me. My street cred battered again.

From our surveillance observations of the suspects regularly visiting Seaforth docks it became clear that a particular port was key to the operation.

The docks are located a couple of miles north of Liverpool in an area called Waterloo. It was built to accommodate the larger container ships. The Customs Maritime Intelligence Teams identified a potential suspect container which was due to arrive at Seaforth docks. A container arrived and we suspected it would be removed from the dock without being examined.

The case officer Mike Ratcliffe dispatched officers to watch the suspect addresses and surveillance teams (from Bs and Cs and Manchester monitored the suspect's movements. Peter Corgan (Bravo 1) arranged with the coastguard to have a Sea King helicopter on standby at Liverpool Airport.

The Coastguard are a search and rescue command based around the coast of the UK. They are called on to go to the aid of ships, yachts and people who have got into difficulties. Unlike HM Custom and Excise, they have no law enforcement remit and no power of arrest. They have always been only too willing to help the police and customs.

I was dispatched to be the officer to liaise with the helicopter crew and to go up with them to follow the container. I spent a whole day waiting for the go ahead to take off. Peter came on the radio and casually almost jokingly asked how much would it cost to have the helicopter on standby. I spoke to the three-man crew (a pilot, navigator and a winchman) and they confirmed the normal charge is £3000 an hour but, in this case, there would be no charge.

I contacted Peter on the radio and transmitted, 'Bravo 1, this is Bravo 6. I have confirmed the charge for the helicopter would be £3000 an hour and we have been on standby for three hours.'

I could hear the pained silence at the other end. I did put him out of his misery after a couple of minutes.

The helicopter crew offered to go up and let me take photos of Seaforth docks as they wanted to reconnoitre the port area in case they needed to return sometime in the future. I jumped at the chance and spent an enjoyable half an hour sitting by the open-door taking photos as it flew over the docks and the city.

It was important to find an observation point where we could watch the Seaforth container port. Dave Thomas managed to get access to a room at the top of a grain warehouse. The grain, imported into Liverpool was used to make breakfast cereals and we nicknamed the building the Kelloggs Corn Flakes factory. We were on the fourth floor and although there was a lift it was slow and unreliable. There was a conveyor belt which took the bags of corn from the ground floor to the sorting machinery on the second and third floor. The quickest way to our location was to jump on this conveyor belt and jump off when it got to the fourth floor. I used this unofficial mode of transport on numerous occasions. Health and safety issues were unheard of at this time. We spent two days in the observation point working twelve hours on and twelve hours off.

The room provided us with a panoramic view of the dock and the surrounding roads and buildings. Dick Palmer had set up a video camera in addition to some WW2 German submarine binoculars on a stand. Myself and Alan, along with other colleagues, manned this position for days, operating a 12-hour shift rota. I preferred using the submarine binoculars, although, unlike the video equipment had no night viewing capability. They were steady and provided a clear focussed view.

When not manning the Kelloggs building and not out on surveillance we based ourselves in a Customs Office in Coburg dock. Gerry Hickey, a senior officer and a real gent was taken into our confidence. He was from Liverpool and knew the docks well. One off his assistant officers, Mark Daniels, "Scouse" approached us and said, 'I will do anything to be part of this operation. I will look after your cars, get your fish and chips. Anything!'

When we finished the case, Mike Ratcliffe asked Scouse what he would like to do - job wise. He indicated he would love to work on the Customs Cutters (patrol boats). Mike wrote to the maritime branch and Mark started a year later at the lowest grade. I met him several years later and he had risen to become the department's senior Cutter Commander.

In the early hours of 30th October, we were watching a recently arrived ship, the "MV Advisor," which had recently arrived from Jamaica. At 04.00 the dockers all retired to the canteen to have a tea break.

Immediately sacks were seen being thrown off the ship onto the dock area where they were transferred to a container on a trailer parked up nearby. I was providing a commentary as to what was happening to the surveillance teams who were waiting outside the dock.

Suspects, Joey Evans and Jerry Bennett, were seen with other males handling the sacks. All vehicle and foot exits were manned by police and customs to ensure none of the suspects were able to leave. We did expect the container to be taken out of the docks but by 07.00 nothing happened. As we had observed the main suspects "with their hands in the till" by handling the sacks a decision was made to call the "knock".

Along with Mike Ratcliffe I drove to the area of the dockers canteen where we had last seen Evans and Bennett. As we parked up, I said to Dave we should wait for backup but he suggested we went in to make the arrests. Dave was senior to me and we were both big lads so I agreed. Evans and Bennett were sitting at a table and as we approached them Dave asked if he could have my handcuffs. To my amazement he arrested Evans, handcuffed him and walked out to the car. I was left at the table with Bennett, Kennedy and another potential suspect, Kelly. They were all wearing working clothes. The canteen area was large enough to accommodate all the dock workers and lorry drivers.

I wrongly assumed Dave had gone to the car to radio up for the "cavalry" to come and help. In fact, he had walked with Evans in my handcuffs to the nearest Customs office in Hutcheson dock. I was left with three suspects in an increasingly hostile environment. I was expecting other colleagues to turn up shortly but as the time went on, I realised this was not happening.

Bennett asked what was happening

'This is a Custom's investigation into a serious matter and I want you to stay where you are'.

Other dockers were having a break and one of them came to the table and said he was a Union convenor.

'This is a dockers canteen and what the fuck is going on?'

I replied, 'This is a dockers canteen but it is a Customs controlled area and anybody obstructing me in the execution of my duty will be in serious trouble'.

This seemed to do the trick although I could see Bennett, Kennedy and Kelly were getting agitated. Kennedy stood up and I said to him, 'Where are you going? Sit back down'.

He said "I am going to get a cup of tea".

Decision time!

I asked him, 'Get me one with no sugar'.

Surprisingly he did return with four teas including one for me. The tray he was carrying was shaking and I realised he was more scared than I was. I moved the sauce bottles away in case they were used to clatter me with and started to sip my tea. My mind was working overtime and I couldn't figure out why the team hadn't turned up. I then saw Alan Griffiths look in and walk past. I gestured to him and shouted.

Alan had seen me shouting at him. In seconds he was by my side and other officers followed. My adrenalin and fear levels were sky high but I was relieved help had arrived.

'What the fuck's happening,' I said. 'I have been here with these three over 20 minutes. I thought I was in for a serious battering'.

Alan had no idea we had gone into the canteen as Dave Thomas had not radioed requesting support. Bennett, Kennedy and Kelly were arrested.

I returned to my car and drove to the Customs office in Hutchinson dock. Dave Thomas was there with Evans and when I could speak to him alone, I asked him why he had left me on my own. He just shrugged his shoulders. What I wanted to say was very short, stern and very uncouth. It would also have been insolent so I never said it.

"The show must go on" as they say and a few hours later I was back at work entering a pub called the Joker in Everton Vale. I was with Alan Lee a Mancunian colleague and we were both dressed as dockers. We were looking for a suspect called Hughes who had been seen helping to unload the sacks of cannabis. I thought I looked the "bee's knees" but after about five minutes the whole pub were humming and swaying to the theme music from Dixon of Dock Green. We both smiled and made a diplomatic exit. Typical Liverpool humour.

A decision was made by the prosecution team to move the trial of Evans, Bennett, Kennedy and Kelly to Mold in North Wales. The accused were well known in Liverpool and it was feared a local jury could be influenced or "nobbled". The accused all pleaded not guilty but after a three- month trial they were all convicted and went to prison for 5 -8 years.

At the trial I had to give evidence on my observations and what happened in the dock's canteen. The Judge made a comment as regards being left on my own.

'So, officer. You were not only handcuff-less you were friendless!'

I have visited Liverpool since and the city has become a truly sophisticated city of culture. On this trip I was not looking over my shoulder all the time.

CHAPTER 9
PLANES, DOUBLE DECKERS and BEETLE WHEELS.

Our expertise at surveillance probably annoyed the other investigation teams, particularly the Foxtrots and Golfs who targeted and investigated heroin importations.

Experience came from covering cases throughout the UK where we cultivated contacts and links with the regional Customs and Police. As drugs came from abroad, they had to arrive at a port, airport or by boat into a remote location. We could often count on a local, someone on the ground who knew the area.

George Atkinson (Bravo 2) had a network of contacts within the Police Regional Crime Squad offices. Valuable contacts such as Chief Superintendent Albert Able from Devon and Cornwall. Chief Inspector Mike Milton, from South Wales, would drop everything to work with us.

A lot has been said about the Police/ Customs rivalry but in many cases our joint investigations proved the right way forward.

Insight, gained over the years into the geography of drug smuggling, often proved invaluable. Spending endless (sometimes unfruitful) time on mobile or foot surveillance for some bizarre reason stays in the memory. Almost like fishing - you wait patiently for a bite only to hook something you were never sure was there. For the most part it may have been boring but you have to be alert and ready. An added bonus, forever in your mind, was that you knew your colleagues sang from the same song sheet.

The Foxtrots and Golfs were part of the overall Investigation Division based in the same office as us. They had the same numbers of officers as us. We knew them really well both work wise and socially and there was a lot of friendly banter as we dealt with importations of "recreational drugs whilst they did "God's work".

In the 70s, having a drink at lunchtime and after work was the norm. The customers in the two pubs behind our office in New Fetter Lane, The White Horse and the Printers Devil, comprised of workers from the Daily Mirror, Fleet Street journalists and Customs investigators.

At that time, mostly Pakistan or Afghanistan heroin entered the country so the Foxtrots and Golfs spent a lot of their time in Southall in West London where there was a large Asian population, many of whom worked in and around Heathrow Airport. As time went on, importations of Turkish heroin increased and part of their brief was to investigate Turkish nationals and Turkish Cypriots living in London (concentrated in the Green Lane area).

Although it was early days of cocaine smuggling two new teams were created; the Romeos and Sierras who targeted cocaine importations. They were also based in New Fetter Lane (the location of all the Customs Drugs Investigation teams and Intelligence). Often there were cross overs as some of the smugglers were involved in cannabis, heroin and cocaine. In the 70s the Investigation Division, including the fraud and drugs teams, numbered about 300. Everybody knew each other and the management quickly resolved any disputes as to which team led the investigation.

The Division only had a handful of official vehicles at this time and to ensure the team had a credible surveillance capability we were encouraged to use our own cars. When using your private car you were able to claim mileage allowance only if you were ten miles outside a radius of Charing Cross. As the Golfs, Foxtrots, Romeos and Sierras were working on London based smugglers they rarely saw the financial perks that we at Bravos and Charlies enjoyed. A few choice words were often spoken between the teams on this arrangement.

'Nice to see you in London for a change. Did you get lost?' was a typical comment from the Foxtrots and Golfs.

'You can't leave London as you will get a nosebleed as well as getting lost,' was our usual reply.

It was a bit of a joke with them as we were mostly outside London so we were the ones earning all the mileage allowances.

The Bravos and Charlies had just completed a successful "Knock" on a light aircraft that had flown a quantity of cannabis to a landing strip in the village of Blyborough, North Lincolnshire. It was a method of importation we had seen only infrequently but it then demanded closer attention.

Our team had been targeting a smuggling gang in London who had access to a light aircraft. Intelligence from Customs identified six potential airfields in and around Retford, a market town on the Nottingham/ Lincolnshire border.

The main suspect, Hugh Hutton was a conman as well as a drugs smuggler. He drove a rented Rolls Royce and would use the vehicle at weekends for weddings which paid for the hire. The other members Michael Glass, Ahmed Mitha, Michael James and Peter Goodsell were based in London and we observed a number of meetings in restaurants in the Queensway. Checks with the police revealed Goodsell was a prolific forger and had the nickname, "Peter the Printer".

Terry sent myself and Alan Griffiths to the Retford area to map out the airfields and landing strips. I picked Alan up at his home and we stopped at my parents for lunch.

As we drove north on the A1, we approached the roundabout for Retford. We couldn't believe our luck a silver Cadillac, owned by Mitha, was two cars ahead of us. The Cadillac turned off towards Retford and headed towards Gamston airfield south of Retford. They slowed down as they passed Gamston. We followed the car for about five miles and we both agreed to abort the surveillance. We could not follow them any more as we didn't want to reveal ourselves and compromise our operation.

For the next few days we continued to look at other airfields in the area and whilst driving passed a farm near Blyborough close to Kirton Lyndsey. I remembered I went there for the Lincolnshire Schools Sports event in the sixties. In addition to Gamston and Blyborough we identified a number of other potential landing strips.

On 25 September 1978 the Bravos and Charlies drove up to the Scunthorpe area. Terry Byrne and Dave Thomas (Charlie 4), the case officer, approached the Army Base in Kirton Lyndsey Camp. The Army's liaison officer agreed we could station ourselves and our vehicles in the camp. Terry said he wasn't sure if he was joking when the army man said, 'We can shoot the aircraft down if you want.'

The following day a light aircraft was reported leaving northern France heading towards the UK. It had been identified by the Customs Intelligence team who followed its progress on UK's radar system.

The previously identified farmer's field in Blyborough became the focus of our attention. Mike Knox and Nick Baker approached the warden of Grayingham church near the farm. Mike and Nick climbed the rickety ladder in the church tower and based themselves on the top of the bell tower. Armed with binoculars and a radio they waited for an arrival. I was in a vehicle with Alan parked up off the main road in a narrow lane. Mike gave a commentary as a light aircraft came into view.

'The target is flying over the landing strip'.

We were panicking that we were at the wrong location.

'The target is coming in to land and a Granada estate is parked up near the landing area. One male is sitting in the vehicle.'

Then. 'The target has landed and one engine - now two engines turned off'.

In anticipation of the "Knock" my adrenalin was flowing.

'A wooden crate has been thrown out and two males are lifting it into the estate car'.

I turned the engine of our car on and we were ready to go.

Mike obviously got caught up in the theatre of what was happening for as I turned the car key he shouted. 'One engine has started up.'

At this point Terry interrupted the commentary and said, 'I think it is time we knocked this'.

All hell let loose as I drove at great speed towards the airfield. Terry jumped out of his car and climbed on the wing of the plane, a twin-engine Piper Aztec. Both engines were on and Terry opened the door and shouted at the pilot, 'Turn the engines off'.

I had a vision of Terry doing "wing walk" as he disappeared into the clouds. We were all thinking the "Knock" should have been called sooner but thankfully Terry seized the initiative.

Alan and I were sent out to look for the silver Cadillac we had been spotted earlier. It was later found outside Mitha's home in Golders Green, London. Mitha was arrested by two officers from Drugs K and brought up to Scunthorpe Police station.

In total six suspects were arrested. Along with Alan, I interviewed Peter Goodsell, "Peter the Printer".

At first, he was willing to talk but when confronted with photos taken of him meeting Mitha and Hutton in Queensway he barked, 'no comment' for the rest of the interview.

The next day we couldn't believe the coverage in the local and national press on the operation.

The Sun had the headline; 'I'm no hero says man who halted drugs plane'.

A photo of me opening the wooden crate containing cannabis appeared in the newspapers.

Mike Knox and Terry Byrne were portrayed as "The Gemini Twins at their base in London."

I knew Geminis are said to have a dual nature, symbolized by twins but I couldn't work out why it was applied to Mike and Terry.

The press coverage was the first real case the Investigation Division had publicised. Normally, we went about our business without attracting or wanting publicity (our division preferred to operate away from the media gaze).

I had to admit I enjoyed the newspaper articles and although it was a view of my back opening the crate, I was able to tell my friends, 'I was on page 5 of the Sun'.

Six suspects were charged and the following year went to trial at Lincoln Crown Court, located on the western side of the grounds of Lincoln Castle.

I had to give evidence regarding my observations, opening the wooden crate of cannabis and the interview with "Peter the Printer".

I was about to enter the main gates of the Castle confines when I was stopped by the police on crowd control. Two trumpeters signalled the arrival of the High Court judge. He was chauffeur driven in as onlookers cheered as if Royalty had graced their presence. It was real theatre which made a great impression on this Lincolnshire lad.

All six were found guilty and received prison sentences between five and eight years.

Instead of taking the time off due to us, we were drafted in to assist Drugs Lima, a heroin team in London, on a major operation.

Given our expertise on surveillance all members of Bs and Cs, apart from Mike and Terry the two SIOs and Dave Thomas, were on the operation. Dave remained in Scunthorpe sorting out statements and preparing the Aztec case for court.

Operation "Big Wheels" involved the discovery of a sizeable consignment of heroin from Malaysia. At the beginning of October 1978 uniformed Customs Officers based at the Royal Albert Docks had identified a Volkswagen Beetle that had arrived from Malaysia.

Dock workers unloading a ship had pushed the car on to the quay and found the wheels would not turn properly. They notified the uniformed Customs staff who initiated some physical checks on the vehicle and the paperwork linked to the importation.

The vehicle was examined and a significant quantity of brown powder was found concealed in the tyres. The powder was tested at the port by the uniformed staff and it was found to be heroin and had an estimated weight of 60 kilos.

This amount was by far the largest amount of heroin seized and all the teams on the ID (Investigation Division) were told this operation was the top priority. In total over 200 officers were involved, from the other drugs teams, tobacco smuggling, VAT and customs fraud.

On the paperwork that accompanied the car was an address in Mount Ephraim Road, Streatham and a surveillance team was dispatched to watch the target address; a four- storey block of flats.

We didn't know the actual flat but deployed an observation van to monitor the movements in and out of the block.

Two males of Chinese/Malaysian origin were seen leaving the premises. They hailed a taxi and Tony Lovell (Lima 1) made a decision to follow them. I was in an official Ford Cortina with Mike Stephenson as the taxi left Mount Ephraim Road. Along with six other surveillance cars they were followed to the Royal Albert Docks a distance of 14 miles.

Travelling by taxi or public transport is unusual for criminals. Normally, they have their own cars, often top of the range Mercedes or BMWs. (Lawbreakers usually have large egos. If they were successful, they wanted to appear successful to their peers).

On arrival the two men went into the building which housed numerous shipping agencies. The mobile surveillance handed over the observations to the Limas who were already in the building. Observation took about twenty minutes before they left the dock and caught a double decker bus back to Streatham.

We had expected that VW Beetle would soon be moved but we later found out from Tony Lovell that they had paid the shipping charges and had arranged with the agent to return the following day about 11.00 to collect the car.

Two officers boarded the bus in case they met with other suspects.

Visually, the bus was not a difficult target to follow but we did have difficulty stopping and starting at bus stops and junctions. We had six surveillance cars (twelve officers) on the job and several 'footmen' who could be deployed when the targets were on the bus and when they got off.

We had four footmen who were passengers in our cars, from Bravos and Charlies and some from other ID teams.

There would be a driver and map reader who consulted the A to Z maps and a plan of bus routes.

Footmen would get on the bus and sit behind the two targets, getting off and swopping with others. They tried sitting close in the hope of overhearing a conversation where names or places might be mentioned.

I was in a car with Stevo.

A fellow investigator, Desmond Chamberlain (November 3), from the "Novembers" a cocaine referred team, boarded the bus with two Deltas as two other footmen got off.

For some reason he decided to pretend he had had a couple of drinks too many.

The bus was driving through Streatham Vale when Desmond asked the conductor if there was a toilet on board.

'No, no. No toilet on the bus.'

The conductor went to the front of the bus and asked the driver to stop outside a toilet with stairs that led down to the facilities.

The conductor pointed out the toilet to Desmond.

As Desmond got out, he radioed in, 'I may have shown a bit. I've had to get off the bus.'

Having got off the bus he went down to the toilet and radioed in again. Stevo told him told him there wasn't a problem - that we would get someone to board the bus at the next stop.

As he climbed back up the stairs to the pavement the bus conductor was shouting at him. 'Hurry up. We've been waiting for you.'

As Desmond got back on the bus everyone on board started to clap including the two people who he was following. It was probably so off the wall, so convincing, that Desmond would never have been identified as a surveillance officer.

The targets got off the bus heading for the block of flats in Mount Ephraim Road. They were followed, at a distance, by two footmen. We stood down and another team, made up from the "Novembers" and "Limas", watched the premises overnight.

The following day, we were back in Streatham at 07.00. I was teamed up with Stevo again. Because this was a massive amount of heroin, thirty surveillance vehicles were deployed to ensure the drugs were not lost. The two suspects left the flats at 09.00 and walked up to a tyre company in Streatham High Road where they purchased two new wheels and tyres for a VW Beetle. After they had left, one of the "Limas" approached the supplier to see if any new intelligence leads were available.

The targets then returned to Mount Ephraim Road and got into a blue Toyota and drove off, with the VW wheels in the boot. We followed the vehicle to the same office in the Royal albert Docks.

As all the shipping costs had been paid, the two suspects were allowed to go to the port warehouse where the Beetle was stored.

They replaced the two wheels which contained the drugs with the spares they had just purchased earlier in the day. "Lima" footmen from a distance watched them jack up the car and swop the wheels. In possession of the wheels containing heroin, they returned to the Toyota. The wheels went into the boot and they drove off, myself and the other vehicles following close by.

About twenty surveillance vehicles from Drugs and VAT investigation teams were in the convoy.

I later joked that we caused an announcement on Capital Radio, highlighting heavy traffic in South London.

Outside a block of flats in Mount Ephraim Road they parked up and the wheels from the boot were taken indoors.

Because in the time available and the sophistication of the concealment it had been impossible for us to remove the tyres from the wheels, take out the drugs and insert a substitute material. To allow drugs, heroin in particular to run live was a risky tactic as the department would be criticised if drugs were lost and ended up in the hands of street dealers. The pressure was on the surveillance team not to lose the car (and drugs) increasing our levels of concentration and stress.

We hadn't identified the specific flat so no audio or video equipment had been installed. There was no way of knowing what was going on inside.

The next twenty minutes were nerve wracking and we knew we couldn't give them too long in case they suspected they had been followed and could easily flush the heroin down the toilet.

Normally we would give them enough time to "breach" the concealment but before that decision had to be made the original driver came out, got into the car and drove around the block. I was giving the commentary as he drove around a couple of times which we thought was a bit strange.

It was the operational team's decision whether to "Knock" it. The operational senior managers, including the Chief Investigation Officer, Peter Cutting were monitoring events on the surveillance radio system in the control Room in New Fetter Lane. Peter Cutting was the head of the Investigation Division and his office was on the sixth floor.

Stevo was driving and I had the 'eyeball' (giving the commentary) and said, 'Look! He's gone around the block twice so we need instructions as to what to do.'

I was happy to continue following the vehicle but given the fact it had gone around the block twice I wanted a second opinion.

A voice said over the radio, 'The Chief says Knock it.'

There were about forty investigators in Mount Ephraim Road and around the local streets and it seemed like Wembley Way on Football's Cup Final day. It must have looked strange to locals to see so many men walking on their own at a gentle pace, around their neighbourhood trying to look like your average pedestrian minding their own business.

So, we had the go ahead to make the arrest. I was with Mike Stephenson (Charlie 7) and I drove in front of the car and grabbed the man out of the car, pinning him down on the bonnet of the VW searching him for weapons and making sure he was restrained. We spread his arms on the bonnet of his car and as I pinned him down Stevo rubbed him down to see if he was carrying any weapons or paperwork that potentially was evidential. He had nothing of interest so he was handcuffed and we handed him over to other officers. He was obviously from the Far East and he refused to say anything.

Although we did not know it at the time, it transpired he was looking for a better parking place.

There were 9 flats in this block of flats and we were not sure which flat they were in. The entrance door was locked so a sledge hammer was used to gain entry.

A colleague John Hector lifted the sledge hammer to hit the main entrance front door. As he did so, he managed to hit one of the other team member Ken Stott, behind him, cutting his forehead.

In order to get in quickly, Reg Low threw a dustbin lid through the front window and tried to climb in, cutting his leg as he did so.

There seemed to be blood everywhere and it looked like scene from a zombie movie.

All the flat doors were knocked on and if there was no answer a forced entry was made. Alan Griffiths knocked on one door and told the elderly owners just to leave the door open and there was nothing for them to worry about.

Eventually we found the right flat. The other suspect was in the bathroom, sitting on the toilet and hadn't heard any of the commotion, not even when his door was smashed off its hinges.

While this was happening, a colleague had observed a car repeatedly driving past. He called it in saying, 'The driver looks Chinese. He's slowed down looking at the block of flats.'

Tony Lovell, the Senior Officer in charge of the "Limas" the heroin investigating team, said, 'Nick him.'

It turned out he was on his way to Sainsbury's to do some shopping when he spotted the melee outside the flat and was curious. It was a case of being in the wrong place at the wrong time. He was held for two days before it was accepted that he was completely innocent.

The heroin was secured and removed to the Custom House.

Although the Bravos and Charlies worked on cannabis smuggling criminals, we ended up investigating a suspect heroin smuggler called Ahmet Velli, who was living in Dongola Road, off Green Lane in North London, an area inhabited by a large population of Turkish Cypriots. We used a plain van parked nearby the target address with an officer hidden inside. A couple of meetings were observed.

Mr Velli met up with a Turkish national in the Regent Palace Hotel in the Strand. I stayed there overnight watching as best I could the movements of Velli. The hotel security gave us access to the adjoining room. The Strand Palace was a typical Central London hotel at the higher end of the market and because it was a few hundred yards from Leicester Square very popular with overseas tourists. I spoke to the head of security who let us have the room for nothing.

Ray Smith (Charlie 7) and I were in the security office monitoring the security cameras that monitored the reception area. On the screen we could see a man walk in dressed in black cowboy clothes and black Stetson hat. He strolled over to look at himself in a full-length mirror. From his holsters he practised quick draws of two toy guns. Satisfied, he tilted his hat back, holstered his guns and walked out of the hotel.

'Who's he?' I asked the security manager.

'He comes in every Saturday evening. He'll be back soon and do it again.'

And he sure did.

Customs officers based at the port of Harwich checked the ferry manifest and found that a suspect car was on board and linked to Velli. The ferry was due to arrive from Holland at 06.00.

Uniformed Customs Officers at Harwich stopped the vehicle in the Green Channel and told the driver to go into the examination bay. Underneath the rear seats were 5 kilos of heroin with a street value of more than £2,000. The driver and his passenger were initially arrested and interviewed by the Harwich staff who were replaced by the investigators from Bs and Cs.

Records showed that the seized car had previously been seen at a meeting with Velli. This was the catalyst to conduct a "Knock" in Dongola Road.

On 3 May 1979 we met up at 5 am on a grey and wet day in the car park for Walthamstow Greyhound Park waiting for the officers at Harwich to give us the nod that the car had been intercepted and secured. We had ten officers and five cars out on the 'plot' (the area being targeted).

Gordon Hall (Charlie 3) was the main officer on the Velli case and we all stood in a circle in the car park, adrenaline flowing, waiting for the word to move on to the target address, not knowing what would be found there.

A plan was in place and I was one of the officers to go to the front door. Others were to be deployed at the rear of the property to prevent anybody escaping.

Gordon had a cup of coffee in his hand as we talked when I said, 'I hope there are no firearms on the premises.'

Gordon had a look of horror on his face but didn't reply.

A second later a passing car back-fired. Gordon threw the coffee in the air and crouched down looking for cover.

Stevo mumbled, 'It's a car back-firing, you silly sod.'

We then got the go ahead on the radio and drove to Dongola Road and entered the target premises using our magic entry key - a sledge hammer. It took a little time but we got inside and arrested Mr Velli, taking him back to New Fetter Lane.

Mr Velli's wife made a complaint that when we bashed in the door it fell on her pet budgerigar that was out of its cage flying around the room. It didn't survive the impact.

None of us could recall seeing a damaged budgerigar or even a bird cage. She also accused Stevo of stealing 50pence pieces from a jar on the mantelpiece.

The Velli linked operation had a spin- off which indicated 5 kilos of heroin were to arrive at Heathrow Airport carried by Sammy Hassan (aka "The Potato Man" as he worked for a company trading in potatoes).

At the airport we spoke to the immigration officers and they would look out for the people with the names we were looking for. Sammy Hassan went through the immigration desk and walked out through Customs Control. He was carrying a hold-all not big enough to carry 5 kilos of anything. He was stopped at the Control and searched. There was nothing on him. He was allowed to go on his way. There was no way of knowing if he had merely arrived from Turkey after making arrangements with others or that his plans had gone awry. He may have been ripped off by shady suppliers.

It was only when all the passengers went through Controls there was one suitcase still going around on the carousel. We took the suitcase off and took it into the Controls office and discovered the 5 kilos of heroin inside. We subsequently found out that an immigration officer looking out for Hassan had written the name on a piece of paper. As Hassan waited to be processed, he spotted this piece of paper so knew he was being targeted. So, he bottled out of retrieving his suitcase and left the airport without it. The only solace for us was that we had recovered the drugs and we knew that he would be answerable to the people behind the operation.

At our Investigation Office at Heathrow, we discussed if we had any options to try and progress the operation. A hair-brained scheme was arrived at by a number of us sitting around in the Customs office at Heathrow. I suggested we could turn up at Hassan's address in Sidcup and pretend we were from BA lost luggage section. We would visit him there and attempt to convince him that we were bringing a suitcase from lost- luggage and delivering it on behalf of British Airways. We thought my basic blue anorak would look like some sort of livery. We cut out a British Airways logo from a leaflet and stuck it on my coat.

I turned up at the Hassan semi-detached Victorian house with six other Bs and Cs officers with a suitcase that contained everything as before but the heroin had been removed. We hoped that he would be there and take ownership of the suitcase. The door was answered by Hassan's partner. She was an elegant looking British woman in her mid- thirties.

'I'm from British Airways lost luggage section,' I said. 'We understand that this suitcase was left on the carousel by mistake and we believe it belongs to a Mr Hassan at this address.'

'He's not here at the moment,' she said, 'He's down the pub.'

As I replied the telephone rang inside the house. I didn't want her to answer it. 'I'm from Customs,' I said walking in and beckoning my colleague Gordon Hall who was sat in the car to come into the house. Gordon didn't move.

I sat the woman down telling her she couldn't answer the phone. After a few minutes I went to the front door to wave at Gordon to come in. This time he saw me and ran to the house.

Gordon interviewed the woman and found out that Hassan had gone to the pub two hours earlier.

I teamed up with George Atkinson in his Marina car and we went along to the pub deciding it would be better to wait for him to come out.

At 11pm we had colleagues in the pub to watch his movements. When he did leave at closing-time we arrested him. He was worse for wear and obviously had had a lot to drink and was slurring his words. He was about 5' 7", stocky build in his late 30s with an olive complexion.

I put him in the back of George's private car. George was driving and I sat behind him with Hassan next to me. We had no handcuffs in those days so had to rely on keeping suspects close to us.

I cautioned Hassan who immediately asked where he was being taken.

'To the Customs Investigation Division HQ,' I replied. 'To New Fetter Lane.'

'Why can't I go to the local police station?' he asked.

'We're not the police,' I said. 'We're Customs.'

You could tell he wasn't very happy about this although his demeanour was much lightened by the alcohol he had consumed.

I'm in the back with Hassan as George's gearbox started playing up. He thrashed the lever up and down trying to find the right gear.

At the first set of traffic lights Hassan tried to open the car door. I grasped him around the throat, George leant over to help and for a short while it became quite physical with George trying to throw punches. At the same time, I was hitting Hassan trying to keep a firm grip going.

The traffic lights changed and changed again as Hassan made another attempt to get out of the car. Impatient motorists were hitting their horns behind us. We then became aware that we were directly outside Sidcup Police Station out of which came a posse of policemen who proceeded to arrest myself, George and Hassan.

I shouted at them; 'We're from Customs. Don't let this man put anything in his mouth. Don't let him reach into his pockets.'

What I didn't want was Hassan swallowing any reference to the suitcase he might still have.

Eventually the Police got my message. Hassan was searched and put into a cell while details were cleared up and we were allowed to take him on to New Fetter Lane. This time Gordon Hall joined us in the car and we sat either side of Hassan.

Regrettably we didn't have enough evidence to charge him with that importation. He denied any knowledge of the suitcase and we couldn't find any paperwork that would challenge his story.

CHAPTER 10
OPERATION WRECKER

Over the centuries "wrecking" was the practice of plundering cargo from any ship that had foundered close to shore. Tradition has it that "wreckers" planted decoy fires to entice ships closer to rocks waiting for the inevitable collision - the shipwreck.

In the 18th Century, on the coast of Cornwall, the activities of wreckers and smugglers were at its peak with peasants (helped by the blessing of clergymen) seizing the opportunity to relieve their poor lives.

Between 1780 and 1783 as much as 2 million pounds of tea and 13 million gallons of brandy were smuggled into the country.

The Custom Officers of the day, the "Preventive Men" were sent to deter them with mixed results for some could not resist the temptation to help themselves. Sir John Knill, Collector of Customs at St. Ives between 1762 and 1782, is reported to have traded in looted cargo as enthusiastically as the next man.

Smuggling has always gone on but in recent years the breed of "smuggler" had changed. Villains who made a living from robbery or hi-jacking lorries saw less aggravation in dealing with drugs. They could use "drug mules" who faced the immediate danger of being caught and they could be hired by third parties. It seemed, and often was, less risky and easy pickings if they were clever enough.

(I suspect the "easy pickings" has now moved on from drugs to computer fraud).

As far as we knew the exercise we called "Operation Wrecker" would not involve ships or shipwrecks but decoys, in the form of tricks and traps, were certain to be employed.

Initially, "Operation Wrecker" was an operation run by Hampshire Police in Cosham, Southampton. At that time, HM Customs and Excise had primacy in investigating and prosecuting drug smuggling. Police forces were obliged to offer smuggling operations to Customs or initiate a joint operation. This led to friction between ourselves and the odd police force although most provincial forces welcomed the co-operation with our department. Some felt it added to the kudos of their operation, others because it assisted in apprehending local criminals.

The Metropolitan Police Force in London were undoubtedly envious of the status we had and the freedoms and facilities that were unique to us.

The "Met" was responsible for law enforcement in Greater London (excluding the "square mile" of the City of London, which is the responsibility of the City of London Police). Their brief included counter-terrorism, protection of the British Royal Family, and members of the UK Government Cabinet. They could spread their activities outside of London but were stopped short as soon as they hit the coastline or any line deemed to be outside UK territory such as those in ports and airports. That's where Customs came in with full access to restricted areas and the constant availability of Customs cutters that patrolled our shores.

Any accusation from the police that Customs only dealt with drug couriers and not the real criminals behind the importation were blatantly inaccurate. Our case book was full of successful investigations that led to arrests and convictions in Court for felons based throughout the UK and overseas.

At the time Customs was part of Her Majesty's Treasury (sometimes referred to as the Exchequer) not the Home Office who were responsible for security and law and order. Statistics show that drug use and small time dealing played only a small part in policing whereas drug importation was a new and growing enterprise for villains. Customs and Excise oversaw importations, were experienced at it with trained personnel. At that time the Investigation Division had about 320 personnel (a relatively small number as part of Customs and Excise 26,000.)

Nine times out of ten we co-operated successfully with a given police force. If difficulties arose the decisions would be settled at a fairly high level between the Treasury and Home Office officials.

At first Hampshire Police were reluctant to hand over the operation but eventually agreed to work with us when they fully realised the maritime nature of the case (much of the investigation would take place at sea and in the port) they agreed to co-operate.

Although we, at Customs, could have insisted on overall control of the operation a route through demanding egos was found.

Drug team "Kilo" was assigned to the operation and Reg Low, a Senior Officer, was tasked with liaising with Hampshire Police. They set up the initial task force and we, the Bravos and Charlies, were brought in later as back up and for surveillance.

At the time we were working at near capacity with our own operations in London, Liverpool and the West Country. The involvement in Hampshire really stretched our resources.

At the end of September,1979 Hampshire Police were tipped off by an informant that a suspect container was heading for Felixstowe. Details of the vessel, it's crew and cargo were flagged up by the Port's Customs Dept.

The Bravos and Charlies were dispatched to Felixstowe and met with Reg Low in the Custom House. The plan was to have the container removed from the storage park by a uniformed preventive Customs officer and covertly examined to see if there were drugs concealed in it. As part of the surveillance team, we took up positions in and around the dock area. As well as the container, we were looking out for any suspect vehicles that may be around. Registration numbers were fed back by phone to our control office in London and checked out through Customs and Police intelligence data bases. Reg Low remained the link between Felixstowe Customs and police. Connections were made between a name on the police files with a shipping agent.

There were 8 of us on the operation and the same from Hampshire Police.

When containers arrive in port, they enter a controlled area. Nothing moves unless the paper-work is right so there is usually no need to observe the container itself. You could also access the Port's computer system to track progress.

HM Customs and Excise had a network of intelligence offices based at the UK's main ports and airports. Eight were in Felixstowe port which was, and still is the largest container port in the UK facilitating over four million containers. It stretches two and half kilometres along the coast with an area totalling 8,360 acres. Intelligence teams would examine ship's manifests, bills of lading and other documents to identify suspect movements. Shipping Agents would have comprehensive detail of the importation they were handling, the ship it was on, about to dock or still on the high seas. They would know when their load was hoisted on to dry land and exactly its position in the container stacks. Customs clearance had to be obtained and any tax or duty paid.

All sixteen of us booking into seafront hotels. Our hotel, The Marlborough, on the seafront was one of the hotels which was used by holiday makers and workers from the port. Despite the fact we were all male we were able to blend in without any problem.

We joined up with the police for a curry that night.

One of the policemen spoke not realising he was setting himself up as a sitting duck.

'I've not had a curry before, he said. 'What's this lime pickle?'

Someone with a cruel sense of humour chipped in, 'It's a fruity flavoured pickle. Delicious.'

'Is it hot? Strong?'

'No. That's a mild one.'

With that the policeman spooned pickle into his mouth. Seconds later he ran out the door crying out for water and mumbling words that were as colourful as the restaurant.

An unmarked building in the Port was our covert examination shed. At our request the Dock authorities would move a given container from a stack and brought on a trailer to the shed where qualified search officers would "rummage". This required a thorough examination of the container structure itself as well as the contents.

This importation turned out to be a false alarm, a villain's trial run to assess the likelihood of discovery. When that was realised, the container received a light touch examination so as not to alert the smugglers. Their thoughts would be that if this consignment went through unmolested a second would probably be treated in the same way. Also, having a "clean" importation would give the importers a satisfactory paper history. If this container was drug free the following would most likely be the same. Regular importations from the same source to the same company with consistent features are less likely to ring alarm bells.

There were times we had, through informants or intelligence, prior knowledge of a "trial" run so a superficial inspection took place. Although we had to be mindful that the "information" we received might well be a "double-take". The drugs were in the first shipment that we let through and not in the following. If we were duped in this way it would be a long time, if ever, that we realised it.

However, it was hoped the next genuine attempt at drugs importation would arrive soon and come through Felixstowe.

On 16 October 1979 I went with Terry Byrne to Felixstowe where another suspect container had arrived. We had just returned from Looe in Cornwall on another joint police and customs operation The Guiding Light (covered in another chapter). Despite working long hours and many of us due some days off, Terry Byrne, who had met with the Hampshire police senior managers, agreed that ten of us from Bravos and Charlies would link in with the officers from Hampshire.

As we were due to be back on surveillance early the next day I went back to Terry's house. After a meal prepared by Terry's wife Pam we sat and had a night cap. Pam said she was going upstairs to bed and I naively said 'I would join her'. (I meant I would retire as well). Terry said 'I don't think you will somehow, Trapper.'

We still laugh about it today.

Little did I know that events over the next 48 hours would be life changing and nothing would be the same again.

The uniform teams at Felixstowe had earlier examined the container by covertly drilling small holes through the floor of the container. It was estimated that a ton of cannabis was hidden under the floor. The actual consignment were shoes destined for a Tesco Supermarket in Saffron Waldon.

Substituting the drugs was impossible without extensive damage to the floor so we had a choice to remove the drugs and not progress the importation, or let it run "live". If we were able to substitute, officers would be sent to a builder's merchant or garden centre to purchase peat or compost. We did not have the luxury of enough time to make a substitution as the paperwork from Tesco's through their own Shipping Agent, had been submitted.

My colleague, George Atkinson and I spent our time driving around the area looking out for any suspicious activity, occasionally stopping off at the Customs House to check on any developments. We were under no pressure, there was no urgency. We just had to be ready for anything unexpected or for a rapid change of focus. There were Customs officers strolling around the tens of thousands of containers who would treat each container the same but covertly noting any movement of the marked container. As soon as it was moved into a position and about to be loaded onto a trailer, they would radio in.

After liaising with the police senior management Terry Byrne, made the decision to allow it to go "live" (meaning we would let the drugs in the container continue on its scheduled journey) and we would keep surveillance on it until we had identified the people behind it.

Travelling in his Ford Cortina, George Atkinson and I kept the container under observations throughout the day of the 18 September as it drove from Essex to Kent. With eight cars and two surveillance motorbikes (one Police, one Customs) in a convoy that switched "eyeball" responsibilities every few miles we entered the small village of Capel, near Tonbridge Wells, Kent. The lorry and trailer then pulled into a yard known locally as Crush's Scrap Yard.

We all assumed the container would be left there or opened up quite quickly.

A police officer and a customs officer in casual clothing went out on foot into a nearby wood to observe what was happening and radioed through that the container had not been unloaded or examined.

Although we were not aware of it at the time, on standby was a Kent police firearms unit. I assume the Hampshire police had arranged this deployment based on a perceived threat of violence. I was in a vehicle with George Atkinson and we managed to park in a farm yard awaiting further instructions. We were ready if the "Knock" was called or the lorry moved off. The adrenalin levels rose as we monitored the radio.

For whatever reason the lorry and container left the yard after about an hour and we carried on with the convoy surveillance through the evening and into the night.

We subsequently found out that the Kent firearms unit had stood down. The police areas were not joined up at this time and armed officers could not cross force boundary areas and therefore the Kent team could not go into Greater London, an area covered by the Met. Police.

Although we were not over concerned, the route through Kent to South London seemed a bit odd. The lorry would drive for a couple of hours and stop for a couple of hours.

There was always the concern that the lorry might pull off into a small layby causing our leading vehicle to drive past, stopping out of sight so someone could get out of the car and edge back toward the lorry on foot and observe from a distance, radioing following cars to find a place to park and wait.

At midnight on the 18 October the lorry pulled into a large car park on the A21 near Sevenoaks.

The park was full of lorries and cars so we drove in and parked near the perimeter. We were some distance away from the target lorry but had an uninterrupted view. At about one in the morning a Mercedes drove in and pulled alongside the lorry. We sat about 50 yards behind the lorry and although it was night time there was some natural light and headlights from vehicles on the A21 helped to see what was happening. The driver was white, medium height, stocky build and balding. He got out of the car and approached the driver of the lorry and handed over a white carrier bag.

Gordon and I looked at each other both speculating what the contents of the bag was. It could have been sandwiches for breakfast or more likely, money as a pay-off. He was only at the vehicle for a couple of minutes and then drove off.

I found out subsequently that the man who handed over the white bag was a south London villain called Freddie Forman who was known as "Brown Bread". He was a fixer and hardman for the Richardson family, a top London crime family on a par with the Krays. Foreman already had a blood curdling reputation of his own. He would later publish a biography calling himself, "The Godfather of British Crime".

The Richardson "Gang" were also known as the "Torture Gang", they had a reputation as some of London's most sadistic gangsters. Their alleged specialities included pulling teeth out using pliers, cutting off toes using bolt cutters and nailing victims to the floor using 6-inch nails. Headed by Charlie and Eddie Richardson the gang included George Cornell (who was murdered by Ronnie Kray), "Mad" Frankie Fraser, and "The hitman" Jimmy Moody. Speaking to The Sun Newspaper, Eddie said: 'The Krays had watched too many US gangster films. They wanted to be like Al Capone but didn't have the brains to do anything major league."

The two gangs mostly operated in different areas of London.

So, we then knew the exceptional level of criminal activity we were facing. The Richardsons and their associates were professional gangsters and as such very rarely got their hands dirty. They also had a number of corrupt police officers on their payroll and considered themselves bomb proof. They came up on the periphery on a number of operations but nothing concrete.

The Richardsons were involved in extortion, robberies and vehicle hijackings and were moving into drugs. They were known to us but at that stage we had no substantial evidence of wrong doing. In 1985 Eddie Richardson was sentenced to 35 years in prison for cocaine trafficking.

We waited for about an hour after the lorry left. George and I followed as it drove seemingly aimlessly through Kent roads eventually arriving in a lorry park in Lewisham. It appeared that the driver was taking a rest so we managed to grab a bite to eat, a "healthy" doner kebab from an all-night cafe and we were able to relax a bit, although we still remained on a high alert.

Four of our surveillance vehicles each took it in turn to watch the lorry. Each one would keep the "eyeball" for about an hour then hand it over to another. After about four hours the lorry started and departed almost immediately and we quickly switched into surveillance mode. At midday, it headed into Central London and parked in a goods yard in Rotherhithe. I was in the right position to go out on foot to try and observe the lorry in the yard. I got out of the car and managed to find a block of flats overlooking the yard and from the stairs I was able to clearly see and advise the other surveillance vehicle what was happening.

After about 20 minutes watching the lorry a blue Rolls Royce turned up and the driver got out. The driver of the roller was smartly dressed in casual clothes. He was in his mid- fifties and had a "Jack the lad" look about him. Those of us involved in law enforcement develop a sixth sense and can usually tell if somebody was a "wrong un". He certainly fitted that bill.

A fork lift truck then lifted the container off the trailer. I thought this was it and I was in the position to call the "knock" if the container had been opened and the floor broken in to. The man from the Rolls Royce and the lorry driver went under the container and examined the floor. I wasn't concerned of a compromise at this stage as I knew the floor of the container had not been tampered with.

Our support Control Office was passed the car registration number and confirmed the driver of the Rolls Royce was identified as George Francis, a man known to law enforcement as a career criminal. It is unusual to pay so much attention to the underside of a container which gave us an essential piece of evidence as it shows a degree of knowledge that the floor was important.

However, they didn't breach the concealment. We needed them to do that so we could prove guilty knowledge and everything they had done so far was circumstantial and they could easily deny all knowledge of the cannabis. We had no cameras with us so we relied solely on notes we took at the time. We did not routinely carry cameras and our "knock" kit would comprise of clear plastic exhibit bags, exhibit labels, property books and a sledge hammer for knocking down doors if it was required.

The lorry drove away from the yard towards the East End of London. The driver parked in a side street off the Commercial Road. He got out, locked the doors and made his way to the main road and waited at a bus stop. This was of concern to us for it looked as if he had abandoned the lorry. We may have been spotted or he may have wanted out of whatever role he'd signed up for.

All the surveillance vehicles were trying to find suitable locations to park up. I was with George in his Cortina. When we tried to find a suitable parking spot we pulled alongside another of our vehicles, both of us trying to get into the same space.

The officer driving the car, Peter Bennett of Kilo 3, wound down his window.

'Don't worry,' I said. 'You park there. We'll find somewhere else.'

'Great fun, this surveillance,' he said. 'All around Kent. All over the shop.'

'See you later,' I replied before driving off across the Commercial Road. We all assumed that the lorry would soon be on the move again.

Our intelligence team in London led by Jim Galloway were collating all the information from Felixstowe and Hampshire police and our surveillance reports. News came through from a senior officer, Phil Byrne who was in our intelligence office in London who suggested to the surveillance team there had been a compromise and the driver should be arrested.

I was then parked in a side street on the other side of Commercial Road when the "knock" call came over the radio from Phil Byrne's office. It was Terry who called the "knock, knock, knock".

I started to run across the road and as I ran past a bus-stop I saw a person laying on the pavement. At first glance it looked as if an old chap had been knocked over. Twenty yards ahead of him I saw two police officers tackling the driver of the lorry, trying to pull him to the ground in unusually aggressive manner - they were going in hard as the driver was fighting back. They needed help. As he was slammed down on the ground, I threw myself upon him. I was able to hold his shoulders down and my larger than average weight helped. An old age pensioner who just happened to be walking past was hitting the driver with his walking stick. I couldn't understand why one of the officers, John Mosely, had handcuffs wrapped around his fingers and was hitting the head of the driver with the handcuffs. He was trying to knock him out. At the time I thought it too heavy as we appeared to have the man under control. John Harvey was the other policeman who had been in a car with Peter and was first on the scene. Two incredibly brave men.

'He's got a gun!' shouted John. 'He's shot somebody down the road.'

I put every ounce of strength and weight I had on this man when I heard that.

A shot was fired during that time but because of the shouting and screaming, horns blowing from passing cars, and the swearing and howling from the man pinned to the pavement, I didn't hear it. I didn't distinguish one sound from another.

'He's got a gun in his pocket,' shouted John.

I quickly moved my efforts to his arms, driving them above his head and away from any pockets. He was a tall, wiry man with a body frame that belied his strength. He thrashed about, his legs and arms flaying in all directions. He was like a trapped animal desperately trying to find a way out of a tightening grip.

Another police officer, Les Templeman, turned up and managed to retrieve the gun. There were moments, seconds, when it seemed like you were watching a B movie, that what your eyes were seeing wasn't actually happening. It was a slow-motion nightmare with blurred, meaningless words filling the space left by approaching sirens.

The man beneath me had stopped struggling and less pressure was required to keep him secure but I could not lessen my control of him. I could see that CPR (cardiopulmonary resuscitation) was being applied to the man lying on the pavement. Someone was obviously in a bad way.

John turned to me and said, 'He's shot one of us.'

Terry Byrne arrived and asked if I was ok.

I said, 'I'm ok but it looks very, very bad further down the road'.

From twenty yards away, I could see one of my colleagues, Gordon Hall, trying to revive the person lying on the floor. I'm no medical man but I could sense the urgency, almost desperation on procedures being carried out. I hoped to God they were going to succeed in saving him. It didn't look good.

The news quickly arrived that shot person was Peter Bennett, Kilo 3. Although throughout the confrontation my brain and bodily strength had been dogged in the single objective in restraining this man, I found myself staring in disbelief at the scene around me. Shapes and colours of people and cars became fuzzy. Time stood still yet raced away. It could have been seconds or minutes before I was hand-cuffed to the assailant. It was only then I knew we had control of the situation.

The area was being sealed off by uniformed police to ensure a smooth route for an ambulance. In those days a "crime scene" didn't exist. DNA tests were a few years off and investigation forensics in its infancy.

The minutes after that seemed endless, a kaleidoscope of images seen through heightened thoughts and emotions. It was only when I saw Peter's motionless body being stretchered into an ambulance and driven away that the mist of fury began to subside. I watched, helpless and exhausted as the ambulance headed off to East London Hospital, only a short distance away in Mile End Road.

The shooter, Leonard "Teddy Bear" Watkins was hand-cuffed to my left hand and we got into the back of a police car with another plain clothed police officer with us. Watkins was conscious, had an open wound in his head caused by the hard metal edge of the hand-cuffs. He required medical attention.

Apart from a few mumbled expletives from Watkins there was an earie silence in the car. The journey seemed to take forever although it was only a few minutes to the hospital. Watkins showed no emotion, didn't speak and just looked forward in the car.

When we arrived, an ambulance drew alongside and Peter was taken out on a stretcher. We stood to allow the paramedics to take Peter in. As they walked past, I got a good look at Peter. My heart shuddered with the realisation that he was not alive. Despite all their efforts the medical team had not been able to revive him.

Watkins had used an illegal lady Barretta gun, not the most powerful gun available but small enough to be easily hidden in a coat pocket. Being shot by a Barretta gun can cause serious injury and fatal if the bullet hits a vital organ or artery.

When Peter and John Harvey went to arrest him, Watkins thrust his hand in his pocket to grab the gun and shot through his coat, hitting Peter in the groin and severing the main artery. I was told Peter would have died within 15 seconds. Watkins had tried a second shot but only grazed his own stomach.

The atmosphere in and around the hospital was electric. People were horrified with what they heard and saw. I was still handcuffed to Watkins, who was gashed and torn, blood already congealing. My clothes were covered in blood stains. Physically I was unhurt but mentally I was in a dark place. My head was spinning and I had had difficulty in comprehending what had occurred on the Commercial Road. I just wanted to get out of the handcuffs linking me and the murderer.

The injuries to Watkins head required stitches so we waited in a curtained off booth for a doctor to arrive and sew him up.

Watkins never made eye contact. He said nothing. He had an unblinking, steely look in his eyes as if planning his next move, a move that would make his current problem a temporary one. We, on the other hand, had exactly the opposite thoughts.

Somewhere in all the bedlam the key to the handcuffs were lost. I wanted the cuffs off. It was the one thing I wanted to happen. I wanted to distance myself from this man who, in my mind, had just murdered an unarmed colleague of mine. My breathing and heart-rate had calmed down but my anger had not.

A doctor examined Watkins and put stitches into the head wound. Watkins screamed in pain and when he complained and asked for something to stop the pain the doctor had no sympathy and just said, 'tough'.

After the doctor left Watkins made a violent lunge for a glass thermometer that was laid out on a shelf with other medical kit items. Before I could pull him back, he had rammed it into his mouth.

I shouted for help as I fell, half sitting on the bed, but able to pull Watkins onto me in a bear hug to get him under control. Restricted by one hand being shackled in the hand-cuffs I fell back on the bed with Watkins on top of me. Somehow, I prevented his free hand from pushing the thermometer further into his throat and try as he would, he couldn't swallow it.

A uniformed policeman rushed in, saw what was happening and grabbed Watkins' throat.

'I could choke you to death,' he bellowed at Watkins. 'But you're not going to swallow that.'

Pinned on the bed by me, his throat gagged by the policeman, Watkins spat out the thermometer. I was not sure why he had made a grab for and tried to swallow the glass. I can only assume it was a theatrical attempt to influence the interviews which were going to take place later. Terry came into the cubicle to check on me and told Watkins he had shot and killed Peter Bennett. 'You have murdered an unarmed Customs officer'.

Watkins did not reply but had an arrogant smirk on his face.

'Tough, are you?' said Terry. 'Not so tough without a gun in your hand.'

Neither I, or any of my colleagues, were easily provoked into a violent act but at that moment it took all of our self-control not to strike out. We knew we had to maintain the standard required when dealing with an arrested suspect. Our training helped but only just.

It seemed an age but someone eventually found keys for the handcuffs and released me. The uniformed police then restrained Watkins, moving the handcuffs from my wrist to his. Another officer cuffed Watkins' other hand to make sure he could not escape.

At that stage I was far from being calm and collected. It again seemed that this was not happening to me and I was a third-party observer watching a horror story unfold.

After leaving the hospital we went back to Limehouse Police Station where we had a de-brief on the operation.

The briefing jointly chaired by Assistant Chief Constable, John Wright from Hampshire police and Alan Taylor, a Customs Investigation Deputy Chief. A plan was discussed to manage the media, as word would get out very quickly as to what had happened. The next stages regarding interviewing the suspects and collecting evidence was also discussed.

A number of us expressed concerns as to our involvement in interviewing those arrested but Alan Taylor came out with a show-biz quote, "the show must go on".

The mood couldn't have been heavier. People close to Peter were highly emotional and none of us, Peter's team, our team and others could find solace in anything.

I realised I was the last officer to speak to Peter.

Our chief, Terry and senior policemen were at the briefing.

It did turn into an ugly farce when a press statement was discussed. Hampshire press officer seemed to be trying to put a positive spin on the role of the National Drugs Intelligence Unit and senior police officers.

It went on until Terry aggressively said, 'Hang on a minute. We're talking about the content of a press release and who should and shouldn't be mentioned, when a Custom's officer had just been killed.'

Terry then stormed out leaving no doubt as to what he thought about these proceedings. He was consoled by another colleague Roly Garrick, and came back into the briefing when it was agreed that a press release would not go out.

It's probable that today we would have been allocated a counsellor to help get over the trauma but not then. We brushed ourselves down, composed ourselves as best we could and went back to the White Horse, a pub at the back of New Fetter Lane.

The pint of beer tasted unlike any beer before, so welcome was it. My shirt was still blood-stained from Watkins' head wound.

We were all exhausted, even spent, but filled with a resolute and strangely calm demeanour.

Gordon Hall, knowing I was single and living alone, insisted I went back to his house for the night for a shower and a meal.

His wife found me a clean shirt to wear.

The very next day we went to the police station at Cosham where Watkins, Michael Bird and George Francis had been taken. We interviewed over the next two days, Saturday the 22nd and Sunday the 23rd of October. Along with the others I looked at documents uplifted during the house searches and details of meetings observed by the police over the previous few weeks.

Terry and Hampshire police detective, Brian Hitchcock spent two days interviewing Watkins where throughout he had stated he had tried to commit suicide and had not meant to kill Peter. Terry got him to admit he broke free from Peter and John Harvey for a few seconds. Watkins could not answer why he didn't try and shoot himself then. He had plenty of time to fire the gun but it was obvious this was just a ruse to divert the interviewing officers from the real reason the gun was fired. That was to kill anybody who prevented him from escaping.

Even today I have difficulty remembering the interview with Michael Bird, a person linked to Watkins and who had been observed with him on numerous occasions. I do remember asking Bird about his relationship with Watkins who he described as his best friend.

Foreman, who had handed over the white plastic bag which we were convinced contained the gun that killed Peter Bennett could not be located. Although we were convinced that was what happened it could not be proved. He always denied he supplied the gun but would never clarify what was in the carrier bag.

Foreman and his son Jamie went on the run not willing to associate themselves with anything to do with the shooting. (Jamie Forman became an actor appearing in East Enders and the film Layer Cake with Daniel Craig).

Freddie Foreman was in the United States for two years but was arrested as soon as he came back to the UK. He was sentenced for two years for drug importation and his involvement with the "Wrecker" case. No charge of accessory to murder was brought.

(Later on, Freddie was involved in the disposal of the body of Jack "The Hat" McVitie (killed by Reggie Kray). He was sentenced to ten years in prison for the crime.

He was also involved in the Shoreditch Security Express robbery of 1983, which at the time was the largest cash robbery in the UK. For his part in it he received nine years in prison.

Foreman also confessed to the murders of Frank "Mad Axeman" Mitchell, and of Tommy "Ginger" Marks in the 1960s in revenge for the shooting of his brother (shot in the legs). He had been acquitted of the murders at an Old Bailey trial in the 1960s. He additionally claimed to have intimidated witnesses to the killing of George Cornell in the Blind Beggar pub in Whitechapel by Ronnie Kray and to having been a hitman for the Kray twins.)

Peter was the first Customs Officer to be killed on the mainland of the UK for 300 years. In the 1700s many Customs officials armed with muskets and swords were killed trying to prevent maritime smuggling from France to the South Coast of England. Probably Brandy.

In the lobby of The Customs House in London there is a plaque commemorating the life of Peter Bennett. The 33- year-old investigator from Leeds, married to Jackie and had a son Andrew, who was one year old when Peter was shot and killed.

In Upper Thames Street there is a church, Old Hallows, near the Tower of London (it is the Customs and Excise church) that has a glass door as a memorial to Peter paid for by contributions from his colleagues in the Investigation Division and Police officers from Hampshire and throughout the UK.

The Customs Office in Leeds, where Peter once worked, is called "Peter Bennett House".

19th October 1979, a date engraved in our minds and hearts particularly when the anniversary comes around. Some of us meet up. If not, we do have a quiet time of reflection.

One of Watkins' associates, Colin (The Duke) Osbourne, was found dead on Hackney Marshes. He was obviously a player in the drugs gang. When found he was sun-tanned and looked healthy but it was concluded he died from natural causes. It had been rumoured he had overdosed, unwilling to add to the 12 years spent in gaol. For us it remained a mystery.

It was a watershed moment for us investigators that we had come across a criminal organisation prepared to kill if someone got in their way. This was probably the first-time firearms played a part. Up to that point the criminals played by the rules, ruthless and violent at times, but not murderous. Watkins was charged with murder in addition to the importation of drugs. George Francis, a well-known South London criminal was also charged. He was the driver of the Rolls Royce and it was he who inspected the underneath of the trailer.

We had to give evidence at Winchester Crown Court over several days. George Francis would travel down by train as we did.

On arrival in Winchester, he would disembark wearing an expensive suit and a trilby hat smoking a fat cigar and if he spotted us, he would throw a quip at us. 'Don't you travel first-class?' was one of them.

He once owned a pub opposite Heaver Castle in Kent and was caught fixing crocodile clips to bypass the electricity meter and pay nothing for the power supply.

The 63-year-old had made plenty of enemies during a long and colourful career in crime, which included laundering gold from the 1983 Brinks Mat robbery.

He did get his comeuppance later by being shot dead on May 14th 2003 as he arrived for work at his courier firm, "Signed, Sealed and Delivered", in Bermondsey, south London. His killers were John O'Flynn, 53, and Terence Conaghan, 54. There was no doubt many people were glad to see him dead.

Harry Richardson, known as Big H, was accused of ordering the murder - but he was cleared by the Old Bailey trial.

Francis had become the latest victim of the so-called "Curse of Brink's Mat Robbery". Seven people connected with the raid had already been killed.

It was reported that Francis had been entrusted with part of the haul from the 1983 Brinks Mat raid at Heathrow airport in which a gang of armed robbers escaped with £26million in gold bullion, cash and diamonds. He was left to look after the finances of those serving time in prison. Upon their release Francis claimed there was nothing left for them.

On the front page of the *Daily Mirror* on Saturday 20th 1979 was the headline -

"Hero shot in one million swoop. DEATH OF A DRUG BUSTER."

Watkins was charged along with Francis and Bird.

Watkins pleaded not guilty and reverted back to his initial statement that the gun had gone off when he tried to commit suicide. He carried a gun for his own protection, he said. He made an attempt to discredit Terry Byrne and the Hitchcock a policeman for the manner they carried out the interview.

When I gave evidence of the two-day surveillance, most of which was accepted, everything seemed to be going well. Watkins' barrister then went minute by minute of my role in the arrest but particularly what happened at the hospital. Through his barrister, Watkins stated that I held him down whilst Terry grabbed him by the throat and hit him. He had been beaten during his disarming and arrest, but he suggested that some of the injuries were inflicted in the A & E hospital examination booth. He also suggested he was beaten up as we were angry that an unarmed colleague had been murdered. A total fabrication. It was Watkins way of attempting to divert the jury's attention from the charges he faced.

Our version (the truth) of the observations, arrest and interviews were accepted and the jury delivered a unanimous guilty verdict. He was sentenced to life with a minimum of 25 years and initially sent to Winchester prison. Soon after, with his brother's help, he attempted to escape by arranging for two ladders to be placed against the prison walls, one inside, one outside. Thankfully, their positioning was off and the ladders were a few feet apart. He was caught before they could move the ladders.

He died in Winchester Prison of cancer after a few years.

We all took a short break returning to work on 24th October 1979.

Six-week's later I was off with what I thought was a flu virus but I suspect it was a sort of after-shock, not Omori's Law of earthquakes but the body and mind demanding a switch off period.

The whole episode never left me up to the day I retired, 33 years later. It came to the fore whenever I sent people out on an operation.

The London Gazette published the following -

CENTRAL CHANCERY OF
THE ORDERS OF KNIGHTHOOD
St. James's Palace, London, S.W.I.
2nd October 1981.
The QUEEN has been graciously pleased to approve

the following awards of the Queen's Gallantry Medal
and for the publication in the London Gazette of the
names of those shown below as having received an
expression of Commendation for Brave Conduct:

Awarded the Queen's Gallantry Medal
Peter, BENNETT (Deceased), Higher Executive Officer,
Board of Customs and Excise.
John HARVEY, Detective Sergeant, Hampshire Constabulary.
John Edward MOSELEY, Detective Sergeant, Hampshire
Constabulary.

Queen's Commendation for Brave Conduct
 James Frederick JARVIE, Executive Officer, Board of
Customs and Excise
For services in assisting in the capture and arrest of an armed and
dangerous man who had shot and mortally wounded his colleague.

On 19th October, 1979, following a protracted
investigation into the importation of cannabis resin,
a surveillance operation was mounted in London.
Mr. Bennett and Sergeant Harvey were engaged in
the action and instructed to arrest the driver of a
container vehicle which was suspected of carrying
the cannabis. After patrolling the streets in a car
driven by Mr. Bennett they saw the driver of the
container who had become suspicious, abandoned
his vehicle and was on foot.
Mr. Bennett quickly stopped the car on the opposite
side of the road while Sergeant Harvey informed
his control that they had located the suspect.
Both men immediately left the car and ran through
busy traffic. Sergeant Moseley who was also in the
near vicinity was alerted and aware that they intended
to arrest the man.
As they reached the man and told him he was
under arrest Sergeant Harvey took hold of his left
arm and Mr. Bennett seized his right arm. During
the extremely violent struggle that ensued, Sergeant
Harvey attempted to handcuff the man who managed
to break away; as the officer grabbed at him again
the suspect was seen to put his right hand inside
the chest pocket of his coat. Mr. Bennett immediately
tried to prevent this by seizing the man's right
arm whereupon he was shot in the chest, fell to the
ground and died shortly afterwards.
The gunman ran off pursued by Sergeant Harvey
who, within a short distance, brought him down with
a rugby tackle. At the same time Sergeant Moseley

arrived on the scene and jumped on the man's back
as he twisted his body and threatened to use the
gun on Sergeant Harvey; a second shot was fired
and the gunman was superficially wounded by the
shot he had intended for Sergeant Harvey.
The officers were then joined by other members
of the surveillance team and, with their assistance,
the violently struggling gunman was finally overpowered
and arrested.
A high order of gallantry and devotion to duty
was displayed by these three individuals during the
events leading to the disarming and eventual arrest
of the gunman. Mr. Bennett and Sergeant Harvey
did not hesitate when, unarmed, they fearlessly
tackled this armed and dangerous man who later
shot and mortally wounded Mr. Bennett in cold
blood. Sergeant Harvey and Sergeant Moseley, despite
witnessing the murder of Mr. Bennett, continued
their pursuit and finally captured his murderer.

CHAPTER 11
GERMAN CUSTOMS. CANNIBIS IN ANGLESEY.

Keeping the many operations going at once, was like spinning plates on
sticks. The Bravos and Charlies had "plates" in Cardiff, Liverpool and
London.
 An operation run by George Atkinson (Charlie 4) focussed on an
importation of cannabis that was destined for Canada with the suspect,
Mohammed Asraf Kahn, based in the UK. Although he lived in Hounslow,
he often stayed at the Excelsior Hotel which was on the slip road to
Heathrow Airport. Records showed that he often stayed there for three
weeks at a time.

I was sent along to stay at the hotel. In theory an easy-going task, enjoying the indulgencies of a well-appointed hotel, lots of sitting around people watching during the day and propping up the bar every evening. It was never quite that cushy. Much of my time was spent with the telephone switchboard operator monitoring calls Kahn made or received. I also tried to guess his movements, to be present whenever he entered the lobby, hoping he might meet up with someone who would add a jigsaw piece to a very incomplete puzzle. I was there from the 26 May until 11 June 1979 and collected an embarrassingly small amount of useful evidence.

Our Intelligence team had received information that a quantity of cannabis resin and cannabis oil was to be smuggled via Frankfurt Airport to Heathrow. This was an inferior resin that had been treated by a distillation process to make a highly concentrated cannabis oil. This is spread by the users on cigarette papers.

This type of cannabis had very high levels of Tetrahydrocannabinol (THC), the active ingredient which gives the user a "high".

The consignment had already arrived at Frankfurt Airport for onward transport to Canada.

Although George and the team had gathered some crunchy evidence, the UK courts would require a sample of drugs to prove an offence had been committed by a UK resident. We also needed a copy of the German law that said it was an offence to import cannabis into Germany. For somebody not involved in law enforcement it appears obvious but for any court case in the UK all these elements have to be covered. Detail, detail, detail. The more you have the less chance of being found short. Defence lawyers have made an art out of exposing gaps, inconsistencies, and weaknesses in the most thoroughly prepared evidence.

George asked me to go to Frankfurt to liaise with the German Customs Investigators ZKA (our equivalents over there). Going to Frankfurt was my very first working trip abroad.

Peter Zimmerman headed up Frankfurt Airport's Customs Investigation team. Colleagues, Harold Frohlich, Jochen Meyer and Norbert Steilen, made up the small but very efficient unit.

We gave them the nickname "the Frankfurt mafia" because they controlled many areas of law enforcement at the airport. I kept in touch with all of them throughout my career.

Peter Zimmerman was an intelligent man, charming and generous. He took me to stay at his home for a week where I met his delightful wife.

In the job we did, we often would stay at colleague's homes and just as often have them to stay at ours. Our long-suffering partners were often required to cook extra food at short notice and make up a spare bed.

The next day I was taken to the Freight Section of the Airport where we examined the consignment of drugs that had recently arrived from Karachi.

On the 18th June I had a meeting at the ZKA with two officers from the Royal Canadian Mounted Police officers Bob Richardson and Ian Gemmell, who had flown over from Montreal.

The Canadian legal system, like ours, needed them to be present when the drugs were removed and replaced with a substitute (peat in this case) by the Germans. The Canadians inserted a light sensitive tracking monitor in the consignment to help with the Controlled Delivery to Canada. They also needed a sample of the drug for their court proceedings.

I took statements from German Customs officers at the Airport who had intercepted the consignment and spent time with the German ZKA, the Zollkriminalamt, the German Customs Investigation Bureau, a federal agency that falls under the German Finance Ministry.

I also met up with the German prosecutor and received a copy of the law that related to the case that was translated into English for me. It confirmed that it was against German law to import drugs into Germany.

I did manage to see a bit of Frankfurt during my time there. Joe Cumberland, a UK police officer based at the Central Drugs and Illegal Immigration Unit (CDIU), Scotland Yard was also visiting Frankfurt for a meeting. When an opportunity arose, our host, Peter, took both of us for a city tour and Joe took numerous photos.

On one occasion, taking a shot of a magnificent old building, he made a comment, 'Our bombers didn't destroy everything then'.

I shrunk down in the back of the car as I watched Peter shake his head in the mirror!

For the court case in the UK, I also needed to bring back a sample of the drugs and the German prosecutor gave me permission to do this. This became my exhibit which was bagged and labelled; a kilo of cannabis and an ampoule of cannabis oil. This evidence would be presented in Court following the arrests in Canada and the UK.

I already had a "Home Office" warrant to allow me to bring drugs into the UK which covered me in case I was stopped by the police in Germany or the UK.

Peter dropped me off at the Airport. I was booked on a British Airways flight, checked in and sat in the departure lounge. I was delayed for five hours due to a technical delay and boarded the plane at midnight arriving (with the time difference) at 1am UK time.

Because I had worked a lot at the airport over the years, I knew many of the Customs officers and investigators there and normally I would be waved straight through.

As the plane was scheduled to land at 6pm the day before the Customs staff shift had changed. After midnight, very few flights would arrive and the small staff left tended to relax a little. I walked off the plane carrying the samples of drugs so I went into the Red Channel (Something to Declare) and rang the bell. An officer came out of a back room looking most unhappy. Underneath his uniform he was wearing pyjamas. He was obviously planning to put his head down for the night.

'What have you got to declare then?' he barked.

'Actually, I've got a kilo of cannabis and some cannabis oil.'

His eyes opened wide.

'Say that again,' he said.

'I've got a kilo of cannabis and some cannabis oil.'

I knew what was going on in his mind. His planned sleep was about to be ruined. It could mean he had to arrest me and a mountain of paperwork will follow.

He looked shocked and then relieved when I showed him my ID card and the Home Office Warrant. I have no idea if he had a good sleep after that.

The drugs were locked in a secure area at the airport to be collected at a later date.

At 2am I found my car, a blue 2000E Ford Cortina with a black vinyl roof parked at the Excelsior Hotel. A tyre was flat! Having to change a wheel on a low slung souped-up 2000E Cortina in the middle of the night in a dark carpark with inadequate lighting only added to the angst brought about by adrenalin wind down and lack of sleep. I then drove robot fashion to my flat in Biggin Hill in Kent. (I have since been to vintage car rallies and when I sit in a Cortina the memories flood back.)

The Canadians successfully arrested and prosecuted the importers in Montreal and Khan was found guilty at Middlesex Crown Court.

I drove Nick Baker's car on my first trip to the West Country. Nick had arrived at the office with a patch over his eye. He had contracted conjunctivitis. We were on our way to Exeter on an operation involving a yacht called the "Cornish Lady" suspected of smuggling cannabis.

At midnight we were deployed at Starcross, a small village situated on the west shore of the Exe Estuary in Teignbridge, home to one of the UK's oldest sailing clubs. It was just getting light when the Cornish Lady arrived at the mouth of the River Exe. Nick made a remarkable recovery, tore his patch off and after consulting a £1.99 Woolworth's map, sent me through the village to get a better view. The most direct route took me through a churchyard and over a wall. In the field beyond I was followed by the intense gaze of a herd of green-eyed bullocks. Not much fazed me in those days but the heavy atmosphere, the silence of the gravestones and the bullocks made me nervous. I eventually reached a stream which I had to cross over. I tried jumping but slid and found myself up to my knees in water. I squelched my way down a slope to reach the river.

The yacht was there but it was not the Cornish Lady.

It took me a while to trudge back to Nick's car and spent the next four hours driving back to London with a dearth of humour.

The Cornish Lady arrived off the coast the next night and detained by the Customs Cutter, "Searcher". A ton of cannabis was seized and three smugglers were arrested.

During this period university educated drug traffickers such as Howard Marks, Graham Plinston, Charlie Radcliffe and Robin Boswell established links with a charismatic Dutchman, Arend ter Horst. Radcliffe rejected the contemporary values of the time and became a radical writer. He revelled in the danger of drug trafficking and in 1974 he sailed a yacht into Scotland with 600 kilos of cannabis. The consignment was sold in a matter of weeks through a reliable north London trafficker, Victor Grassi. Grassi was in a unique position having well established contacts with the groups supplying cannabis in Morocco and the customers in London. Arend ter Horst was close to a fearless yacht skipper called Robin Thompson.

Most importations by yacht were undertaken during the late spring/summer period. Thompson wanted to beat the competition and attempted to smuggle of over 1 ton of cannabis from Morocco to the UK. This trip was a disaster and the yacht limped to the Isle of Wight where it promptly sank. Despite almost drowning, Thompson and the crew managed to salvage the cannabis which was hidden in a cave. Grassi subsequently retrieved the cannabis which he went on to sell through his contacts.

In June 1979 a neighbour of Thompson took a note of numerous vehicles that turned up late at night. He also saw Thompson remove a brick from a garden wall, place something in a space and put the brick back. The neighbour managed to examine the concealment and saw a quantity of cash. He immediately told the Sussex police. Dave Wolstenholme, a police Regional Crime Squad officer took on the initial investigation.

Records and intelligence from the police and customs confirmed Thompson owned two yachts called "Eloise" moored in Lymington, a port town in Hampshire and the "Woodwind" in Falmouth on the South coast of Cornwall.

Checks in the maritime community revealed the Woodwind was about to sail to Morocco. It is perhaps a sweeping statement but sailors only go to Morocco in a yacht for one thing - to pick up drugs and bring them back to the UK. Chris Hardwick (Bravo 3) was appointed as the case officer and liaised with Dave and his team. The Bravos and Charlies were called on to follow Thompson and identify who he was meeting. Six of us went down to Falmouth to take a closer look at.

The Customs had a fleet of patrol vessels called Cutters. Each region bid for the cutters to patrol the coasts locally. However, the Investigation Division had first call.

We kept in touch with one of the Custom's Cutters, a 24metre vessel costing around four and a half million pounds. This was manned by ten crew members. These vessels were unarmed but equipped for lengthy postings on the high seas. They regularly carried out exercises with their French and Spanish counterparts.

Should force be needed out at sea Marines or Special Forces would be taken on board. Deployments would be agreed at a senior customs and military level and liaison officers from both departments would agree an operational plan and operational tactics.

The Cutter crew were tasked by the Investigation Division with tracking and following target ships on our behalf. Should the Woodwind set sail the Cutter would chart their speed and route, which hopefully would predict the next port of call. With such a report we could then put people in place before the yacht's arrival.

In Falmouth, myself and Alan Griffiths, went onboard the Cutter Valiant in order to get a closer view. It was a grey misty morning and the waters in the large yacht harbour were a bit choppy.

We asked the Cutter Commander Arthur Dunlop if we could get closer to the yacht and he suggested we went out on their 10-foot RHIB (rigid-inflatable boat). It was launched with myself, Alan and two maritime officers. The RHIB driven by Arthur was speeding and zig zagging through dozens of boats moored in the Marina. I looked at Alan and we both realised Arthur was trying to dislodge Alan and myself from the boat, to pitch us overboard. An investigator in the water would be a talking point for the Cutter staff for years. We hung on in what became a white-knuckle ride. We did insist that speed was reduced so we could take some close-up photographs of the unoccupied yacht.

Arthur was expecting us to say something but I just commented, 'I was surprised how smooth the waters were.'

The Woodwind remained in Mylor Harbour near Falmouth for most of August but there was no sign of Thompson. With Ray Smith and other officers, we stayed the whole of August watching the yacht. We managed to find a small family run bed and breakfast and the owners knew we were Customs they asked no questions as to what we were up to. It might have been an idyllic place to be among the holidaymakers and attractive surroundings but it was so boring watching a motionless yacht day and night. There were no signs of preparations for a voyage. No cargo being loaded aboard, no shifty men lurking around the bobbing boats, nothing that would suggest we were anywhere but in a typical seaside resort on the Cornish coast. The holiday makers milling about all day and half the night meant it was less likely for any of us to stand out.

We were joined by Mike Stephenson and we spent most of our time wandering around the marina trying to blend in. We sauntered around, took in views and facilities, but never allowing the yacht to be blocked from view. Cafes were visited and revisited. You can only eat so many pasties and cream teas!

Towards the end of our stay, I was in a bar with Mike Stephenson when he decided he'd had enough.

'I'm fed up being in Cornwall,' he announced,

Mike was a Londoner, born and bred, and felt out of place. He liked the hustle and bustle of city life, the varied hordes of people hurriedly heading in all directions, the buildings, the noise, the smells. Sea breezes, fish and chips, candy floss and hats made from knotted hankies were not for him. And, like most of us, missed being closer to the centre of activity. In London you felt at the hub with many spokes. You were "in touch".

We were observing a meeting between Thompson and two of the other crew members in a harbour bar when Mike said,' I've had enough of this. I'm going to talk to them. Find out when they're leaving.'

I wasn't sure if he was joking but I held on to his arm and for a while held firm. I said, 'Don't be daft Stevo, you will show out'.

'Leave it to me,' he said. 'It will be OK'.

Eventually he did go up to the bar and asked Thompson for a light. He then started a conversation with him. I looked on in horror as Stevo chatted away. He didn't get anything out of him but at least he didn't show out.

Thompson, and two crew members, Bob Campion and Stephen Lloyd were on board as the Eloise left Lymington, heading out to sea on a journey with a sailing time of nearly two weeks to Morocco. "Operation Yashmak," the initial name given to the operation by Dave Wolstenholme was up and running.

With the yacht on the high seas, we turned our attention to the other members of the organisation, particularly Victor Grassi, Charlie Radcliffe and Bob Campion.

On 21 February 1980, six months after the Eloise had left the UK, a full surveillance team of five cars and ten officers were out following Grassi. He was driving a pristine red Jaguar and headed from his home address in north London on the M4 west. I was driving a car with Alan Griffiths as a passenger. As we approached the junction with the M5 south and M5 north we assumed he was heading South-west, back to the West Country. But instead, he headed north up the M5. After Birmingham he turned westward through North Wales, through Snowdonia.

Following a target by car is not the same as portrayed in films. Two men in a following car filling up the target's rear-view mirror is not a practice carried out by any UK security force. With a few cars and occasionally a motor-cycle you would let colleagues overtake you and sometime later, after a few passing manoeuvres you tried to allow two or three "civilian" cars to drop in between. The idea was to avoid the target seeing us and showing out. Through our radios we would give out a commentary about road and building details we passed so that any colleague following would know they were still in touch.

If you felt you had been in one position for any length of time you would pull over for a colleague to head up the surveillance. This swapping would be carried out as often as thought necessary to dodge detection.

If traffic snarled up you would spend no more than ten minutes behind a vehicle before backing off. On motorways you could stretch distances and the occasional weave in and out of lanes helped to disguise your pursuit.

Every now and again you would pull off at a junction and re-join at the rear, becoming the "Tail-end Charlie".

We had driven about five hours when Grassi stopped at a hotel near Capel Curig, North Wales and booked in for the night; we had to do the same. Thankfully, it was in February so the hotels had several vacancies. Six of us piled into a small hotel, Bryn Tyrch in Snowdonia wearing trainers and heavy jackets trying to convince the hotel staff we were rock climbers, ramblers and ruggedly ready for any terrain the countryside could throw at us. The look on their faces showed quite clearly that they hadn't bought that story.

We expected the next day to be problematic as the hotel was on the main A5 and to find a position to watch Grassi's departure. None of us were dressed for the rainy conditions but thankfully a bus shelter provided Ray Smith with cover, both from the elements and Grassi.

Surveillance in rural areas is very challenging. The scarcity of other cars, the narrowness of roads with many, many turnoffs you don't see until you're upon it. As a team you have to work very closely.

At one point the target car went through the green traffic lights at road works followed shortly after by our lead vehicle. The lights changed to red as some of our cars went through and quick thinking by the driver of the third car in the convoy. He got out and stopped the oncoming traffic radioed that we could come through which enabled the rest of our team cars to drive through the then red lights. The oncoming motorists were not amused but it was over in a couple of minutes.

The surveillance route then took us toward Bangor, over the Menai Bridge to Anglesey. Grassi visited several harbours and marinas throughout the island. The case officer, Chris Hardwick was convinced Anglesey was the location for the importation. What he didn't know was when or exactly where.

Later in the month, I was part of a surveillance team in the Shaftesbury area of Dorset where Charlie Radcliffe was staying in a hotel. The team followed him from there into London, eventually arriving in Earls Court Road. Radcliffe went into a pub called the Boltons. After a few minutes I was told to go into the pub by Chris Hardwick. Unbeknownst to me the Boltons at that time was a favourite haunt for homosexuals.

Remarkably, my surveillance outfit of leather jacket, trainers and jeans coupled with my long hair and 70s moustache resulted in me blending in well. I looked like one of the members of the American disco group the Village People well-known for their on-stage costumes, catchy tunes and suggestive (gay) lyrics.

I was standing at the bar trying to catch glimpses of Radcliffe and a person we later identified as Malcolm Woolfson. A few people came up to me with obvious chat up lines such as, 'You're new. Have you been here before?' and, 'Are you drinking alone?'

I managed to mumble something and turned to order a pint. I spotted a pay phone in the bar so I called the office.

I whispered my request short and clear. 'I need someone here with me. I'm on my own in a bar full of homos!'

I avoided eye contact with everyone until Gordon Hall arrived.

Mindful we were still keeping an eye on Radcliffe and Wilson we sat and drank a couple of beers. Radcliffe only stayed in the pub for about an hour and eventually left. Woolfson left the Boltons Pub and hailed a taxi which was followed by the team waiting outside, to the Holiday Inn, Edgeware Road.

I linked up with Alan Griffiths and went to the hotel. We both approached the Head of Security and sat in the reception area. Woolfson had a visitor to his room and about 8pm they both left and took a taxi. Chris instructed us not to follow them but to try and gain access to the hotel room to look for evidence. The Head of Security opened the room and let us in. He returned to the reception area and he told us he would ring the room's phone twice if Woolfson returned.

I remember the double bed had both pillows on the one side and an empty bottle of champagne with two glasses together on the bedside table.

I looked at Alan and said, 'No prizes for guessing what has been going on here'.

On the floor was an unlocked suitcase and we were both amazed when we found bundles of cash, not hidden but just in the case. We counted £50,000 and took photographs of the notes in situ.

In those days there was no money laundering legislation so we had to let it go. It was ten times my yearly salary - a large amount of money. The photographs of the cash were important pieces of evidence.

Sometime later we discovered that this money was taken to Holland, to be somehow forwarded to Morocco as payment for the drugs.

Several weeks went by and Chris and the team thought there was a problem in Morocco or the importation had already taken place, either into the UK or another country. Radcliffe had links to the US and had successfully imported cannabis into the east coast of America before.

On Easter Sunday 1980 along with Bruce Letheren (Bravo 3) I drove to Anglesey. Ten other members of Bs and Cs also made their way from London to the area. Chris had approached HMS Indefatigable, a training establishment for young people looking to improve sea-fairing skills. This became our headquarters allowing us to park our cars safely and to have briefings.

We stayed at various hotels across Anglesey and the Bangor area. Bruce and I stayed at the Maelog Lake hotel in Rhosneigr, a village some 10 km south-east of Holyhead. We had different people over different parts of the island. It was a Welsh speaking area so it was often problematic in keeping a low profile by sounding as though we were casual tourists. The Maelog Lake Hotel was owned by an ex Regional Crime Policeman from Manchester. He got suspicious about us going out and about thinking we may be thieves casing properties to rob. He contacted some of his ex-colleagues in Manchester.

One day I realised I was the subject of a surveillance team from Manchester. Two cars were appearing in and out of my rear-view mirror – dropping back every now and again which is a sure sign that someone doesn't want to be noticed. It's a technique we, in Customs regularly use if we only have a couple of vehicles out on surveillance.

I stopped in a layby, waved them down and explained the situation. Embarrassed, they accepted my story which I repeated to the landlord when I got back to the hotel in Rhosneigr.

I was satisfied that being ex law enforcement he would not compromise our activities. In fact, he could not have been more helpful cooking breakfast at 3 in the afternoon when some of us woke up after a sleep following a night shift.

There were a couple of "choke points" on the island, intersections or junctions which must be crossed to get to a destination. The first was the entrance to the Menai Bridge, the crossing from Bangor to the Isle of Anglesey. We knew that if we had control of that point, we could monitor all traffic going on and coming off the island.

Two colleagues from Birmingham including Terry Delahunty booked into a hotel on the Menai crossing.

He asked the landlady if he could have a room for a week but keep the booking flexible.

'I have a beautiful room overlooking St Georges Channel with Snowdonia in the background, the Menai Straits.'

Terry's reply must have mystified her. 'A lovely room but can I have one that overlooks the roundabout.'

She knew that something was not quite right but didn't say anything.

The position of the hotel meant it was used by visitors exploring a wide area in Snowdonia and Anglesey as well as people working in Bangor. However, not many of them chose to stay in a room overlooking a roundabout.

After a couple of days Terry thought it was best to tell the manager he was working for Customs. She was relieved they were from the right side of law enforcement and not felons planning a robbery or worse.

Colleagues were booked in hotels throughout the area and each had an area to investigate looking for potential landing spots. One of the key crossroads was in a small village of Pentraith at the junction of the A5025 and B5109, the roads to the south, north, east and west. We took it in turns to monitor the known target vehicles, particularly the Jaguar owned by Grassi.

I was parked up in a layby on the A55 in my new car an SDI Rover (earning mileage costs) when a local police panda car pulled in behind me. He walked towards my car looking into the rear passenger seats and parcel shelf.

'What are you doing here?'.

(Chris had established contact with the local police at a high level and had devised a cover story that we were working for the Home Office testing radio reception in the area.)

'I work for the Home Office,' I said, 'testing radios.'

He stared at me. 'Why have you got a copy of The Bangor Times on the back seat of your car?'

I couldn't understand his reason for asking that but replied 'I've been reading it.'

I can only assume he was on the lookout for Welsh nationalists who had been setting fire to holiday properties owned by English people. Whether he thought I was an arsonist looking out for holiday homes I'm not sure but he was not a happy man. He wanted to get me out of the car and carry out a search.

He seemed to be determined to carry out what he saw as his duty so I had to tell him; 'Speak to the Chief Inspector at Bangor Police Station who knows why I am here.'

He got on the radio and got a very short reply. He nodded to me, walked back to his car then drove off.

Many of the pubs and restaurants were Welsh speaking so their evening was interrupted by English and Scottish accents. Ray Smith and Gordon Hall were Scots, the rest of us from across England. Holiday makers were there but we were the only group of men who were obviously not hill climbers bird watchers or ramblers.

I spent 10 days driving around Anglesey, parking up for about an hour, clocking car registration numbers, passing any suspicious ones to the control room in HMS Indefatigable.

The yacht Eloise, skippered by Thompson was spotted by the Cutter Swift a few miles off Anglesey. They were able to follow the yacht on radar, ensuing they were far enough away as to not be seen.

On the 14th April all our surveillance vehicles were circling the area the yacht was heading for. We did not have to get too close as the cutter had the yacht under observation. We were on the lookout for the shore party who were responsible for collecting the cannabis and driving it away to London. A Landrover was seen several times in the area of Newborough beach in the south west part of Anglesey. The sloping beach was about a mile wide and ideal for running a dinghy ashore. Chris was happy the cutter's radar would be able to tell us if there was any movement by the Eloise which was moored several hundred yards from the beach.

In the early hours of the morning the Land Rover was seen on the road down to the beach. Dave Wolstenholme, the police officer, jumped in my car and was a bit anxious.

'I want to be there when the job goes down and the arrests are made', he said.

'Dave, I can assure you will be there, as I want to be there as well.'

Terry Byrne instructed the surveillance team to drive slowly down to the beach. 'Can you all drive with your car lights off and keep the noise down as much as possible'.

No matter how good your surveillance and navigational skills are, driving in pitch black was quite scary. I parked up short of the beach and got out on foot. Dave stayed by my side as we tiptoed down towards the beach.

The cutter had seen on the radar an image that confirmed the yacht's small inflatable had been ferrying packages ashore, so we were sure some drugs had been carried inland and hidden between sand dunes. As they landed and began unloading more packages ashore the decision was made to "knock" by Terry Byrne.

As we moved, we kept losing sight of our target in the dark so, more by instinct and hope, we set out to find them in the sand dunes and gorse bushes.

George Atkinson (Bravo 2) was walking along the sand when he heard a voice, 'Quick,' it said, 'there's a police-boat out there.'

One of our Customs Cutter was on its way to intercept the yacht. We could see its comforting lights.

George answered, as if one of the gang. 'Where are you?' he whispered. 'Down here, to your right.'

With that George rushed down and grabbed the man. 'You're under arrest.'

There was no resistance.

Another customs officer was handed the smuggler as George went on looking for other people. A few steps later he was falling down a dune only to crash into another gang member who was promptly arrested.

I met up with Terry Byrne when we spotted a dark shadow coming toward us. 'It's one of them, Trapper,' Terry whispered.

With that we both charged and rugby tackled the man. Terry got out and shone a beam in the man's face.

'Get off me, you idiot,' said the man, 'it's Reg Lowe.'

There was a suggestion that as Terry and Reg didn't get on Terry gave him a whack after Reg identified himself. I don't know if that's true and Terry never admitted anything.

One of the shore party had decided to wade out into the sea and made his way in the shallow water toward a caravan site further along the beach. This took him an hour or so to reach the site and clambering ashore he was arrested by a uniformed police officer who had been scrambled to help us securing the area.

We had arrested all the suspects on the beach and the cutter had intercepted the yacht. Thompson and two other crew were arrested. The suspects were taken to Holyhead and Bangor police stations and were interviewed over the following 24 hours.

We all needed a break and the restaurant in the Anglesey Arms was booked for about 15 of us. The owner then realised what Terry and the rest of us were up to and she couldn't be more helpful.

She said, 'This is the most exciting thing to happen in Anglesey for years.'

Halfway through the meal the hotel received a call from the police at Bangor police station. They told Chris they were holding in a police cell a person brought up from London who was suspected of being involved in the importation. He had been locked up for 24 hours and nobody had been to interview him. Alan Griffiths and I volunteered to drive over to Bangor and sort it out.

At Bangor police station the sergeant wasn't concerned. The Police and Criminal Evidence Act was not yet with us and there were no legal time limits when an arrested person had to be interviewed, charged or released.

We were led down the steps to a corridor containing old-fashioned, almost Dickensian, cells. As the door creaked open the male, Malcom Woolfson, I had observed at the Bolton's Pub weeks earlier, flounced out.

As we led him to an interview room he complained 'I'm not very happy.'

'I'm not happy neither,' said Alan. 'I was in the middle of my first proper meal in two days.'

We looked through his belongings that had been found in his home address started the interview. He denied all knowledge of the cannabis importation and said the money seen in the Holiday Inn was not payment for the drugs. Among his belongings were numerous photographs of scantily dressed body-builders in various poses.

At one point, Alan whispered, 'I think he's taken a shine to you.'

For a while it was a bit bad cop, a bit good cop. Alan would ask normal questions, not in an aggressive manner but focused and sharp. Alan left the room and I said in a sympathetic voice 'Malcolm. I just want to be your friend and I want to help you out to avoid anything. I simply want to know your role in all this.'

Not getting anywhere Alan burst back in as if in a very bad mood, sat down and stared fiercely at Woolsfon.

'I'm talking to you,' Alan shouted. 'Look at me when I am talking.'

Both Alan and I knew that we did not have enough evidence to take it much further. He had been in possession of £50,000 in cash but there was no proof it was intended for a drug's pay off.

It was at midnight he was told he could go.

'I've got no money,' said Woolfson. 'I was brought here from London. I've got to get a taxi. Can you cash a cheque for me?'

'No,' I said. 'I can't do that.'

He was going to Bangor Railway station and we made it clear that no one was going to help him out.

In a search of his extensive paper-work we found letters that had responded to his complaints about officials to the United States Immigration and Customs. We had expected a complaint to wing its way to our Customs House.

He was not charged and he never complained about his treatment.

Charlie Radcliffe was interviewed by Roly Garrick (Bravo2) a genial Geordie who was an experienced investigator. Radcliffe admitted his involvement in the importation and agreed to provide a statement as to what he knew. Roly started to write down the words dictated by Radcliffe.

Radcliffe said, 'This is painful, can you get me a type=writer and I will sort it out'.

He typed out pages of a statement which confirmed his involvement.

Thompson also admitted his role and Grassi and the shore party had been caught red handed on the beach.

The gang were charged and remanded in custody.

Each week Chris Hardwick had to take a train from London to Holyhead to attend the remand hearing. Thompson and the others were bussed over from Strangeways prison in Manchester. At one of the hearings and much to everyone's surprise, the trial judge agreed to accept guilty pleas from all the accused. They were all sentenced to three years in prison which was a disappointment to Chris Hardwick and us all. With court cases, defendants are given credit for an early guilty plea which can dramatically reduce the cost of a trial.

Robin Thompson's barrister at the time was Alex Carlile QC who later became a liberal peer Lord Carlile of Berriew. He was famous for defending Diana Princess of Wales's former butler Paul Burrell who was charged with stealing some of her belongings. He was appointed as the Government's Independent Advisor on counter terrorism and I escorted him on a tour of the port of Felixstowe. He remembered the Thompson case and we had a good discussion about the operation and the trial.

CHAPTER 12
"CUSTOMS VENDETTA WITH POLICE". FAST CADILLACS.

In June 1979 the Bravos and Charlies attended a briefing at Scotland Yard regarding a police operation, "Cyril" which involved a large importation of drugs by a London crime group.

The Metropolitan Police Drug Squad had built up the intelligence but they were legally obliged to involve the Customs Investigation Division. Chief Superintendent John Smith was the police lead and Terry Byrne headed up the Investigation teams, the Bravos and Charlies.

At that time our department had the lead on drug smuggling and, as such, any drugs operations which involved an importation had to be run through the UK Customs and Excise, so a strategy for a joint operation had to be agreed. On some occasions the department will give the police permission to investigate but it was recognised we had the expertise and knowledge on ports and airports. Normally we would adopt the case or play a major role on joint operations. (The laws on drug smuggling were covered in the Customs and Excise Management Act 1972)

The Met had put a lot of time and effort into an operation they named "Cyril" which was headed by two London criminals, Robert Mills and Ronald Taylor. As they knew the suspects and their associates, they played the main lead on surveillance having tracked them for several weeks,

The day after the briefing the Met Drugs Squad deployed a full mobile surveillance team including two motorbikes and a helicopter to follow two of the suspects in a blue Mercedes driven by Mills. The Bravos and Charlies were on standby in vehicles at the start of the A3 motorway in west London. We were effectively observers, stepping in to help the Met if required. A police officer was a passenger in one of our vehicles. He maintained a radio link with the main surveillance team which in turn kept us all updated.

The Mercedes pulled into Fleet services on the M3 and I drove off the motorway near Frimley to await further instructions.

At most motorway service stations in the UK there is normally a service road for restricted traffic to travel from one carriageway to another. They are used by the police, ambulances and motorway staff. Not open to the public we knew about these service roads as they are often included in our surveillance training.

We heard on the radio the driver of the Mercedes had met with another male. We were instructed to drive into the service area in case arrests had to be made or help was needed. To our surprise the Mercedes drove across the motorway on the service road and headed back to London.

As the vehicle drove at speed down the slip road the driver had his arm out of the window and was giving a 'V' sign to cars but in particularly towards the police helicopter that was hovering above. Not the result the investigation team was expecting. Obviously, the Met surveillance team had been compromised. The helicopter looking down on their cars had got too close. So, the surveillance was aborted.

Following the "show out" a Land Rover and pick-up truck registered in the names of Mills and Taylor were found abandoned at the Fleet Service Station.

Terry had sufficient information to make a decision that two Customs vehicles would drive down to the Torquay area to liaise with a Customs Cutter to see if there had been any suspicious maritime activity that may have been a link to the Mills Taylor group. I was happy to drive down to Torquay via the M3, A303 to Exeter and on to Torquay. I boarded the Cutter along with a police officer and spoke with the Cutter Commander. He reported that nothing untoward had occurred in the previous 24 hours that would help the investigation.

Dave Hewer, an experienced investigator had previously worked on the Cutters and had a wealth of maritime and navigational experience. He liaised with the Met team who were labouring over information supplied by informants, people we didn't know. They had mentioned a place of importance referred to as "The Villa".

Dave suspected this related to Vilamoura, a marina in the Algarve area of Portugal. His hunch was right and a yacht linked to Mills and Taylor, "The Guiding Lights" was discovered, moored up there away from prying eyes. Dave acquired nautical details which appeared to be sets of coded numbers. Using his maritime knowledge, he recognised them as tide dates and times. The tide data identified an area between Looe in Cornwall and Plymouth in Devon.

Crucially Dave Thomas (Charlie 4) had been looking at the properties on the coast, remote ones that could house both villains and merchandise. He identified a café located in Talland Bay near Looe. The cottage and café had recently been purchased by one of the Mills-Taylor gang, Rodney Eagleton.

The pieces of the jigsaw were falling into place.

To say the Met team were impressed was an understatement. Without the Customs they would have never got anywhere near the importation. It highlights why the government at the time, despite pressure from the police supported the position that Customs had the lead on drug smuggling. Instead of trying to follow the targets and risk another "show out" Terry Byrne persuaded John Smith of the Met team to have confidence in the intelligence secured by Dave Hewer and Dave Thomas. They agreed and the Bravos and Charlies and the Met team drove to Looe in Cornwall on September 14 1979. It was the end of the high season but there were a lot of visitors in the town. There were 30 of us and we booked into various small hotels and guest houses.

We thought we would standout like sore thumbs so we tried to act as tourists as best we could. The Met teams were made up of people from different ethnic backgrounds, employed because of their London work. Ideal for a big city but not for a sleepy Cornish town like Looe.

"The Guiding Lights" had been sighted by a French Customs patrol boat, heading towards the UK and was at least two days sailing away. By regularly driving past the café in Talland Bay and the occasional stop for a coffee and lunch, we observed vehicles, including a Nissan pick-up truck, parked near the target cottage.

Myself and Alan Griffiths booked into the Anchor Lights Hotel and posed as tourists. We had maps and binoculars which we hoped gave people the impression we were twitchers. I don't know what we would have said if we had been asked a bird watching question.

We discovered that two of the Met officers carried firearms, probably usual practice for them but not for us. At that time the issue of firearms (normally a Webley and Scott revolver) was tightly regulated.

One of the policemen staying at a small hotel went up to the receptionist and asked her if she would put his gun in the hotel safe.

On seeing the gun, the female receptionist was close to fainting. It took an age for her to recover and for the officer to explain who he was and why he carried a gun. He stopped short of revealing details of the operation.

One of the firearm officers and I were in a pub when he realised that he had 20 bullets in his pocket. They were his full allocation, every bullet accounted for. He made a joke of it until the moment he reached into his pocket for some change and a couple of bullets fell out and fell to the floor.

Instead of helping him, his colleagues, who by then had enjoyed a few pints, started to kick the bullets across the packed pub floor. He then spent an age on hands and knees trying to retrieve the bullets. The laughter that accompanied his scrambling just about muffled the cussing and cursing.

Talland Bay had few houses and only one road in and out. The surrounding hills hindered our radio communications and Terry asked for a base repeater station with aerial to be sent from London. It took a day to arrive.

At the top of one hill was a bungalow, with very few houses around, making it an ideal location to transmit and receive.

We decided to knock on the bungalow door and seek permission to erect our equipment. An elderly couple answered.

Phil Matthews explained that we were the police and customs carrying out an operation in the area and asked if we could park the base station in their back garden.

At first, they were reluctant not wishing to be involved.

'It will be no trouble,' I said. 'You won't hear it and nobody will see it from the road.'

Eventually they agreed and Phil, Len Watson and myself unpacked and assembled the kit. It was an aerial that you needed to inflate with a large hand pump. Phil and Len were reading the assembly instructions and continued pumping. There came a point when they couldn't get any more air in but the aerial was not moving. Consulting the instructions and scratching their heads they were convinced they were doing it right. Len, curious about a wing nut, decided to undo it. With that the aerial shot out of its base, blasting out a whheeeee sound. It then landed on the roof of the bungalow.

Having told the owners how quiet and discreet we would be, we had to knock on the door asking permission to scramble across their roof.

Far from happy they reluctantly accepted the need for us to retrieve the aerial. A little while after that the base station was complete and working.

Along the western end of the single-track road seven of us were in a caravan and eight in a rented holiday home on the eastern side waiting for the "knock" to be called.

Customs and police were on the headland looking out to sea.

Info from the Cutter said the yacht was approaching land. Ray Smith (Charlie 7) and Chris Hardwick (Bravo 3) were hiding in the gorse bushes, two of the suspects came onto the headland and stood within a few feet of them looking out to sea. So close they could almost reach out and touch them as they walked past. They both hoped they would not get cramp or have a sneezing fit.

Ray and Chris could see "The Guiding Lights" moored a few hundred yards off Talland Bay. I waited in the caravan with the others listening to the whispered commentary from Chris as a suspect signalled to the yacht. A small inflatable boat went out to the boat, returning to the shore near the café.

It was just before dawn and we knew the "Knock" was imminent and the adrenalin was flowing.

About 2 tons of cannabis was brought ashore over six trips in the inflatable. According to Chris on the headland the inflatable was overloaded and looked as if it was about to sink. The drugs were loaded into the pick-up truck and driven off to the cottage.

Terry and the Met Police called the "knock". Our teams then started walking down the road toward the cottage. The distance of half a mile was further than some thought so a very quick running march was called for. When the two teams met at the cottage, the door was kicked in. The south London criminals were taken completely by surprise.

I said to one of the suspects called Lake, 'What are you doing here?'
'We're down here for a few days fishing.'
'Okay, where is your fishing equipment, your rods, your tackle?'
The look on his face told me that he knew his story was blown,
They were all arrested, including Taylor and taken to Plymouth Police Station.

Dave Hewer was on the Cutter when "The Guiding Lights" was boarded. He spoke to one of the disgruntled crew who asked, 'You have found the concealment I suppose".

Although we hadn't Dave suggested they had.

'You'll get credit if you confirm it,' said Dave.

The crewman took Dave to a bathroom and a chord near a mirror when pulled opened up a lock of a bulkhead. Behind the bulkhead were two large tanks where the cannabis had been concealed. It was a sophisticated set up which had obviously been used previously.

The following day I interviewed Lake with a police officer, Ron Boarder. Because of the detailed knowledge Ron had on the gang he led the interview. Lake denied everything but had no answer to the fact that he was arrested with over two tonnes of cannabis. A further 2 tonnes were found in a lock up garage in Penge. A total of 4.5 tonnes were seized; a massive amount at the time.

Later the same day I went to "The Guiding Lights" to help with the search.

Robert Mills thought he was being clever lying low well away in a hotel in Leeds. Detail of the hotel was discovered when Taylor's pockets were searched. Mills was arrested by police in the Leeds area.

I returned to London and on 18 February continued the interview with Lake at Rochester Road Police station.

In total 16 suspects were charged and the main players were found guilty at the Old Bailey.

Although it had a difficult start with the compromise on the M3, it turned out to be a really successful joint police and customs operations.

There were a number of "turf wars" between Customs and police but in the majority of cases we successfully worked with the police. A minority of police forces, but particularly the Met, who have always considered themselves international crime fighters, didn't like the Customs and Excise's legal and operational control of drug smuggling.

Resentment grew when Customs seized head-line amounts of drugs when the Police were left with "busting" small term users.

Rarely though did it reach the animosity of the 1971 "Sands" case that lasted 30 days in Court. A Detective Chief Inspector, the Head of the Scotland Yard Drug Squad, had been observed by Customs officers associating with members of the drug gang. The claim that the meeting was to obtain information and that there was no intention of hindering the on-going Customs investigation, it publicly revealed the damage caused by non-cooperation between the two organisations. In the end five conspirators were found guilty but the national head-lines were less satisfactory. "Customs Vendetta with Police" was one example.

It was often the case when the police would turn up at a freight depot or ferry terminal where they would have no knowledge of the port procedures or the customs paperwork required to clear a consignment.

The police invariably would be noticed and show out to the port employees who would notify the local Customs. Stories about the police turning up at airside warehouses, flashing their warrant cards, often alerting corrupt officials were numerous. When they did come to us, we would ensure that the proper procedure was adopted, reducing the risk of a compromise.

Whenever we out on operations we were always mindful that the next criminal we came across could be armed.

This was taken up by the powers that be, for we were issued with bullet proof vests whenever a "knock" was called for. These vests were rudimentary, bulky and cumbersome made from Kevalar, a ballistic nylon spun into aramid fibre and woven into cloth.

The early ones stretched from your neck to your hips making it difficult to drive a car as the vest rose up under your chin.

On 13th November 1979 the Bravos and Charlies had a spin off operation (intelligence identified on another venture) looking at two Turkish males who were driving a Mercedes car out of London but we were not aware of their destination. They then headed north towards Liverpool.

On the North Circular Road Terry Byrne radioed from the office to say he wasn't sure how far we should follow - that the suspect's purpose wasn't known. It would not be worth the trip. We didn't really know enough. It was too much of a wing and a prayer to deploy a surveillance team with the incumbent costs.

Six of us ended up in Liverpool driving on the M1 and the M6.

I radioed into Terry to ask advice. Although he had his initial doubts, he would support the decision to follow the targets.

The event started banter around the office that stayed with me throughout my career. Colleagues would say I tuned in to the radio and if there was any opportunity to leave London on surveillance I would jump at the chance. They were of course correct as I loved the art of surveillance and the gathering of intelligence evidence.

The joke was that whenever a call went out for someone to respond to a situation, not just by the Bs and Cs but other investigation teams, my reply was always, 'I'm on my way.'

The two targets stayed at a hotel in the centre of Liverpool and we booked in to a nearby hotel and took it in turns to watch the vehicle. We convened at 06.00 and waited for the vehicle to depart.

The hotel was in the Upper Parliament Road, close to the docks. The car with the two occupants left the hotel car park at 09.30 and headed south down the M6. We had no intelligence to confirm drugs had been collected so we were operating 'blind'. It was a spin off operation and whatever action we took it wouldn't have an effect on the main case.

Between junction 7 and junction 6 of the motorway there were road works where we were directed into a contra-flow. As the traffic slowed down, we decided to stop the suspect's car. I accelerated past and braked in front, boxing the car in, forcing the driver to turn in through the security bollards.

We ran to the Mercedes and dragged out the driver and passenger and spread-eagled them over the bonnet. We told them who we were, cautioned them and asked why they had been to Liverpool.

One turned up his hand and shaped it like a gun, pointing it at us. We acted quickly and aggressively, unwilling to take any chances. We pinned the two suspects down even harder with other colleagues rushing forward to restrain them. It was the first time I had arrested anybody since the tragic events leading up to the murder of Peter Bennett.

Later they said they had been to Liverpool to look at petrol pumps, those used in petrol stations and his hand action was an attempt to emulate a working pump, not aiming a firearm.

We searched the men and the car and finding nothing we let them drive on.

Our team's target were cannabis importation and the criminals behind them. Two of the other teams numbering 20 officers were the Foxtrots and the Golfs, two teams that investigated heroin importation. Their work was primarily in London where heroin trafficking was widespread, distribution carried out by Turkish and Asian smugglers. They operated in Southall and Gooding Lanes in north London.

On the 6th July 1980 I was called out to assist in a heroin operation. Information was passed on to us from the Customs Intelligence teams, the Bravos and Charlies. They had carried out surveillance in the Shepherds Bush area. On Monday 7th we observed the handover of 3kilos of cocaine from one vehicle to a Cadillac car. We were told by informants that there would be a meeting of two suspects in one of the streets nearby. Surveillance officers from the Golfs and Foxtrots observed a briefcase being handed over by two males. The suspect that received the drugs got into the Cadillac.

The "Knock" was called by Senior Investigation Officer, Tony Lovell.

I drove towards the Cadillac and joined other cars surrounding it to stop it moving. The Cadillac was being driven by Anthony Moxley, an ex-rally/racing driver and although blocked in he crashed and shunted his way out of the block and sped off. The passenger in the Cadillac was Douglas Morden, a former mercenary in Africa.

Bill Stenson had thrown himself on the bonnet of the Cadillac as it sped away and was holding on for dear life. There was a traffic jam at the end of Addison Road, Bill held on until the car stopped at road works where he got off visibly shaken but in one piece.

An armed police officer from the Met was in my SDI Rover. I cannot remember his name but we jokingly called him "Triffick" as every time we spoke, whether to him or between ourselves, he replied, 'terrific'.

As the car sped down Addison Road he got out of my car with his gun and shouted, 'I can shoot the tyres out.'

'You can't shoot here,' I said, 'they're too many civilians around.'

There were. Parents taking children to school, men and women on their way to the shops. Instead of fleeing the area some had stopped to see what was going on.

It seemed to me that the policeman's adrenaline had risen too fast, too high.

Thankfully, my car was still intact so I picked up Tony Lovell who had got out of one of our smashed-up surveillance cars and we drove off looking for the Cadillac. Down one road we could see it coming towards us the wrong way down a one-way street going very fast, exceeding, we thought, sixty miles per hour.

'Pull in front of him and stop the car,' screamed Tony who was pumped up with adrenaline.

Although he outranked me, I shouted back at him, 'You've got to be fucking joking,' I said. 'He'll go straight through us at that speed. I'll turn and follow him but I'm not going to put our lives at risk.'

My adrenaline levels were off the scale but I wasn't that cavalier.

As an ex racing driver Moxley knew how to get the most out of the roads, the tight corners, break through traffic lights. Eventually we lost him.

He was later arrested at his home address but Morden had left London.

I was asked by Tony Lovell to go to one of the suspect's home address in West London. The house was owned by Martin Bendelow. He had been a high flyer in the UK Conservative party, being placed years before on a parliamentary candidate list for Hull East by Sir Keith Joseph, himself a high flyer in Margaret Thatcher's election team.

In the search of the house 6 kilos of cocaine was found in the back of speakers. Bendelow was arrested and I had great difficulty clamping the handcuffs around his very thick wrists. He wasn't a dangerous or nasty person. He was polite and respectful but even with the most compliant suspect, handcuffs were obligatory.

It was not our operation so we handed him over to Tony Lovell's team, the Limas, who were pulling the evidence together in preparation for a trial.

An informant suggested that Morden would leave the UK in a light aircraft from a small airfield near London. On the 12 and 13 July I was sent with another officer Reg Low to cover Biggin Hill airport to observe departures by light aircraft.

We eventually stood down and we had no success in locating him.

I found out later he somehow had managed to get to the United States where he was arrested in New York and taken to the tough Rikers Prison. His finger prints matched the record we had circulated internationally. He tried to convince the US authorities that he wasn't Dougie Morden from the UK but a citizen of South Africa.

It was reported that a NY policeman advised him not to claim he was from South Africa – this was 1979, over a decade before apartheid was abolished. Morden, being an arrogant man, persisted in his story and made the reckless mistake by repeating it in the mainly Black American holding cells. The result was a severe beating by other prisoners and unconfirmed reports that he had been held down and raped.

Hugh Donagher (Golf One) received a call from Morden's solicitor in the US who confirmed Morden screamed at him, 'I want to get out of here and I won't contest the extradition.'

Bendelow, Morden and Moxley all pleaded guilty and received six years in prison.

CHAPTER 13
"THE MARCO POLO OF DRUGS".
HOWARD MARKS (MR NICE)

In April 1980 the Bravos and Charlies started looking closely at the activities of Dennis Howard Marks, a former Oxford University man from South Wales who it was suspected to be illegally smuggling cannabis to the UK, the United States, Australia and other countries of the world.

He was known to believe that his behaviour was socially and mentally beneficial to mankind at large and, as a reward for all his "good" work, made himself a whole lot of money.

His story would later become a famous one through the publication of his book, "Mr Nice". This was made into a film in 2010 directed by Bernard Rose with the actor, Rhys Ifans, playing the part of Marks.

Howard Marks was born in the small village of Kenfig Hill, near Bridgend, Glamorgan, South Wales in August 1945.

He obviously was very bright and was the first member of his family and close friends to go to university. Even more impressive was the offer to attend Balliol College Oxford to read physics. During this time, between 1964 to 1967, he became friendly with the epidemiologist Julian Peto and the journalist, Lynn Barber. He also became a prolific user of cannabis and spent most of his time attending wild parties and smoking drugs.

In the final few weeks before graduating, Marks found he hadn't completed sufficient practical physics experiments. He copied the work of other students and got access to his attendance record and filled in the blanks. Through a mixture of cheating and last-minute cramming, he passed his finals achieving a second-class honours degree; this was despite months of taking drugs rather than attending classes and a serious blood infection caused by stepping on a rusty nail a few weeks before the exams.

One of his professors said he was one of the brightest students to attend the college. They must have despaired thinking what Marks could have achieved if he hadn't fallen under the influence of cannabis.

He met up with fellow students and street level suppliers who were importing relatively small amounts of cannabis from Holland but enough to sell in commercial quantities so that some money could be made to fund their own use.

The drugs were often sold as "wraps", a small folded piece of paper containing the drugs. Each wrap would then have cost the user £5 to £6, not a small amount in those days.

Mark's inexhaustible demand for personal cannabis use would have stretched his finances beyond breaking point so becoming a "wholesaler" was a godsend for his addiction.

At that time, only small amounts of cocaine or heroin came into the country. Heroin addicts have existed since the opium poppy was cultivated in lower Mesopotamia as long ago as 3400 BC so drugs other than cannabis would have been available, but it seems played no part in Mark's activities.

So, Marks chose an alternative direction from physics. He chose drug smuggling, firstly from Holland and later from Kabul and Pakistan. Consignments were smuggled from Pakistan via Frankfurt through Shannon Airport in Ireland, facilitated by fair means or foul by James McCann. McCann was a well-known IRA (the Irish Republican Army) member, who, in the early '70s, threw a petrol bomb into Queen's University in Belfast. He was also described as "possibly the most effective arms supplier" for the IRA. He was also involved in what the Irish Police called the biggest "burst" of drugs in Ireland amounting to half a kilo of cannabis.

In his thick Belfast accent, he always referred to Howard Marks as H'ard Marks.

He was introduced to McCann in 1968 by Graham Plinston who Marks had met at Oxford. McCann, it appeared, didn't like Plinston, calling him "soppy bollocks" due to his plumy English accent. Mark's Welsh accent would have appealed to McCann being valued only because it was obviously not English.

Marks was a regular visitor to Plinston's cottage in Oxford where they reported to smoke up to 20 joints a day.

Plinston had a criminal record. Marks didn't.

The two men, Marks and Plinston, persuaded McCann that a lot of money could be made by smuggling hashish into Ireland from Kabul.

James McCann soon had Shannon Airport Customs and other officials on his payroll so drugs were easily and speedily unloaded from aircraft and secreted out of the cargo sheds, by-passing Customs controls and off the airport limits.

At this time (Marks disclosed later at his trial) he was approached by a former Oxford student "Mac" Hamilton who said he was an agent for MI6 and was interested in Mark's drug smuggling activity and latterly McCann. Up until recent years the security services tended to recruit from the top of top universities, not your average white-collar worker, not your blue-collar worker and certainly not a full-time drug dealer, however well educated.

The story that Marks was approached by "Mac" was never confirmed by the authorities but that is not unusual. One of the main responsibilities of the "Secret Service" was to remain "secret".

According to Marks he was to be provided with a "safe house" and a "letter drop" facility to pass on any information that might be of interest to the security services. Hamilton had made it clear that Marks' involvement with drug smuggling was known to them, information that would be kept classified should Marks cooperate.

It seems clear that Marks kept his contacts stringing along without getting too involved. He even told McCann about his new "employer". Marks revelled in the idea of being a secret service James Bond agent. Not a licence to kill but a licence to smuggle!

Marks first came on the Customs radar in 1970 when he returned to Heathrow Airport from a trip to Frankfurt. He had illegally smuggled out £5000 of Plinston's money to a man known as Lebanese Sam. On his return at UK Customs he was stopped and searched. Marks' fee for the job was £300 which he had hidden in a sock, along with a receipt made out to Kenneth Graham Plinston. Marks was unaware that bringing such a sum into the UK was legal. The then currency restriction of £25 applied only to money being taken out of the country. (He knew that by taking the £5000 out of the country he had already broken the law).

After extensive questioning the Customs Officer advised Marks that duty was to be charged on a small amount of perfume he had bought, but the £300 was legal.

'We can't touch you on that,' the Customs Officer said. 'But we do know of your friend, Mr Plinston. We know how he makes his living. We advise you don't get involved.'

Needless to say, Howard Marks did not take that advice.

He was one of the few to recognise the increasing demand for cannabis use in the UK and USA. In the early 70's America consumed 28tons of marijuana and hashish a day. England smoked 3 tons a day.

So, in 1973 he decided to branch out on his own ventures not involving McCann. Marks became involved with James Morris, a friend of Plinston, who operated a scam smuggling hashish from Pakistan to the UK and Switzerland to the United States. At that time British pop groups, Pink Floyd, Genesis and the like toured America. Their equipment, amplifiers and speakers, would be air-freighted separately by others. The pop groups were totally unaware that prior to shipping, the drugs were weighed and secured inside their equipment. At US customs they were weighed again and with little or no scrutiny of paperwork. On arrival on US soil the drugs were taken out and distributed. At the end of the (normally short) tour the equipment was loaded with bricks to match the incoming weight and flown back to the UK.

As the first consignment were successfully smuggled to the US, Marks and Plinston planned another delivery of 1500 kilos of cannabis into Shannon Airport, some of which would then go by ferry to the UK and some air-shipped to the US using Morris' rock group equipment method.

Through a Dutch contact and using a truck with 400 kilos of Lebanese cannabis resin (hash), concealed in loudspeakers was delivered to Schipol airport Amsterdam. The load was air-freighted to Las Vegas. Unfortunately for Marks and the others a Drugs Enforcement Administration (DEA) team had busted the consignment and arrested the US importer, Gary Lickert.

On a separate deal, a car with cannabis hidden inside had been left parked on a street in Hamburg. McCann sent his girlfriend Anne McNulty, to Hamburg to collect the car (using the spare key supplied by Plinston). McNulty was arrested by the German Police and held in custody. When McCann heard about it, he flew into a rage and stated "he had declared war on the Nazis and he would give them a fucking reminder of World War II" if she was not released. She was not and served a short custodial sentence in Hamburg. World War III didn't happen.

In March 1974 Marks, using an Irish passport in the name of Peter Hughes, was arrested by the police in Holland who asked him, 'Are you Dennis Howard Marks?'

His reply was recorded. He replied, 'Yes I am, why do you want to know?'

Although Mark's Dutch solicitor protested Marks was put on a flight to London where he was immediately arrested, charged under section 20 of the Misuse of Drugs Act 1971 with assisting in the UK in the commission of a United States drugs offence (rarely used charge at this time as most of our cases involved an importation into the UK).

At the time of his arrest Marks was the owner of many false passports. Peter Hughes was one, Donald Nice another and Anthony Tunnicliffe. In his life of crime, he had 43 aliases, 89 phone numbers and owned, or part owned, 25 companies including a dress shop, "Annabelinda".

By this time, he was well known in the UK and in Europe. The case officer, Robin Eynon, was compiling the case against Marks. Marks was granted bail with sureties totalling £50,000 and within eleven days of his scheduled trial he had disappeared somewhere in Italy, often travelling in a Winnebago motor home.

News of Marks' "disappearance" made the papers with headlines suggesting he had been executed by the IRA or a crime syndicate.

Marks himself, his activities and his slippery manoeuvring was of great public interest, not quite in the "Robin Hood" mould, but that of a clever bounder able to charm or outwit any "Sheriff of Nottingham" that stood in his way. There was little coverage given to the social, physical and emotional costs his "business" generated in society or the company he kept of murderous gangsters such as Dave Courtney. Marks is described in Freddie Forman's book, The Godfather of British Crime, as "Dave's driver". There was no evidence that Marks was a violent man but he certainly rubbed shoulders with men who were.

Marks had business links with the American Mafia, the Colombian trafficker Pablo Escobar, as well as the IRA. It is said that at one stage he controlled 10 per cent of the world's cannabis trade.

In the Daily Mirror newspaper of May 2nd 1974 was the headline front page "Where is Mr Marks?" Under Mirror Exclusive "Police hunt for drugs case man who was a Secret Service Informer."

On 19th April the Daily Mirror, under the headline "The Face of A fugitive" was a photo of a moustached Marks in London.

In 1975, unspotted by us, he returned to the UK using one his numerous passports.

On 4 July 1975 Marks organised the importation of "Nepalese Balls", small black balls of cannabis resin. The drugs left Kathmandu to Bangkok to Tokyo and on to New York. This incursion into the USA would later prove to be his downfall.

When, in early 1980's, Marks again came to the attention of HM Customs and Excise Investigation Division when the Bravos and Charlies were following a well-known West Country smuggler, Raymond Humphries. He was arranging his own importation of cannabis from Morocco and he was followed from Paddington railway station to a restaurant in Hyde Park where he met an unknown male. The discussion was overheard by colleagues sitting at a table nearby and the male offered to sell Humphries 5 tons of cannabis.

Nick Baker, the most senior officer out on the day made the decision that we should follow the second man. We followed him to the Dorchester Hotel. Checks with hotel security identified the male as an American, Walter Nath. Checks also revealed he had checked into the hotel with another American called Joel Magazine. A third male, as yet unidentified, met Nath and Magazine in the Dorchester Hotel and when he left the meeting Nick instructed us to follow this third man. He made his way to a flat in Hans Court, an exclusive area next to Harrods.

Checks with the utility companies and the electoral rule confirmed the third man was the elusive Howard Marks. The fact it was Marks, a new operation was initiated and it moved up in the list to become our number one priority. The drugs teams Bravos and Charlies (although two teams they were effectively one for operational matters) were tasked to investigate a report that Marks and his associates were arranging a drugs importation. Terry Byrne (Charlie 1) agreed that Nick Baker (Charlie 2) should be the case officer. Bs and Cs and our intelligence teams were aware of Mark's "links" with the Security Services and we were not sure if he would use this to "get himself out of jail". It was of paramount importance that this operation was on a need-to-know basis and kept within a tight nucleus of officers. All of our operations began with a B or a C (the same with others teams in the ID) and Operation Cartoon was named and began to evolve in February 1980.

Because of our concerns there was a risk of a compromise we gave all the suspects nicknames and the operation name lent itself to us using cartoon characters.

Howard Marks was Donald Duck, James Goldsack was called Goofy, Patrick Lane, the financier, was Pluto. It was amusing but it had a serious side - we referred to them by their nickname in case we were overheard. Even in the office we referred to the suspects by their cartoon names. It was slow but we were slowly building up a picture of Marks' group and their activities.

We knew Walter Nath and Joel Magazine were in London. They, it was thought, were part of a United States drug trafficking group. Nath, a Sicilian-American, was a suspected Mafia member. Magazine, a Miami defence lawyer.

Although we were not aware of this at the time, they were acting on behalf of Colombian drug suppliers. A large quantity of cannabis had been delivered to the UK and there had been concerns by the Mafia in the US and the Colombians regarding the delay in distributing the drug and, of course, receiving payment.

Nath and Magazine were sent over to the UK to find out where the drugs were, to make an inventory of the drug haul and to "persuade" with any means available, those in the supply chain to move things on quickly. They were concerned the two organisations had been ripped off by the distributors in the UK. If they were not being ripped off it was far too slow for their liking.

I can only imagine what frighteners were being used by the Mafia to "persuade" people! The combination of a Colombian Drugs Cartel and the Mafia is a mix that no sane man would displease.

At that time, we had no information how or where the drugs were imported or how much remained in the UK. There was a suggestion some of the drugs were going to be moved to Norway and other parts of Northern Europe.

Joel Magazine was in his forties, medium build and looked middle European. He was staying in a suite at the Dorchester Hotel in Marble Arch. Nath, who was younger, shorter and slim but again looking middle European, was booked into a normal room at the same hotel. This gave us a clue as to the pecking order of the group.

On the evening of the 12th November Nath and Magazine had met up with Howard Marks (aka Donald) at The Dorchester, a meeting they repeated the next day. Marks was followed by Mike Stephenson (Charlie 7) and saw him go into the hotel room occupied by Nath. We were able to establish the meetings took place but we were never in a position to hear what was being said. Most of our time was spent in parked cars in case they left.

When they had returned to their respective hotel rooms, a skeleton cover of the reception area was maintained, while the rest of us got a few hours' sleep.

Marks was now an important equation in our investigation. For two days officers tried every avenue available to them to try to find out who he lived with and who he associated with.

The Dorchester Hotel Security people were tasked with passing on any information on comings and goings and would press a panic button if Nath or Magazine checked out. Our intelligence team at Heathrow monitored airlines for any bookings connected to the three men.

Early on the morning of the 14th Nath did check out the hotel and got into a black BMW driven by Marks. We moved fast. By the time they hit the road we had assembled three unmarked surveillance cars to follow him.

Alan Griffiths drove one of the cars and I handled communications. We stayed three to four cars behind the BMW.

They headed west past Harrods and the British Museum along Cromwell Road to the M4.

The Case Officer for "Cartoon", Nick Baker agreed to stay at the Dorchester to search the vacated hotel rooms for any evidence left behind (written notes that had been thrown away etc.) So, Nick was likely to be at least an hour behind us.

We quickly adopted our surveillance procedures where one vehicle would be behind the target vehicle for a short period of time, giving a commentary throughout. The "eyeball" would then be handed over to the next vehicle in the convoy and so on. Because we regularly changed over the surveillance vehicles we were satisfied we had not been spotted. The commentator in the 'eyeball' vehicle would advise of the road name, direction of travel and the direction which, in this case, appeared to be Heathrow although we couldn't rule out the West Country.

Terry Byrne, had given instructions to follow Marks and Nath wherever they go and, if they split, stay with Nath.

When they turned off towards the airport it became apparent this was going to involve a flight for one or both of them.

Terry's instructions were at the forefront of my mind when we approached Terminal 1 of Heathrow Airport.

A few of us hoped that Nath would head for the US or the Caribbean and we would be required to follow, a thought that would have Terry Byrne climbing up a wall and probably back tracking on his 'follow them wherever they go' instruction.

In our conversation with Nick Baker, we taunted him with the prospect of six of us heading halfway across the world and that he had given us authority to do so. Alan Griffiths wanted to wind Nick up by telling him on the radio we had checked in on an Air Canada flight to Montreal. The rest of us thought that was just too cruel.

In those days some of us might carry passports but we always had our ID cards. The Customs ID card was like a "warrant" card giving the bearer permission to go anywhere at airports, even board aeroplanes. Security was more relaxed and we could, if necessary, talk ourselves onto a flight. We all knew that once aboard a flight a phone call to our office would result in everything being sorted out with the airline and the arrival destination authorities in whatever country we landed.

Nath was dropped off by Marks at Terminal One, which handled near Europe and domestic flights. As Nath entered "Arrivals" the surveillance 'footmen' were dropped off to follow Nath into the terminal and we parked our cars.

I quickly jumped out of the car to follow Nath into the terminal.
I watched as he walked up to the check-in desk that handled the British Airways Shuttle service to Glasgow. Immediately after he booked his flight, details were passed to colleagues on a radio handset.

Not long after Nick joined us.

We had no idea why Nath was going to Glasgow. No information had been received that flagged up that connection.

Eight of us bought tickets on the shuttle, telephoned our office in Glasgow and they would have six fully manned (driver and commentator) surveillance vehicles waiting for us when we arrived. We then boarded the plane.

Had the plane been full we had the legal clout to demand a number of passengers be taken off the flight to accommodate our team. In this case seats were available but we did insist on being spread around rather than together in two rows. Six men sitting together, even dressed casually, would stand out however hard we tried to blend in with normal travellers.

Surveillance on an aircraft was new to us. We spread ourselves throughout the plane ensuring we could see if Nath met or spoke to any other passengers. Alan Griffiths sat in the row behind Nath in case any opportunities arose to overhear any conversation. As it was a domestic flight there were no "Border Controls." It was effectively like getting on and off a bus.

Our colleagues in Glasgow had already been briefed by our London office and were waiting our arrival, cars and footmen at the ready.

After disembarking we kept Nath in constant view as we blended in with the other passengers keeping as close to him as possible.

Nath was met by a man who was driving a white Volvo which checked out to a Stuart Prentiss. Prentiss was late thirties, slim and tall. He had not come to our attention before and was a "clean skin", somebody that had not come on the law enforcement radar. Although he was not known, the very fact he had met Nath rang alarm bells.

(It turned out that Prentiss was a key player in Mark's current venture.

Prentiss and Nath headed up the west coast of Scotland. I was in a vehicle with Jim Conroy, a colleague from our office in Glasgow. It was the 14th March, a beautiful day, clear and sunny with snow on the distant hilltops. We drove through the ancient village of Luss, with its stone cottages, then up the side of Loch Lomond, beautiful scenery all the way. We spent over two and half hours tracking the suspect car ending up at Oban, a town on the west coast of Scotland.

It's a very long journey from Glasgow to Oban with less than perfect roads that made it unusually difficult for surveillance. Although the winding narrow roads meant the car went out of sight for short periods of time, we were happy that we were able to follow him without too much difficulty. We used the same method of surveillance, regularly changing over the "eyeball" car.

We arrived on the outskirts of Oban and Prentiss stopped for petrol. We immediately found places to park that were hidden from the petrol station while Ray Smith and Len Watson got out of the car to observe the situation. We spent those minutes plotting the next moves, what car went where, what car would take over, what car would pull back, who would cover what exit, who would hold back. The "eyeball" car instructed all the others.

What we didn't know at the time was that our radio transmissions could be heard by the intercom system of the petrol station so as Nath paid his bill, he could hear what could only have been surveillance talk, surveillance references. Although unaware if the conversation was about him or something entirely connected with him, he was, however, alerted. Caution was paramount. No way could he risk continuing with his current plan of action.

We followed as the car drove through Oban then north toward Fort William. At no point did we think we had been compromised.

At Fort William he started to head South through barren landscape with very few buildings on heather covered open land and across Ranoch Moor. We were hanging back at least half a mile behind him still believing all was well.

After two hours we began to feel uneasy. The handover of eyeball and the swopping of vehicles continued but Nick asked if the Volvo was driving normally. Although it was a long, drawn-out route Prentiss was not driving erratically. There seemed to be no logic to Nath's route, no reason to take the roads he did other than to expose any vehicle that may be following. He wasn't heading for the coast, for an airport or a city.

Eventually he did drive into Glasgow City Centre and Nath was dropped off outside the Glasgow Central railway station. We followed him inside and he immediately went into a telephone booth. I walked quickly and entered the booth next to him in the hope of overhearing his conversation. What I did hear made my heart sink. Three words; 'Your dog's sick.'

He put the phone down and made his way to the train heading for London.

In Cockney dialect the telephone is, "Dog and bone".

Even though he was an Italian American he used that expression and what he was saying was "don't use the phone, we're being watched and the wheel's come off. Keep your head down."

Those three words had made it clear. Our surveillance was compromised, perhaps wrecked. We reported back to Terry who decided we should stand down and let Nath go back to London, which he did by train.

Under these circumstances, when any advantages you thought you had turned into disadvantages, you stepped back as far as you thought expedient, to give your suspects space and time so they would reason their activities were safe and back on track. They probably spent the next few weeks looking to see if they were being followed, which of course they were not.

Terry and Nick knew, as we all did, that the people behind the drug smuggling had invested a huge amount of money. They were unlikely to abandon their plan A completely without a plan B, especially if the Mafia had been let down. Those deemed to be at fault would face the wrath of the suppliers and those financing the importation.

Experience told us that in spite of a possibility of a compromise, those involved in serious criminality do not give up their investment easily and that certainly applies to the Mafia. They were notorious at having snitches everywhere whose job was to gain insight into any law enforcement investigation that might include them. A snippet of good information would help them take back control of the situation.

From our point of view the fact Nath had met Prentiss made it clear that Prentiss was a key player. A link had been established between Marks, Nath, Prentiss and the Mafia. And Scotland itself was on our radar.

On our behalf Scottish Customs Investigation colleagues carried out discreet enquiries in and around the Oban and discovered that Prentiss had rented a house on the Isle of Kerrera (Seal Island), a small island off Oban Harbour. Another of Mark's associates, Peter Whitehead, a film director, had rented Conaglen House, a mansion at the entrance to the Caledonian Canal near Fort William only an hour and a quarter from Oban.

Given that it was March with average temperatures hovering just above 5 degrees in the middle of the day, long days and nights were not the best working shifts for our Scottish colleagues camped out in make shift shelters on hill-sides. Heavy snow, rain, sleet and raging winds tested the best of humour.

They were paranoid about using words that could give us away. We developed a word code using deer instead of persons (there were lots of deer all around). So, meaning that a person was on the move we would say, 'The deer is stirring'.

It worked well until two suspects emerged from Conaglan House and got into a car. Our observation officer came on the radio in a loud whisper, 'Two deer have surfaced and climbed into a Mini and are driving off.'

Down south we had observed James Goldsack (Goofy) and Patrick Lane (Pluto) meeting with Martin Langford. Langford lived in a house in Pytchley, a small village near Kettering, Northamptonshire. From there he bred falcons for the Saudi Royal family.

Over the next few weeks there were reports of 25 kilo bales of herbal cannabis were being washed up in various locations on the West Coast of Scotland quite near the Oban area. These were spotted by members of the public out walking their dogs. The police put out a message through the media to warn people not to touch or tamper with any bales washed up on the beach. That they may contain prohibited or dangerous material. Under no circumstances can they be removed other than by the authorities.

It was calculated that over half a ton of cannabis had been washed up along the west coast. A story circulated that a farmer picked up a bale thinking it was animal fodder and fed it to his chickens. It was reported that chaos ensured with riotous chickens "as high as kites", taking off in a manic fashion and crashing into fences only to get up and do the same again.

The story became a national issue with the Scottish Daily Record running a cartoon series called "Angus Og" on the arrival of cannabis bales.

It never reached "Whiskey Galore" notoriety but it became part of the local folklore.

It became evident that these bales were linked to our investigation as a Government Chemist identified the drug as Colombian Red, the same as had been seized elsewhere. And although there was a significant amount of cannabis washed up it was unlikely to be the complete haul, the complete importation. The probable connection between the discovery and Walter Nath and Joel Magazine's presence in the UK, burdened with Colombian links, backed up the theories that were rapidly forming, theories that could be developed and investigated.

We stored the bales in a secure Customs Office in Glasgow although after a short while the office was evacuated because of the rank smell. The cannabis, wet with mould and sea water, was a noxious combination and at one stage the office above the store had to be evacuated on health grounds. I checked the drugs at an early stage so the stink didn't get to me.

The bales were then sealed and transported to London to a more secure Government warehouse.

UK security forces had little evidence of Colombian cannabis reaching the streets. It was known as a high yielding plant that produced medium-sized buds full of red hairs and street talk had it as good for morning and day time use.

We were convinced that more cannabis was on its way. Nick Baker, the case officer, decided to hold back and do a limited surveillance on other parts of the criminal organisation, leaving the main players alone. They would be the ones looking over their shoulders. Their movements were observed at a distance; houses and other premises were watched, details of cars, regular haunts, meetings and visitors were observed – anything that helped build up a picture. Not exactly painting by numbers but colouring in unconnected parts and hoping to number them later.

Nick Cole, a former barrister who lived in Daniels Farm, Laindon in Essex, was thought to be a middle rank member of the organisation. Cole was a man with a drink problem and was no longer practising law.

Observing Whitehead's comings and goings at Conaglen House were difficult. There was no vantage point that provided adequate cover. The only thing we could do was to infrequently drive past in different cars hoping to spot any movements of people or vehicles.

Alan Griffiths and I were in Kettering doing a drive pass checking out Martin Langford's address to see if we could see any suspect persons or cars when we spotted a car owned and driven by Goldsack.

We were hoping that some of the drugs were still located there, in addition to that washed up on the beach. Also, we were almost certain that some had ended up at the house near Kettering.

We had no idea of the quantity of drugs in any one location.

I was in the office when I received a tip off that Patrick Lane was about to be visited by Goldsack in Bayswater. It turned out that Patrick Lane was the money man for the organisation. He later co-authored a book with Howard Marks; "Recollections of a Racketeer: Smuggling Hash and Cash Around the World."

It was just before 5pm – rush hour around New Fetter Lane. We knew the traffic would be heavy so Dave Thomas offered me the back seat of his 1000cc motorbike. Dave was six feet five, I was six feet three so apart from vans and taxis our line of sight was above most cars. It was worse than any helter-skelter ride I'd ever been on. We zig-zagged through the traffic over and under-taking everything before us. It seemed only a few minutes to cover the four and a half miles.

We arrived in time to see Goldsack arrive at Patrick Lane's house. This gave us a piece of real information that could prove useful as evidence. Should we ever interview Goldsack we had an indisputable fact to throw at him.

A few days later, on the 13th May, I observed Goldsack at Cole's house. Again, more evidence.

On the 14th Goldsack was seen meeting with Lane and Howard Marks in Queensbury, an area of northwest London. Our evidence file was growing day by day.

A day later Terry and Nick held a briefing at our office in New Fetter Lane and it was decided that all the addresses we had identified would be searched and suspects arrested. I was asked to be one of the officers to go to Cole's home, Daniel's Farm in Laindon, Essex a substantial farmhouse.

The "knock" was scheduled for Saturday 17 May.

Chris Hardwick lived near Billericay about 14 minutes' drive from Laindon. He invited me and other officers to stay at his house for the night of the 16th.

Some of us slept on the floor, some in chairs. Some stayed awake preparing to leave at 4am the next morning.

In the early hours we drove in convoy to Laindon, parked our cars near Daniel's Farm waiting for the arrest of Prentiss and Grey in Scotland which was the catalyst for the rest of the operation to kick into action. The operations, north and south had to be synchronised to the second. Any delay, even a few minutes, could result in one phone call between villains and a stack of evidence being destroyed.

The team in Scotland waited for daylight. At that time of year, it was a lot lighter in Scotland than in the South east England.

So, at 5am in the morning, when we received the signal from Terry Byrne and Nick Baker in our Fetter Lane Office to "knock" as it was just getting light. "Knocks" usually happen at that hour as half asleep minds tend not to make efficient criminal minds.

A decision had been made to include a local police officer from the drug squad as we were more than likely have to use police offices for interviews, Scenes of Crime forensics to take fingerprints and photographic evidence. Although he was rather miffed at being dragged out in the early hours, it would turn out to be the largest case he ever got involved in. We drove into the grounds of the farm-house just after 5am.

Vehicles were parked across all possible exits. Chris and I headed for the main door as footmen ran around the back to cover rear and side doors.

As we banged on the front door hoping for a quick entry a West Indian guy leaned out of a bedroom window.

This came as a surprise as this man had not been seen before.

'Can I help you,' he asked.

I identified myself and said, 'Open up now. Otherwise, we'll knock the door with sledge hammers.'

Within a minute we were let in the house by Nick Cole wearing his dressing gown and we all piled in to search the house.

On the way in I had spotted a newly built large shed. I left colleagues in the house to inspect the building. The wooden doors were padlocked so I returned to the house and asked Cole for the shed keys.

'That's not my shed,' he said.

'It's in your garden. It's obvious that it's your shed.'

'I haven't got the keys. I don't know who owns the shed. I don't know anything about it.'

I said, 'I've got a sledge hammer. It won't take me a few seconds to bash the padlock in.'

'Go ahead,' he said. 'I don't have the key.'

I inspected the shed lock. With Roly and Alan we prepared to crash our way in. As I swung the hammer at the lock I slipped on the grass and instead of demolishing the lock, the hammer clipped the metal edge and the lock sprung open.

The police officer was aghast. 'What a fantastic shot that was,' he said. I did point out that if I tried to do that a thousand times, I would not achieve the same result.

In the shed was 4 tons of cannabis all wrapped in fertiliser sacks. Scales hung from a beam ready to weigh out and sell on wholesale to dealers in London and other cities. There was a strong smell of musty herbal material which we immediately recognised.

In addition to the drugs, we found the inflatable boat (now deflated).

On seeing the quantity of drugs, the policeman contacted his sergeant who then turned up at the farm within half an hour. The sergeant then phoned his Inspector who raced to the scene, arriving in about 20 minutes. He phoned his Chief Inspector who got in touch with his Chief Superintendent. Eventually the Deputy Chief Constable of Essex turned up a few hours later and waited around to give interviews to the press.

The black guy who we saw first was interviewed and his account of being merely a visitor was accepted.

It transpired that Nick Cole's mother was the owner of the farm who was completely unaware of what her son was up to. She was polite and well spoken. At one point during the house search she insisted on making us all duck egg sandwiches. Although she had to be treated as a suspect initially and taken to Basildon Police station by Steve Frodsham to be interviewed. The station sergeant was a typical station custody officer who treated lowlife and worthies exactly the same. After answering basic questions, she visibly reeled when asked if she had distinguishing features.

'What do you mean, distinguishing features?' Her voice echoing Lady Bracknell's outrage from "The Importance of Being Earnest."

The sergeant's words were a few octaves lower, 'Any tattoos,' he said.

'Tattoos!' she bellowed, 'Tattoos!'

The interview was promptly terminated.

Scenes of crime and forensic people visited the farm and found cannabis seeds in the bottom of the inflatable boat. Evidentially this was very important because when our Scottish colleagues busted the address in Kererra Island tracks were found where the trailer had taken the drugs to the house spilling seeds as it went. Cannabis plants were growing in the grooves of the tracks.

To link the seeds to Oban and to other premises was vital.

Simultaneously with the farmhouse raid, Alan Griffiths, Tony Lovell, Tom McKeown and others went to Langford's house in Pytchley and found 3 tons of cannabis in the loft of a charming old cottage. To gain entry Tom climbed on the fence which collapsed. As he gathered himself and looked up all he could see was the chilling stare of a live falcon perched on a garden post.

We had been to addresses guarded by rottweilers, Alsatians and Great Danes but never one by a bird of prey.

It was then 5am and, disturbed by the unusual hullabaloo. the next-door neighbour arrived in his pyjamas, dressing gown and a night cap to see what was happening.

'What's going on here?' he asked.

'We're police and customs conducting a drugs raid.'

'Drugs!' He said. 'There's no drugs in Northampton. I'm on the Police Watch Committee and we've been discussing if we should disband the drugs squad in Northampton.'

The local policeman took great delight in taking him into the cottage and up to the loft and pointing out 3 tons of cannabis less than 100 yards from where he lived. Martin Langford was arrested at the house.

Needless to say, the proposal to disband the drugs squad was shelved.

George Atkinson was the lead officer in Scotland when they raided a bungalow owned by Alan Arthur Grey in Glengarry, near Inverness. They found almost 4 tons of cannabis in the bungalow roof.

Grey was heard to say, 'Thank goodness you arrived, my roof was about to collapse' (not sure he really meant it)

Most of us on that operation have an iconic photograph of the pile of cannabis stacked in front of the bungalow dwarfing it.

From the three locations, one in Essex, two in Scotland and the sacks that washed ashore we had recovered over 11 tons of cannabis. It was the UK's biggest seizure of cannabis up to that time and to this day remains one of the biggest busts ever.

It transpired that the drugs had arrived on Kerrera Island on New Year's Eve 1979 on board The Karob, a salvage tug, that had sailed to Colombia, loaded the drugs, and sailed back. Prentiss' two 40 feet yachts, the Bagheera and the Salombo were used to transfer the cargo nearer the coast and the inflatable found at Laindon was used to bring the haul to dry land. We assume their rationale was that Hogmanay celebrations would be the sole focus of law enforcement. The Karob was later found abandoned in Bermuda and during the search, paperwork indicated the crew had been heavily armed when they made the crossing from Colombia to Scotland.

Peter Whitehead from Pytchley turned out to be an interesting character. He married Dido Goldsmith, the daughter of Teddy Goldsmith and niece of Sir James Goldsmith. Howard Marks was Peter's best man. Bianca Jagger was a bridesmaid. He was born in Liverpool, became a writer and filmmaker who documented counterculture in London and New York in the late 1960s. He also made promotional film clips including a version of "Interstellar Overdrive" for Pink Floyd and several clips for The Rolling Stones. He was not involved in criminality but being in Mark's circle of friends demonstrated the people Mark's liked to mix with.

Alan Grey was brought down from Scotland much to the annoyance of The Crown Office and Procurator Fiscal Service in Inverness, Scotland (who was responsible for the prosecution of crime in that region.) Unknown to The Procurator Fiscal we put Grey on the shuttle to London with George Atkinson. We wanted to have them all in one locality to be interviewed simultaneously by officers who could immediately exchange details of the suspect's responses and any fact needing confirmation.

We had information that Marks was on a weekend break in Suffolk. On Friday 16th May Terry and Nick went to the historic Swan Hotel in Lavenham, Suffolk where Marks and his wife Judy, where staying.

As they walked in, they saw Howard Marks in the bar ordering a sherry. They decided to act.

Terry walked up to Marks.

'Have you got the time?' Terry asked.

As Howard Marks lifted his arm to look at this watch Nick quickly clipped handcuffs around his wrist.

'We are Customs Officers,' said Terry, 'and we are arresting you.'

'Why?' Asked Marks.

'On suspicion of being involved in a drugs offence. Do you understand?'

'Yes.'

'What is your name?'

'I'm not saying,' said Marks.

After fruitless questioning a driver's licence was found in Marks' pocket.

'This licence has John Hayes on it. Is that your name?

'Yes.'

'What do you do for a living, Mr Hayes?'

Without a hint of a smile or smirk Marks replied. 'I'm training to be a Customs Officer.'

The hotel room was searched and a notebook was found listing the details of the drugs at each of the locations. This was the equivalent of a "smoking gun".

He was taken back to New Fetter Lane and interviewed.

(In the film "Mr Nice" Terry and Nick were portrayed by two actors wearing Customs uniforms which was undoubtedly a case of artistic licence, the director being either ignorant or choosing to ignore the (normal) dress code of investigating officers.)

With Marks being arrested we had captured most of the organisation including Stewart Prentiss. They were charged at Snowhill Police Station in Holborn with bringing in controlled drugs to the UK and to appear at a magistrate's court the next day.

I sat in with Nick Baker when a moustached, long-haired, Howard Marks was interviewed where he denied anything to do with drug smuggling. The interview room was one of our small offices in New Fetter Lane which was just big enough for a desk and three chairs. There was no lock on the door or bars on the window but as we were on the third-floor jumping out was not an option. Marks was handcuffed when he went to the toilet.

We wanted to establish what role Marks played in the whole operation. We were forever mindful that what went on in the interview would probably go before a jury at trial. If Marks decided not to answer specific questions the jury might ask why?

All the usual questions were asked. Nick asked most of them and made the notes.

'Where do you live?' we asked.

'Hans Court, London,' Marks replied.

'How can you afford to rent such an expensive property near Harrods?'

'No comment.'

'What do you do for a living?'

'No comment.'

'How do you fund your lifestyle?'

'No comment.'

'What were you doing at the Swan Hotel?'

'Enjoying a night out with my wife.'

'Are you involved in importing drugs into the UK.'

'No comment.'

'You drove Walter Nath to Heathrow Airport.'

'No comment.'

'The best man at your wedding was?'

'No comment.'

'What is your relationship with Goldsack?'

'He's a friend of mine.'

It was always part of our thinking that Marks should be given the opportunity to answer tricky questions at the interview stage rather than at trial. In Court the defence could argue Marks was not given the chance at interview where he could well have given a convincing reply. Nick asked Marks about the meetings with those in charge of the drug stashes but he declined to answer. The same applied to the incriminating notebook found on Marks.

Marks was a charming, intelligent and articulate man but refused to co-operate, revealed nothing and did not respond to our questions other than the ones he knew we already had knowledge of. Someone counted the "no comment" Marks had made during questioning – 65.

As Marks held a number of passports in different names and had a record of going on the run in the early seventies. Nick, at the first court appearance, opposed bail and Marks was remanded initially in custody for 24 hours which could be extended to 36 hours by a Senior Customs Officer. Beyond that, permission would have to be granted from a magistrate.

Marks' wife, Judy, was arrested and questioned but released due to lack of evidence.

Marks was later remanded in Brixton prison until his trial.

The number of passports found in different names and the fact he had absconded previously made it impossible for him to get bail at the Magistrates court' There was evidence against him. In particular a key was found on Marks by Nick Baker on the day he was arrested at Lavenham. It wasn't a conventional domestic door key so it had to be identified. Marks was asked about the key whilst being interviewed but refused to say what it was for. Nick suspected it was for one of the stashes and sent one of the team to Pytchley and tried the key in the lock. To our delight the key opened the lock securing the loft door where the cannabis was found. Another "smoking gun"!

Having identified gaps in our evidence with Nick Baker, I spent the next few days in Scotland with George Atkinson in Oban, gathering new detail, and taking statements. This included following paper and money trails of who rented the properties, how it was paid, local estate agents, suppliers who sold goods to the newcomers, any record that put an individual in a place, at what time and date and what activity were they up to. Local people were only too pleased to help, not wishing to be associated with drug smugglers. Had they been uncooperative they could have been charged with Obstructing a Customs Investigation.

Most of the transactions I found were innocent and of no interest but some did provide links between separate events.

We discovered that Nath and Magazine had returned to the US and out of our grasp.

In Marks' rented flat, in Hans Court, near Harrods, a suitcase containing £30,000 was found under a bed. There was a photograph of an ice sculpture which was purchased for of one of his daughter's birthdays. It cost £1300 which was a lot of money and indicated the sort of lifestyle he lived and the amount of money he had at his fingertips. In the photo was Bianca Jagger!

To transport the three tons of drugs in a large van from Laindon a police escort was arranged to ensure its safe arrival at The Customs House in Central London.

The drugs were again examined to establish by an expert, that it was cannabis and where it probably came from. A sample amount would be kept as evidence and the remainder destroyed as agreed by all parties.

If the defence objected to destruction it could backfire. Heaving 11 tons of cannabis into a courtroom would have a massive visual effect on a jury as to the scale of the operation.

Marks solicitor, Bernard Simons, appointed Lord Hutchinson of Lullington QC as his barrister, a well-known socialist with a reputation of defending spies and society trouble makers. The Russian spies, Blake and Vassels had benefited from his legal distinction and Penquin Books when they were prosecuted for publishing Lady Chatterley's Lover and Fanny Hill. He also defended Christine Keeler, an English model and topless showgirl, who at the height of the Cold War, became sexually involved with a married government minister, John Profumo, as well as a Soviet diplomat.

In a pre-trial meeting with Lord Hutchinson, Marks outlined his defence which centred on his alleged recruitment in 1972 by Hamilton McMillan of MI6 to help them capture James McCann, the IRA arms dealer by bringing him into drug deals. In 1973 this led to McCann being arrested in County Kildare for being armed and handling a consignment of Thai sticks hidden in a cargo of bananas. McCann claimed he was set up by British Intelligence. In March 1980 Justice Gannon directed a Dublin jury to acquit McCann of all charges against him.

McMillan thought that a few overseas outlets of Mark's dress shop "Annabelinda" would be a good "front" for intelligence work.

Marks also stated that MI6 asked him to work with the Mexican Secret Service who sought the capture of McCann as they believed he was aiding a Mexican terrorist group known as "The September 23rd League" in drug dealing and arms acquisition.

'The Mexican Secret Service supplied me with a passport in the name of Anthony Tunnicliff,' explained Marks. 'I tracked down McCann in Vancouver but the authorities were too slow and allowed McCann to flee the country and travel to France.'

'I carried on giving information to the Mexicans,' Marks added. 'The narco terrorists in South America, the drug lords of Colombia and the activities of "the Golden Triangle", Laos, Thailand and Burma.'

Marks said he was responsible to the British and Mexican Governments and his main job was to infiltrate the Colombian hierarchy along with the arrest of McCann.

After giving his version of events Lord Hutchinson said it was the most ridiculous defence he had ever heard.

'Don't you believe it?' asked Marks.

'I'm obliged,' replied Hutchinson,' to represent you in the Court even if I find your defence idiotic.'

Marks also announced that the Head of Mexico's Intelligence was willing to travel to the UK to corroborate his story.

The trial started on the 28th September 1981 at the Number One Court of The Old Bailey. We all felt that this Court was the most impressive Court in the UK housing trials as diverse as Dr Crippen and the Kray Twins, Jeremy Thorpe and the Yorkshire Ripper, Ruth Ellis and Lord Haw-Haw. All have risen to the court usher's instructions of "silence and be upstanding". The judge's stern command - "take him down" seemed to echo as soon as you entered however innocent you were.

The Crown prosecution expected to take six weeks to present the case in front of Judge Mason, known as "Penal Pete". John Rogers QC was the prosecuting Counsel. The case officer, Nick Baker was present through all the Court proceedings.

Nine men were in the dock. Marks was shoulder to shoulder with Martin Langford and Bob Kenningdale (from Pytchley) Stuart Prentiss and his worker Alan Grey (from Scotland), James Goldsack with his worker Nick Cole (from Laindon) and Hedley Morgan (Patrick Lane, the money man's assistant).

Asked by the clerk how they pleaded Goldsack, Cole, Langford and Morgan replied 'guilty'. A good start to the case but Marks was the number one and he and the others pleaded 'not guilty'.

Following the pleas those who pleaded guilty returned to prison to await sentencing.

Prentiss was accused of running the importation and made a written confession. He claimed that the Mafia had threatened to kill his wife and family and his defence was one of duress.

Morgan was responsible for banking £2 million in cash. 'For a tax avoidance scheme,' he suggested. He in fact was working for Patrick Lane and ultimately Marks.

As the trial went on, we produced evidence of meetings observed (including photographs, the cash under his bed and the key to the premises in Pytchley). Mike Stephenson (Stevo) gave evidence that he was in the corridor at the Dorchester Hotel when he saw Marks exiting the room occupied by Nath. The defence lawyer came out with a string of detailed questions, some of which Stevo couldn't answer and others only a passing reference. The lawyer persisted, giving no consideration to Stevo's circumstances, criticising and sometimes ridiculing his account of detail.

Marks then produced a witness, a man called Leaf who ran a pub in Oxford. Leaf testified that Marks was staying with him that night where they watched a rugby match between Wales and Ireland on television so Marks could not have been at the Dorchester Hotel.

A lengthy cross-examination of Stevo's account at the Dorchester Hotel managed to make him look a liar and tied him up in knots.
This going over effectively cancelled out Stevo's observation.

In spite of that we all thought we had presented a very strong case against Marks and the rest. Our evidence was robust enough to put Marks in prison.

At one stage in the outpourings the judge halted proceedings to state that he had got lost in the mist of detail and feared that the jury could not cope. Marks smiled charmingly at the jury and got a few smiles back. Judge Mason was not impressed.

The only outburst of Marks' questioning came when it was alleged, he had agreed that cannabis use could lead addicts to try harder drugs. 'No, I didn't,' he shouted. 'That's a lie.'

During the trial 28 pounds of Columbian and two kilos of black hash was escorted into court. Judge Mason sniffed a cigar-shaped bud and inquired at the lack of smell. 'It wears off,' he was advised.

He caused great if muted amusement when he asked, 'How is it ingested?'

He was swiftly and quietly informed.

The last defence witness was a guy called Jorge Rios who said he was a Mexican Government Law Enforcement Officer. We thought then and since he was an imposter, a handsome actor brought in with prepared lines. He gave his evidence "in camera" when members of the public and press are removed from the Court. He confirmed he knew Marks as Anthony Tunnicliff and that Marks was in Mexico at the time of the crimes working for the Mexican Secret Service. He was so impressive with his account the jury, as it turned out, was swayed. We asked The US Drug Enforcement Administration to check out Jorge Rios and were advised that he was a convicted cocaine smuggler. Unfortunately, this arrived too late to inform the court.

For a reason we did not understand, Lord Hutchison summed up by saying, 'If ever there was a case for the legalisation of cannabis, this is it.'

In the judge's summing up he conceded that Marks had charisma, intelligence and an encyclopaedic grasp of detail and evidence. 'As for his guilt or innocence,' the judge said to the jury, 'you must decide if he was party to this conspiracy or not. Either he knew nothing about it or he was up to his neck.'

We were stunned when the jury came back with their verdict on Marks; "Not Guilty."

I think we all lost a few hours of our lives, going over and over detail, small and large, trying to make sense of what had just happened.

After the trial cleaners went into the jury room and found a piece of paper with a drawing of a heart with an arrow through with Marks' initials, DHM. So, one member of the jury must have been besotted by Marks.

The result of the main trial caused real misery in our team, particularly with Nick and Terry.

After the trial and acquittals Nick and Terry were outside the Court when they were approached by a member of the jury who had heard all about the previous drug dealings of Marks in 1973/1974.

'We made a terrible mistake,' the person said.

Terry just about held himself together, his anger festering just below the surface.

Two weeks after Marks' acquittal a Superintendent of the Thames Valley Police committed suicide by plunging a kitchen knife into his heart. He had confessed to leaking information to the press on Marks' alleged work for MI6 and knew he would face charges under The Official Secrets Act. The period of time Marks had spent on remand the charge of possessing false passports was dropped though he was far from being out of the woods.

Marks had forgotten, or chose to forget, that back in 1973 he had absconded from the charge of drug importation when acting as a pop-band "roadie" so a date was set for that charge to be heard so Marks was refused bail.

The trial for the importation in 1973 was set for the Old Bailey in front of The Recorder, Sir James Miskin. He had been approached in Chambers by Lord Hutchinson in an attempt at plea bargaining although such a manoeuvre was not strictly part of the justice system (an unofficial plea bargain, might enable an accused individual to plead guilty to a lesser crime than the one they are charged with). Miskin advised that the maximum sentence Marks would receive was three years, a duration that Marks saw as acceptable given that the period would be reduced when his remand time was taken into account. He pleaded guilty which resulted in spending only three months in prison. He was released on the 6th May 1982.

For two years he was mostly off our radar living, though we knew through photographs and recordings taken by Thai police that he had spent some time there.

There was no question in our minds that Marks would walk out of prison a reformed man. History told us that the top criminals invariably return to their old ways. The higher up the crime ladder you were, the lower you dropped. This was an anathema to us. Prison, to most hardened criminals, was an occupational hazard, a time to gird loins, to organise the next racket to make money from.

From the year 2000 money and assets gained through illegal activity could be seized by the authorities. This hurt the guilty. It's one thing doing time when a large amount of cash lies in wait for you to collect. It's another thing doing time and have all your assets taken away from you.

Our team never gave up on Marks. We knew that by continuing his drug career Marks would likely surface back in the UK.

We still had in our possession, in our secure office in London, the £30,000 found under Mark's bed in Han's Court. Nick Baker and Customs solicitors went to the Royal Court of Justice in the Strand for a financial hearing as we were determined that the money should be seen a part of the drug trafficking activities. We didn't want Marks to have it back!

To our dismay the High Court decided that the money be returned to Marks. Our solicitors appealed, advising that the case would be taken to the House of Lords. This all came to nothing and the money was eventually returned to Marks on the understanding that outstanding debts with the Inland Revenue was settled.

For us it was a defeat. For Marks yet another victory over the system.

In March 1985 we had a visit from Major Surachet from the Metropolitan Narcotics Unit of the Thai Police in Bangkok.

I spent a lot of time with him building up a rapport. I took him to the various Customs Offices and to Scotland Yard, did the sights and museums.

My idea was that we could establish a direct and reliable contact in Bangkok. This proved to be the case as over the next few months I was able to consult with Surachet and his colleagues on a number of matters, including sightings of Marks and others on our suspect list. I was also put in touch with Surachet's boss, General Bam Roon who was in charge of the country's Narcotics Unit. Our telephone conversations were not regular and failed to provide information we could use. It was, however, friendly, which in my mind could lead to something substantial. The following successful co-operation was not the sort I was hoping for.

I had a phone call from the General.

'I'm looking for a favour,' he said. 'My daughter is going to a private school in Bangkok and needs some material for her school uniform. Can you help?'

'Of course.'

'I need a bolt of Oxford Blue cloth to be sent over.'

'Of course.'

Obviously, doing a relatively small favour leads to additional friendship and trust so I was more than happy to track a bolt of Oxford Blue cloth down for him which I found in a tailors in London.

A colleague at Heathrow Airport put the package on a Thai Airways flight.

All this cooperation with the Thai authorities eventually led to them advising us on a number of people operating in Bangkok. One was Philip Sparrowhawk, from the Epsom area who was a known drug trafficker. Also, Lord Antony Moynihan, a 3rd Baron who had gone off the rails unlike his brother, Colin Moynihan, 4th Baron Moynihan, a Labour Government Sports Minister. All of whom were close associates of Marks who was spending a lot of time in Thailand. We had no doubt he was back to what he knew best ...smuggling cannabis!

Late 85, early 86 Marks was living in Karachi when an American drugs agent, Harland Bow, was there. Somehow, they got into conversation and Marks casually asked him if there were any UK Customs people in the city.

'Mike Stephenson,' said Bow.

Marks was taken aback. 'Stephenson! From London!'

'Yes, he's the drug liaison officer at the British High Commission. Do you know him?'

Marks lied. 'No. I don't.'

Marks didn't know Stephenson but his wife Judy did. Geraldine Stephenson and Judy would meet up at the school their children attended.

Normally this would have spooked Marks but his privileged position in Karachi society made him practicably bomb-proof. There were so many cronies, straight and crooked, in the company he kept, it made sure he was not going to be investigated by Government Officials, the security forces and the like.

In 1985 Marks travelled to Thailand to meet Sparrowhawk and Moynihan. Intelligence teams at Heathrow had identified a booking for him from Karachi and through my contacts I was able get Marks tracked by Thai police.

Information was sent to us in London and to the DEA in the US. A DEA agent in Miami took particular interest. Craig Lavato was heavily involved in keeping track of Marks activities, naming him "The Marco Polo of drug trafficking".

Evidence of drug importation in the US had been gathered going back to the 70s of the comings and goings of pop groups and the roadies that transported them.

We were able to confirm that my colleague Peter Nelson, who took on the UK's interest in Marks was able to pass the details through to Lavato.

Lavato took ten years to build up his case against Marks, even writing a book about it, "Chasing Marco Polo".

Lavoto visited Portugal in 1988 where I was a liaison officer. I met him socially and facilitated his enquiries with the Federal Police. They identified premises in Lisbon which had the equipment to switch and disguise the origin of telephone calls.

By that time Marks was living in Palma, Majorca where the Spanish police picked him up following an extradition request by the US. He was eventually transported to mainland Spain along with his wife who was also under arrest for aiding and abetting including taking and re-directing phone calls.

The affair was taken up by broadsheets in the UK and America. The Attorney's Office in Florida announced, "The biggest drugs bust in history". The Daily Express in the UK suggested that Marks ran a 2-million-pound cannabis empire. The Daily Mirror wrote of Marks being "the most sophisticated drugs baron of all time, with a ruthless organisation matching anything operated by the Mafia or Columbian drug lords".

Early one morning three US Federal Marshalls arrived at Marks' prison door and whisked him away to Madrid Airport. At gunpoint Marks was taken aboard an empty Pan Am 747 with the Marshalls seated in front and behind him. As the aircraft was considered to be American territory, he was read his rights. His wife was transported separately.

Marks wasn't granted bail by the Miami Court and news reached him that some of his own people were willing to give evidence against him. This corner was tighter than any Marks had been in.

Judy pleaded guilty to her small part in the racket and was released, having already served some months in prison in Spain. She was deported and advised she would never be allowed to return to America.

On July 13th 1990 Marks pleaded guilty to two counts of racketeering and conspiracy to racketeer. He was sentenced to 10 years for the first one, five for the second and another two counts of 10 years and five years. The judge mistakenly said the counts would run concurrently meaning Marks would be imprisoned for 15 years not 25.

Marks may have been pleased with the outcome but the judge returned, admitted his mistake, and announced the sentences to be consecutive. Marks went down for 25 years.

In January 1995, Marks was granted parole after a prison officer testified that he was a model prisoner who spent much of his time helping his fellow prisoners pass their General Educational Development exams.

He was released in April 1995 after serving 6 years.

After leaving prison Marks came back to the UK and took up speaking in halls and clubs throughout the UK including a "tour" with the "reformed" gangster, Dave Courtney who he worked for at the beginning of his lawbreaking career. The two of them are featured on a "You Tube" video.

In 2011 Nick Baker went to see his performance in Saffron Walden and at the interval chatted with Marks. There was no animosity between them. In the second part of the evening Marks announced that Nick, a prosecuting officer, was in the audience. Some of the audience booed. Marks silenced them. 'No, no,' he said. 'I was treated properly. The legal system worked its bizarre magic and acquitted me.'

Marks may not have been a vicious man, calling himself a "gentleman smuggler" but he chose to ignore the brutal nature of the people he worked with as he did with the damage done to many of the victims of his trade.

'I'm a fanatic advocate of the legalisation of cannabis,' Marks once testified. 'I feel it is essentially harmless and because of the illegality of it, we have a situation whereby extreme terrorists can fund themselves from it.'

CHAPTER 14
PAULINE

In 1982 my life changed dramatically when I met my future wife, Pauline.

When I first joined the Customs Investigation Division, I was living with other colleagues in a house owned by John Green another investigator. The property was on the Forestdale Estate in Addington, south of Croydon.

Like many of colleagues the job was my top priority and the hours we worked resulted in a chaotic social life. Long term relationships were hard to cultivate and the divorce statistics within the ID, as with the police and military were sky high. I was in the typical bachelor rut of work, pub, takeaway, few hours sleep and work. It was probably the reason why most of us were happy to work away when we could stay at a hotel. Our beds were made, meals were provided and even laundry done if required.

Staying with colleagues did have its funny moments. John was an enthusiastic jogger and ran for 45 minutes every day before breakfast. He would come home and boil two eggs for four minutes thirty seconds. Myself and John Chapman, another lodger couldn't understand this precise approach and after a night in the pub we returned home and took all of John's eggs out of the fridge and hard boiled them. We replaced them in the fridge and at breakfast the next day watched in fascination as John boiled his eggs for the same time. Of course, they were rock hard and for the next few days John complained about the timer, the cooker and the quality of the eggs. Eventually we had to admit what we had done and, for a few minutes, he was not amused.

One Saturday night I went with John to a nightclub in Croydon called Sinatra's. I was on call that weekend so I was restricted to how much I could drink. The nightclub was running a promotion- pay £10 entry fee and drink as much as you want. Sounded fantastic but I could get a call anytime to go to work. I had to leave the club every 30 minutes and radio the Investigation Division control room to see if there were any messages for me.

As the night went on John was in deep conversation with a female. I stood at the bar but noticed a girl dancing with her friend. I was immediately attracted to her and thought she looked stunning. I wasn't a shrinking violet but it took me a while to pluck up the courage to ask her to dance. The fact it was one of the last dances which invariably were slow the possibility of rejection was high. I was philosophical but was chuffed when she accepted. We chatted as we danced and as we left the nightclub. I walked Pauline and her friend, who had her leg in plaster, to her car, a minivan. My Rover SDI was parked nearby but I didn't want Pauline to think I was flash. We exchanged work telephone numbers and a few days later I rang her at Adhesive Paper Products.

Using a cross between Kenneth Williams and Arthur Mullard accent I said 'Hello is that APP?''

'It is,' replied Pauline. 'How can I help you?'

'I would like to order 500 metres of fly paper'.

'Sorry?' said Pauline. 'What do you mean?'

'You know the sticky paper you hang up to catch flies.'

Just as she was about to hang up, I said, 'It's me, Jim, the guy you danced with last Saturday'.

Pauline agreed to go for a meal at the Grasshopper Pub in Westerham, Kent. We got on like a house on fire and we arranged to see each other again. I was always conscious that the demands of my work could destroy a relationship but I did have high hopes it would not snuff out this one.

Pauline was honest with me from day one. She was divorced with a seven-year-old son, Robert.

I didn't give it much thought to her situation but I was determined to develop our relationship. Things were not helped when I transferred to Birmingham. I bought a house in Kings Heath but although it was a four bedroomed detached house, I couldn't persuade Pauline to move to Birmingham.

I took Pauline for her first curry in a restaurant in Stoney Lane, Handsworth. I knew the restaurant well. It was basic and you had to eat your curry in a "balti", a dish with chapatis using your hands. I did tell Pauline not to go to the toilets as they were very basic. That said it was a fantastic and popular restaurant. After a year in Birmingham, I returned to London on promotion.

Our relationship had developed and we decided I should move into Pauline's flat in Tadworth, Surrey. Luckily, the hours at Kennington VAT office for the nine months before I returned to the ID allowed me to have a normal home life. We bought a property together in Addington and Robert joined us and went to the local school.

On 21 September 1985 we married at Sanderstead United Reform Church. The wedding was attended not only by friends and family but also colleagues from work. Pauline has had to put up with a lot, particularly when work took me away to other parts of the UK and abroad.

On one occasion, when Pauline was six months pregnant when we decided to have a bedroom plastered. I arranged a cut price deal with a local plasterer on the proviso I would be his labourer. On the day he was due to complete the work I had to go to Thailand. Pauline ended up mixing his plaster and helping him out. He gave Pauline a box of chocolates for her efforts.

I have been incredibly lucky to have met Pauline and she is a great Mum to my three boys, Alex, Alistair and Jimmy as well as my step-son Robert. She kept our home together when I was "gallivanting" all over the world. She is and will always be my soulmate.

CHAPTER 15
ALAN

I first met Alan Griffiths in 1978 when I first joined the Customs Investigation Division. We hit it off immediately. We had the same sense of humour and we were both new to Investigation. Alan moved to the Bravos and Charlies at the end of 1977 to become Bravo 7. I joined him and the team in January 1978. Alan Griffiths - "Griff" as we knew him had a sharp sense of humour and he was a typical "Scouser". In our office in New Fetter Lane a potted plant had an infestation of fruit flies. Ray Smith (Charlie 7) sprayed the plant and Nick Baker (Charlie 2) started to complain. Alan wittingly replied, 'It's ok, Nick, it doesn't kill crawlers.'

Nick was close to the team Senior Officer Terry Byrne and we always joked Nick could do no wrong.

As we were the junior officers on the team we invariably were called out at a moment's notice. These early jaunts created a "bon homie" that never left us.

I met Alan's family, his wife, Sheila, and his young children Ian and Helen. I saw them often as I picked him up from his home when we were deployed on surveillance.

In 1982 I had spent six years working on drugs and I was due a transfer to one of the fraud teams. I was desperate to continue working on drugs and applied to join a newly created team in Birmingham. Alan decided to transfer as well, as did Chris Hardwick.

Working in Birmingham allowed more social contact with colleagues and we often met up in the evening for meals and drinks at pubs. The Birmingham office was in a building above the Night Out night club and one year we had our Christmas meal with entertainment which turned out to be the Grumbleweeds, a comedy group who regularly appeared on the TV and radio in the eighties.

For over ten years Alan and I worked together, laughed together and the relationship grew. What was important to me was that we trusted each other as brothers.

In 1983 I was promoted and transferred from Birmingham to our VAT office in Kennington in South London. This procedure, from Officer to Higher Officer, meant that I had to leave the Investigation Division, the outfield, and go back under the Customs and Excise division. A similar "promotion" happens in the police force when "plain clothes" offices have to don the force blue to gain spurs to climb the career ladder.

The date was 6th February 1884. At 3am the telephone rang. It took me only a few seconds to fling off the bed clothes, sit up and reach for the phone. It stopped ringing. When the phone rang in the early hours it was always a horrible feeling. One second you are in dreamland with a loose mind with no boundaries, the next, disciplined and focused.

Decades before mobile phones or pagers, the house phone was the only instant link with the outside world and the ring tone at two, three or four in the morning was always loud and harsh, foretelling bad or urgent news.

Mechanically I got back into bed, my mind racing with the premonition that something was wrong. The phone never rang that early when I was with Investigation, so this was a new episode for me and one that left me restless and troubled. Few people had my number and there was no way of knowing if the call was from home or from a colleague.

I was far from falling asleep when the phone rang again. It was my associate, Nick Baker, who told me that Alan Griffiths, had been killed in a car crash. Alan was on his way up to Felixstowe when it happened.

I immediately got up and robot like got dressed and made ready for the drive. I left home at 3.20am.

I had been with him at 6pm the evening before in the Smithfield Pub in High Holborn under the Viaduct near the Smithfield market. As he knew he was about to drive ninety odd miles he didn't drink alcohol. We talked a bit about work, about moving to London and how I was going to re-join the Investigation Division within a couple of weeks. Alan chatted about Felixstowe where, on the Delta Division, he spent a lot of time working with uniformed staff stationed at the port. There he advised and encouraged them to look out for drugs and what to focus on. And, most importantly, don't charge in if a suspicious cargo if found. They were told not to touch or move anything but to contain the situation until Alan or a Delta colleague arrived.

Alan worked for Deltas, the cannabis referred team, and he was going to inspect a "cargo" that had arrived at Felixstowe Port. Road works on the A12 had reduced multi-lanes into one and the inexpertly erected sign-posts were unclear. In bad light and distracted, Alan hit a lorry head on and was killed immediately.

I had recently been told that within weeks I would be returned to Investigation and be part of a "Heroin Referred" team which was "Drugs L for Lima".

At 6.30 in the morning, I had parked my car and was on my way to our office in Atlantic House, Holborn when I bumped into one of my Deputy Chiefs, Mike Newsom.

'We're really looking forward to you coming back and working on "Drugs L",' he said through a broad smile.

The smile lasted only seconds as he noticed the mournful look on my face had failed to soften.

'Alan Griffiths . . ,' I said, faltering.

'I heard,' he said. 'Terrible news'.

We nodded our goodbyes and I made my way into our office. Close colleagues were there; Nick Baker and Cedric Andrew, Alan's Senior Officer.

Inside there were few words and no smiles. The atmosphere was awful with some showing signs of being emotionally upset.

The whole team's thoughts were with Alan's wife and their two young children.

Cedric Andrew, had the dreadful task of informing Sheila of Alan's death.

Sheila was distraught. Their marriage was sound, happy and close. Both from Liverpool, both with a wonderful scouse sense of humour. They truly were a marvellous couple, with two lovely children.

At the time I hadn't thought through the professional consequences of Alan's death but others had and a decision was made that I should carry on Alan's work on the Deltas operation so my transfer to "Limas" was cancelled and I was posted to become "Delta 4".

I was partly based in the Kennington VAT Office so I found myself going back and forth to my home in Birmingham. Whilst there I visited Sheila, her family and some of their friends.

On the day of Alan's funeral at the Solihull Crematorium I travelled in the vehicle behind Sheila and her family. At a steady speed along the half a mile approach to the Crematorium we slowed to walking pace as, to our left and to our right, dozens of investigators and ex colleagues of Alan stood straight and true in silent tribute to their dead comrade and friend. At moments like this the mostly unspoken but indisputable loyalty between team members is there for all to see. It was very moving.

I did the eulogy at the Service. I found it difficult to talk about a close friend. When you work with someone, laugh with someone, when you share remarkable triumphs and bitter disappointments, you never think that one dreadful day you would be called upon to "sum" up his short life. I did get through it. I did my best but there was no getting away from the injustice and cruelty of such an event.

At the time Sheila was inconsolable believing that she too had died that day. Alan's death had created a gap that would never be filled. Of course, it was, but only slowly. With the ever-loving support of family and friends she began to cope, stability and hope gradually returning.

Some years later she met Don who she later married. I didn't contact Sheila as much as I would have liked as she was forming a new relationship and, in a way, a new life. My voice would only bring back painful memories, unnecessary I thought. We sent Christmas cards but only met up at Mike Ratcliffe's house.

On the 25th anniversary of Alan's death, Sheila and her grown-up children met up with Alan's ex-colleagues, including me, so that his memory would be celebrated. We recalled Alan's humour, his jokes as well as his humanity.

The accident in which Alan died caused extensive damage to his head and body, details, I think, were kept from Sheila.

Inside his jacket pocket was a wallet with a blood-stained pound note. Although most of Alan's belongings were handed over to Sheila, Mike Radcliffe (the liaison officer) had kept hold of the pound note unable to decide what to do with it. Eventually, as Alan's closest friend, Mike gave the note to me.

This note I placed in my wallet with my I.D. and Investigation Badge. I carried this throughout my 25 years in Operations.

We all met up in a pub in London, just below Harmsworth House just off Fleet Street. Ian, his son, was the spitting image of his father. So much so that when he walked into the pub I went back on my heels. It took a few intakes of breath for me to be certain it wasn't Alan approaching.

Over the next hour or so we chatted about many things (Ian was two years old when I last saw him).

When the time was right, I took out the pound note. 'Look,' I said, 'this was on your dad's body when he died. It does have some blood on it. I think you should have it.'

As he took hold of the note, we both became very emotional. Although Ian couldn't remember his father, he was well aware how important he was to his and his mother's life.

'I've carried that around for the last twenty-five years,' I said. 'I'm hoping you will carry it for the next twenty-five years.'

He did not have to answer. His love for a relatively unknown father was evident.

CHAPTER 16
OPERATION; DEVOTION
"The Bankers of Cosa Nostra".

For UK Customs in the nineteen seventies the Mafia rarely came on the radar. We had all seen the Godfather films, all read the stories of Alphonse Gabriel Capone, nicknamed "Scarface", a Chicago based gangster operating in the USA's prohibition era of the 1930s and 1940s.

But when we started our working day, the drug villains we cogitated on were usually home grown, usually city born, city based, plying their trade in relatively small unconnected units, carving a lucrative income from well-defined areas of activities.

The modern-day Mafia were a secret organisation, that we knew. They were close knit with tentacles stretching across generations and continents. For law enforcement in the UK and abroad the well-structured gangs were difficult to penetrate, similar in many ways, to the Chinese Triads.

In those early days the term "Mafia" applied to the "Sicilian Mafia" that began in the 19th century. There were others with a similar history; the "Russian Mafia" formed in the 1720's who stole from government entities and divided profits among the people and survived Vladimir Lenin's attempt to wipe them out. Close ties with "East European Mafia" were established during the Soviet era.

The "Japanese" Mafia, the Yakuza, emerged in the mid-Edo period (1603–1868).

Accounts did reach us through our colleagues in the US and Italy of the widespread bonding of Italian mafia members and their code of silence. This had severely hampered the Italian Police in making any inroads into rupturing the organisation's protective shield, often reinforced by corruption in high offices.

The UK had a sizeable Italian population in the decade after World War 2 made up of refugees and ex-prisoners of war, many of whom had found work or married locals. London had the most, 50,000 or so followed by 25,000 in Manchester and another 20,000 in Bedford, mainly as a result of labour recruitment in the 1950s by the London Brick Company in the southern Italian regions of Puglia and Campania. Most were law-abiding citizens.

In December 1984, news reached us from Customs officers that a suspect consignment had arrived at Felixstowe Port.

We had freight targeting teams based at all our ports and airports twenty-four hours a day, seven days a week, comprising of experienced uniformed officers, well acquainted with the workings of a port or airport and the paperwork required to import goods into the UK.

They not only studied the travel movements, current and historical, of passengers and crew, they scrutinised the paperwork that accompanied cargo and carried out background checks on new or potentially suspect companies. An unregistered, first-time importer from certain parts of the world would notch up curiosity levels.

On this occasion a shipment of wooden carved dishes and bowls arrived from Bombay with documentation that stated the goods originated in Kashmir in the north of India. It was addressed to a company, Elongate Ltd, in Mitcham in Surrey. Elongate appeared to have been recently set-up with no history of importation and no history of artefact distribution, retail or wholesale.

Following the identification by the Customs Intelligence team the uniform staff conducted the first examination of the consignment to see if it contained drugs.

Once they had decided that it did, they were obliged to notify the Delta Investigation Team.

Peter Finch, who had joined the department the same day as me, drove to Felixstowe to assess if an operation could be progressed. It was, so a plan to remove the drugs, install a substitute material, delve into the background of the importer and names behind it and organise a controlled delivery. The operation was given the name "DRESSER".

We knew we had a few days to manage the task and set out a time frame. This would give us the degree of "control" we needed.

The team was made up of Senior Officer, Cedric Andrew, Peter, Adrian Owen, Mike Gough-Cooper, John Philips, Eddie Jones, Dave Piper, Andy Miller and myself.

Although we had only a limited number of tools; jemmies, hammers, screwdrivers, pliers, chisels, pinchers and the like, we were sufficiently skilled to open the crates without causing damage and reconstruct with no sign of intrusion.

Hidden among the artefacts were slabs of cannabis resin weighing about 250 kilos in total. These were removed and replaced by wrapped plywood material, similar in size and weight to the drugs. Most of the wooden artefacts were then put back into the container.

From a legal point we had to leave a sample of the drugs in the consignment because there might be a legal get out when the delivery contained only wooden items. The importers could later argue that they merely imported wooden carvings and nothing else.

It was common practise to leave incriminating evidence inside controlled deliveries.

Dave Piper, saw an opportunity to acquire some of the wooden bowls and dishes as souvenirs of the operation (all of which would have been destroyed at the end of any Court case). He put a few selected items in a black plastic sack. While he was out of the room, we swopped the sack for one containing rubbish. Returning to our office some hours later we had difficulty controlling our laughter as Dave sat with the bag on his knee singing the Aussie folk song 'Once a Jolly Swagman' made famous by Rolf Harris. He went ballistic when he eventually opened the sack.

Peter approached the landlord of the warehouse which enabled us to enter the premises when it was not occupied. The Investigation Division photographer, Dick Palmer, was able to install a camera, light activation and audio equipment that would allow us to listen in for a few hours to any activity once it had been delivered. The camera, hopefully, would allow us to see who was inside the building and what was going on.

On 18th December 1984 a controlled delivery took place and the consignment delivered to the suspect company address, Elongate Ltd., Unit 5, Batsworth Road, Mitcham, Surrey. This Unit was on a small non-descript industrial estate which made surveillance Difficult. We dressed as workers in jeans and work jackets and tried to look as busy as possible.

We knew that the light sensitive and audio equipment were basic. The camera equipment covered only part of the warehouse. As a backstop officers listened at one of the fire doors at the rear of the premises.

Although there was some movement inside, we could hear nothing that suggested they were opening the shipment. There was shuffling and some banging but the light sensitive device remained inactive indicating the consignment had not been breached. In those days we were all old school, not yet completely trusting recently invented electronic devices. If we could see something with our eyes, hear something with our ears we were happy. Eyes and ears were devices we could rely on.

There was an option to observe the warehouse day and night but this would have been resource intensive. Some "stake outs" can take days or weeks.

Peter discussed the situation with us and the options available – keep up the observation or call a "Knock".

The police action call is "Strike, Strike, Strike". Customs have always used the term "Knock, Knock, Knock." A television series called the 'The Knock' ran from 1994 until 2000 and centred on a customs Investigation unit in south London, London City and South. Each Customs region throughout the UK, from Aberdeen to Plymouth had Investigation Units. They investigated more minor cases and those not adopted by the Investigation Division. We were all amused at the time when the Unit featured in the programme took on high level international investigations but I suppose it made interesting viewing.

Eight of us stood by for the "Knock", mostly near the main entrance and two at the back door to prevent any runners. Although we wanted to create a swift and dramatic entrance, we didn't have to smash the door in. For whatever reason the door was opened and two of the suspects were attempting to leave. We simply rushed through the open door apprehending the two males as we did.

Excitement and fear coupled with sharp focus and physical daring contributed to the adrenalin rush that followed the call to "Knock". We had to impose ourselves on the situation and take control and we had to do it instantly. At that moment we had no idea if the people carried weapons. They could be dangerous psychopaths armed to the teeth, prepared to pull triggers or throw knives. This danger, this risk, I have to admit, was almost relished, bringing into play a heightened body and mental readiness that was never replicated in day-to-day living.

To generate a degree of fear we would grab hold of the nearest "villain" bellowing instructions while making sure they knew who we were. Because we had to react instantly to what was in front of us the complete trust in each other enabled everyone to have the choice to act as they saw fit. We never failed to "click" as a team.

'Customs and Excise Investigation Division' was shouted followed by 'You're under arrest.'

The caution we used then was, 'You are not obliged to say anything unless you wish to do so. Anything you say may be taken down and used in evidence.'

Events unfolded very quickly and the two suspects were caught off guard. They were speechless either by design or because our actions were so swift. They said nothing.

We then secured the building and contents realising there was no intention to open the consignment but to "re-address" for onward shipment to Canada.

At that stage we did not know who was who, who may be behind the importation and who had devised the scam.

We closed the door and kept a low profile. It was quite possible that another member of the "gang" would show up. Had they done so they would have been arrested long before they entered the warehouse.

With this sort of operation, it was likely there were people involved who we had no record of. We called them "clean skins". Not innocent people but those villains as yet undetected.

Inside were two Italian men, Alberto Gualtieri and Francesco Siracusa. Both were late thirties, slightly built with a Mediterranean appearance. They were told they were under arrest on suspicion of being involved in importing drugs into the UK.

Using a stencil and black paint they had been covering over Indian lettering replaced with ones that suggested the shipment originated in this country. It read "MADE IN THE UK".

In our search of the building we found, under a piece of carpet at the entrance, a dead blackbird. We all thought it strange at the time but it was only later Peter was told it was left as a warning by senior Mafia bosses of what would happen if they were double crossed or betrayed. A bit similar to the dead fish being left to indicate someone is with the fishes, at the bottom of a lake or river. A fate to be avoided!

It became apparent from paperwork we found in the office that the consignment was destined for a Canadian company called Santa Rica, in Montreal.

With the "MADE IN THE UK" markings it would then seem that the shipment came from a "non-drug source country". This could have meant that the Canadian Authorities would not have looked at in the depth as it would from some other countries. Some countries were seen as "drug source or transit countries" and any imports would have been looked at closely. Drugs imported from "non-source" countries, such as the UK would not be deemed suspicious and as such could sometimes slip under the radar.

Alberto Gualtieri and Francesco Siracusa were arrested. Siracusa was a Director of Elongate and Gualtieri was an employee. Both appeared to be temporary residents of the UK, Montreal being their permanent home.

During the search of a bedroom in Francesco Siracusa's home a brochure for Thai furniture was found along with a number of references to Canada in copies of invoices and in address books.

At that stage other Investigation Officers were called to assist with the search of home addresses whilst the Deltas conducted interviews. The warehouse had been secured, photographs taken and the crates made ready to be transported to the Custom House.

The Company, Elongate, was now a suspect importer and intelligence officers were able to look for previous importations, particularly those from Kashmir.

The paperwork that accompanied each and every importation into the UK had to list Company details, the contents and value of the cargo. Usual practice of importers was to use one of the many shipping agents, whose job was to facilitate the smooth transfer from ship to onshore transportation.

By extensive searching we were able to identify another company possibly linked with Elongate, ITAL Provisions in Clapham. This company imported Italian foods to their warehouse in Ellerslie Square, South-West London.

Shipping logs revealed that the exporting company, Shalimar Enterprises in Kashmir, was responsible for previous shipments into the UK, with ITAL as the delivery address.

It was then discovered that soon after, ITAL had exported two consignments of furniture to Montreal describing it as originating in London.

Peter Finch contacted the Royal Canadian Mounted Police and the Canadian High Commission in London. He was told that Alberto Gualtieri and Francesco Siracusa were known by the Canadian authorities and were linked to, if not part of, the Mafia. It was thought they could be the "London" end of the Mafia organisation with a "head office" in Canada. A decision was made that no action would take place in Canada. The suspects there would not be approached, merely observed.

(We learned that anti-Mafia prosecutors in Italy had uncovered the new face of the Mafia in Toronto, alleging there were seven dominant mob families in the city, each with a boss who sits on an influential board of control.)

OPERATION; DEVOTION.

In May 1985 a shipment of ornately carved tables and furniture arrived in Felixstowe originating in Chang Mai, Bangkok and addressed to ITAL Provisions a company identified during the cannabis operation 'Dresser'. Uniformed Customs officers made an initial examination and suspicions were raised. The container was loaded onto a Customs trailer and taken to the Custom House in Lower Thames Street London for further examination.

Initially the test didn't indicate any drugs inside the tables but we were all convinced the consignment was suspect. The Government chemist was called in to use the latest x-ray equipment which clearly showed packages inserted in the table tops. A small drill hole in the underside revealed white powder. We worked out a way to remove the tops without causing obvious damage and mindful of the need to re-construct. In all we removed 36 kilos of top-grade heroin with 90% purity levels worth around half-a-million pounds.

We were really buzzing as this amount of heroin was massive and certainly in the top ten of recent law enforcement seizures. The quantity and purity would give the importers the leeway to swell up the volume by adding non-toxic powder. On the street heroin content can be as low as single figures, the balance added to bulk up the weight when distributed to users on the street. 30 kilos can be as much as 200 kilos when bulked up.

Nothing was found in the legs of the table.

As this shipment was destined for Canada, Peter contacted the RCMP in the High Commission in London which led to two officers from Montreal arriving on the first possible flight. On arrival they examined the haul in the Custom House.

We did leave one of the tables intact as the Canadians pleaded that one of the tables arrived on their shores untouched (leaving 26kilos of heroin inside) so they would have the opportunity of arresting the recipients in Canada. And with an untouched table placed to the fore in the container they would not suspect any tampering by the authorities.

For the rest, wooden blocks covered in tape were used to substitute the drugs.

The tops were re-fixed so expertly that you couldn't tell they had been removed. This was undertaken by officers from the Deltas and uniformed staff from Felixstowe.

Peter and I approached Jim Galloway, our Assistant Chief Investigation Officer, and convinced him that we had examined the table-tops and had removed all the heroin.

He looked at me in quite a quizzical way and repeated the question; 'Are you sure you've taken all the heroin out?'

'I'm convinced,' I replied. We examined all the shipment and removed all traces of the drug.'

I am not sure if he suspected at the time, we had been a "bit economical with the truth" but he certainly was aware after the UK and Canadian operations had been successfully concluded. I am sure we would have been hauled across the coals if things hadn't turned out so well. That said, throughout my career I had nothing but praise from my senior managers who gave us enough leeway to progress our investigations.

The Royal Canadian Mounted Police deployed some of their own sophisticated tracking devices into the consignment. This was programmed to be activated when it reached dry land in Canada and not start working on the high seas and using up battery life.

The RCMP office in the Canadian High Commission London advised Peter of the consignment's arrival at a warehouse in Montreal on 19 June 1985. We had a co-ordinated "Knock" with the Canadians to ensure either end could not alert the other.

Their report said they could hear the table tops being sawn up. This was followed by bangs and thuds as the smugglers loaded the slabs of the heroin into the boot of a car. The car was followed by the RCMP to premises in Montreal where arrests were made.

Parked outside was a Rolls Royce car which was identified and connected to a number of people in Canada, the main gang members being Gerlando Caruana, 56 with his brothers, Alfonso 54 and Pasquale 51.

In the 1980s both Alphonso and Pasquale lived in a luxurious villa in Lugano and had visited their UK arm in the Woking area,

(The Cuntrera-Caruana Mafia mob was a Mafia clan of Cosa Nostra. Leonardo Caruana's son, Gerlando Caruana, was considered to be the head of the family in Sicily (according to the Italian authorities).

With intelligence gathered from observations and surveillance, the Mafia clan were identified by our RCMP. The people paying for the shipment and those operating at the delivery address were identified and checked out on law enforcement data bases. As the intelligence was collated, links with the mafia were established.

When the heroin was stashed in the car, those at the scene were arrested and later charged by the authorities.

As the Canadians were about to go "live" we limited our activities to covert observation of suspect addresses, logging comings and goings of occupants and visitors.

The Deltas called the operation, "Operation Devotion" (as it started with a 'D' for Delta. And something to do with the devotion to the job, the hours worked. Well not exactly!)

One of my colleagues who had just arrived on the Deltas from Tilbury where he was a uniformed search officer, Ken Head, liked the odd bet on the horses. Just prior to the operation, he told us as a member of a horse owning syndicate, he had been invited to a stable and had a red-hot tip on a horse called "Morning Devotion." One, he suggested, was worth putting a few quid on having received a red-hot tip. We put a fiver each and true to form (ours and the horse's) we all lost a fiver!

Ken had recently arrived on the team. He was a likeable cocky, Essex lad in his twenties, six-foot-tall, skinny and wearing horn- rimmed spectacles. He, like the rest of us, wore casual clothes.

He announced his arrival over coffee one morning. 'Hello, I'm Ken Head.'

Dave Piper said, 'Not any longer, Dick.'

From then on Ken was known as "Dick" Head.

We attempted to identify the people behind ITAL Director Filippo Monteleone who had been staying at a wine bar in London which was owned by Francesco di Carlo who was known as part of the Mafia. Di Carlo was known as "Frankie the Strangler".

We suspected Monteleone of being involved in heroin trafficking and kept him under surveillance. We learned later di Carlo was wanted in Italy for various murders. He and Monteleone were arrested along with Antonio Luciano, who was the front man for ITAL Provisions, and Siracusa.

I interviewed Luciano in West London whose line, up to then, was that they were merely importing vegetables and provisions from Italy. He was a short, good-looking man in his thirties with a swarthy complexion and a full head of wavy black hair.

No recording equipment was available so I had to take notes. My approach was always to attempt a non-intimidating atmosphere, to create, if possible, some sort of repartee.

'I'm Jim Jarvie. I'm investigating the importation of an amount of heroin into the UK for onward shipment to Canada.'

I then asked simple questions that were easy to answer.

'What is your full name?'

'What is you date of birth?'

In a voice that was easily recognised as Italian, Luciano admitted he was a director of the company, ITAL Provisions.

'What was your role at ITAL,' I asked.

'I import food for the Italian market in the UK.'

I then asked for details of suppliers and customers of the business.

He did reply but would not or could not give names.

I had reached a point that I had reached in dozens of interviews where you know that all the real and penetrating questions were not going to be answered.

'Were you aware that drugs were being imported?' I asked.

'No comment.'

On arrest he had been told that he was not obliged to say anything so he chose not to oblige.

The notes I took down would later be discussed with Peter Finch and within days the hand-written notes would be typed up. A final comparison with my original notes would see it through as a final typed version.

With four colleagues we searched his office taking away any documents hoping that some would prove useful. These papers were placed in named "exhibit" bags to be logged as part of the case we were building. All exhibits were carefully labelled and recorded as part of an evidence chain.

Adrian Owen led the team tasked with arresting Di Carlo and search his home premises in Woking. At that time, they had no safety concerns as the links to Mafia crime including murders had had not been established.

During the interviews it was established that Di Carlo had links to the wine bar run by Filippo Monteleone. Although the evidence linking Di Carlo to drugs was thin, he would normally have been released on bail but was prevented when Peter Finch received a phone call from Snow Hill Police telling him that Di Carlo was wanted in Italy for murders he had committed. So, this gave us a lot more time to dig around the connections in Kashmir and Thailand. Peter and the team required more time to sift through the evidence. Bags of potential evidence were uplifted from the various addresses, all of which had to be carefully sorted and researched further. All this can take days or weeks, particularly if overseas links were found.

As well as the Canadians, the Italians (particularly those investigating the Mafia in Palermo and other parts of Italy), were all very interested. It was thought Di Carlo was a high-ranking member of the Mafia. He was sent to London in 1976 to control the Mafia finances in the UK. He purchased the house in Woking and a hotel that was used for meetings. He also ran a travel agency through which he made travel arrangements for couriers and accomplices. Also, a Bureau de Change which was used, we thought, to launder money. This was still a time when money laundering legislation was limited. Although in the 70s there was restrictions on money movements this was lifted and large amounts of money could be moved abroad for genuine but also illegal activities. If we came across large amounts of cash, we had no authority to seize it and, in certain cases, we would want the money to move on, to re-enter the planned smuggling operation. With money, things start to develop and with any luck we could follow its movements and spot the activities of those who received it.

The head of the Palermo Flying Squad visited us along with two police officers. His name was Doctor Cassara. He went through our files picking out detail that would assist his Mafia investigations. A lot of people worked in dangerous environments so Doctor Cassara would have bodyguards most of the time who were armed. They knew there would be people eager to "take out" investigating officers. When he was told that three unarmed officers, including Adrian Owen and Eddie Jones had raided Di Carlo's house in Woking he was astounded. In the same situation in Palermo, he would have commandeered an army tank unit to accompany him.

The mansion in Woking in 1984 was valued at over four hundred thousand pounds, an incredible sum in those days. It featured a swimming pool, a heart-shaped lily pond, a sauna, landscaped gardens and paddocks. Gardeners, handymen and cooks saw to their needs. Parked in the garage was a £25,000 Ferrari.

Alfonso Caruano travelled back and forth from his house in Lugano to his house in London.

When Di Carlo was arrested, Caruano fled to Venezuela.

It wasn't thought Di Carlo conducted operations from his house but there was no signs of any illegal activity when we searched it.

There was no complaint or resistance when Adrian and the team arrived at Di Carlo's house. They had in their possession a HM Customs and Excise, "Writ of Assistance".

These were first authorized by an act of the English Parliament in 1660. For Customs, writs of assistance served as general search warrants that did not expire, allowing customs officials to search anywhere for suspected prohibited goods without having to obtain a specific warrant. They were most useful because they called upon public officials and loyal subjects to "assist" any Customs official in carrying out his duties.

As these "Writs" are issued at the beginning of a Monarch's reign the document we had in our office was dated December 1952 when Queen Elizabeth 2nd succeeded to the throne.

Within the Writ is the following – "YOU ARE NOW COMMANDED to [enter the said land and eject the defendant (name), his tenants, servants and accomplices, each and every of them, from the said land and every part thereof and put the claimant (name) and his assigns into full, peaceable and quiet possession thereof] [or put the claimant (name) and his assigns into full peaceable and quiet possession of the said goods] and defend and keep him and his assigns in such peaceable and quiet possession, when and as often as any interruption thereof is at any time effected, according to the intent of the said orders. And herein you are not in any wise to fail."

So useful was this Writ to Customs and Excise that it was a well-protected tool for our organisation. Police forces, by law, had to apply to a magistrate or judge for every single search warrant whereas we would show up whenever, wherever, flash the Writ and enter premises, using force if required. If we were ever questioned by savvy villains about the validity of our "warrant" a quick glance at the "oldie English" nature of the presentation they were put off reading further. It looked official so it was official.

Each of the investigation teams would have two "writs" locked away in a safe and only released by a Senior Officer.

I was never sure if it was bravado, naivety or whatever that motivated us to carry out such a potentially dangerous procedure or if it was that we mostly lived in a tolerant society without the need for violence. Of course, the Mafia was thought to have much less influence in the UK than it did elsewhere.

Although we had no concrete evidence of Di Carlo's involvement with drugs he was interviewed by Peter and Adrian Owen in Snowhill Police Station. This station "housed" our prisoners that were being held overnight. It was an uncomplicated procedure with no red tape. A call would be put through advising we had suspects in custody and had to bed them in for the night. There was rarely a problem.

With Di Carlo safely locked away for the night we were able to make calls and send telexes to Interpol and other law enforcement agencies to gather as much background as we could. As Di Carlo had his eight hours sleep by right, we had to make do with two.

News came through that Di Carlo was wanted for murder in Italy. The police were called in and obtained the authority to hold him while an International Arrest Warrant was issued in Italy.

Three days later, in February 1986, we received information from the Italian police via Interpol to our office, that there were three Italians coming through the Port of Dover. We stopped them and discovered they were carrying two hand-guns, one silencer and 120 rounds of ammunition. They had paperwork on them relating to Mafia figures in the Woking area, including Di Carlo who obviously had become a nuisance to the Mafia.

Two days after he returned to his office in Palermo, Doctor Cassara and his assistant was machined gunned and killed. He was a very nice, honest and professional police officer. This action, along with many others, illustrated the extraordinary influence the Mafia had on the authorities' pursuit of justice.

Di Carlo was remanded in custody in London's Brixton prison and he was tried in his absence in Italy for a previously committed murder.

After the trial Peter went to see Di Carlo at Leicester prison. In the presence of a solicitor, they chatted until a part Italian warder arrived with three cups of tea.

With a wry smile the solicitor joked, 'Mr Finch is not going to drink a cup of tea made by you, Mr Di Carlo.'

'Well, he will do,' said Di Carlo, 'as you are going to have the first cup.'

There was a recent history of Mafia members to inform on others and so avoid a 25-year sentence. They were given false identities and housed safely. A door of opportunity for some was opened for them. For others it remained shut.

When we investigated possible connections with Di Carlo they flagged, in 1980, a half ton seizure of cannabis in Dover concealed in a consignment of peeled tomatoes and, in 1982, the attempt to smuggle 250 kilos through the Italian/Swiss border. In 1984, 47 kilos of cocaine were found on a vessel in Hamburg Harbour. A telephone number found on one of the crew was that of a Di Carlo employee.

Di Carlo wanted to serve his time in the UK and not be sent back to Italy where his attempt at sentence reduction would have met with little success. He really wanted to go to Canada where he had his closest contacts.

After Peter had eluded to Di Carlo's murder charge in Italy and his association with the drug importers in Canada, Di Carlo realised he was in serious trouble and decided to assist the Italians and the Canadians and turned "super-grass" against the Italian Mafia group. In 1996 Di Carlo decided to collaborate with the Italian authorities. He was transferred from his UK prison to Rome. He was hailed as the "new Buscetta". Di Carlo mentioned several politicians to be members of Cosa Nostra, among others: the Christian Democrat politician Bernardo Mattarella, the former president of Sicily, Giovanni Provenzano, and Giovanni Musotto, father of Francesco Musotto, former president of the Province of Palermo who has been accused of Mafia association.

He also testified about the murder of journalist Mauro De Mauro. The investigative reporter had been kidnapped and killed by the Mafia in 1970. Di Carlo testified in 2001 that De Mauro was killed because he had learned that one of his former fascist friends, Prince Junio Valerio Borghese, was planning a coup d'état (the so-called Golpe Borghese) with like-minded army officers determined to stop what they considered as Italy's drift to the left. Di Carlo became an important witness in numerous anti-mafia trials and also testified in the trials against former Prime Minister Giulio Andreotti and Silvio Berlusconi's right-hand man Marcello Dell'Utri. He gave up tremendous insights into what was happening in the Mafia throughout the world.

It took a few months to gather and sieve through the evidence and make it presentable for prosecution. It became clear that a couple of overseas trips were required to "beef" out skinny evidence. All countries have to be advised that a UK law enforcement officer wishes to visit. Permission had to be sought and gained, usually at Embassy levels. This took time. There was also the possibility that our accountants (we called them the bean counters) may question the validity of expensive operations particularly when overseas travel is concerned.

My Senior Officer, Cedric Andrew, came into the office and asked who had a current passport. Peter Finch and I put our hands up.

Peter drew the short straw by going to Kashmir to find the source of the cannabis. During a visit to Shalimar Enterprises in Kasahmir he managed to obtain a lot of evidence linking the group with the shipment,

Peter recalls going up to Srinigar, a large city that lies in the Kashmir Valley on the banks of the Jhelum River. It is a city known for its gardens, waterfronts and houseboats and for its lawlessness. On arriving at a police-station he noticed seemingly cultivated cannabis plants growing in the back garden.

'Jim, I want you to go to Kenya next week,' said Cedric.

I felt I had got the long straw by going to Kenya rather than India. In the house search in Woking, we found a photograph of Di Carlo standing in front of what seemed to be a hotel. Written on the back was "Mombasa".

So, I was tasked to go to Mombasa visiting hotels to see if any of the group had stayed there.

I made the arrangements for vaccinations for hepatitis A, typhoid fever, yellow fever, and polio, as well as medications for malaria prophylaxis and travellers' diarrhoea and requested our departmental travel section to book a flight. It turned out that it was cheaper for me to go on a 10-day package trip than to book flights and hotels separately. I flew British Airways to Nairobi Airport then on a connector with Kenyan Airways to Mombasa Airport. Mombasa Airport at that time was nothing more than a large Nissan hut. The luggage was brought from the plane to a hall by a tractor and flat-bed trailer. Suitcases were collected by the passengers until only mine was left. The whole hall had emptied except for me and my suitcase waiting to be met by I didn't know who. Thankfully a Kenyan policeman called Joseph came marching into the hut, came to a halt, saluted, stamped his foot and shouted 'Jambo, Mr Jarvie, bwana. Mr Jarvie.'

I said, yes and he took me to his official car, an old Nissan and drove me to the White Sands, a beautiful hotel situated north of Mombasa on one of East Africa's most stunning beaches. Palatial grounds, Arabic architecture and facilities made it "the" place to stay on the Kenyan coast.

There were security officers armed only with long bamboo canes throughout the hotel but particularly near the beach. They prevented Kenyan nationals from entering and pestering the hotel guests by begging or trying to sell them various items. They wore uniforms and hard hats. I did ask one of them why, in the heat, did he wear a hard hat.

'Falling coconuts.' he said and pointed up into the trees.

I had registered into the hotel as a regular tourist.

During down time a stroll along the beach was regularly interrupted by people trying to sell you things or asking for money. I found it annoying mainly because it was non- stop and I didn't expect it, not having been to a third-world country before. They were obviously poor and hungry.

The large bed had a huge mosquito net over it - a first for me. I took anti-malaria tablets but that didn't stop the agitation at hearing the mossies flying about.

A note was pushed under my door saying the holiday rep would meet me in reception at 10am the following morning when I could enjoy a glass of champagne as the local attractions and excursions would be illustrated.

After breakfast the next day, wearing my jacket and tie, I attended the meeting where fellow tourists wore sandals, shorts or summer dresses. I did have some strange looks.

I had a copy of the black and white photograph of Di Carlo taken outside a hotel in Mombasa.

My first port of call was the hotel I was staying in. I could not just approach the staff myself and had to wait for my policeman, Joseph. The manager of the White Sands confirmed it was not his hotel.

Joseph allowed me to ask the questions and he was there to ensure those interviewed answered the questions and I conducted my enquiries whilst ensuring it was in accordance to Kenyan law.

We then drove to a couple of nearby hotels which proved negative. We then called into the Dana Hotel and met the manager, a Scot, who did recognise his hotel in the photograph.

He made available the hotel register and found Di Carlo's name. A member of the hotel staff recalled that he was accompanied by a woman of Thai appearance.

I photocopied the relevant pages plus the back copy of Di Carlo's hotel bill and any telephone calls he had made from his room. These could well serve as useful evidence.

In addition to Di Carlo's name there were many other Italian sounding names registered. All of this could potentially become evidential at the trial, in Canada, Italy, or the UK or for the general intelligence picture on the Mafia.

For us it was worthwhile going to Kenya as in the mid 80's the country was becoming an emerging money-laundering centre. Di Carlo had been looking to buy hotels and casinos in Mombasa and other parts of Kenya to enable "dirty money" to be invested in legitimate enterprises.

Italians first began flocking to Malindi, two and half-hours drive north of Mombasa in the 1980s. It was said that "they thought they had found an Eden in Africa". They swept up nearly all of the prime real estate; a construction boom followed a decade later. Alongside legitimate activities came the crime. Several thousand Italians still live there.

I spent most of the evenings in the hotel but one evening the police officer picked me up and we went to a fantastic restaurant overlooking the Indian Ocean, the Tamarind Restaurant serving delicious seafood, including crab, lobster, salmon, prawns and fish fresh from the ocean. The police officer managed the menu for me but I paid the bill.

Having the paper work I came to Kenya for, I was kicking my heels so I became a genuine tourist for a few days. I was tempted to go on a three-day safari but decided to remain in and around the hotel in case any other evidential opportunities were identified by Peter and the other officers in London who were examining all the documents uplifted during the house searches.

On my arrival one evening the hotel receptionist asked if I had confirmed my return flight booking in 10 days' time.

'No. Not yet.'

'You need to do that quickly. The flights get filled up.'

So, I rang British Airways only to be told that the flight from Mombasa to Nairobi was fully booked and I would be on a reserve list. So, I told Joseph of this problem that I might miss my connection back to the UK.

We looked at the possibility of going by train which was a 24-hour trip. Although a slow train travelling through mostly rural landscapes I, for a moment at least, relished the thought of an overland journey. This daydream was soon halted by a telephone call to the hotel from BA saying a seat had been allocated for me.

On the day of my departure from Kenya I got picked by up by Joseph at 5am to catch a flight to Nairobi. We passed hundreds of people walking and cycling all carrying baskets of fruit and market goods on their heads on their way to central Mombasa. Hotel life and escorted journeys bypassed the real life of the people.

The centre of Mombasa was a hive of activity, hundreds, thousands of people hurrying about their business. The heat, the colours and the smells were way outside anything I had experienced. The air was full of smells; spices, fragrances, cooking food and the odd whiff of something (or somebody) unpleasant.

At the time the President of Kenya was Daniel Toroitich Arap Moi, the 2nd President after Mzee Jomo Kenyatta's term of office. The government had strict limitations on cash leaving the country and even if you had a few Kenyan shillings you had to declare the fact at the airport. I was vigorously questioned on the matter but had no Kenyan currency at all.

On my return all the witness statements, copies of the hotel registration document and the details of phone calls made by Di Carlo were handed over to Peter. The witness statements and exhibits (for example copies of the hotel records) became part of the prosecution case.

It was most important that we find a link with the makers of the table tops in Chiang Mai to the company in London.

I had already established contacts with the Metropolitan Narcotics Unit in Bangkok and the Thai police so a few weeks after returning from Kenya, Peter and I went to Bangkok with a plan as to who we needed to speak to and what witness statements were required.

After our initial meetings with the Thai police in Bangkok we flew to Chiang Mai in the north of the country and visited the company who had made the furniture. We were able to take a statement from them to say that they had exported the tables.

We concluded that in the previous few years the organisation had exported sixty million pounds worth of drugs. The Thai police took an active interest in the company and monitored future exports although the owners of the company quickly disappeared.

The trial was at the Central Criminal Court, The Old Bailey in 1986. The Old Bailey is half a mile from New Fetter Lane, crossing over Fleet Street. The trial lasted from January to July.

I received a letter saying I was required to give evidence at the trial. The Custom's solicitors were similar, but independent of the CPS and it was their role to put the case papers and evidence together and to be the link between the investigation team and prosecution barristers.

In those days the Customs Solicitors were on call to an organisation 27,000 strong and based on the lower-ground of New Kings Beam House in what was Thames Television on the Embankment.

Peter Finch was the case officer for the entire trial and as case officer it was decided the days when I should attend court.

There was a lot of sitting around waiting (you can wait for hours, sometimes days). If they call your name you have to be there or the prosecution side would be seriously criticised by the judge.

The waiting is a nerve-wracking time - similar to going to the dentist.

Giving evidence chiefly from my notebook sets the scene of my involvement. The defence barristers will then have the opportunity to cross examine you on your evidence, your notebook, on your witness statements.

Four defendants were in the dock. As the three walked up to Di Carlo they took his hand and kissed the ring. It was a real scene from the Francis Ford Coppola's epic 1972 film The Godfather, as well as Mario Puzo's novel of the same name. An iconic moment when the Don's ring is kissed.

Ring-kissing is also tied into religion. Most of the Italian and Sicilian gangsters came from Catholic families, and despite living as criminals, still held the tenets of Catholicism dear to them. Ring-kissing is a deep part of Catholic tradition.

The trial went on for several weeks their defence being that they imported only genuine foodstuffs and had nothing to do with the importation of drugs.

Along with other colleagues I was called to give evidence. It lasted two days.

Number one court at the Old Bailey is incredibly impressive even on the outside where the dome above the court supports a bronze statue of Lady Justice, executed by the British sculptor F. W. Pomeroy. She holds a sword in her right hand and the scales of justice in her left.

The Great Hall is decorated with many busts and statues, chiefly of British monarchs, but also of legal figures.

The main Court, Court One is on the ground floor.

Everywhere in the building you get a sense of history, sometimes a forbidding reminder of judgements that initiated someone's death. Within the court the trial was presided over by a High Court Judge. He sits facing the barristers and solicitors. The jury are located at one side and the defendants on the other. The witness box where I gave my evidence was below the judge and facing the barristers and jury. There are a few seats for the press and a public gallery.

Judge Hassan and the jury were given 24-hour protection when the case had links to the Mafia, more than justified when news came through of Dr Cassara's death.

The police would provide this security following a request by the Court.

Peter was advised by the then Chief Investigation Officer, Richard Lawrence to vary his times and route into work. He also said, 'if you are at a railway station, don't stand close to the edge of the platform.'

The Prosecution Barrister was Richard du Cann, brother of Edward du Cann who, in 1974, played a part in the elevation of Margaret Thatcher to the leadership of the Conservative Party.

Michael Mansfield, the well-known barrister, acted for the defence.

Mansfield's reputation was formidable. He had represented plaintiffs and defendants in famous cases including the Guildford Four and the Birmingham Six and others accused of involvement in IRA bombings, the families of the victims of Bloody Sunday, Mohamed Al-Fayed in the inquest into the deaths of his son, Dodi and Diana, Princess of Wales, the inquest into the death of Jill Dando and the families of the victims of the Hillsborough Disaster.

His line of questions to me was that I had already had a conversation with Antonio Luciano before I had officially interviewed him. He was referring to a conversation we had regarding tin tomatoes. What happened to them when they arrived in the UK? Were they sold wholesale or direct to retail shops? That sort of questioning.

As Mansfield pressed, I flippantly said, 'There's not a lot you can do with a tin of tomatoes.'

Although the jury and courtroom laughed at this, Mansfield's eyes became steely. He was not amused. He visibly straightened in readiness for action.

He had been given a copy of my notebook and read out the questions I has asked Luciano. He would then ask why I had asked them. Even the most uncomplicated questions were dissected.

Also, he was trying to say that I had interviewed him prior to the one I had recorded, that in the first interview I had somehow compromised his client's position.

Although you know that what you did and your account of what you did is 100% right it is a nerve-wracking experience. Mansfield gave me a hard time continuing to analyse every question I asked of the defendant, trying to deconstruct my words to the point they meant nothing or very little. I was well and truly grilled. Much of the barrister's fees are valued at his or her ability to make you look an idiot.

The wait for the next searching question was like being a nervous batsman at a cricket crease watching a skilled and very fast bowler blasting a solid object at you at over ninety miles per hour.

In a curious way appearing as a witness in court is a bit like being a batsman. Surrounded by others it is you who is the centre of attention. You have supporters who must remain at a distance, silent and inactive, you have the judge acting as the umpire, the jury the ultimate evaluators of your performance and the opposing team eager beyond measure to demolish your defence. Being stumped in cricket is the same as in Court. You're out!

On a more sinister note, a young female Italian interpreter Maria (not her real name) was selected to act on behalf of the court. She would interact with the defendants, in particular Di Carlo. During the trial, whilst picking her children up from school she was hit by a car. The vehicle had mounted the pavement (similar to recent terrorist atrocities), crashed into her and sped off. The driver and vehicle were never found.

To her credit, despite a serious leg injury she carried on as an interpreter for the trial (she was in a wheelchair). No firm evidence could be found linking the incident to the defendants.

"Half time" is the point after the Prosecution have presented their evidence and before the defence give theirs. This gave the defence lawyers the opportunity to approach the Judge suggesting that the prosecution had failed and there was no case to answer. We heard that Di Carlo had arranged for Champagne to be on ice at his home in Woking so certain was he of walking out of the court a free man.

During the period prior to the trial, we had a magistrate called Giovani Falconi who was the most important investigating magistrate in Palermo. He arrived with a number of colleagues. He had a small army of people protecting him in Italy. He looked at all of our files and took copies of relevant issues. He was taken to the Cheshire Cheese pub off Fleet Street where he and his body guard insisted on sitting in a position facing the wall. He had good reason to fear for his safety.

He returned to Italy and was murdered on 19 July 1992.

Salvatore "Totò" Riina, known as "Totò the Short"; succeeded Luciano Leggio as foremost boss of the Corleonesi faction of the criminal organisation in the early 1980s and achieved dominance by a campaign of violence. He was known for a ruthless murder campaign that reached a peak in the early '90s.

Giovanni Brusca had been tasked by Riina with killing Falcone. Riina wanted the murder carried out in Sicily in a demonstration of Mafia power; he instructed that the attack should be on Highway A29, which Falcone had to use to get from the airport to his home on his weekly visits. 400 kilograms of explosives were placed in a culvert under the highway between Palermo International Airport and the city of Palermo, near the town of Capaci. Brusca's men carried out test drives, using flashbulbs to simulate detonating the blast on a speeding car, and a concrete structure was specially created and destroyed in an experimental explosion to see if the bomb would be powerful enough. Leoluca Bagarella assisted at the scene during preparations.

Brusca detonated the device by remote control from a small outbuilding on a hill to the right of the highway on 23 May 1992. Giovanni Falcone, his wife Francesca Morvillo and police officers Rocco Dicillo, Antonio Montinaro and Vito Schifani were killed in the blast. The explosion was so powerful that it registered on local earthquake monitors. Riina reportedly threw a party, toasting Falcone's death with champagne, according to the pentito (repentant) Salvatore Cancemi.

There is a tall, red memorial to those victims erected by the highway that circumvents the Sicilian mountains to connect the capital, Palermo, to its airport.

Falcone's colleague, magistrate Paolo Borsellino, was murdered only two months later when a car bomb filled with 90 kilograms (200lbs) of explosives killed him and five police officers in his escort on July 19, 1992. He was killed just moments after he rang the doorbell to his mother's apartment building in Via D'Amelio in Palermo.

Borsellino was only 52 years of age.

The airport in Palermo is now called the Falcone/Borsellino Airport.

Both men were deemed heros in the fight against the Mafia.

It was thought that the murders signalled a point of no return for the authorities. 'A great awakening,' it was said. 'A great conscious awakening.'

The trials that followed the murders of Falcone and Borsellino convicted the people who planted the bombs and planned the assassinations, but a wider investigation into powers behind the attacks had to be closed for lack of evidence. However, it still had an impact on the Mafia's power and the way it operated.

In the late 90's Riina was tried and convicted of over a hundred counts of murder, including sanctioning the slayings of Falcone and Borsellino.

In February 2000, The Canadian newspaper, The Globe and Mail, had the headline; "Canadian mob kingpins jailed."

The drug seizure was described as "near-staggering proportions," by Mr. Justice David Watt of the Ontario Superior Court as he handed out lengthy prison terms to the brothers.

Gerlando and Alfonso drew concurrent 18-year terms for conspiracy to import and traffic in cocaine, Pasquale got 10 years on the same charges. And Gerlando's son, Giuseppe Caruana, 29, received four years on a related charge of transferring drug-payment money from Toronto to Montreal and eventually to Miami.

Aided by an Italian translator, all four men entered guilty pleas under a deal struck with prosecutors. Plea bargaining in the US and Canada is an often-used tactic which can result in guilty pleas thus saving lengthy and costly trials. Plea bargaining is not officially accepted in the UK's courts although credit is given to those who plead guilty at an early stage. Reduced sentences can also be secured if defendants turn 'Queen's Evidence' and provide a testimony against fellow gang members.

The Caruana brothers admitted to successfully smuggling approximately 1.5 tonnes of cocaine into Canada in the two-year period before their arrests in July, 1998.

The Italian press baptized the clan as "The Rothschilds of the Mafia" or "The Bankers of Cosa Nostra". They were the brains behind a multinational octopus whose tentacles reached around the world from its lair in quiet Woodbridge, a large suburban community in the City of Vaughan, 349 miles north of Toronto.

Whilst in prison di Carlo decided to co-operate with the Italian and Canadian authorities.

At one point he had admitted to the police to being behind the death of Roberto Calvi, the banker for the Vatican who was found hung under Blackfriars Bridge.

Initially it was thought of as suicide but the police quickly realised that nobody could extend their reach to tie the knot around his neck.

Calvi's clothing was stuffed with bricks, and he was carrying around $15,000 worth of cash in three different currencies.

Roberto Calvi had been an Italian banker dubbed "God's Banker" by the press because of his close association with the Holy See. He was Chairman of Banco Ambrosiano, which collapsed in one of modern Italy's biggest political scandals

Claims have been made that the Mafia may have used Banco Ambrosiano for money laundering.

Banco Ambrosiano collapsed in June 1982 following the Discovery of debts of up to 1.5 billion US dollars. Money had been siphoned off via the Vatican Bank. In 1984, the Vatican Bank agreed to pay out 224 million US dollars as a "recognition of moral involvement" in the bank's collapse.

In the months before his death Calvi had been accused of stealing millions being laundered on behalf of the Mafia.

Although Di Carlo had admitted to Calvi's murder by strangulation he later retracted that by saying he had been approached but soon after was told that it had been sorted.

Sometime later he issued a statement; "I was not the one who hanged Calvi. One day I may write the full story, but the real killers will never be brought to justice because they are being protected by the Italian state, by members of the P2 masonic lodge. They have massive power. They are made up of a mixture of politicians, bank presidents, the military, top security and so on. This is a case that they continue to open and close again and again but it will never be resolved. The higher you go, the less evidence you will find."

I don't know what the truth is.

The trial at the Old Bailey had lasted six months, from January to July 1986.

'One only has to state those mind-boggling facts to realise the gravity of this case,' said Judge Hassan, sentencing the four men. 'In some countries of the world, the death penalty would be imposed for such an importation.'

Di Carlo publicly protested his innocence. 'I came to England because I didn't like the Sicilian mentality,' he said. 'I like the civilisation in England. It is eight years that I have been here. I don't even have a traffic offence.'

All defendants were given 25 and 22-year sentences.

25 years jail in UK: Francesco di Carlo. The main defendant. Born 18.2.41 in Altofonte, Sicily. The Sicilian Mafia's top man in London.

25 years jail in UK: Filippo Monteleone. Di Carlo's right-hand man. Born 5.4.44 in Palermo, Sicily.

25 years jail in UK: Francesco Siracusa. Middle-ranking Mafia 'fixer.' Born 25.11 54 in Sicily.

22 years jail in UK: Antonio Luciani. Believed to be a "bag man", responsible for moving Mafia cash in and out of UK. Born 22.12.44 in Palermo province, Sicily.

Deported to Canada: Alberto Gualtieri. Low-ranking Mafia soldier. Born 3.10.54 in Sicily.

The combined sentences in Canada and the UK were the longest in the history of law enforcement.

Di Carlo, on finishing his time in the UK was allowed to go back to Italy and then to Canada. He would be looking over his shoulder for the rest of his life. He knew there would be a contract out for him.

According to a Daily Mirror article in May 2012 di Carlo had left Canada and was "in hiding" in Italy.

This was probably the most important case we had taken on, both nationally and internationally. Although we rejoiced at the end of the trial, we did not have any real idea of the magnitude of the case, its triumphant and its tragic consequences. A Mafia godfather and his three lieutenants had been jailed for a total of 97 years at the Old Bailey after being convicted of running the biggest drug-smuggling ring ever found in Britain.

However, with a truly stressful trial behind us the taste of a celebratory pint could not have been more satisfying.

CHAPTER 17
PORTUGAL

In August 1986, almost a year after my marriage to Pauline, I was told by Jim Galloway, my Assistant Chief Investigation Officer that the Customs Investigation Senior Management Team were considering opening an drugs intelligence office in Bangkok in a year or so. With my connections in Thailand, he added, I could be the man to go there and set the operation up.

It would be a big move for us. We had to balance my enthusiasm at the idea of working in Bangkok with the needs of Pauline and my stepson, Robert, then eleven years old. Pauline shared the attraction of experiencing a different and colourful challenge but the ex-patriot lifestyle was unknown to us and Robert's educational needs were paramount.

We had plenty of time to ask questions, investigate as best we could and try to find answers that would reduce or increase doubts.

As this was going on, I was informed that an office was about to be opened up in Lisbon, Portugal where a position of Drugs Liaison Officer was being created.

Jim called me into his office.

'Someone has been teed up for the Lisbon post,' he said, 'but I suggest you to apply for it. It will be a good experience for you. Something may come up in the next year or two and you'll know what's required in these interviews.'

I knew the way Investigation worked and if somebody was earmarked for a position, they generally got it. I ran it past Pauline and she agreed it would be worth putting in for, if only for the experience of a Drug Liaison Officer interview.

I put my application in and on November 14th I joined 5 other investigators that had been short-listed. Although I was 33, I was the junior amongst them and had spent the least amount of time as an investigator.

In the 45minutes allocated for each interview we all expected to be grilled mercilessly - in those days "caring management" did not apply.

I recall waiting with the others, all of whom had dark suits on. I wore a light grey with a white shirt and tie and the obligatory shiny shoes.

'Mistake there, Trapper,' said one of them. 'Wearing that colour suit.'

The others all agreed.

When I was called in, I was quite relaxed. In the back of my mind was the thought that, no matter how well I did, I would not be offered the post. I was interviewed by three senior officers, two from Investigation and one from Human Resources.

I had, however, done my homework into why Portugal was an important transit country for both cocaine from South America and cannabis from Morocco.

When asked, I told the panel I would look to engage with the police and customs as well as establishing links with shipping and airline staff. I thought the interview had gone well but was realistic enough to know I wouldn't be successful in getting the post even though it was a storming interview. I was told later that the favoured candidate had completely messed up his interview.

Five days after the interview I was asked to accompany an American informant known as "Uncle Jack" to Turin. Uncle Jack had persuaded the powers that be that he was in direct contact with illegal suppliers of missiles, based in Italy. At Turin airport we were met by a US Customs Official who, like us, was concerned about the movement of rogue armaments throughout the Middle East.

After booking into a hotel Uncle Jack left to meet up with the missile suppliers.

We had no way of knowing who Uncle Jack was dealing with. They could be part of a chain emanating from the US, they could be agents from a Middle East country or they could be a terrorist group wanting to fund their cause.

The tentative negotiations took a few days and seemed to be going well.

This ground to a halt when news reached the world that the Ronald Reagan administration had been selling arms to the Islamic fundamentalist government in Iran in order to gain the release of American hostages in the Lebanon. The profits of the deal were then used to supply the anti-Marxist Contra guerrillas fighting in Nicaragua

It immediately attracted the headline of "Irangate" resulting in all relevant operations being instantly reassessed including ours.

In agreement with the US Customs there was no choice other than to abort our operation. Uncle Jack headed back to the States and I checked into my flight for London.

Before my departure I called the office and was told that Nick Baker wanted to speak to me urgently.

I rang Nick's office.

Nick came to the phone. 'Jim,' he said, 'You've got the job. You are the new Liaison Officer for Portugal.'

Standing in Turin Airport my mind was racing in overdrive. The thought that we would have to move to Lisbon was quite a shock. What would Pauline think and what affect would it have on Robert, my stepson. Robert, aged 12, lived with us during weekdays, spending weekends with his father.

Our lives would be significantly changed for the better or worse. There was no way of knowing. It was a mixture of sheer delight and trepidation.

As it turned out Pauline was delighted and we celebrated the news and cracked a bottle of wine picked up at the Turin duty free shop. The next day I spoke with my boss Cedric Andrew who was also delighted I had got the job.

I knew that I still had to do my day job but much thought was given to what was to become.

So, my life changed completely on my work front as well as domestic. In December 1986 it was confirmed that Pauline was pregnant with my first son, Alex.

I worked through December attached to the National Drugs Intelligence Unit at New Scotland Yard and started my first of 25 hours of language lessons at the Diplomatic language School in Whitehall. I also started to look at the logistics of moving to Lisbon, finding a home, finding medical facilities and working daily from a UK Embassy, something very new to me.

We decided that Robert would come with us so schooling had to be sorted. I couldn't find anyone who had intimate knowledge of the Portuguese environment I was diving headlong into. There had never been an international Drugs Liaison Officer in Portugal. I was the first.

I was to be part of a fledging overseas network. There was one officer in Pakistan, Mike Stephenson. Brian Flood was in the Hague and Len Caley in Cyprus

Today UK Law Enforcement has over 100 liaison officers based throughout the world.

I spoke to my future boss, Warwick Preston, an experienced SIO who managed the Investigation Overseas Network telling him I had no language skills.

'No problem,' he said. 'I've been on holiday in the Algarve. Everybody speaks English over there.'

Prior to going I had 25 hours of Portuguese lessons. I was a long way off being fluent. I could say hello, goodbye and thank you in Portuguese but not much else. "Ola". "Tchau". "Obrigado".

I made contact with the European Desk of the Foreign Office in Whitehall picking up any information I could. This desk managed all the British Embassies, High Commissions and Consulates based in cities outside of the capitals.

To work in a British Embassy, you had to be vetted in a procedure called "Developmental Vetting". Your background is looked at, your colleagues and friends are interviewed. I was interviewed by a security officer whose name, title and employer were never revealed.

He went through my life, schooldays, social habits, sexual predilections. I got the feeling that you could admit to being a cross-dresser or whatever, the importance, to him, was that you were completely honest. Any hint of covering something up would fail you. Blackmail is out there waiting. The Iron Curtain was still drawn across Europe and spies, real or otherwise, were thought to be everywhere. British and European diplomats were considered to be fair game.

I was asked about my overseas travel, business and holidays.

In 1973 my best friend, Paul Warrington, and I went to Barcelona on a one-way ticket. Armed with a tent we moved around the Costa Brava area until other friends drove down to pick us up in their Bedford Dormobile.

'I went to Spain for a month,' I told the security officer.

'No, you didn't. You went for six weeks and two days.'

'How do you know?' I asked.

'I just know.' He said with a wry smile.

I was amazed they had such precise details. The only thing I could think of was on our way back from Spain we had a crash south of Paris. The vehicle was a write-off and one of my friends broke his arm. One of us lost his passport in the milieu, a fact that must have entered the records of Special Branch.

Early 1987, although I was still waiting for my vetting results and a start date, we made arrangements to rent out our house.

Also, on my mind was the continued relationships I had built up with contacts in Bangkok so I went to see Cedric Andrew, my Team Leader, based in London.

'My contacts at the Thai Police have been vital. I have to find a way this can continue. I'll need to brief whoever takes it on.'

'I agree,' he said. 'Mike Gough Cooper will be assigned as the Thai link officer.'

It was agreed that Mike and I would fly to Bangkok so I could introduce him. We flew out to Bangkok, economy on 16 February 1987 and remained there until the 25 February.

We had meetings with The Metropolitan Narcotics Unit, the Customs, Embassy Officials and all relevant police officers in Bangkok and Chiang Mai.

A lot of our work in Bangkok was channelled through a Brit, Richard Darkin, from the Hong Kong police and their Counsellor in Thailand.

He provided the link between the Hong Kong and Thai police. Being based in Bangkok he had daily contact with all the Law Enforcement agencies and he introduced us to them and members of the foreign attaché network. He was able to open a lot of doors for us.

We met with liaison officers from the US, Australia, Germany and Italy in their embassies and other police and Customs teams. At that time, due to the communist threat in the region the US had the largest DEA station outside of the US. There were around twenty-five liaison officers from other countries.

The law enforcement community in Thailand had worked closely and successfully together and they welcomed representation from the UK and they hoped there would a full-time deployment soon.

We had a surreal meeting with the two Italian police liaison officers in their Embassy. One was from Sicily and the other from Turin and it became obvious they didn't trust or talk to each other. We had to hold the conversation with their long-suffering assistant as each officer used her as a conduit for them. It was a general conversation about establishing a working relationship with them going forward.

It was some relief to me that Mike was able to carry on the good work and had regular telephone and face to face meetings with the Thais and the law enforcement community in Bangkok. I missed dealing with the Thais but had many new challenges as I was going to set up a new office in Portugal, a country I had never visited.

I went on various Foreign Office and Security Service courses, primarily in Whitehall on general security, informant handling and firearms training.

On this course they showed a film of full-size dummy holding a letter bomb (a method favoured by the IRA). It spectacularly blew the model to pieces.

'This could be sent to you at an Embassy,' the lecturer said.

Pauline, as my spouse, had been invited to this course. She couldn't attend as she was working. Just as well. Had she seen the exploding dummy she would probably have chosen to stay in Croydon.

The prospect, at times, was daunting. Foreign Office, Ambassadors, diplomats, special attaches, strict protocol and the like. It was an environment that you can't practice at.

My vetting was successful so we stood ready to go.

I announced to my boss, Warwick Preston, that I was going to go on the 6th April 1987 unless he told me different.

He didn't. I was cleared. I called the Embassy in Lisbon telling the day I would arrive on my own as my wife is now pregnant and schooling must be arranged for my stepson, Robert.

I flew to Lisbon from Heathrow and was met at the airport by an Embassy Official, a Portuguese man, Joao Pedro Mendes known as "JP" employed by the Embassy as their "go to man" their "Mr Fix-it", who carried out important duties, dealing with all the contractors working on the embassy and diplomatic properties, sorting out transport and official flights picking up people from the airport.

As we left the airport the heavens opened, rain I'd rarely seen and just the opposite to what I expected.

The first thing I bought in Portugal was an umbrella, bought from a small shop in one of the old cobbled streets near the embassy, the purchase negotiated by JP. (umbrella is guarda chuva in Portuguese). It one of the words you learn in basic lessons but very rarely used.)

I arrived at the Embassy on a Monday evening, an imposing four storey building on the cobbled street of Rua Sao Domingos in the Lapa area. Trams trundle up and down the road within a few feet of the embassy's entrance. These trams were built in the UK early in the 20th Century and covered most of the city as far as Belem (the well-known tourist area). I had been on trams in Glasgow in the sixties which were more modern than the ones in Lisbon.

To this day they are a popular tourist attraction.

The Embassy building outside was obviously old and classical but once into the main reception area it had the usual security desk and a double lock system where you had to go through one door which closed and the second one opened. I signed the "visitor's book" and because we arrived about 17.30 and was taken by JP out of a rear entrance through a beautiful garden with an adjacent swimming pool and into a small club house and bar.

I entered and found many of my future colleagues to be having an after-work drink. The club opened for just for a couple of hours on a Monday. I was introduced to Doug Martin, Head of Chancery, the highest- ranking person in the administrative side. At the "grand" head was the Ambassador, an "old school" career diplomat, Michael Simpson-Orlebar and his Deputy Head of Mission, Charles Drace- Francis. The Chancery oversaw the work of departmental secretaries, first and second. I was a second secretary ranked as a Vice Consul, a title that sounds a lot more important than it is.

These titles conjured up a few hundred years of history with the Anglo-Portuguese Treaty of Windsor dating back to 9th May 1386.

Doug Martin was a career diplomat in his late 30s (and a Crystal Palace supporter like myself when I lived in Croydon) was effectively my boss while under the Embassy roof even though operationally I continued to be managed from London, reporting to Warwick Preston. My daily contact was with my desk officer, initially Kevin Harrigan and more latterly Christine Hughes. Doug and I got on straight away and he was a great support to me, particularly in the early months and helped me navigate the ways of the embassy and FCO staff.

I was introduced to Doug's wife Jill and during the conversation he said, 'I've heard you are good at darts.'

'I'm rubbish at darts,' I said. 'I hate darts.'

'Never mind. You're in the team.'

There I was playing darts on my first night in Lisbon. I had to pinch myself to ensure I wasn't having a crazy dream.

Doug and I sat chatting after the darts match.

'You've probably heard,' he said, 'that the Foreign Office is full of absolute plonkers.'

I thought it would be diplomatic not to comment.

As time went on Doug's words echoed as I did indeed meet some plonkers. You did wonder how they got their jobs, presumably on a written application only, not on a face-to-face interview. Newcomers started complaining as soon as they entered the building, too hot, dirty streets, unpleasant smells, surly locals. Some explained that they never wanted to live abroad, ignoring my question as to why they joined the Foreign Office.

I did, however, meet many non-plonkers, non-complainers who got on with the job with efficiency and good humour. I became very friendly with Chris Glynn, Bill Kelly and Mick McMaster who worked for the defence section. At that time, I looked a bit like Nigel Mansell, the motor racing driver. I had the same facial features and moustache and during the lead up to the Portuguese Grand Prix. Chris insisted I wore a Marlborough bomber jacket when we went to some pubs in Cascais. Some of the locals thought I was Mansell and one even asked for my autograph. Did they really think I would be out drinking the day before a race?

I was given an Embassy spare car, a clapped-out Ford Escort and initially stayed in a nearby hotel before moving out to Estoril Town located along the railway from Lisbon to Cascais. Part of the Portuguese Riviera, Estoril is famed as a luxury entertainment destination and home of the Casino Estoril.

I stayed at a small guest house, the Belvedere, run by a Brit, John Shaw.

My first day in the office, the Tuesday, was spent organising paperwork, obtaining passes for the Embassy and applying for my diplomatic pass which gave me accreditation for Portugal.

JP took me from the non-secure area to the secure area where the Head of Chancery, The Defence Attaché and highly vetted people had their desks.

JP opened a door and said,' This is your office', then quickly closed the door.

'Can I look in?' I asked.

'No! No!' he said rather too quickly. 'Not now'.

Curiosity got the better of me and I opened the door to a broom cupboard complete with brooms and cleaning equipment. It was, however, larger than I first thought and had a window.

I rapidly decided that this room would do as I had every expectation of spending little time there. My job, although as yet far from being defined, would take me out and about for most of the time.

I did have a dilemma as to what to do next, to whom should I speak about things I knew little or nothing about.

I had to resort to finding a telephone directory to find out where the Lisbon's law enforcement agencies were and found the Judicial Police Drugs Squad in Rua Condo Redondo in central Lisbon.

I didn't know how the local Drugs Department was organised and to whom I should speak to. I received no real briefing from London apart from a contact of Jim Galloway one of the senior managers who knew a Dr Botelho who worked for the Portuguese Alfandega (Customs).

I did get some useful leads from the Embassy's Consular section who helped Brits arrested in Portugal, but also spent a lot of time ringing around different officers.

My most used phrase at that time was "falar Inglese?" (speak English?) and "falar mais devegar se faz favour" (speak more slowly please!)

My first meeting was on the 29th of April with the Policia Judiciaria (Federal Police) who handled drug trafficking and smuggling throughout Portugal.

I met the Maria Alice Fernandez, the senior Delegado (Chief Inspector), a formidable police officer. She was quite short and stocky, a very strong character. It soon became clear that after my 25 hours learning Portuguese, I was in no position to discuss operational matters. Fortunately, Maria's English was very good and I quickly realised she would be a valuable contact. She was very knowledgeable on Portuguese and international drug trafficking. She was prepared to share information and opened many doors for me with the Federal Police offices, particularly in the Algarve.

'For all drugs matter you must deal with us,' she made clear.

I then went to see the Customs Investigation Division, who had the competence to deal with any initial drug seizures at a port or airport but under Portuguese law they were obliged to hand the case over to the Judicial Police for them to investigate and prosecute. Many countries have the same process.

Doctor Botelho, head of investigations, said that if I picked up any information it must be passed on to him and he would speak to the Federal Police.

'I don't see that working,' I said.

'But you are Customs.'

'I represent Customs and the Police.'

It was a bit of a Mexican standoff.

I didn't want to tread on any toes but I knew I had to handle my contacts with diplomacy (another skill there is no course for).

I was introduced to a Customs investigator Fanguiro dos Santos who fully understood the difficult position I was in but was willing to help me as much as he could. He quickly became a trusted colleague and friend. I visited both the police and the customs as much as I could.

Fanguiro looked like me, facially (similar moustaches) and size wise. I joked that he was my long-lost brother and we had been separated at birth.

He knew I would have to deal primarily with the Judicial Police with specific information but I was reliant on Customs for access to the airport and shipping data, yacht movements and the like.

It was important to keep the Customs onside.

The police Drugs Squad comprised of twenty officers with offices in the other towns in Portugal. The Customs investigation service numbered about six.

In May 1987 I was in the Belvedere guest house having breakfast when I received a call from Heathrow Customs Intelligence Team who look at airline reservations and movements.

They had identified that a drugs courier was about to arrive having travelled from South America to Lisbon in transit to Rome and there was an important question to ask. Will the Lisbon authorities allow the courier to carry on to Rome so the Italians can follow him, and arrest the organisers.

This was a month in since my arrival. It was a Saturday morning. I couldn't find an English speaker in the PJ office in Lisbon to try and convince the Customs that it was vital they let it through the airport.

It took some time and a lot of self-control on my part but the broken Portuguese I clumsily voiced was enough for them to be convinced and the Police and Customs allowed the courier to catch his flight to Rome without being stopped.

I heard a few days later I heard that the Italians had arrested the courier and two other higher up in the gang.

At lunchtime that day John, the owner of the hotel, commented on my appearance as I walked in the door red faced, sweaty and ruffled.

'You look flustered,' he said.

I obviously looked as harassed on the outside as I did on the inside.

'I am,' I said.

'Have a brandy.'

It really hit the spot as did the two others that quickly followed.

I was expecting a lot of intelligence and specific information to be coming in daily from the UK but I was quickly disappointed. I realised I would have to generate my own intelligence. I kept asking myself what I could do to build up the intelligence picture. A thing I had to do was to have ready access to all the facilities at Lisbon Airport.

Many flights from South America to Europe would land in Lisbon in the early hours, passengers would come off – some in transit to other European cities including London. For example, a flight would come out of Bogota to Caracas then onto Lisbon. Those passengers would wait in a transit area for their ongoing flight to other European cities. Each day there were two or three arrivals from South America (the major source of cocaine destined for the UK and Europe).

I spoke to JP who, although he was not a diplomat had an airport pass to meet and greet inbound staff and UK government visitors. The pass allowed him go through the airport staff gate into the "airside area".

I knew this sort of access would be valuable to me and my effort to identify drug smugglers destined for the UK.

'Look,' I said to JP. 'I really need a pass to go airside, bypassing police, immigration customs and security controls.'

'Leave it with me,' he said.

Two days later he produced a form for me to sign that would give me an Airside Pass. This proved invaluable.

I informed the Policia Judiciaria (PJ) I wanted to look at the flights coming in to look closely at passengers going on to the UK.

They agreed and for the first few mornings they came with me but my habit of arriving at the airport a 6 in the morning was too much.

'If you see anything let us know,' they eventually said.

So, I had the run of the airport making contact with the senior Customs Official, Joao Rapaseiro. He managed all the uniformed Customs staff at the airport.

I was able to build up a fantastic relationship with Joao who introduced me to all the airline managers and facilitated access to the airline computers to assist in tracking potential smugglers.

During this time Pauline and Robert were living in our house in Addington Village, South Croydon.

I was keen for Pauline to join me, to see and feel what Lisbon has to offer and where we were going to spend the next three years. I began looking for somewhere for all of us to live. The Foreign Office had stringent rules on "staff" accommodation with regulations that included not only size of houses and number of rooms but how many chairs you have around a dining table. I looked at many properties to rent but none had the requirements needed for the three of us increasing to four after the baby was born. Convenient shops and schooling were paramount. The baby was due in August.

In June 1987 Pauline flew over and stayed in the Belvedere for a month. During this time went looking at potential houses. I would work in the mornings and late afternoons we drove around searching for the right sort of home.

I didn't get on with the Embassy's Admin Officer who I found an arrogant man and a real jobsworth. He found fault in every property we were interested in. Instead, it seems he was trying to fob us off with a housing list supplied by his favoured estate agents, none of which were suitable.

I did agree to meet him at a house in Carcavelos, between Cascais and Lisbon and close to St Julian's, an International School, so the location was ideal.

The estate agent was there on time and 45 minutes later, all of us suffering from the heat, the Admin Officer arrived.

The front door was opened. He took one step in and one step out.

'It's too big,' he said. 'You can't have it.'

I stood in front of him as he attempted to leave. 'We've been here for 45 minutes. It's unreasonable to make my pregnant wife stand around waiting in this heat.'

I knew I had some clout. Customs Investigation back in the UK would be paying for our accommodation.

The longer I stood there the angrier I became.

So later on, I requested a meeting with the Ambassador, Michael Simpson-Orlebar.

I explained to him that it was critical for my wife, my baby and step-son to be with me as soon as possible so we can be settled allowing me to concentrate on work.

'Leave it with me,' he said. 'Don't make waves over the next few days. I promise it will be settled.'

It turned out that the Admin Officer had to return to London to account for his appointment of a homosexual young man to work behind the Embassy bar and it was revealed that they had been in a relationship. This was deemed to be unacceptable so he was dismissed and the returned to London. Any behaviour that could be subject to blackmail was swiftly dealt with, being a serious security risk.

With help from Embassy staff, I was able to rent a bungalow north of Cascais, in a small village called Birre. This was about 15 miles from my office but there was a local supermarket in Cascais along with bars and restaurants. On our first visit to the village, we observed a number of local women washing their clothes in a large concrete basin full of water. Some parts of Portugal were still very poor and had few trappings of the 20th century. The school was about twenty minutes away and we registered with an English-speaking doctor.

It was further out than most Embassy people lived but because much of my time was spent at the airport and docks it was convenient.

We moved into the house, Pauline went back to the UK, stayed with my parents when our son, Alex was born in August 1987. I was able to get back for the birth, arriving a few days before.

Two weeks later the four of us flew out from Gatwick Airport. Robert had stayed with his father in Arundel during the summer holidays and in September 1987 he started at the International School in Carcavelos. We agreed with Robert that if he didn't like the school or living in Portugal, he could return to the UK to live with his dad. He was determined to return to the UK after year in Portugal, a decision he latterly said was a massive mistake.

Surprisingly, for us, the weather during the winter months can be wet and cold in the Lisbon area although warm when the sun did come out.

The local shops were geared up for the Portuguese and we missed the usual things from home. Visitors, both family and colleagues would bring over Stilton cheese, Branston pickle and HP sauce.

We had to buy bottled water but the other services were similar to the UK.

It wasn't long before we settled in, making a new life for ourselves. Pauline made many friends, mostly the Embassy wives Wilma Glynn, Tina McMaster and Carol Kelly. We also met a young recently married couple John and Julie Buck. He was a rugby playing, ex-Navy diver who worked in the docks making underwater repairs to ship's rudders.

My working day started at 05.00 when I drove to the airport to cover early morning flights from South America. I did take my turn at nappy changing and bottle-feeding Alex during the night but thankfully he quickly settled into a routine. The Customs office was on my way back to the Embassy and most days I would call in to examine paper copies of ship's manifests to try and identify suspect consignments. I would also visit the two local marinas in Belem and Lisbon and jot down the names of any UK yachts.

Any significant intelligence was either phoned back to Kevin, my desk officer in the Custom House, London. If urgent (specific air passengers for example) were sent by telex through the Embassy's communication system. After a few months I received information on yacht movements through the islands of the Azores which lie halfway between Europe and South America. Yachts transiting the Azores or mainland Portugal were checked out by the ID's intelligence teams and suspect couriers stopped and searched on their arrival in the UK. At least once a fortnight I would visit the Algarve, liaising with consulate staff and looking at the yachts moored up in Vilamoura. The resort is known for its large marina, golf courses and casino, and for the sandy Vilamoura Beach.

If a particular yacht was of interest to the UK, I would go to the Guarda Fiscal who kept information on ship's movements, similar to the Guarda Civil in Spain, and get details of route, ownership, crew and passengers. They would have a full list that included nationality, names and passport numbers. The Guarda Fiscal handled all immigration checks outside of the airports.

Thankfully, my Portuguese was improving all the time and I was able to conduct my work without having to rely on somebody who could speak English. At the airport I was dressed in civilian clothes (jacket, shirt and trousers) as was the head of Customs, Joao Raposeira.

If drug courier arrived at Lisbon airport the Portuguese Customs used a similar tactic as we did in the UK. Suitcases were checked before being released. If drugs were detected they would watch the suitcase go through and wait to be picked up off the carousel. They hoped to discover the next link in the drug distribution chain. They would follow the courier on to the concourse to see if they were met by someone, possibly an organiser or financier or to track their onward movement.

Joao would often say to me, 'I've got a courier coming through. Give me a hand.'

He would reach into the top drawer of his desk and take out a revolver and give it to me.

Prior to moving to Lisbon, I went on a week's Foreign Office sponsored DLO induction course to learn about such things as informant handling and dealing with local law enforcement. I also received training on handling and firing a weapon. Although Portugal was not considered high risk, unlike Colombia and Pakistan a few years later, things could change quickly abroad and training was considered essential. Although I had been taught how to handle a gun. I had never been issued with one to carry on duty.

As I accompanied Joao at the airport, I carried a small cabin bag as cover. We chatted as if we were tourists as we followed the suspect through the concourse.

Often the couriers were young South Americans, dressed in an ill- fitting suits and oversized shirts (obviously bought by somebody else). Uniformed officers wearing jackets were standing by to make arrests which happened if the suspect met someone.

Every day I would look up the arrival of transit flights, flagging up those from drug source countries. At times I was alerted to a smuggling possibility by the experienced Customs Outward Intelligence Teams (OITs) at Heathrow and Gatwick who had picked up potential suspects from airline company computer searches.

In May 1988 the OITs identified a man who arrived from Caracas in a wheelchair appearing to have two false legs. He was travelling on his own and was aided by the airline assistance workers (not suspected).

I was on my own in the transit area. It wasn't a huge area (about the size of a tennis court) so I sat as close as I could to the suspect. He was waiting for a connecting British Airways flight to London. I posed as a transit passenger reading a newspaper and he sat quietly, staring into the distance. Once he had caught the connecting flight, I went to the Customs office and called Kevin my desk officer in London.

'He's left Lisbon on the BA flight,' I said.

Although he would be fairly obvious in a wheel-chair I described his appearance and advised the seat he had been allocated on the plane. His suitcase had been tracked and loaded onboard.

Prior to his departure I went with the staff to the transit baggage carousel and inspected the suspect suitcases. Inside amongst a few clothes was a plastic bag containing about 5 kilos of cocaine.

When he arrived in the UK, he was followed by our Cocaine Investigation teams (the Romeros and Sierras) into central London where he booked into a hotel on the Edgeware Road.

A team staked the hotel inside and out until he received two visitors in his room. The team burst in to find the courier sitting on the bed, his false legs on a table next to two 2.5 kilo bags of cocaine.

They were all Columbians and were arrested in the hotel room. They were charged with importing cocaine and received eight years following their guilty pleas.

The job was mightily diverse, every day was different.

On one occasion I accompanied the Ambassador in his bullet proof, armour plated, Jaguar car. It had been shipped over from Colombia and it was so heavy it bounced violently over the cobbled Lisbon streets, often scraping the exhaust system. We went to the Egyptian National Day, formally dressed in a dark suit, shirt and tie. It was the usual diplomatic event with a lot of small talk and a good supply of canapes and cocktails.

Two days later, another courier from Bogota had been identified by the Heathrow OITs who had examined the airline computers and found he was booked on a flight to London. My office in London wanted me to take the same flight. I was able to call Pauline at home to tell her I would be away for a few days and would ring her when I got to London.

He was booked on a TAP (Portuguese Airline) so I booked a seat. It was thought he was to meet someone on the plane and perhaps handing drugs over. There was no specific intelligence but it was a "backstop" position.

So, my job was to keep a close eye on his movements. I sat a couple of rows behind him and watched his every move and who he spoke to. He kept himself to himself and I believed he was travelling on his own.

At our arrival in Gatwick, I followed him off the plane and linked in with officers from the Romeros and Sierras who took on the surveillance. I jumped into one of the surveillance cars.

The suspect caught a taxi and was followed to a hotel in Kensington.

I was in London for 24 hours without a change of clothing so I went into a police station and washed myself down as best I could. I remained in the surveillance car overnight grabbing a bit of sleep. A striking change of circumstances over the three days since sipping Champagne at the Egyptian party.

I flew back to Lisbon the next morning but the team followed the courier for another 24 hours. He was eventually arrested and received five years in prison. Unfortunately, no other suspects were identified. It was good to have a proper shower and a decent night's sleep.

There was no doubt I thoroughly enjoyed the variety of duties and the people I mixed with. It had become very clear that my limited understanding of Portuguese was hampering my work, not necessarily for the leading edge but for the casual conversation that could contribute a small but vital detail. There was no chance of me detecting a Portuguese "slip of the tongue".

It came quickly as I forced myself to ask questions in Portuguese, to chat to taxi drivers, to shop keepers, to go over a word or phrase I hadn't understood first time. I talked and listened to Portuguese staff at the Embassy, to barmen and waitresses.

I visited a British prisoner in Faro jail arrested for being part of an attempt to smuggle drugs into or through Portugal. It was the responsibility of the Consular section to look after Brits arrested in Portugal. I had a really good relationship with the Consul Tony Abbott and Vice Consul Andy Kirk. We often joked it was my job to lock people up and their job to look after them.

Unlike some prisons in the UK, Portuguese prisons in the early 1980's were far from being holiday camps. Prisoners of all nationalities would share a very small basic cell (often two or three at a time). The food was very simple and invariably the prisoners had to rely on friends and relatives for money and an enhanced diet. I would take cigarettes in, which even today, is a form of currency in prisons, or give them a small cash payment if they supplied some useful information.

The intention was to gain any intelligence, either regarding those higher up the chain and the people who had recruited them. I would sit with them in a casual, unofficial manner, talking about what and who they missed from home, their circumstances and so on. I then slipped in a question or two about their arrest, their contacts and the make-up of the gang they worked for. I wanted to know who paid for their flights. They would often supply details of contacts and telephone numbers because they felt badly let down and they were the ones that took all the risks and suffered the consequences for being caught.

Visitors to the prisoners were rare. Family once a year, although many were disowned by family members because of their involvement in drugs. Embassy staff visited infrequently.

Occasionally a snippet of information came forth but it was more often than not a bit historical and not to an evidential standard required by the UK Courts. It was however, rewarding to me as it gave me an insight into background and motivation behind their involvement in trafficking. How they were recruited, what they were instructed to do and who in the organisation decided where the couriers were to collect drugs gave me a valuable insight into international drug smuggling.

In October 1987 I handed back my loan car and took custody of a white Ford Sierra, brand new with diplomatic plates. This was to be my car for work and so that Pauline had independence we purchased a red Seat Ibiza. I flew over to the UK to take delivery and with Kevin Harrigan (my "go to" person at HQ) we set off to for Plymouth to catch the ferry to Santander. Kevin drove the Sierra and I drove the Seat.

Leaving Santander, we drove through beautiful and dramatic country-side of the Basque region and northern Spain. We booked into a hotel in the historic town of Salamanca where we stayed before driving south to Lisbon. I think I played a Lucian Pavarotti cassette the whole way reliving the recent football world cup. To this day, if I hear Nessa Dorma, it reminds me of that journey. Kevin flew back to London the next day.

My boss, Warwick, had advised that it wasn't necessary to have air-conditioning. 'Never gets that hot,' he said.

How wrong he was! In Lisbon the temperature could reach 38 degrees in the summer.

Many countries had Embassies in Lisbon, including America and France which was in the same road ours and it wasn't unusual to see a car on diplomatic plates.

I often took the three-hour drive to the Algarve to meet the Central Police, visiting the Consul in Portomao and gleaning any information on suspect boats.

On many occasions I was asked to assist the MI6 official (a spy) "Charles", not his real name based in the Lisbon Embassy. His role was different to mine but he didn't have the same degree of access to the airport and marinas.

On one occasion I was asked by the Embassy to meet up with the British crew of a cargo plane in the airside area of Lisbon airport. The cargo plane was in transit to Africa. I was to hand over a package that contained cash. Quite rightly, I was not told the full story but I trusted my embassy colleague and was willing to hand over the package to the captain who had drunk a couple of beers before he flew off. I never did find out what happened but I was happy to be a small cog in the UK Government's fight against crime and terrorism.

In January 1988 my team leader Cedric Andrew came to Lisbon because he had received a phone call from an informant in Vilamoura, in the Algarve. A converted fishing boat linked to an IRA sympathiser Adrian Hopkins, was moored there. At the same time a freighter called the Eksund was intercepted by the French navy. The skipper of Eksund, Adrian Hopkins, and three other men were arrested when an arsenal containing 150 tons of weapons and munitions were found, supplied by Libya's Colonel Gadaffi and heading for the IRA.

There were 1,000 mortars, a million rounds of ammunition, 20 surface-to-air missiles, 430 grenades, anti-aircraft machine-guns and 120 RPG rocket launchers. (Hopkins later revealed he had landed another four arms shipments in Ireland and that the weapons were hidden in a network of bunkers.) It was the first time the security forces realised the IRA had enough hardware to equip a small army.

Hopkins, the skipper, was arrested by the French Customs, tried and later sentenced to five years.

Hopkins jumped bail in France but in 1990 was arrested in Ireland.

Cedric Andrew and I went to Vilamoura with a Portuguese Customs officer. We met the British contact, obtained the keys, went on board the converted fishing boat after meeting up with a Brit who worked in the marina.

There was no intelligence to suggest that arms or explosives were on board but as much information on the vessels itself was sought. We took the ships log and all the charts and took them back to Lisbon where they were sent in a diplomatic bag back to London. The Security Services in London were able to confirm their suspicion that Libya was the source of arms.

In April I was driving along the Marginal, the major coast road from Cascais to Lisbon. It was reputed to be the most dangerous road in Europe. It was dark and unpleasant weather and as I was trying to overtake a slow -moving lorry when a car suddenly appeared behind me, lights flashing, horn blasting- trying to get me to move over.

I waved gently back but as the headlights continued to flash my fingers jerked a V at the driver. I even gave a middle finger gesture – a most undiplomatic sign.

I overtook the slow lorry and pulled over to let the car past. As it did so a blue light flashed on its roof. My fears of facing a diplomatic incident lasted only as long as the car drew level and two faces laughed at me; Herbert Bauer, also a liaison officer, (I jokingly referred to him as Herman the German) was one and the other Luis Bordadagua, a Portuguese colleague and friend. As they passed, they both raised their middle fingers and mouthed the words, 'and you'.

They told me later that the look on my face was priceless.

The Judicial Police were very good to me, particularly those working for Maria Alice. Machado, Mario Marques and Luis Bordadagua were great colleagues. We would visit each other's homes and our families socialised. Luis lived in a village a couple of miles from ours. He and his wife Dada (he always joked about his wife's name. Dada Bordadagua; a real tongue twister). He introduced me to a number of local restaurants including one in our village of Birre. The Portuguese are so family friendly and they would move table and chairs to accommodate prams and pushchairs. The staff in our local restaurant would occupy the children while their parents had their meal.

Mario Marques's grandfather was from the UK and an ardent Liverpool supporter but had spent most of his life in Portugal. Mario came to our house with Herbert Bauer, the German Police Liaison Officer. Mario had just been promoted to become a Delegado (Team Leader). He obviously had already been celebrating for he staggered into the house, ate half his meal, half asleep.

He rallied enough to say he was going home.

'How are you getting there?' I asked.

'I'm driving.'

'You can't drive, Mario. You can hardly stand let alone drive.'

'I've got to get home,'

'Look,' I said. 'I've had two drinks but I'm nowhere near drunk. Leave your car here and I'll drive you home. I'll get your car to the police station in the morning.'

'Fantastic,' he said then hesitated. 'Would you look after this?'

Mario unclipped his holster and pulled out his gun.'

I locked the gun away and took Mario home.

The next morning, I had a phone call from Mario. 'Jim,' he said, 'I'm in terrible trouble.'

'What's the problem?'

'I've lost my car and even worse, I've lost my gun.'

'Mario, I've got both of them here. I looked after them for you.'

'Jim, you've saved my life.'

'I'll bring them over to you.'

Still hung-over, Mario was all smiles as I handed over the car and gun.

There were times when information from police officers and other sources were filtered through Kevin or came directly to me although the direct arrangement had to be cleared by Kevin.

A valued colleague Mike Milton, Chief Inspector from the Regional Crime Squad in Cardiff phoned me to tell me he had an informant called "John" (not his real name) who had been contacted by a group of Colombians based in Madeira. They wanted "John" to go to the island and meet them with the view of purchasing a large quantity of cocaine.

I informed Mike I would advise my office in the UK and the Federal Police and tell them what I knew. We had to quickly establish if they would allow the meeting to take place and to conduct surveillance. In a matter of minutes, they agreed to do this.

I told Mike to send John over and he arrived in Lisbon where I met him at Lisbon Airport and booked him into a hotel. The following day we both flew on to Madeira on a day trip leaving at 08.00. Two officers from the Federal Police joined us on the flight. They would link up with Madeira police.

We arrived at Madeira Funchal Airport (now known as Madeira International Airport Cristiano Ronaldo). John made a telephone call from a telephone booth to a contact number he had been given and went off in a taxi. The taxi was kept under surveillance by the Judicial Police until it stopped in Funchal City where he met some Columbians in a restaurant. After about three hours he took a taxi back to the Airport where I was waiting.

'I need to speak to you really urgently,' John said.

'What's wrong?' I asked.

'It's over.'

We went into the gents' toilets and checked all the cubicles.

'Tell me what's wrong,' I said.

'We had a great meeting but they're trusting me so much they've given me a sample of drugs.'

'That's okay.'

'No, no,' said John opening up a duty-free bag.

Inside was a kilo of pure white cocaine wrapped in plastic. I estimated its worth about £40,000.

'I'm not going to carry it through,' he said.

'Give it to me.'

John handed me the bag before leaving the toilet. I followed.

I found Machado and told him that Joe had been given a sample of drugs.

'That's okay. Let him take it through.'

'No,' I said opening up the bag.

His eyes bulged, his head shook.

After a short discussion we started to fear there may be a rip-off (the cocaine would be stolen somewhere along the line). So, we all boarded the flight back to Lisbon just in case I was being ripped off.

So, I arrived at Lisbon airport carrying a briefcase and a duty-free bag.

Domestic flights rarely have Controls stationed but as the flight was to fly onto Madrid it docked at International Arrivals. The Customs officers I spoke to on a daily basis were everywhere.

As I walked through the green channel someone said, 'Hello Jim, how are you?'

'I'm fine, thanks.'

'Where have you been?'

'Madeira for the day.'

We chatted for a while, the bag getting heavier and heavier.

It was the one and only time I had smuggled drugs through Customs.

A long deep breath took me outside and I climbed into a taxi. I was followed by several police cars as I drove to the Police Station.

After handing over the drugs to the police it was placed in a secure safe. The police had a lot of leads including the contact numbers and Colombians John met with in Funchal.

It was a month before I heard from John. He had been invited back to Lisbon by the Colombians to purchase several kilos of cocaine. He wasn't keen to take part himself so advised that a drugs expert from the UK crime group would fly over to verify the quality of the cocaine and discuss the details of the purchase.

We then had the opportunity to deploy a trained under-cover officer who could carry out that task by meeting the Colombians in Lisbon.

Kevin Harrigan from my support team in London had trained as an under-cover officer and had the legend (identity and passport) to take this on.

It was Cup Final day on Saturday 14th May 1988 and my hopes of watching the game on the Embassy television was dashed when Kevin and John arrived back in Lisbon. John had told the Colombians that Kevin was a high up member of the UK crime group with the authority to purchase the cocaine. Kevin received instructions from the Colombians and was instructed to go to a block of flats a few miles outside Lisbon. He went inside and appeared to go down to a basement.

I joined the Federal Police surveillance team of eight officers who were watching the premises.

It was the most worrying hour I had. We had no radio cover, nothing to help him in a jam. Was it a set up? Was he in real danger?

To our relief Kevin emerged out of the premises and calmly hailed a taxi that took him to Lisbon.

The Police surveillance team stayed on site covering any move the Colombians may make.

Sometime later the suspects left the flat and they were followed to another address not far away and once inside the decision was made to "bust" them. The police were satisfied they had seen enough and went in arresting all inside.

Kevin said later that it was a typical "drugs buy", the procedure you saw in films and tv. The drugs were tested with equipment he had brought with him, weighed and weighed again.

'They bought it,' said Kevin. 'They were convinced I was the real thing.'

The Colombians had moved across town where the rest of the cocaine was stashed.

Kevin went back to London to his desk job with a broad smile on his face.

It was the first time I had experienced seeing a colleague going into a dangerous position while having to stay on the side-line. You always want to be the one on the front line, to face danger head on, not have someone in your place.

In July 1988 I received a phone call from our office in Birmingham office who were running an operation and were looking at a yacht importation that was heading for the coast of the UK with the drugs eventually ending up in Birmingham. It was thought the cannabis would be collected off the coast of Morocco by the yacht.

I was tasked the investigators in our Birmingham office to see if I could find it in Portugal. I only had a limited description. It had a white hull, three masts and a distinctive wooden deck and was called "Pegasus". It was like looking for a needle in a haystack.

On a Saturday in July myself Pauline and Alex who was nearly a year old went into the Embassy for a bar-b-que. John Bartlett, the Security Officer and his wife Beryl lit the charcoal in a 45-gallon drum cut in half. John and Beryl provided salads and we would take our meat in. It was always a happy day by the Embassy swimming pool. My love of bar-b-queuing started there.

On a weekend we took the train from Cascais to Lisbon. We passed through Belem the historic part of Lisbon where the statue of The Navigators is located, the Tower of the Belem.

As the train went through Belem Station, I looked over the harbour beyond I could see a yacht that stood out from the others.

'That's the yacht,' I said to Pauline. 'The one the Birmingham lads are looking for.'

We got off the train at the next station and caught one back to Belem.

Pushing Alex in his buggy we walked down to the Marina and as I got closer to the yacht, I realised the yacht fitted the description and eventually I could make out the name "Pegasus" and it was the one we were looking for. It matched the description to a tee.

The three of us walked closer to the yacht. There was a man washing down the deck.

Showing interest, I got chatting to the man and said, 'The yacht is magnificent. Can I take a photo of my son in front of it?'

'Course you can.'

I took a few photographs and after thanking him I asked about the British flag.

'Are you sailing back to the UK?' I asked.

'No, we're going to Vilamoura Algarve, tomorrow.'

Vilamoura, a popular holiday destination for Brits, is in the Algarve and one of the closest marinas to Morocco.

I wished him a good trip and we left.

I rushed back to the Embassy and rang the Birmingham office and spoke to the case officer and told him I had close up photos of the vessel. I put them in the Foreign Office diplomatic courier bag but did ask, 'If you ever use them as evidence make sure my son is taken out.'

'What happened then?'

'I walked up with Pauline and my son enjoying the view. It was a family outing. The guy didn't bat an eyelid.'

'Blimey!'

'The yacht leaves tomorrow for Vilamoura '.

'How do you know that?'

'I asked him.'

'What! You've compromised the whole operation.'

'For a surveillance officer,' I pointed out, 'it was the most natural thing to do. The more natural you are the more you blend in.'

The operation was not compromised, although it was aborted as the group could not raise sufficient funds to pay for the cannabis. I learnt a valuable lesson as regards surveillance. The more natural you are the less likely you are to show out!

In September 1988 the Embassy held a gambling night at the Ambassador's residence to raise money for Great Ormond Street. I attended on my own as Pauline was looking after the boys. I was responsible for handling the cash and to place it in the safe. There was a raffle with the first prize being a return flight from London to New York. This was won by the Ambassador's wife Rosita and we were all mildly surprised when she didn't ask for it to be re-drawn. The second prize was a return trip from Lisbon to Madeira. To my amazement my number was called out! I immediately rang Pauline at home to give her the good news, forgetting it was three in the morning.

A few weeks later we flew over to Funchal in Madeira and stayed in an apartment arranged by the Honorary Consul for Madeira, Richard Blandy. He was a valuable contact for me, particularly as regards shipping movements and a nice man as well. He was part of the Blandy dynasty who owned numerous businesses on the island including Blandy's Madeira wine and Reid's Palace, one of the most iconic hotels in the world.

We used a small Fiat car owned by his wife Rosemarie and we had a letter of introduction signed by him allowing us to use the facilities at Reid's Palace.

My parents flew over for a few days having booked into the Reid's Palace hotel. As we drove from the airport, we looked like the Clampits (from the TV show The Beverly Hillbillies), the two boys and my parents crammed into the small car. Somehow, we all squeezed in with luggage and baby buggy across passenger's laps. A pile of nappies and towels rested on the rear window shelf alongside an inflatable rubber ring in the shape of a duck.

The Hotel commissionaire watched us drive up and grudgingly approached us.

'Are you sure you have the right hotel?' he said.

I handed him the letter of introduction and his attitude changed immediately. He helped us into the hotel and showed us the swimming pool area. Most of the guests were elderly, wealthy pensioners.

We realised we were, perhaps, in the wrong location when two-year-old Alex, who was in the pool shouted, 'I want a poo'.

On 1 October 1988 I received a phone call from Desmond Chamberlain, who was then based at Heathrow Airport Investigation Unit telling me that a courier had been identified transiting through Heathrow with 6 kilos of cocaine on his way to Lisbon. Desmond wanted it to go through so we could find out who was behind it.

I spoke to the Federal Police who agreed to follow the courier when he arrived in Lisbon to identify the gang members. I phoned Desmond with the news.

'I'm sending a junior officer on the same flight as the courier,' said Desmond. 'He'll contact you as soon as he arrives.'

I told Desmond I would meet him at Lisbon Airport.

John Kay arrived and immediately pointed out the courier to me and I notified the police surveillance team and they followed him away from the airport to a hotel in Lisbon. He was met at the hotel by a Portuguese man and both were arrested by the police.

John stayed with us and the next day he joined me as we entered the drug squad office in Rua Condo Redondo. We walked up the stairs to the 2nd floor there was a set of hand-cuffs fixed to the bannister.

An officer I knew well walked past.

''What's the cuffs doing there?' I asked. 'What's going on?'

'One of the people we arrested on cocaine charges was hand-cuffed to the bannister when we brought him in. He slipped out of the hand-cuffs and jumped out of the window.'

'Did you catch him?'

'Oh, no. At that height he'll have broken a leg or something. We'll pick him up at a hospital at some stage.'

Both John and I were staggered at the lack of concern. If we "lost" a prisoner in the UK there would be endless paperwork and gruelling interviews in front of disciplinary boards.

The Cocaine target teams, the Romeros and Sierras, based in London ran an operation "Redskin" which resulted in a yacht "Kula" being intercepted in Cornwall UK and was found to be carrying 50 kilos of cocaine. On its journey back from South America it called into the Azores a group of nine islands nearly 1500km west of Portugal in the mid-Atlantic.

I met the case officer, Bob Grey, an experienced Higher Customs Investigator based in London at Lisbon airport and I took him to meet my contacts in the Judicial Police. Bob needed to get statements and evidence on the yacht's visit to the Azores before it sailed to the UK.

A close contact Jose Corrollo a Judicial Police officer based in Lisbon, was assigned to go with us to the Azores and ensure we got the evidence and to iron out any problems we may have incurred with the locals. On 27 October 1988 the three of us flew to Ponto Delgado, hired a car and met with the local police. Jose told them we would be visiting the marina in Ponto Delgado. We drove to the yacht marina and met with the port captain (harbour master) and took a statement from him regarding the Kula.

By that time my Portuguese was good but the local people's dialect was beyond me.

'I can't understand what they're saying,' I said.

'Neither can I,' Jose replied.

We understood a few words but had to ask them to write important stuff down. The statements taken in the Azores were essential to prove the vessel had travelled from South America and who the crew were.

That evening we indulged in a local meal cooked in a ceramic pot carefully dug into the ground where the scorching thermals were just below soil level. We sat in a restaurant overlooking the Atlantic Ocean and had a plate of the stew and a few glasses of the local wine.

My second son, Alistair, was born in December 1988. Because we were uncertain of the maternity care in Portugal, Pauline went back to the UK to give birth, staying with my parents in Lincolnshire, Alistair was born in Peterborough Hospital on the 9th of December 1988.

On our return we discovered that the baby's milk we bought in Lisbon didn't suit Alistair at all and he had picked up a chest infection. He slept very little and was coughing a lot. The chest infection did clear up eventually but he still didn't take the milk. I ordered milk to be sent from the UK.

Kevin Harrigan arranged for a large quantity to be sent to Heathrow Airport and flown out on a TAP flight. My colleague at the airport Joao Cabrito collected it off the aero-plane for me.

When the box arrived, it was addressed; James Jarvie, British Embassy, Lisbon. Urgent Medical Supplies.

Eventually Alistair came to like the local milk and got into a sleeping routine.

There was fourteen months between our young sons and it was difficult to cope particularly for Pauline who took the brunt of sleepless nights. When I could I did take my turn.

A few weeks before, Joao Raposeira, the Head of Lisbon Customs, had asked me if I could get a part for a Fiat car from the UK.

'No problem,' I said. 'Give me the model and part numbers and I'll ask my colleagues.'

What I didn't realise was, it was a complete exhaust system. It duly arrived on an Air Portugal plane. In those days you could do such things. Not now!

I often socialised with the police officers, particularly one of the agents, Luis Bordadagua. When we were driving home at night, a tad later than usual, I insisted he made no noise near our house as Pauline and the boys would be asleep.

I closed his car door gently and entered the house as quietly as I could but as Luis accelerated away, his tyres broadcast a hail of small stones against the door, waking up the whole family.

In June 1989 the Embassy hosted an exhibition of British gardening equipment and furniture organised by UK based companies wishing to promote their goods overseas. Several stands were erected in the Embassy Garden and swimming pool area. On the Monday night of the event most of the exhibitors attended an informal reception in the small club.

I was talking to one of the representatives and I noticed he had a chain with a gold gnome round his neck.

I said to him, 'That's an unusual necklace.'

He replied, 'It was made from gold from the Brinks Mat robbery.'

I laughed out aloud and said, 'Very funny'

He said he wasn't joking and the smirk that spread across his face suggested he really was not joking. My alarm bells started to ring.

After about 20 minutes I discreetly left the club and went to the Embassy's reception area. I checked the visitor's book and obtained the person's name, date of birth and passport number.

I made a phone call to the National Drugs Intelligence Unit at Scotland Yard, and asked them to see if anything was known about him. I called them back twenty minutes later and it transpired there were six arrest warrants out for him for alleged contrived liquidation, on paper a legal process in accounting by which a company is brought to an end but, in the hands of criminals, a means to fraudulent activities.

I returned to the club and engaged him in conversation where he confirmed he was travelling back to the UK on Thursday.

The following day I spoke to the Ambassador's secretary and told there was a potential diplomatic problem with the garden furniture event. I was immediately called in and explained what I had found out. The Ambassador consulted the Commercial Secretary, the FCO official responsible for promoting UK business.

When he was told of the situation he said, 'I asked the Department of Trade and Industry (DTI) to check the companies out.'

I was a bit sarcastic and commentated, 'You would have been better off asking my Mum as she would have had a better idea than the DTI.'

The Ambassador was really worried that the press would find out about this breach of security.

A few days later, much to the embarrassment of the Embassy, the Daily Mail wrote an exposé on the event. Where they got the story, I don't know but the suspect party was arrested on arrival by the police on his arrival in the UK.

On the 27th June 1989 the Federal Police called me to say they had received information from the British Captain of a cargo ship that was in a dry dock in Setubal, a town south of Lisbon. He also had telephoned the British Embassy to say he believed a bomb had been clamped to the bottom of his vessel.

We doubted it was a bomb but I went along with the Judicial Police into the dry dock.

Although there were far bigger cargo ships nearby this one seemed enormous as I stood underneath it.

Attached to the bilge keel, fixed with G clamps was a large metal object shaped like a torpedo. We were certain it wasn't a bomb so a couple of men removed it and took it back to an office. Inside was 60 kilos of cocaine.

The drugs smugglers in Colombia would build a torpedo like container and pack it with cocaine. Divers in the main ports of Turbo and Cartagena in Colombia would clamp it to a vessel that was known to be sailing to Europe or US.

Once the vessel arrived at its destination dock, corrupt divers would be ready to remove the package. They would dive down to the torpedo and release the clamp, allowing it to float to the surface for collection by the traffickers.

We had no intelligence on the seizure – it could have been destined for Portugal, the UK or even onto Miami. Because it had been underwater forensics revealed nothing. If it had been kept dry there may possibly have been fingerprints on the torpedo. We had to be satisfied that a large quantity of drugs had been removed from the market. No arrests were made but the traffickers had lost a lot of money. Intelligence regarding the ship and the crew was sent via Interpol to Columbia to help them identify the South American criminals.

On 20 July 1989 I was in the Judicial Police office with Maria Alice and an Agent Machado who advised me that a male suspect was staying at the Vilamoura Marina Hotel in the Algarve. According to the security staff he had three Samsonite hard back suitcases in his hotel room. The suitcases were locked and very heavy. The suspect did not leave his room and relied on room service. House-keeping staff were not allowed in.

I drove to the Algarve with Machado and we met up with Faro police.

We found out that the suspect was travelling on a Maldives Diplomatic passport in the name of Cetian. I spoke to Kevin my desk officer back in the UK, who did some checks. He found out he was once a diplomat but had ceased being so 10 years before. It was suspected he just flashed his red Diplomatic passport (which was out of date) and waived through by immigration staff and never stopped.

He was due to check out of the hotel the following day. The hotel was watched by undercover officers all night. Cetian eventually left the hotel at midday and placed the three suitcases in a locally rented car. We followed as he drove towards the airport and after an hour he stopped at a restaurant. He ordered lunch so we all did the same in a restaurant next door. This was totally against my surveillance training but, "when in Rome" as the say.

After an hour he left the restaurant and drove towards the Spanish border. He had a booking for a flight to Luton airport and if he had gone to the airport he would have been allowed to fly to the UK.

Unfortunately, he drove past the airport, so a mile from the Spanish border his car was pulled over and he was arrested at gunpoint. The suitcases were open and they were full of packets of cocaine. Cetian was taken away to Faro. Machado and myself took the drugs away.

Machado wanted to confirm how much there was so we stopped at a local butcher who agreed to weigh the packages. In total there was 90 kilos of cocaine, a considerable amount at that time.

We drove to Faro and I was allowed to speak to Cetian. I wanted to find out who he was working for. He was incredibly arrogant and refused to assist us relying on his so-called diplomatic status. I did tell him it was worth nothing and showed him his passport which had expired several years before. When he eventually appeared in Court, he was sentenced to six years in prison.

In September 1989 I met with American DEA officers based in Madrid on one of their regular visits to Lisbon (they did not have a permanent office in Portugal). Agent Craig Levato was the US based investigator who had taken on the international investigation into Howard Marks. Craig had information that Marks was using Portugal as a switching centre for phones. This effectively meant that calls from Spain to Pakistan and Thailand would appear to be made to Portugal. It was good to talk about how the Marks case was developing and he did appreciate the effort I had made in regards to the intelligence in Bangkok. The acquittal of Marks was painful to us all and the fact that after ten years it was the DEA who captured him.

The recruitment and handling of informants was considered crucial and encouraged by the UK management I took on two informants, "Frank" a British national based in Morocco who visited Portugal and Spain. He had left his details with the Consular section in the Embassy and I agreed to meet him. He said he could provide sound information about yachts leaving Morocco, destined for Europe and if expenses were provided, he would feed us detailed movements.

Money for expenses was small and payments were usually made after intelligence received led to drugs seizure. Final fees were paid on substantial information or for a successful prosecution. Actual sums were always a grey area and we paid out rewards in dirhams, the Moroccan currency.

He would phone me on my direct line in the Embassy or at home almost always asking for more "deary-mes" (Dirhams). I'm not sure the few hundred pounds we gave Frank was value for money but he did give me a few snippets of helpful information. He provided the names of the Moroccan suppliers and the coastal areas where the cannabis was collected.

We did, however, see the value of having someone in Morocco who could, if asked, carry out an errand or assignment. He was in Morocco on and off for about six months. He phoned one night and spoke to Pauline on my home phone. Pauline was savvy enough to arrange a time and place I could call back.

Every now and again my long-suffering wife Pauline would assist and nudge circumstances to my benefit – all while attending to the constant needs of the family.

It wasn't long before "Frank" was dropped, his use to us fading to zero.

"Bob" was the next informant I recruited. He had made the initial contact with the Consulate, a sub office of the Embassy and they contacted me. He lived in Portugal at the time. I went down to meet him on the coast. He looked a sea-faring man, rough, ruddy exterior, an ex-sailor. He convinced me that he knew a great deal about yachts arriving and leaving Portugal, from Morocco and onto Spain, Contacts in both places.

Bob was recruited to be our eyes and ears in Portugal and Spain and through his access to marinas could identify suspect yachts. He passed us a lot of information and over time became a creditable informant. And, important to me, trusted most of the time. Like Frank, he was paid reward money after he had fed us movements that led to arrests and prosecution.

On one occasion we wanted to put a tracking beacon on a yacht called "Blue Mist" in Sotogrande in Spain. Although I was not accredited in Spain, Bob proved his worth having access to the vessel itself.

I flew from Lisbon to Gibraltar via the UK where I collected the tracking beacon.

Back in Gibraltar I was met by John Ballantine a trusted Customs colleague. I stayed in the Caletta Palace Hotel located on a beach where the cigarette smuggling boats left in the early hours of the morning to collect their contraband from Morocco destined for the Spanish market. The next day I walked back to the Customs office at the airport to meet John Ballantine. I had the tracking device with me and I walked across the border to the town of La Linea a few hundred yards into Spain.

I met Bob who was waiting in a car (he had spoken to me at my hotel the night before to arrange a meeting at 10.00).

The border between Spain and Gibraltar has been fractious for many years and if you are in a vehicle, you will be stopped and searched but foot passengers are mostly ignored. There were no stops, no controls as I walked through.

I had put the tracker which, because of the battery, was the size of a house brick, in a camera bag which I slung in full view over my shoulder.

As Bob and I drove to Sotogrande we were pulled over by the Guarda Civil on what appeared to be a routine stop, the military face of the police in Spain. They looked at our passports, asked a few questions and began searching the car. I had a flash of scandal with my career being crushed by importing a tracking device without authority. They did open my camera bag, saw the camera on top and closed the bag up.

I had been warned by a Duncan, the Drug Liaison Officer in Madrid, who, on hearing on my plan, said, 'On your head be it!'

The yacht was of particular interest to the Spanish as well as the UK.

Although we knew the yacht crew were not around, it was quite nervy climbing aboard the yacht. It was just possible that someone would turn up unexpectantly and find us.

Bob had somehow acquired keys so we were able to find a very good position behind a projection in a cupboard in the galley to conceal the tracker.

Being on board reminded me of searching hotel rooms when you know for sure no-one was there or about to arrive - you still had this apprehension that you were about to be discovered. Although, I suspect that Bob would have talked our way out of a difficult situation.

Bob continued to be my informant when I left Portugal in 1990. It turned out to be a successful relationship with Bob sending valuable detail to me and to the Spanish National Police.

Back in London the Bravos and Charlies had a joint operation with the Spanish Police and I was sent to Alicante to liaise with them and meet up with Bob. He had been offered a job as a crew member on a yacht heading to Morocco, returning to Spain. I had to get agreement from the Spanish police for Bob to go to Morocco which they did. He remained in Alicante and joined the other crew on the yacht and I flew back to London. He was due to leave on the Friday and he called me from a call box to give me an update and to receive any new instructions.

'What happens if I get caught in Morocco?' he asked.

I said as a joke, 'Have you seen the film, Midnight Express?'

(A young American caught by Turkish police while attempting to smuggle hash out of Istanbul. He's tried and sent to prison for four years, where he endures all manner of privation and abuse. As he finishes up his time, he's shocked to learn that the Turkish High Court has added a further 30 years to his sentence. Escape is his only option.)

We both laughed nervously when we recollected the story-line.

The plan was the yacht would keep to international waters, out of reach of Moroccan patrol boats.

The Spanish Police had been able to place a tracking device on board when it was docked in Alicante.

On the Monday morning I had a phone call from a Lieutenant in the Moroccan Gendarmerie in Casablanca.

'I have somebody here called Bob in our custody who needs to talk to you urgently.

Bob came on the phone. 'We've been arrested,' he said. 'But there's no drugs on board. No drugs were picked up.'

'If you have no drugs, they're can't be a problem.'

'They found a tracker. The Gendarmes are asking me about it.'

'Put me back to the Lieutenant.'

I explained that the tracker was part of an operation sanctioned in Spain that did not include the yacht going into Moroccan waters.

Thankfully he did accept my explanation. 'If this happens again,' he said, 'call me direct. If you don't take the official route your operation could be compromised.'

Bob was let go and he later returned to Spain. He wasn't compromised so returned to work soon after.

I had kept my Assistant Chief Investigation Officer, Ken Paterson up to date. His thoughts were that we had to avoid a diplomatic incident so I may have to fly to our Embassy in Rabat to put pressure on and sort it out. Thankfully, my conversation with the Moroccan Gendarmerie resolved a potentially a difficult diplomatic incident and I didn't have to go to Rabat.

I have changed the name of the informant to protect his identity. He provided invaluable information to me for over 10 years which led to tons of cannabis and numerous arrests in the UK, Gibraltar and Spain.

One such seizure of about half a ton of cannabis had been stashed in one of the many tunnels within the rock of Gibraltar. I drove with the Gibraltar Customs to the location I had been given. After an hour searching the tunnels at the side of one of the main roads, we found the cannabis. Although there were no arrests at the time, examination of CCTV cameras identified potential suspect vehicles and drugs were prevented from entering Europe and the UK.

My tour of duty in Lisbon was for a fixed period of three years but a few months before I was due back, I received a call from London to see whether I would be willing to go straight from Lisbon to Miami to fill a vacancy. I didn't need to speak to Pauline as I knew what her answer would be. We would have jumped at the chance.

Unfortunately, for me at least, the Trade Unions had to give their agreement to all postings and they ruled the Miami post, along with other overseas posts had to be through an open competition. In addition, the Investigation Division rules confirmed returning DLOs should go back to frontline work for two years before being posted again.

In January 1990 an advert for posts at a Senior Officer (Team Leader) within the wider Customs and Excise Department came out. As with most Civil Service positions the opportunities are open to all Higher Officers. I completed an application form and waited to see whether I was successful in the paper sift. In the pre-email era I received a typed letter advising me I had been successfully sifted and would have to undergo the next phase, an interview. My interview was set for the 10th of May, just two days after we had arrived back in the UK.

We really enjoyed our time in Portugal and we had many visitors, particularly my parents who came over to see their grandchildren whenever they could.

We were all in the Embassy one Saturday and my dad Alex was playing with the boys throwing a plastic football. I noticed his shirt had a green scuff mark on the shoulder. I said, 'Did you fall over?'

'No,' he replied, 'the ball went over the Embassy's next-door neighbour's wall and I climbed over to retrieve it.'

'What! That is the private residence if the Iranian Ambassador and it's crawling with armed security guards.'

Dad's answer was typical. 'It's just a ball.'

I couldn't tell anybody in the Embassy as I suspected our security was exhaustively tested by our own protection people. I thought at the time they should use my Dad for future assessments.

Chris Harrison was appointed to replace me and we had a couple of weeks handover period where I introduced him to my contacts and informants. I still was able to manage Bob from London as he no longer lived in Portugal but had access to the maritime community in Spain. He continued to pass on intelligence and I met him on several occasions in the UK and Spain.

On the 5th May 1990 my parents came over to Lisbon and flew with our sons back home. Pauline and I started packing.

On the day I left Portugal, Loius, Machado, Jose, Mario, Machada and the German liaison officer, Herbert Baur turned up at the Embassy and presented me with a box of Pastais de Belem, the famous Portuguese custard tarts. I was really touched by this thought.

The day after, the 6th of May, Pauline and I said our goodbyes to Lisbon, stayed one night in Guarda in north east Portugal and drove up through Spain in the official Sierra (Chris had obtained a replacement). We took the 24-hour ferry from Santander to Plymouth, the exact reverse of the trip I made in 1987.

Within days of arriving back in the UK I was at Wembley Stadium with my brother-in-law Brian, watching Crystal Palace in the FA Cup final against Manchester United. I was a season ticket holder for a number of years at Selhurst Park, mainly during the bleak years and it was great to see them reach a major final.

At full-time it was three all and the replay was scheduled for the following week. Brian was at work and I volunteered to go to Wembley to queue up for tickets. Once again Pauline stepped in to supervise the delivery of our personal effects from Portugal. After 3 hours queuing at Wembley, I secured the tickets and returned home. I lost a few Brownie points that day and Palace lost the replay.

CHAPTER 18
PROMOTION. MY FIRST AND LAST ADVENTURE ON THE HIGH SEAS.

Our heads were spinning. There were so many things to think about, not least the move back into our home and sorting out a school for the boys.

I attended the interview for Senior Officer at Harmsworth House in London. It was conducted by a panel of three, none of whom were part of the Investigation Division. It consisted of a person from Human Resources, one from headquarters and two from the general Customs and Excise area.

After the initial introductions I was asked, 'What was your greatest achievement in the last 12 months?'

That really fell well for me. I described opening up the office in Lisbon, having to learn and work in a foreign language, assimilating a different culture, working with people who had received training that differed greatly from my own. I detailed a number of operations, including facilitating controlled deliveries (allowing drugs intercepted in Portugal to carry on its journey to the UK.) and hosting visiting Foreign Office Officials and police officers. I also made a point of successfully achieving a good working relationship with the Ambassador and Embassy staff.

The interview was 30 minutes long which flashed by.

Later in the day in the Custom House I met one of my colleagues from Manchester, a chap called Alan Ward who was also faced with the same interview panel. Alan was a real character.

We chatted about the interview and I asked him how his interview went.

'Did they ask you about your greatest achievement?' said Alan.

'They did.'

'What did you say?'

'I've just got back from a posting in Portugal. I told them about that. What did you say Alan?'

'I told them my greatest achievement was my Crown Removal from London to Manchester. (A Crown Removal is where a government employee is moved from one part of the UK to another. It gives government departments the flexibility to move officials to where the work is. All costs, such as solicitor's fees, stamp duty and removal costs are paid for officially. I was able to secure a Crown Removal when I transferred from Birmingham to London.)

Alan thought the panel were not impressed with his answer.

We did have a chuckle but thought Alan's reply wouldn't help his cause. I found out later he didn't get the promotion he was after. What a surprise!

The move back to the UK was quite an undertaking. I had little knowledge of changes within investigation and the Criminal Justice System during the time I had been away. Long-established procedures having been scrapped and modernised. Rules were replaced by the guidelines of the Police and Criminal Evidence Act of 1984.

The Investigation Division was one of the lead law enforcement agencies to trial the use of tape-recording suspect interviews.

I suspected that role duties and responsibilities could have been turned upside down by unknown fresh faces with unknown fresh ideas. Would I like them? Would they like me? Would I fit in and be able to follow a path I knew suited me best.

I decided to start using up my holiday entitlements so we could move back into our house and get the boys settled into schools.

I thought that having worked abroad in a British Embassy any red tape on returning to home shores would be kept to minimum. I had been taxed on my income as if I had been a UK resident and settled a shortfall on my National Insurance contributions. The Council Tax for our house was paid for during our absence.

I went along to the Education Department in Croydon explained that we had just returned from Portugal and that we wanted our children to start school as soon as possible.

The lady in charge gave me a disbelieving stare. 'It's not that straightforward,' she said.

'What do you mean by that?' I asked

Her reply was such a shock that it took me seconds to recover. 'Your children will have to be tested to see if they can speak English properly.'

'Hang on a minute,' I said. 'I've been working for the British Government. Look at my records. All taxes have been paid regularly including National and local council tax. I've already paid money toward your Education Department.'

As my blood rose to the point of spitting feathers her demeanour didn't change at all – a happening that only increased my rage. I suspect I would have made matters worse had I not previously realised we lived on the border between Kent and Surrey (about two hundred yards from the Kent border). This, I had been advised, entitled me to apply to a different Education Authority in Bromley.

Thank goodness the Bromley Authority were accommodating, admitting our boys into a school in West Wickham with the assistance of a headmaster who couldn't have been more helpful. The school was about a mile away from our house in Addington Village. Our youngest went to a nearby nursery school.

I was enjoying being on leave at this point knowing that the 9th July was my return date to work.

Hugh Donagher, a close colleague and friend, had a holiday home in the south of France so as soon as we could we drove down spending three weeks there.

Procedures at work had indeed changed. Familiar personnel had left or moved on. The atmosphere, the bon ami, the feeling of belonging from my time in the 70s and early 80s, had vanished and it was like my first day in a new school.

Terry Byrne had moved up the ladder to become the Deputy Chief Investigation Officer in charge of all the drugs operational and intelligence teams. Nick Baker, Mike Knox, Chris Hardwick – all the colleagues I had previously worked with had moved on and replaced by fresh faces from the Bravos and Charlies – the teams where my heart lay, and do so even to this day.

The years 1978 to 1982, prior to moving to Birmingham, were halcyon days for me and it was a passionate (perhaps foolish) wish to recapture those days.

However, I was delighted to see that George Atkinson was still part of the Charlies having been promoted to Senior Investigating Officer. He was Charlie One. George was keen for me to re-join the team.

The office was the same but the majority of the team were new. For the first time Bs and Cs had female officers, Liz Haines, Lesley Martin and Janette Lawson. However, my initial apprehension was short lived and the new team made me so welcome. The girls quickly proved they were "one of the chaps" and were brilliant surveillance officers and ones you would be happy to go through a front door with.

Large drug trafficking groups were still the main targets including a die-hard south London gang led by Tony White. White was interviewed and charged with activities linked with the Brinks Mat robbery at Heathrow Airport but later acquitted at trial.

Like many of his associates, he concentrated his efforts on drug smuggling which became his main activity and source of income. Both Customs and Police had intelligence on White and for the Bs and Cs he was number one target. Along with John Zanelli and Stephen Dalligan, both career criminals, they moved from robberies to smuggling. They all lived in the Bromley area. Zanelli lived in Keston two miles from where I lived, and a few hundred yards from where my boys went to school.

I recall looking at the school list of pupils to see if any surnames corresponded with our list of villains. Thankfully I found none.

It took me a few weeks to understand the new ways of doing things and get back to target work. I remember getting a phone call from our intelligence teams on 21st of July about 6 o'clock in the morning to say could I go to Catford Railway Station where Tony White was meeting Zanelli and Dalligan.

So, I arrived there on this Saturday morning and hung around the railway station. As I smelt the damp air mixed with diesel fumes, I thought to myself that only a few weeks previously I was a "king" of Lisbon going with the British Ambassador to cocktail parties. I had no management in Lisbon, nobody telling me what to do and making all decisions, small and large, myself.

So, I was back doing the real work where uncertainty and patience ruled my day. Deemed to be a senior investigation officer I still had to get myself immersed in day-to-day target work which sometimes can be a boring and mind-numbing toil. To outsiders, sitting in a car watching a suspect house sounds exciting. After days and days, the shine certainly wears off.

At Catford railway station, White turned up in his Bentley convertible and got into a BMW driven by Zanelli. They sat talking for 20 minutes and both left in their own vehicles.

A lot of criminals liked to meet on open parkland, large areas where they cannot be watched closely. If they met in a café or pub they could be overheard. And distance is an enemy of incriminating photographs even with zoom lenses.

On the 28th of July we had an opportunity when Tony White had a meeting near a coffee house in Hyde Park near the Serpentine. We had four footmen in the area, dressed in very casual clothes. There were many joggers and walkers around so it wasn't too difficult to blend in. Things had moved on technically and the four of us had covert radios. The radio was clipped to my belt and a transposer sent a signal to a small ear piece. It took time to get used to it as I still thought the transmissions could be heard as they were so loud in my ear. The system had a range of about a quarter of a mile. Andy Devine, the case officer, Colin (Lou) Tennent and Andy (Lanky) Lawson) were the other footmen.

Keeping a sensible distance on the other side of the Serpentine, I followed Tony White. After a while, as I tried to inch closer, I recognised one of my ex-colleagues from the Lisbon Embassy. Charles Drace-Francis was a Deputy Head of Mission, second only to the Ambassador and he was a real eccentric.

As he approached, I realised I could not avoid him and he recognised me straight away. I started to talk to Charles on where he was working and living whilst listening to the radio transmissions. This provided me with excellent cover and if White had turned around to see who was in the vicinity, (lawbreakers have a habit of looking over their shoulders) he would not have seen anything to worry him.

We had a very complicated and bizarre conversation between myself, and Andy over the radio and Charles who thought everything I said applied to him. There were a few "sorrys", "pardons" and "I didn't get that".

Eventually I managed to get across to Charles that I was actually working and communicating with another officer. He stood back mumbled some sort of goodbye and marched away.

As we carried on watching, Tony White met up with two other potential suspects. We didn't know who they were but Lou managed to take some photographs. The meeting ended after one hour and the suspects left the area. As with all target operations, observations and photographs are collated to build up the evidential picture.

My informant, Bob, in southern Spain, was in regular contact having responded to tasks I set him regarding off-beat behaviour of individuals or yachts. I would forward details to our intelligence team who would flag up any possible illegal connections however tenuous. I knew from day one Bob would prove to be a stellar informant, but also knew he had to be on a short rein, for his and our welfare.

On the 10th August George Atkinson, my SIO team leader called me into his office closing the door to would be eavesdroppers.

'As part of Operation Bacardi,' said George, 'Tony White, Zanelli, Dalligan and so on - we've come across an off-shoot concerning a ton of cannabis from Morocco to the UK. A Customs undercover officer had been approached by the crime group to provide a boat to pick up the goods and sail it back to the Plymouth/Brixham area.'

This was a Bravo/Charlie operation but it was news to me. Although as Charlie 4 and a senior member of the team, I understood that I was not told about every element of an operation.

'It's been on a need-to-know basis,' George continued. 'The case officer knows, of course. The solicitors who gave the okay for the operation and me.'

George filled in the detail. Three of my colleagues, from other teams, acted as crew on the yacht that sailed from the UK, via France and Spain to the coast of Morocco where they would take the drugs aboard. All three were experienced sailors (two of them had worked on the Cutter fleet).

The caveat from our lawyers was that unless urgent, they should remain in international waters for the whole of the journey. Diplomatic incidents with France, Spain and Morocco were to be avoided. Although, George told me, the French were aware of our activities.

'The yacht hit bad weather,' said George. 'The steering has been damaged and some sails ripped. So, the yacht limped into Leixoes, the marina in Porto.'

'So, Jim,' George added, 'we want you to go back to Portugal to make sure there are no problems with the police or authorities.'

'Chris Harrison is out there,' I said.

'Chris has just arrived. You know the ropes. You've got the contacts. They know and trust you. If things go wrong Chris would be in a difficult position. It could threaten his post as liaison officer.'

The next three hours were taken up driving home, stuffing a bag of over-night clothes and arriving at Heathrow to catch a flight to Lisbon.

I was met in Lisbon by Chris Harrison and we drove directly to Leixoes where we met up with the skipper of the yacht. The skipper, Dave Randles, had been working undercover with the crime group for several months. Dave Ross and John Manley made up the crew. They were all undercover customs officers from the Investigation Division. John Manly had to return to the UK for domestic reasons and was due to be replaced by Nigel Eccles. For different reasons Dave was unable to go any further on the yacht.

I telephoned George in London. 'We have a problem,' I said. 'We're down to two crew including Nigel, who has just arrived in Portugal.'

'Paul Dunne can crew, Trapper. I'll try and get him to join you.'

I pointed out that it would be too late. The vessel had to leave that night so that it could meet up with another vessel at Start Point near Plymouth as arranged on the 18 August 1990.

As we sat at a bar trying to find a way around the problem of man power Dave asked me if I was willing to sail back with them.

'We need three crew,' he said. 'We've got to have three crew.'

'I've never been on a yacht in my life, I said. 'I could be sea sick. The only time I've been on water was on a pedalo off the coast of Wales.'

'It'll be a piece of cake,' said Harry.

Dave Ross interrupted: 'If you go on this boat, you're mad. It was the worst nightmare I've ever had.'

I was in quite a quandary in spite of Harry's assurances.

We had a bite to eat early that evening. Dave confirmed that the yacht had been sorted out, the ripped sails repaired, the faulty steering gear replaced so everything was good to go.

I pulled him aside. 'Dave,' I said. 'I want you to be perfectly honest with me. Is it safe for the journey?'

'Look,' he replied. 'I wouldn't be on it if it wasn't safe.'

I called George who said he would like me to speak to Terry Byrne. He was the Deputy Chief in charge of the drugs operational and intelligence teams in the UK.

Terry had been briefed on the situation. Niceties were kept to the minimum.

'If you don't go,' he said, 'I'll fully understand – but if you do go on the yacht I'll be delighted. It's been a big investment for all of us.'

'Got it,' I said.

I then called Pauline.

'Are you coming back tomorrow?' she asked.

'No, not tomorrow.'

'When are you coming back?'

'I don't know.'

'Will you give me a ring when you know.'

'I won't be able to ring you either. George Atkinson will call with an update and assure you I'm all right.'

Obviously, Pauline was wary of what was going to happen.

'I'll be okay,' I pressed. 'It's just an operation we've got to keep under wraps. It's important and I can't talk about it on the phone.'

We spent the next few hours stocking up as best we could with food and drink. This mainly consisted of the basics, drinking water, tinned fish and vegetables, pasta and potatoes from the local bar. At 10 o'clock in the evening we sailed out of the harbour.

It was quite interesting because some of the Portuguese police officers who I knew really well saw I was climbing aboard staring with disbelief. It may have confirmed something they thought all along that this Englishman had a touch of crazy about him.

There was a Mexican stand-off with the Guarda Fiscal (similar to the Guarda Civil in Spain). Both were border control military. They had aspirations to arrest everyone concerned and stick two fingers up to the Federal Police. The Federal Police who were the lead police force took them aside and over-ruled any hostile act but we all felt their eyes looking daggers at us as we sailed out of the west coast of Portugal toward the Atlantic Ocean.

The yacht, a 32-foot "Rival", was not luxurious by any stretch of the imagination. There were two cabins in the forward part, one of which had two bunks. I took the top bunk which was tiny for somebody who is 6' 3". I couldn't stretch out fully and it was very narrow. Nigel was in the bunk below. There was a small cooking stove in the galley and Harry was the main cook. I was happy to prepare what little vegetables we had and wash up with cold sea water. The ton of herbal cannabis was placed in a storage area which we named the "Queens Warehouse" after the secure location within the Custom House in London. It was really claustrophobic in such a small space and at night it got cold. My clothes were permanently damp as at sea there is nowhere to dry wet clothing. Personal hygiene fell by the wayside as water was rationed and used for drinking only. We gave thanks the night was calm and uneventful and at 8 o'clock the next morning I stood looking at the vast expanse of sea as if I were on a holiday cruise. The sun was shining and it was warm and dry and the sea was calm.

Early evening Dave called me over. 'It's now your watch.'

'What do you mean it's my watch?'

'It's your turn to steer the boat. It's not under sail. Its straightforward. Just keep the boat heading in this direction as he pointed to the compass (that I recognised at least). Keep an eye out for containers that have fallen off ships. Fishing boats with no lights. Give me a shout if there's a problem.'

Dave and Nigel disappeared into the cabin and I was left gripping the steering wheel as if the whole British Maritime industry depended on the course I was setting. It was getting dark but the weather was mild.

The yacht was not a large boat by any means, its size shrunk to almost nothing by the distant views in front, behind and to the sides. It had over 400 square feet of sails, 2 cabins and could sleep six.

We had a roster of 2 hours on, 4 hours off for the whole journey back to Plymouth.

On my watch during the evening, I started glimpsing lights ahead. I had no idea what lay ahead and I couldn't determine if the lights were static or moving or, worst of all, moving towards us.

I shouted, 'Dave, Dave! There are some lights ahead.'

Dave sleepily but rapidly arrived at my side. He stared at the lights, yawned and said, 'Not to worry. They're four hours away.'

As well as aching hands and arms from gripping the wheel my eyes were watering as I constantly saw shapes in the waves that could have been an up-turned container diving and surfacing in the waves.

We were heading in the direction of the Bay of Biscay. For four days I saw nothing, no ships, flotsam or jetsam, no seagulls, no sardines, no anchovies, no mackerel - fish that the Bay is famous for. The feeling of isolation was incredible. We could have been on any ocean in any part of the world, miles from land, completely out of any comfort zone. If you were in trouble there was no-one to reach out to.

All these were thoughts of a typical land-lubber and not, thank goodness, thoughts that crossed Dave's mind. He would regularly tune into shipping forecasts. Vital information that covered the weather of the next few days however experienced a sailor you were.

Halfway across the Bay we encountered force 4 or force 5 winds, not considered turbulent enough for concern, but scary for me. As the yacht started to list 15 to 20 degrees I tensed up and gripped onto anything to hand. At times, a large wave reared up and bucked the boat it seemed as if we were about to be swallowed up. But the boat did its job. Every twist and turn were followed by an automatic balancing procedure, rehearsed thousands of times. It took me quite a while and many bucks to convince myself we were not about to be swept out to sea. I'd never considered drowning as my route out of this life so, as I clung on with all the strength I could muster, I didn't mull over the possibility.

One night, during Dave's watch I tossed and turned on my top bunk. I couldn't sleep. Nigel, on the other hand, snored and snorted his journey on the bunk below me.

I must have eventually fallen asleep as I was rudely awoken by a loud scream and a muddled shout. 'The boats on fire!'

As I sat up, I cracked my head on the ceiling and I immediately saw streaks of light and stars, stars in my head and flashes in the dark cabin.

My head still clanging like an out of tune bell the situation became crystal clear in my mind. We were on a boat in the middle of the Bay of Biscay with no help to hand and our boat was on fire. All the water around us and we were going to burn to death.

I half fell to the deck as Nigel shouted again, 'Fire, fire.'

Dave appeared in the cabin, looked around, looked at me then stared at Nigel still fast asleep. I then saw the torch in Dave's hand, that flashed its beam as he steadied himself.

'It's this,' Dave said. 'It was the light off my torch flickering. I turned the cabin's light off. Nigel's having a nightmare.'

So am I, I thought. I tried to recall the exact moment I agreed to come on this voyage or what was going on in my brain when I did so. I've made a few mistakes in my life but none seemed as calamitous as this present one.

A lighter note came the next morning at 4 o'clock. It was my watch as the day started. As I stared and stared at nothing in particular an unusual shape appeared about half a mile away. Suddenly the shape zoomed out the water in a perfectly formed arc. It was a whale diving, flapping its tail as it did so. I was amazed at the sight. I'd never seen or expected to see such a phenomenon in real life. In pictures, yes, but nothing had come close to watching it for real.

'Look,' I shouted.

By the time Dave arrived the whale had submerged but I had to share my experience. 'It was a whale, a giant whale, magnificent.'

He took a cursory glance at the ocean. 'Probably a beaked whale. Hundreds around here, perhaps thousands.'

We had spent nine days travelling and our stocks of biscuits, tinned beef and vegetables, tinned fish and rice were limited. To bathe we threw a roped bucket over the side and haul it up. This went a little way to feel washed.

Our unwashed clothes had begun to deteriorate early on. What fabric there was left smelt horribly. I wore a pair of slacks, a T-shirt and a jumper and not shaving for two weeks completed my fashion looks. I was sure it would not catch on.

The "Searcher", one of the UK's Customs Cutters, had flagged us up near the Brest Peninsular and had tracked our progress from a distance.

We arrived off Start Point, 20 miles off Plymouth on July 10 at early evening and followed our instructions to anchor down and wait for radio contact from a fishing boat that would be ready to depart from Brixham. We would meet them in international waters twenty miles from the coast to hand over the drugs. Our story would be that we would directly sail back to Spain and transport another cargo of drugs.

We waited hours for the call. We were really tense waiting for the radio to crackle into life, but to no avail. We sat around drinking tea and "swinging the lamp" about drugs jobs and the characters we worked with.

At this distance from land, I thought I may be able to get a signal on the boat's mobile phone. I climbed a few feet up the main mast and managed to get just two reception bars.

I managed to get through to George and I am not sure who was more elated; him knowing we had arrived safely or me knowing my ventures were coming to an end. He told me that a fishing boat had been identified as the one destined to meet us. Although the crew were around there was no sign that the vessel was about to move. The Bravos and Charlies were watching the boat day and night, seeing who was onboard and gathering evidence.

'The forecast is bad tonight,' said George. 'If you have to come into land at Plymouth, you can. The weather is too bad for the Cutter and they will be going into port but they'll be keeping radar cover on you'.

I had a quick chat with Dave and Nigel and we were in complete agreement. 'That may wreck the operation,' I said. 'We've come all this way. We'll ride the weather out.'

In the evening the winds indeed got up and the sea increasingly choppy. It was a topsy turvy night with no calls from shore. We continued with the two hours on four hours off watches. Despite the rough conditions I managed to get some rest.

We remained at the same location for all of the next day and none of us slept and the nerves started to kick in again. On one occasion we were killing time and had the main sail up. I was at the wheel when there was a sudden strong gust of wind and the boat turned around.

Nigel shouted at me, 'We have just jibed'.

'I haven't a clue what you are talking about, are we going to sink?'

'No, but the wind has turned the boat around and was putting strain on the sail'.

I just shook my head and shrugged my shoulders.

As time went on, we were getting a bit despondent as we had heard nothing from George or the fishing boat. When the mobile phone did ring it made us all jump.

'The fishing boat had left the harbour and had gone out to sea,' said George.

It was game on and we listened avidly to the ship's radio. At 10 o'clock we were tuned in to Channel Sixteen, the basic channel for maritime users when a voice asked us to retune to another channel, channel 8.

The reception was very poor but we could just make out through the crackling sound, 'White Swan. White Swan. This is Blue Lady. Do you receive us?'

Dave replied. 'Blue Lady, Blue Lady, this is White Swan. We are receiving you. We are in position.'

About 20 minutes later we could see a search light on a moving vessel that was heading toward us.

We assumed that this boat was our contact so we started moving the bales of drugs from The Queen's Warehouse, one of the cabins used as storage. We heaved the sacks of drugs on deck.

We were buzzing and the adrenalin flow was difficult to contain. We were 20 miles out to sea holding drugs worth about half a million pounds on the street. An unknown number of villains were approaching on a boat. They could have a quantity of serious firearms at the ready. Back up was non-existent and the Cutter was about an hour away.

Unlike the movies Battleships were not steaming over the horizon, fighter jets were not being scrambled and Apache helicopters with cannon and guided missiles were not hovering overhead. The stakes were high for them and for us.

The fishing boat pulled alongside swinging back and forth with the swell. It was dark so we were relying on the floodlight on the fishing boat.

Dave was aggressive with them. 'Where the fuck have you been? You were supposed to have been here last night.'

'You yachties are all the same,' was the surprising reply. 'You can't take a bit of rough weather.'

They all burst out laughing but we maintained our displeasure which helped with our cover. We wanted to act how smugglers would behave.

A few words were shared that included a number of expletives.

Formalities over, they threw a securing line which modified the movement so we were able to hand over the bales from our boat to theirs.

As they were so close, I picked up a 25-kilo bale and threw it onto the deck, narrowly avoiding the wheel-house. Not sure what their reaction would have been if I had broken a window but thankfully, it just bounced on the deck.

It took us 15 minutes to transfer all the drugs.

In the arrangement that had been set up by Harry and the crime group, they were supposed to supply us with enough water and food to get us back to Spain.

They handed over a carrier bag containing a loaf of bread, butter, a pint of milk, six eggs and bacon rashers.

'Where's the rest?' asked Dave. 'We can't get back to Spain on this.'
'Yea,' was the reply. 'That's all we could get.'

Dave had planned to hand over a bottle of brandy as a good will gesture but good will instantly vanished.

There were no goodbyes. They unfastened the rope, drifted off and started their engine. We watched as they disappeared into the darkness.

Our instructions from the investigators were to sail onto Cherbourg where we were going to meet up with the French Customs Investigation Service who had been kept informed of the operation's progress. It was they who had sourced the supply of the yacht.

From being on an adrenalin high it was almost an anti-climax to know the delivery had taken place.

As calm descended, we decided to open the bottle of brandy we were going over to hand over to the fishing boat to celebrate. All of the things that could have gone wrong didn't, and we were safe (but still on a small yacht on the high seas). Although we avoided back-slapping we all relished the success. The brandy bottle was empty after 20 minutes, time spent giggling, a little singing, all done as we crossed one of the busiest shipping lanes in the world.

We arrived in Cherbourg's marina the next day expecting to meet the French Customs Investigation Service (DNRED). The marina was fairly busy with yachts and we could not find a berth. We eventually moored up alongside another yacht. There are certain protocols within the yachting world and Nigel had to ask the other yacht's skipper to tie up alongside.

We waited for about twenty minutes and to our horror we could see uniformed French Customs heading towards us. They came on board and obviously had no idea of who we were and what we were doing.

They carried out their checks, looking at passports. Harry and Nigel had new passports in different names with no stamp. Mine had plenty suggesting I was rather more than a leisure sailor. Stamps included Thailand, Venezuela as well as southern Europe.

They asked for a copy of the ship's log. Dave knew that I had put it up my jumper as we didn't want the uniformed officers to see it.

Our arrest was minutes away when six plain clothed officers from the French Investigation Department pulled alongside in two cars and quickly jumped on deck.

The uniformed officers were told to leave as the affairs of this yacht were covered by higher authorities.

We eventually made our way off the yacht onto dry land. I broke another unwritten rule and did not ask permission to cross over the yacht we were moored next to.

Nigel admonished me and I replied, 'Piss off, Nigel, I just want to get off this boat'.

I, like many novice sailors, started crabbing, with no ability to walk in a straight line. I aimed in one direction but veered in another.

Dave and Nigel fell about laughing and it took me 24 hours to get my land legs back.

We were taken to a hotel for the night enjoying our first shower and shave for ten days though I did that after I had phoned Pauline who told me that George had called her daily to say all was well. We had to keep our clothes that were close to falling apart, the seams just about holding. But a shower and a shave, with a hotel supplied razor, made us feel so much better.

The freshly cooked hotel food was extraordinary, my taste buds bursting back into life having been by-passed by the poor mainly tinned food we had consumed aboard.

The next day we were taken to Cherbourg Airport where the three of us boarded a French Customs surveillance plane to Bournemouth Airport.

Colin Tennant, from the Bravos and Charlies, picked me up.

On the way back to London he said, 'Jim, you've just missed a fantastic job. We've had a yacht come up from Morocco met by a fishing boat from Brixham to pick up drugs. We watched them land the drugs and load into a van. We followed them to Exeter Services where they waited for people from London, Liverpool and Scotland. We nabbed them all as they were divvying up the drugs.'

I was still obligated to keep all the facts to myself.

'Yes,' I said. 'I was away on an operation with the French.'

(It was a few days later when Colin twigged as to my involvement in the case.)

Over time people asked me if we had a legal basis to carry out and participate in the operation. I assured them that everything had been run by our official solicitor and given the okay providing we remained in international waters.

The villains were found guilty of importing drugs into the UK receiving sentences of 4 to 6 years. Others were charged with "intent to supply".

I have once been on a yacht since that time. Alan, a friend and neighbour, owns a yacht in Woodbridge. I have been out with him but thankfully it was only on the River Deben and certainly not out to the high seas. A short trip, thank goodness.

I was back at work a couple of days later. My yachting clothes were consigned to the dustbin. The main "Operation Bacardi" continued and a man called Robert Mills, a well-known drug smuggler in the 70's and 80's, came on the scene. He had a close association with Tony White. His home was in Bermondsey just over the Thames from Customs House. We would walk over to observe him at home or down the local pub to see if we could pick up something or observe him meeting other suspects. Mills had a mobile home in the Hastings area.

We had been in Hastings when Mills met up with a person who, through car number plates checks turned out to be the owner of a fishing boat in Hastings.

Hastings is very distinctive in that it has no marina. Boats are dragged by machine and chain up the shingle beach to the fisherman's huts where the fish is processed.

We singled out a boat to keep an eye on, its movements, its crew, its visitors. We also wanted to establish the limits of their fishing trips, logging routines, noting anything unusual.

A house in Hastings, owned by Valery Strachan, the Chairman of The Board of Customs, was made available to us. Negotiations higher up the chain of command enabled us to gain entry to her house whenever we needed to.

Observations continued in Hastings and Bermondsey. The evidence against White, Dalligan and Zanelli was accumulating.

On the 20th October, in the Blackheath area of London we were expecting Tony White to meet up with Dalligan. Two weeks previously Dalligan had been shot in a London night-club. Five bullets entered his body but none proved fatal. He was compos enough to instruct the attending police for the bullets to remain in his possession, effectively removing a vital piece of evidence. His argument was they had come out of his body and as such the police could not take them away. Like most criminal groups they have their own methods of discovering who the perpetrators were and how to deal with them.

Blackheath Park is a large area of common land covering over 210 acres, an open expanse that made close surveillance impossible. We were able to gain entry to the Park Ranger's house and set up our cameras on the roof.

Through binoculars we could easily identify White and Dalligan. The fact that two suspects met up in the middle of nowhere did show intent to avoid scrutiny. It could add relevant evidence to a bigger picture.

We were all dressed for the late October cold weather and it was freezing on the roof. Heavy coats, gloves and bobble hats proved to be inadequate.

Dalligan however, was not feeling the cold. He strolled across the grass in a short-sleeved shirt and a light pair of trousers. A hardy fellow, we decided, as well as a ruthless one. Just 14 days after five bullets had been fired at his body from short range he sauntered and chatted along at White's side not needing to rest or catch his breath. The photographs and observations were recorded as evidence against the group.

In the time I spent in Portugal a number of changes had taken place in our department including a range of new surveillance vehicles and a fresh look at terminology, intended to thwart any unwanted insight into our minute by minute, hour by hour endeavours. We no longer used overt conversations on the radio stating actual road names or directions to colleagues. You now couldn't say, 'Back of the White Swan pub down The Old Kent Road.'

A surveillance system primarily used by the military in Northern Ireland was introduced. These advanced techniques were completely different to the training I had received.

I was sent on an Advanced Technique course on the 1st to the 17th of November. For me it was a real culture shock. I felt I had accumulated some expertise on surveillance. Replacing street names and junctions we had an Ordinance Survey map book that had been adapted for the departments specific purpose. A junction would have a red spot with a number. A roundabout could have a green spot with the number 7. So that roundabout whose name was known to everyone in the area was now "Green 7".

Should a spot and number be missing you would give a map reference number using the OS map. For those of us who were so used to the old system this new way of working was rather difficult. For me it seemed a bit showy. You had to have two people in the car, one to drive and one to map read. Instead of, 'the vehicle is on the A4 heading West towards Cardiff', you would make the call, 'vehicle 9 – one, green – 7.'

For short distances we had two map books, more for longer journeys. Giving correct grid numbers was vital so continuous concentration was needed, so much so that I, for one, was worried that there was little focus on other matters. For large groups of villains some sort of anti-surveillance measure was used. You were following someone but you had to ask if someone was following you. From day one in the service, we knew that a wide-ranging grasp of your surroundings was central to any quick decision you may have to make. I, like many of my colleagues had to make the best of it.

The police had their own systems in place, differing dramatically from the one Customs were now using. This, of course, did prove problematic in joint operations. Their "spots" their "colours" their "references" were unrelated to ours.

The new Vauxhall Cavalier motor-cars looked like your average family saloon but the works under the bonnet had been souped up with 2000cc engines. Ideal for our work, common-place on the outside, unique and surprising on the inside.

One type of vehicle, (nick-named the Star Fighter) stood out as it contradicted our ideas of a basic, unadorned mode of transport that no one would give a second look. Five 2.8cc fuel injection Ford Capris were purchased, light silver/blue in colour. They were so gaudy you could see the gaudiness before you saw the car itself. I was less than impressed with the department head who bought these for a largely covert division. Probably they were purchased by some Investigation "boy racer" who enjoyed being seen in the car.

In April 1991 I was asked to join a surveillance team in the Clapham/Brixton area of London. I went to our resources cupboard where a "pouch" would be found containing keys for one of our cars and discovered only one – keys for a Ford Capri. I made enquires and was told that was it, the Capri or nothing.

'Starfighters are go!' I shouted as I sped off to an address where a Scottish suspect, Robert McCloud, was staying. McCloud was a "heavy" from Glasgow and known as an enforcer for the criminal underworld. Checks with the police in Scotland revealed he had been charged but acquitted for murder in Glasgow.

McCloud was driving a Ford Granada along Wandsworth Road towards Brixton and pulled in at the side of a pub. I was a couple of cars behind so I drove past the pub for a half a mile, turned left into a cul-de-sac and spun around.

A call came over the radio from one of the Bs and Cs officers. 'He's started his engine . . . he has lifted off and heading in the same direction towards London . . he's coming your way.'

As I stared ahead, ready to drive off, I couldn't believe McCloud had turned into the cul-de-sac and driving towards me. He parked across the road twenty yards ahead. I locked the doors, turned my radio off as two men got out of the car and walked toward me.

'Are you following us?' A burly bloke said.

'No,' I said.

'Yes, you are and you're fucking useless at it.'

'I don't know what you mean. I'm not following you.'

'Get out of the car!'

'No, I'm not getting out.'

With that I slipped the gear into first, accelerated and mounted the kerb as I did so.

I reached the Wandsworth Road as they ran back to their car. I had no idea if they carried weapons so I put my foot down along the main road, breaking all the speed limits, thankful I was driving the Capri. Reaching 80 mph along the road I was sure I wouldn't be caught.

Later, as I approached our garage in Harmsworth House, I radioed into Control, 'Control, this is Charlie 4. Please contact Harmsworth House and get them to open the garage door. I need instant access. I need it quick.'

Even though I hadn't spotted McCloud's car in my mirror I drove as fast as conditions allowed until I was safely inside the compound, sighing a big sigh as I turned the engine off.

McCloud did not figure again on our operation. I can only assume it was too hot for him in London and with my showing out he was persuaded to return to Scotland.

On the 15th July I was with a colleague, Roly Garrick a jovial Geordie and a real character, on the way to help Hampshire police search a property in Bournemouth. It was thought that there might be a link to a drug importation that happened a few weeks before.

We had been told to get a move on so on the M3, the Capri primed and ready, Roly said, 'I wonder how fast this thing can go.'

'There's only one way to find out,' I replied.

Ahead was a totally clear road so I slammed down on the accelerator pedal with swift glances at the speedometer. I eased off after the reading told me we were travelling at 130 miles per hour.

Obviously, we exceeded the speed limit of 70mph and all went smoothly until I started to apply the brakes. It did slow but as it did so the back end of the car started swaying and only stopped when we reached normal speeds. Both Roly and I were pleased we had tried it out but both of us decided once was enough. I still didn't like the car and after a couple of years they were replaced with conventional, dull cars such as Vauxhall Cavaliers and Ford Sierras, ideal for surveillance work.

On the 30th May 1991 the Tony White element of Operation Bacardi was coming to fruition. Andy Devine (his nickname was Big Daddy) was the case officer and it was his job to pull all the evidence of observations together.

I was nominated by George Atkinson as the arresting officer for Tony White. He lived just off Catford one-way system. Part of his life was taken up by the wine bar he owned with his wife Margaret called, Biancos in Catford.

White and Zanelli had been observed at a lorry park in Kent which was suspected of being used to build concealments to smuggle drugs into the UK. The evidence against them was strong particularly when a lorry arrived in the park and a ton of cannabis unloaded. This was the event we were waiting for and it was decided by George and Andy to act.

The plan was to arrest him as soon as his location was established. Information reached us that he was inside his wine bar that evening. I had a briefing in Old Street Police Station from The Met's firearms team SO19, a group of incredibly brave officers who were brought in whenever there was the possibility of villains using guns. The Met team were one of the few teams at that time authorised to carry and use arms. They were sometimes compared to the SWAT units of the United States.

Just before 10pm four Range Rovers containing four officers and equipment in each approached the area. I was in one of them.

As this was a Customs operation, I had to be the legal arresting officer. The role of the SO19 team was the physical stop, restraint and securing of White himself.

Once White was constrained, I would caution him and he would be handed over to the Customs teams.

The four SO19 Range Rovers parked up in Catford's one-way system. Cedric Woodhall who was watching the entrance to Biancos radioed in to say that White's green Bentley convertible was parked outside the wine bar. We had decided not to arrest White inside the building to avoid a public disturbance but to wait until he left even though it was then pouring with rain.

A message came through that White had emerged and got into his car and was heading towards us.

The Range Rovers were started up and as soon as the Bentley appeared, they accelerated into a well-planned manoeuvre. I've rarely seen anyone move so fast. One second the officers were in the vehicles, the next they had surrounded White in staggered formation, their machine guns raised as if about to fire.

'Get out of the vehicle – now!' was shouted and repeated a few times.

I jumped onto the road as the Bentley's door opened.

My heart sank as out stepped Margaret White, Tony's wife.

Our man eye-balling the bar had mistakenly thought Mrs White, cloaked up against the driving rain, was White himself.

The traffic was stopped as I ran up to Mrs White's side and asked, 'Where's Tony?'

The reply was short. 'You can fuck off.'

'Where is he? We'll find him.'

'He's at home I will call him.'

'Give me the keys to your house.'

'I'm not giving you my fucking keys.'

A mobile phone was taken from her bag.

'Look,' I said. 'These people are going to your house. They're going in one way or another. Let's keep it calm and civilised. Give me the keys.'

She wasn't moved. 'Fuck off.'

A team of four secured Mrs White and the Bentley as the rest of us drove around to White's house just off the Bromley Road.

The house sat in a large plot behind a tall iron gate. This was scaled easily and the gate was opened up from the inside and I was beckoned in.

I heard the instruction, Armed police. Lie down. Lie down.'

As the front door came into view the police had already pinned Tony White to the ground wearing nothing more than his underpants.

I went up to White and told him who I was.

'We are investigating the importation of controlled drugs. You are under arrest.'

White was pulled to his feet and handcuffed. I cautioned him.

When I had done so he looked straight at me. 'Officer,' he said. 'Can I put some clothes on. I'm freezing.'

A policeman went into the house and retrieved a track-suit bottom, a jacket and a pair of shoes.

'Have you got any money in the house?' I asked.

'Yea. A bit of spending – pocket money.'

'Where is it?'

'Bedside cabinet.'

White was put into one of the vehicles and transported to Harmsworth House where he was interviewed by colleagues.

I went into the house and with the help of other officers conducted a search.

In the cupboard was about £4000 in cash. For me, a large amount of "spending money".

It was 6am in the morning when I had to drive the Bentley back to the Custom House trying to ignore the people who gawped at the sight of an open-topped luxury car purring leisurely down the road at break of day in bad weather.

White, Dalligan and Zanelli were charged with importation of drugs.

By the time the trial came around in February 1992 I had been posted to Brussels so I had to fly back to give evidence.

I had been promoted to SIO (Team Leader) but I had to leave investigation. Nick Baker and Mike Knox persuaded me to see my time on a secondment to the European Commission as a National Expert. I was to be the co-ordinator for the Customs Information System which was a messaging system. It was amusing to me as I had never used a computer.

White's trial was held in Croydon Crown Court and I managed to get a flight from Belgium at 06.30 to Gatwick and arrived in Croydon at 9.30am.

As I waited outside the Court, I was suddenly aware of a number of doubtful looking characters hanging around. I had a long white mac on to ward off the steady rain. As I strolled around outside the court-room I heard a voice say, 'He's one of them. They all wear "nonces" raincoats like that.'

Various swear words were uttered along with forced laughter.

I didn't look at them. I didn't move an inch. I wasn't going to be intimidated. I pulled myself up to my full 6'3" and pushed out my chest.

Tony White, who had been given bail at a previous court appearance at Croydon Crown Court, turned up at the courtroom with his wife. His followers, to a man, stood quiet and upright as if on parade.

As White walked past me, he spoke. 'Morning officer.'

'Morning, Mr White.'

I have no doubt that White or any of his followers would have knee-capped me at the drop of a hat even though his gesture would be seen as a bit of "gangster" class. A romantic view would be that we had respect for each other but there was none from me and I doubt White had showed respect to anyone during his life. He didn't get the nicknames "The Bull" and the "King of Catford" for his contributions to the local community. Zanelli, who also was on bail, failed to turn up for his trial which meant a lot of the evidence of association with White was not put forward. We were distraught that White was acquitted. His brother David and eventually, Zanelli, received 10 years in prison (reduced to nine after an appeal).

White moved into smuggling cocaine and a Customs case in 1996 he pleaded guilty to smuggling 21 kilos of cocaine through Dover, where he was sentenced and received eleven and a half years in prison.

He was one of nine smugglers sentenced to jail terms totalling 167 years for their parts in an international drugs ring aimed at flooding Britain with top-quality Colombian cocaine.

A few years after his release White was arrested in Spain in possession of 60 kilos of cocaine. He was on his way to his 60th birthday party organised by his wife Margaret. As the saying goes, "a leopard never changes its spots".

In 1992 Alan Huish (Charlie One) told me I had been successful at my interview to be a Senior Investigating Officer. This was good news as I was unsure how I had performed in front of a panel of three, made up from Headquarters and HR senior managers.

A few days later, Richard Henry Lawrence's secretary called me to arrange a meeting. Richard was "number one", the Chief Investigation Officer.

'Jim,' said Richard, 'You must have had a very impressive interview. Well done.'

'Thank you, Chief.'

'The panel chairman suggested your interview was so good we should put you forward as a fast-streamer,'

'They must be joking'.

'Funny that,' said Richard. 'That's exactly what I said to them!'

I wasn't upset by his comment as I always considered myself an operational frontline officer, feet on the ground, dirty hands. For some strange reason I always preferred my working days to have an uncomfortable edge to them.

The Civil Service fast stream process was designed for "bright youngsters" who were catapulted into a middle management position.

I have worked with some of the fast streamers who were academically sharp but most lacked common sense. As George Atkinson would say, 'I wouldn't send them out to buy fish and chips!'

In those days if you were promoted you had to take the higher-grade position in a different discipline; a Customs and Excise VAT office or an Airport. You were not allowed to remain in the investigation service. After a while, if you wished, you had to re-apply to be an investigator again.

The Civil Service and in particular the trade unions, were keen to avoid any suggestion the Investigation Division would look after their own and not open up opportunities to the wider department.

My friend and colleague Nick Baker had recently transferred to a European Fraud Team covering very expensive scams in agriculture and misrepresentation of grants application throughout consumer goods.

'Trapper,' said Nick.' 'There's a possibility the powers that be may want you to go to Brussels to work with the European Commission, based there as a national expert. Come to the office and we'll meet up with Mike Knox. Mike is the HM Customs and Excise senior liaison officer with the European Commission.'

Mike had been my Senior Officer in my early days on the Bravos and Charlies. He became an Assistant Chief and in the early nineties spending many years working with his European counterparts.

Mike Knox was waiting for me in Harmsworth House.

He came straight to the point. 'We'd like you to go over to Brussels. There's an EU-wide computer system being developed. It's to help combat Europe-wide crimes generated as a result of the free movement of goods and people.'

The system, Mike Explained, had been funded by DGXX1 the Customs and Indirect Taxation Unit of the Commission. There were nine Member States at this time and the proposed system would be put in Customs offices throughout the EU.

'We would like you to be the coordinator for this high-tech installation.'

I had to admit. 'I don't know anything about computers. I don't own a computer. I wouldn't know where to start.'

'That's not a problem,' said Mike. 'We want someone who understands the business. To look at what others are doing and assess if it works for us. A private technical company is building the system on behalf of the EU. There will be clear guidelines as to what the Commission could get involved in but the system is designed to provide an instant messaging system between all European Customs stations as regards drug smuggling and frontier fraud.'

I realised that if I took on the position it would mean moving abroad again with all that meant to family life although I was comforted by the fact that I would still be closely linked to the Investigation Division. As well as Mike Knox there was John Chapman and Nick Baker who had explained his interest in what Brussels was up to. I was keen not to divorce myself from the Investigation side of our business.

Later that day I approached Pauline. 'Look, we've got the opportunity of going abroad again, to Brussels.'

'Doing what?' asked Pauline.

'I'm going as a national expert on an EU wide computer system. I'll be promoted to Senior Officer and receive my salary directly from the Commission. All costs will be covered.'

There was a lot to think about. Our third child, Jimmy, born in April 1992 in Croydon, added to the weight of responsibilities.

We knew it would be a few months before we moved to Belgium so Pauline and I had some time to discuss yet another overseas undertaking. Our sons were still young and adaptable so the matter of changing schools was less intimidating than it would be when they were older – approaching important examinations. After much discussion over a few glasses of wine we decided I should take up the secondment for three years. We would live in Brussels although neither of us had been there.

Over the years I had met colleagues who had been seconded to Belgium to work with experts from many European countries who were working in different fields. Neither Pauline or I thought we were going into a complete unknown.

Curiously, it was a double-edged sword that I had been promoted. The requirement to leave the Investigation Division and join another Customs branch was, in a way, disheartening. The change would also mean the loss of the Investigation allowance which amounted to a quarter of my salary. In Investigation you did have unsociable hours and spend hours or days in inhospitable surroundings but the compensation payments for this had boosted the level of my income – a level I had got used to.

But this was how it worked. To achieve a higher-grade job, to start climbing the career ladder I had to move and face a cut in my pay. From day one I hoped that one day I would return to the Investigation Division. Many of my colleagues from Investigation had taken new roles only to be selected again in their old departments. Time varied but it usually took two years to return to investigation.

When I was offered the Brussels position, I had to admit that I was up for the challenge of working in a different law-enforcement environment although not a hands-on environment, not front-line operational work.

Obviously, the new duties set out by the European Commission was likely to be a cultural shock.

The department I was about to join was a customs and indirect taxation unit (taxes other than PAYE, Income Tax) Excise Duty, VAT, Customs Duty on Imports. The Indirect Taxation office was a large organisation. I didn't have a clue about the workings of the EU and the Commission but given the other challenges I have faced in my career it couldn't be that daunting...could it?

Throughout my career the "coal face" was always my chosen place of work. I had never sought a position that was mostly desk-bound, where the telephone and fax machine were my tools of trade, where the only crisis was the breakdown of a paper copying machine. Facts and figures were always a necessary evil. And statistics were a mysterious testimony designed to bamboozle the powers that be.

Statistics, drug smuggling statistics, were important but they never failed to remind us that for all the local successes we achieved, there were a whole world of criminal activities we had failed to detect and eradicate.

Drug cultivation, drug trafficking and drug usage was, of course, a global problem. In the mid-nineties an estimated 12.8 million Americans, about 6 per cent of the household population aged twelve and older, used illegal drugs on a regular basis.

USA Federal funding for the war on drugs reached $17.1 billion dollars a year. According to DEA estimates less than 10 percent of all illicit drugs were seized. (a 90% failure rate).

There were many estimates and guesstimates for the amount of illegal drugs that entering Europe. Billions of pounds were mentioned, vast amounts tripping off the tongue rather too easily.

In the United Kingdom the fight against the importation of illegal drugs had been broadened by units tackling tax and economic frauds, human trafficking and firearms. There was even an upsurge on the importation of endangered species of wildlife.

France's geographic position in the centre of Europe had made it a "transit country" for the movement of illegal drugs along drug trade routes, specifically cannabis and cocaine from North Africa and neighbouring Spain to Northern Europe. The heroin trade there gave rise to the film "The French Connection".

Since the collapse of Communism, heroin was smuggled through Hungary and Czechoslovakia for Western Europe.

Zurich, Switzerland's largest city had become a magnet for the country's heroin users, whose numbers skyrocketed from just 3,000 in 1975 to 30,000 in 1992. The New York Times reported that up to 3,000 drug addicts a day frequented the city's Platzspitz Park, dubbed "needle park".

Spain ranked first in Europe in revenues from cannabis smuggling arriving from North Africa and South America. Most was quickly moved northwards through Europe. The country's tourism and real estate markets, especially expensive beach area homes along Costa del Sol, served as attractive outlets for money laundering.

So, the computer system designed to combat Europe-wide crimes by providing a speedy messaging system between every Customs unit throughout Europe would soon be tested. And I was to become an expert!

On the 24th of February I flew from City Airport to Brussels Airport and caught the train to my new office close to Place du Luxembourg. My office was not part of the Europa Building (the seat of the European Council and Council of the European Union) on Wetstraat/Rue de la Loi but about half-a-mile away in a sub-office.

After a day or two I met up with an ex-customs colleague, Dick Stone, who I had worked with on a few occasions. Dick had been an Assistant Collector in Dover. The Investigation Unit in Dover, as in all other Units around the UK, and "The ID" always had a friendly rivalry relationship. Accusations flew that we would skim off the cream of cases and take all the glory. We would accuse them of holding back the facts, complicating matters and over exaggerating statistics.

There was, however, a very productive rapport that, in spite of the jesting, generated excellent results.

Dick introduced me to the team headed by Pierre Faucherand, a senior officer from French Customs.

Thankfully he spoke remarkably good English. It was evident as he explained the work of the department DGXX1. He clarified the work of the Directorate and how the whole of Commission adhered to strict parameters.

The UK in particular was keen to ensure the Commission did not take on roles assigned to individual Member State governments.

The Commission did not get involved in the operational decisions or investigations.

I shared an office with Dick Stone spending my first day writing down what I thought my immediate tasks would be, what actions I might take, what questions I should ask and from whom.

When my list filled a page, I asked Dick where I could get it typed up.

He couldn't hide his amusement. 'Getting it typed up?'

'The typing pool,' I said. 'Where is it?'

Dick stopped laughing. 'There's no typing pool here. You type it up yourself on a computer.'

Dick didn't know that I had never worked on a computer using word-processing, spreadsheets and the like. I had entered data on a Scotland Yard machine but I was never required to turn it on or off.

We painstakingly went through the process of switching on, keying in essential commands and opening up a new file or page.

A document was created using my one typing finger (the same one I use today). I've got quicker and a recent attempt at a long document drew the attention of my wife and two sons.

'I can't hear the television,' Pauline shouted. 'You sound like a pecking woodpecker.'

Guffaws of laughter from my sons echoed around the house.

My task in Brussels turned out to be as described; to oversee the planning, development and dissemination of a Europe wide Customs Information System which would allow officers from remote parts of Europe to have direct contacts with colleagues based at ports and airports in other EU countries. There were nine member states in 1992. UK had just joined the Single Market.

31st December 1992 was to be the last day before the Freedom of Movement came in to practice. Each Directorate would have a senior official responsible, a Commissioner.

The German Commissioner made it clear that he was going to travel by ferry to Dover that evening of the 31st to arrive in the UK just after midnight without a passport or any other identification. Under the Freedom of Movement Act he would be able to stroll over the "border" without hindrance.

(The process of establishing freedom of movement for all nationals of Member States was finalized with the signing of the Maastricht Treaty in 1992, which created the European Union (EU) and introduced the concept of a common European citizenship.)

Bearing in mind the UK and Ireland had not signed up for this Schengen agreement I was asked to explain what would happen when he set foot on British soil.

'He'll be arrested,' I said. 'He'll be turned around and sent back to on the next ferry.'

The Commissioner saw sense and didn't take the ferry.

I rented a room from Dick Stone who had an apartment in the centre of Brussels, walking distance from my office.

Dick was very helpful, supplying a crash course on the workings of the Commission and insight into the EU's international relationships.

The creation of the Single Market in 1993 afforded drug smugglers a border free area throughout the majority of the EU. Drug shipments would cross the external EU border, for example from Turkey (a source country for heroin) into Greece. There was no border control until the goods arrived in Calais.

My working week was Monday to Friday and the first time I had weekends free without the likelihood of a demanding telephone call from head office. So, I was able to travel home to spend two days with the family flying into City Airport from Brussels on the Friday evening and early the next Monday fly back. I was acutely aware of the weight of responsibility that Pauline carried during that time, running the house and caring for the boys.

And – on a Friday evening I would arrive with a large bag of dirty washing which required washing, drying and ironing by the Monday morning.

The intention was for me to assess how it would be when all of us moved to Brussels.

I always thought of Brussels to be the centre of the Freedom of Movement legislation. For me it seemed quite the opposite.

When I rented the room from Dick his name was on the doorbell outside.

Dick advised that my name would have to be listed next to his.

'Why is that?' I asked.

'Because the police will come round and check. They'll ring the bell to find out who is living in that room. If you live here and your name is missing there could be serious problems.'

'How free is this movement?' I asked.

'Brussels,' said Dick, 'and Belgium have the most bureaucratic structure in the EU.'

Later, when I came to rent a house, their officiousness became clear.

The rubbish collection (although mostly going to landfill) was paid in advance by purchasing tokens that you stuck on rubbish bags. "Rubbish" police would regularly inspect bags for correct recycling material.

The Commission held daily meetings on all aspects of the Single Market, including the free movement of people and goods. The theme of my first meetings I attended was in relation to Data Protection. My Directorate, (the DGXX1) attended the majority of meetings along with officials from the Member States.

The centre of Brussels was a hive of activity with all the restaurants full up with delegates from across the EU. I always wondered if there was anybody back in their own countries doing real jobs.

The meetings were so well organised. The nine Member States took it in turns to hold the Presidency for a six- month period and would call and chair the meetings.

The proceedings of the meetings were available in the nine EU languages. Translators would occupy sound proof booths at the sides of the meeting area. The attendees would all have earphones to listen to the translation. The main languages were English, French and German.

In addition to EU meetings, I represented the Commission at World Custom Organisation which was also based in Brussels. The WCO is an organisation which represents Customs administration throughout the world. It is similar to Interpol for the police although, unlike the UK, Customs in the majority of countries have no power to investigate drug trafficking. If Customs discover a consignment of drugs, they legally have to hand over the case to the police. When I attended the meetings, my participation was generally "on the hoof" particularly if it related to EU politics. I could however, give my opinion based on my experience as a frontline investigator. I found after a short while, issues would be run past me to see if they were possible and, more importantly, legal.

My experience as a front-line investigator gave me an advantage. Intercepting illegal drug smuggling and fraudsters, the pursuit of traffickers, the assembly of evidence for Court proceedings were factors not readily present in other delegates as most were from a civil service background. Dozens of delegates attended the meetings and there would be several meetings on various topics on the same day, all funded by the European Commission.

It soon became evident that those of us with hands on experience in the drugs trade could provide the knowhow to give these meetings substance. Often the chairman of the meeting would ask for my input and if the proposal was viable.

The EU Commission could not get involved in drug policing as this was down to member states to deliver. The Commission would facilitate meetings between parties that wouldn't normally assemble. Interpol, Europol, Customs and Police policy makers and practitioners would regularly meet.

The Commission had a European Anti-fraud Unit (OLAF) which was tasked to investigate fraud against the EU budget, corruption and serious misconduct within the European institutions. A number of officers had been seconded from the UK to investigate European fraud including fishing quotas and mis-description of goods. Tuna would be labelled as bonito which had a smaller tax rating. Chilled garlic had a different duty rate to frozen garlic which had a different rate to fresh garlic. Millions of Euros were being lost through mis-labelling. Producers and shippers were ruthless in this sort of fraud. Taxes and duty collected in the UK on importations would eventually end up in the EU. If the duty level was not correct the UK company would pay less to the Government and the EU.

At Europol meetings took place in The Hague. They supported EU Member States in their fight against terrorism, cybercrime and other serious and organised forms of crime. They also work with many non-EU partner states and international organisations such as Interpol, World Customs Organisation and national law enforcement agencies.

One of the Europol meetings I attended in Brussels with 30 or so delegates who were all suffering from an air-conditioning breakdown on a very hot day. Chaired by a high- ranking Greek official who, before speaking, took out a handkerchief, tied knots in each corner, and placed it on his head. To me it was if I was watching a Monty Python sketch but the majority there, either ignored it or saw it as normal.

The hilarity continued at another meeting when a French MEP, using an old French expression, said that this was thanks to "la sagesse normande" (the wisdom of the people from Normandy).

The translation came through in English as "all thanks to Norman Wisdom". No one of any other nationality could quite understand why the British and Irish members were in stitches!

These were rare moments of amusement, contrasting with hours and hours of dull, boring speeches that had no insight into anything worthwhile.

Continuous debates went on for three days on word usage. Should "shall" be used or should it be "may"?

To my relief the customs system I was to test and teach was straightforward. It was designed to assist operatives at ports and airports 24 hours a day simply and quickly and in their own language.

I worked with a private company who had successfully secured through the EU tender process to develop the system. If specific or trend information on smuggling movements were identified by a country the system was initiated. All the computers had a specific page where a Customs official could type in the details they have, knowing that it would automatically be translated.

Not all of participating officers throughout Europe would speak another language.

On one case the Dutch Customs intercepted a consignment of rice from Suriname which contained 200 kilos of cocaine. The details of the consignment including the exporting company was sent to Customs offices throughout Europe. As a result, the UK identified another similar importation and over 120 kilos of cocaine were seized at Felixstowe.

At the beginning of May I purchased a left-hand drive seven-seater Chrysler Voyager SUV a vehicle needed to accommodate our family of five. I also rented a house in Rhode Saint Genese, a suburb of Brussels, halfway between Brussels and Waterloo and about 10 miles from the office.

A good friend and colleague, Andy McCreadie, from the UK had transferred to the anti-fraud unit. His wife Gerry, and their two children, Helen and Alex, came with him. They lived just around the corner from our new home.

When I signed the rental agreement, the agent asked if I spoke Dutch or French.

'Neither that well. Why?' I asked.

'We have to have a balance of Dutch and French speakers,' he replied. 'If there is a majority of Dutch speakers in one area no more will be allowed to move in. The same with French speakers.'

Another example of bureaucracy blocking any idea of Freedom of Movement.

On the 14th May we went back to the UK for two weeks. Pauline and I started packing up the house, putting furniture into storage. The movers were thorough, wrapping and packing everything including the rubbish bin that I'd forgotten to empty. I was feeding my youngest Jimmy a bottle whilst sitting on the stairs (all the furniture had been put into the lorry). I put the bottle down which was almost immediately wrapped up by one of the packers. Thankfully I managed to stop him and carry on feeding my son.

We all flew to Brussels and moved into our rented home.

For me, but particularly Pauline, it was a new adventure. However, the gloss soon wore off as Pauline had no friends and family nearby

Andy had told me that we all had to register as Belgian citizens. 'Every piece of paper you have,' he said, 'your birth certificates, marriage certificate, passports, driving licence, anything you can find that says who you are. You take all this to the Town Hall in Rhode Saint Genese.'

Soon after we moved in, we walked along to the Town Hall and joined the queue. I always thought the British were the queuers of the world but the people of Brussels would challenge that.

The forms we had to fill in were in Dutch and French so we had to be helped by one of the town hall officials. I was constantly impressed with the Belgians with their ability to speak different languages as and when called to do so. Dutch, French, English and German.

All of our papers were photo-copied and noticing that Pauline's father had died a few years before, he said he would need a copy of his death certificate.

'Why do you need that?' I asked.

'To be registered,' he said. 'We need to know everything about you and your family.'

It meant, of course, that after we obtained a copy, I would have to arrange another meeting. I am afraid I left this for Pauline to sort out.

'Typical,' said Andy after I complained about the red tape,' no matter what you hand over they'll always demand something you haven't thought of and haven't got.'

Having registered as Belgian citizens we were issued with ID cards. These ID cards enabled travel between European countries without the need for a passport. Even today some EU nationals can travel to the UK on an ID card. We have to pay £80 for a passport. Italians use an ID card costing a few pounds.

We did all the things you have to do when settling down in a new residence; finding schools, a doctor and dentist. Jimmy was only a few months old but Alex and Alistair (who was only four) caught a bus near our house and went to the European School in Uccle (a school attended by Boris Johnson years before).

Soon after a health visitor called in to look at Jimmy who was coming up to twelve-month old.

'What food do you give your son?' she asked.

'Mostly what we eat,' said Pauline. 'Liquidised, of course.'

'How much meat? We recommend that a child of this age has meat no more than twice a week.'

'He seems a strong baby,' I said. 'He's never had any colds or coughs. Is there anything wrong?'

'No. That is our recommendation.'

Needless to say, we had to comply.

I took the train to work which only took 40 minutes. I was so impressed by the train system in Belgium as you could set your watch by the train arrivals and departures. My hours were civilised, mostly nine to five something I had not experienced for over twenty years.

I did go to every one of the EU countries and other European countries to meet up with Customs officials.

I was told I could go anywhere in the nine member states but travelling to Switzerland required getting permission from Jack Delor, the then President of the European Commission to travel outside of Europe.

John Smithson was the project manager for technical company. His team established terminals in all the Member States. A training programme for a group of 20 or so Customs officials and investigators from each nation lasting a week was initiated. All expenses were met by the Commission including travel costs and hotels.

With my understanding of the Portuguese language and limited French I was able to get across my lectures in a colourful mix of languages. At least, they showed every sign of understanding what I was saying.

In keeping with my usual style, I presented my section off the cuff.

If a linguistic problem arose, we always found a colleague or student who could help out.

A man called Spyros was our main contact in Greece. He was the person we turned to resolve any technical issues in the country. I knew Spyros was severely physically handicapped and found travel difficult. Although physically handicapped he was incredibly bright and was a top-class technical Customs and computer expert. His French, Italian and English were perfect. He oversaw the installation of terminals in Greece (about forty in total) and mentored his colleagues.

The Port of Piraeus is the chief sea port of Athens, Greece, situated upon the Saronic Gulf on the western coasts of the Aegean Sea, the largest port in Greece and one of the largest in Europe. It is also a key location for the movement of cannabis from Afghanistan and heroin from Turkey.

Spyros also played a major part in having the terminals up and working in other Greek ports and airports.

Whilst in Athens checking the implementation progress of the system, I eventually met Spyros. I asked if it was possible for him to attend a training course in Brussels.

'It will be beneficial to you,' I said. 'And we would benefit from your input.'

'It is too difficult,' he replied. 'I cannot travel alone and my mother is my carer. She looks after me every day, every night, week after week.'

When I next met up with Dick Stone I said, 'I would love to get Spyros over here.'

After much discussion and quite a lot of scheming we arranged for Spyros and his mother, to come to Brussels as an additional Customs Officer, paid for by the Commission.

When it happened, it was a success. A wheelchair was always available and there was never any shortage of volunteers to spend time with him.

His mother spent the working day in an adjoining office. A charming lady devoted to the well-being of her son. The group of 21 stayed at a hotel in the centre of Brussels. His Greek colleagues carried him everywhere his wheelchair would not go. We could see the look on his face that he was so delighted he had been allowed to travel out of Athens for the first time in his life.

A question was asked how much trouble we would have been in if it was revealed that we financed his mother's trip. Both Dick and I would have been happy to face any cross-examination to justify what we had done. It was the right thing to do.

In 1994 I was called in to see my head of unit, Pierre Faucherand. 'I want to talk to you about a delicate matter,' he said. You were in Lisbon as a Liaison Officer.'

'I was. 1987 to 1990.'

'We have an official working for our team who came from Portuguese Customs. There are rumours that he is not all he seems. Would you mind checking out who he is and find out about his background.'

I took the man's name and other details and telephoned one of my former contacts and friend in Lisbon, Luis Bordadagua and asked him what he knew.

'He was in charge of customs at Lisbon Airport after you had left. He had been arrested for facilitating 30 kilos of cocaine for a courier from South America. He met the courier on arrival and escorted him through customs to ensure he wasn't stopped. He spent six months in prison before the charges had to be dropped as the courier died. There was no evidence to go on.'

He had already applied to the Commission for a job but delayed his application due to "domestic issues".

'Where is he?' Luis asked.

'He's working for the EU Commission.'

'What! I cannot believe it What does he do there?'

'He is in charge of controlled deliveries, (a law technique to allow drugs if intercepted to allow to continue in a controlled manner to its ultimate destination).'

I recall an expletive or two.

When I relayed this information to Pierre he said, 'I don't know what to do.'

'Sack him,' I replied.

'I cannot sack him. He has not been convicted with anything and he has been posted to Brussels using the correct process.'

'In that case just make sure he does not get involved with anything operational. Give him a supervised desk job with menial tasks, like issuing paper clips. Don't let him near any sensitive material.'

A demonstration of the fully implemented system took place on the 25th October. I flew over to Heathrow and met Mike Knox where we had the first live transmission of a message from the Customs office in Paris to the Customs office at Heathrow. Journalists and tv reporters were there. The Chairman of the Board of Customs, Valerie Strachan and other senior Customs officials watched on as observers.

Praying there would be no glitch in the plan and the equipment we waited as telephone connections were made. Thankfully, it worked.

We all observed on a large screen the completed form being relayed from Paris. London responded by return with their own message. It took less than a second to arrive and the same time to send the reply.

I set up a similar demonstration to the European Parliament in Brussels. The Parliament building is vast. Inaugurated in 1958 it houses the legislative assembly of the European Union (EU). Beginning in 1979, members of the European Parliament (MEPs) were elected in their own countries for a term of five years. There are more than 700 members.

There were many well-known figures present; Ian Paisley and Jean Marie Le Penn were just two. It was a surreal moment. Luc Wanten and Mike Knox were on the stage with me but I did most of the talking. We didn't have the luxury of a trial run and we kept our fingers and everything else crossed.

I had a few minutes of panic when I thought the whole process had broken down and I would be unable to continue. We were there a couple of hours before the presentation was due to start and we had all left the parliament area. Because there was no movement or microphones being used the electricity went on to stand-by. The whole arena went dark and only came "back to life"' when the sensors monitored some movement. The presentation lasted about 20 minutes and everything went smoothly. I was even applauded at the end which was even more surreal.

Luc Waten and Eddie Weynes, who we nicknamed Rock Steady Eddie, were from the Customs in Antwerp and were excellent operators with a wealth of international experience.

I went with Luc to Dublin to give a presentation to Irish Customs Officials.

Unlike my travels from HQ in London, air-flights from Brussels taking over an hour were paid for by the EU. They were always business class, luxury seating and an endless supply of free booze.

By the beginning of 1994 it was evident that it was becoming difficult for Pauline and the boys to properly settle in Brussels.

Although I had my work colleagues it was a very lonely existence for Pauline as there were few friendly Brits around. Pauline and the children went back to the UK to live. They were closer to other family members and friends. Pauline had lost her father in the early 80s but her mother and siblings all lived in south London and Kent. Given the office hours I was working I was able to travel home most weekends. After Pauline and the boys had left, I gave up our rented house and rented a room in David Murphy's house, an Irish Customs Officer. Like me, David would travel home most weekends to see his family.

I would stay on in Brussels until the end of my contract in February 1995.

When I handed over the keys of our rented house the agent insisted on an inspection. Pauline had kept it spotless and somehow, we had kept the garden in good order. I presumed we would get our deposit back without fuss.

The agent painfully checked his inventory and on finding a small cobweb in the otherwise spotless lounge advised me one Euro would be taken off our deposit. I was flabbergasted but not altogether surprised. I found the French speaking Belgians humourless, not warm at all.

In May 1994 I gave presentations in the Channel Islands, flying direct to Jersey and then an island hopper plane on a ten-minute flight to Guernsey.

It was such a small plane that the pilot arranged for passengers to be evenly distributed to ensure balance.

The Guernsey event took place on a Thursday just as a very dense fog arrived, preventing our departure flight. Our moods were as heavy as the fog when it was announced that it was going to be Sunday when the skies cleared.

In need of a few days off with my family I took action by booking a ferry to Bournemouth, train to my parent's house in Stamford where Pauline and the boys were visiting during half term.

Towards the end of my contract, I was approached by Pierre Faucherand who said they were recruiting for the Commission and he would like me to stay on as a full time "functionaire" (a full time EU official.)

'You just have to sign this form,' said Pierre, 'and you will be a full-time employee of the EU.'

Although the conditions, pension and renumeration were very attractive I saw it as a gravy train – a journey you stay on forever.

I thanked Pierre but had to be firm with my reply. 'Thank you, Pierre, but it is my wish to return to work in the UK.'

I knew in my heart that returning to the UK Investigation Division was my only route in my working life. I knew I would be welcomed back.

Throughout my secondment I had kept in contact with Nick Baker and Terry Byrne. Terry had always wanted to be Investigation's Chief Investigation Officer. His initial disappointment at not securing that post was short lived when he was appointed as Director General of Customs and Excise Law Enforcement. He was the head of uniformed Customs, Intelligence and Investigation, probably the most powerful position in the department.

February 1995 duly arrived and I packed my bag, basically a small holdall, for my return to the UK. It was an easy journey because the "feelers" I had put out looked very positive.

I was now a Senior Investigation Officer (team leader) and looked forward to the next phase of my career. An SIO is the position most investigators aim for and I for one would have been happy seeing out my career at this level.

My arrival back to Customs was pivotal but another twist changed my career path dramatically. Instead of joining a drugs team I was assigned to the recently established Customs fraud team.

I was to be an SIO, a team leader in a discipline I had no experience of.

CHAPTER 20
DRUGS PLUS FRAUD, OBSCENE AND PAEDOPHILE MATERIAL.

On returning from Brussels, I took up my promotion within Investigation as a Senior Investigator/ team leader. Running your own team, although challenging, provided me with an opportunity to lead and manage a group of investigators.

My future had been decided by a senior management team who met regularly to discuss appointments and moves within the Division.

So it was to my surprise in February 1995, I was appointed to Customs "F" a newly created team tasked with investigating EU fraud, obscene and paedophile material. It was a new work area for me but my recent secondment to Brussels gave me a good insight into the workings of the EU.

Prior to this an established team, Customs E, had an intelligence and prosecuting role. My team took on the investigation and prosecution of offenders. Handling of intelligence, managing trade contacts and informants processed, remained with Customs E, managed by an experienced investigator, Bob Snuggs.

My initial disappointment at not returning to investigate drug smugglers soon disappeared when I was told about the top- level criminals who had moved into frontier fraud. It was less risky and if caught and found guilty the prison sentences were normally in single figures. I had previously worked on the Deltas with my new Assistant Chief, Cedric Andrew and I knew he was a very experienced and supportive manager. The major fraud I was asked to concentrate on was the diversion of spirits, wine and beer, destined for other countries within the EU. In 1993 The European Single Market, or Common Market was established. It is a single market seeking to guarantee the free movement of goods, capital, services, and labour – the "four freedoms" – within the European Union. Under this arrangement goods were allowed to travel tax free until it arrived at its destination in a European country where the tax would be accounted for and paid.

Transporters of goods would carry an "AAD", Accompanying Administrative Document, to be stamped up at its destination to be followed with a tax payment by the recipient.

It was thought to work satisfactorily until organised criminal gangs thought up the idea that products such as beer and spirits, could be diverted from its intended destination and illegally be distributed throughout the UK. On paper these goods were to be delivered to other countries where duty would be paid. Arriving in the UK by stealth enabled the criminals to avoid any payment of tax. This was assisted by the use of false Custom's Stamps which eased the flow of goods between countries.

It was estimated that tens of millions of tax were avoided with the loss being funded by the UK taxpayer.

In many ways it was a licence for fraudsters to print money.

Company A would sell a consignment of spirits to Company B. They would be charged tax and VAT. This could be tens of thousands of pounds depending on the load. Company B would then export to Company C who were based abroad and therefore zero rated. Company B would then claim back all tax paid. Company C paid no tax either because they didn't actually exist or a trail of false paperwork hid their existence. The scheme helped, of course, by the false Customs stamps.

So, tax would be claimed back from Customs and Excise on the transaction between A and B but nothing paid on the transaction between B and C.

This resulted in millions of pounds unnecessarily being paid out as repayment every week. A huge loss to the UK Exchequer which was spiralling out of control.

Customs F were tasked to obtain evidence on fraudulent activity.

It seemed to us that the EU regulations were far from perfect. Finding a profitable weakness in the system became the focus of fraudsters and, it seemed, a quest that required a painless effort to exploit. No arms were needed, no one was going to get hurt and their illegal activity demanded no more than falsifying paperwork and willing beneficiaries down the line. Money was there for the taking.

But we still had to prove that an offence had taken place.

In addition to excise fraud, we were charged with tracking down those involved with pornographic and paedophilic material that had been imported into the UK. It is hard to imagine that in a time when the internet was in its infancy, obscene magazines tapes and films were still being smuggled from places like Amsterdam and the Far East. Police forces investigated paedophiles within the UK but Customs prosecuted importations.

There were 13 members of my team some of whom I had worked with before. There was a mixture of experience and youth but all had an insight into investigation work. The three Higher Investigation Officers were Ian Donald, Dave Piper and Norman Trew, I already knew. The Investigation Officers were Paul Roden, Gary Bishop, Debbie Richards, Maxine Crook, Nick Matthews, Danny Clifford, Dave Hill, Pete Harvey and Kim Stalabrass, our team support manager.

I convened a team meeting on my first Monday morning. I am sure the team were weighing me up as much as I was trying to get to know them. My office was based in the Custom House, Lower Thames Street, London so I was at least familiar with my surroundings.

'Look,' I said. 'This is my first role as a team leader. I've spent most of my career working on drugs. I know nothing about excise fraud but I'm determined to treat fraudsters in the same way I treated drug traffickers. We relentlessly pursue a lead until we identify the villains and their organisations.'

I was heartened by the response from the team. They were new to each other and seemed pleased an experienced investigator would manage them. They also welcomed my admission that I was new to this area of work.

At the meeting, the activities of a predominately Asian smuggling gang, was raised by Ian Donald. "Operation Fluke" was at an early stage and progress was limited.

Previous attempts at surveillance entailed conducting observations and surveillance on the gang and the bonded warehouses they were using to move the alcohol. Tofail Ahmed and three brothers Avtar, Kulwant and Sohan Singh Hare were well known in the drinks trade. No tax was being paid so their organisation was able to undercut genuine traders. Many of these complained to Customs and Excise.

The Hare brothers flaunted their wealth with top of the range BMWs and property including a motel in Canada which they called "Hare Creek". They relished in the nickname given to them "the Millionhares".

Hare Wines had their warehouse in River Road, Barking an industrial area in east London.

A container of whisky would have a tax element of £150,000 so Hare Wines could sell the load on at a reduced cost.

Operation "Fluke" had ground to a halt due to the absence of a satisfactory observation point on the suspect addresses, particularly the River Road warehouse. The team had tried every angle and couldn't find a useful surveillance position.

They had approached the police Flying Squad Office to ask if they could use one of their offices to watch Hare wines.

They received a frosty reception. 'We get our booze from them when we have our Christmas party'.

I have to say I wasn't surprised. It was typical Met police.

'That's near the control room for Thames Barrier,' I said. 'Can you not see their yard from there?'

'We can see the yard but too far away to follow movement or read vehicle registration numbers.'

'We could solve it by having footmen nearby. When movement is spotted from the Thames Barrier you warn the footmen. They can be standing at bus-stops, shop doorways or just strolling up a road. If we get registration numbers, we can follow them. If they go to Dover or Folkstone we may be on to something and we would have to notify local Customs to see if the lorry and load returns to the UK market. We'll be able to build up a picture.'

Some lorries had already been tracked by the team. Paperwork suggested they were destined for Europe but none did. It was thought the loads were delivered to UK cash and carry outlets.

When I asked if we had the home addresses for all the suspects, I was told some did not appear in police records or customs databases. One suspect, who was arranging movement of the lorries for the Hares but the team could not find his home address.

'We even tried the electoral register.'

'What about the telephone book?' I asked.

A few eyebrows twitched.

I went on. 'When I joined the service there was no such thing as databases. We ploughed our way through telephone books, electoral registers, council records or we would visit police station intelligence units who kept card indexes on local criminals. Unusual names were welcome otherwise it could take hours or days if the name Smith or Jones were searched.'

A couple of days later a sheepish Paul Roden came back with a London telephone book. 'We found the suspect. Right here.'

'I'm really pleased,' I said. 'I'm not trying to look clever. Sometimes, the most simple of routes is the shortest. If that doesn't work move on to other tactics.'

In the early days I did find my new role rather strange. I had an office to myself (an old small room with a fireplace) about 20 yards from the team's two open plan offices. I suspect they got fed up with me constantly asking what's going on. I did have a habit of commenting, giving advice, recollecting similar circumstances and offering solutions to a case problem that I knew little about. I was in danger of becoming the sort of leader that I rubbished when I was a rookie investigator. Over time I reigned myself in and contributed only when I thought it completely necessary.

Early March 1996 Customs Officers at the port of Tilbury office telephoned to say they had intercepted a container from Japan. In their search they found 109 obscene, including 70 containing hard paedophile material of young boys being abused.

'This one is down to you,' the officer said.

'Why is that?'

'The contents of the containers belong to a diplomat returning to the UK. The diplomatic status ends when he returns. Is that right?'

'That's right.'

'A C3 form was completed. (a C3 form is a document which accompanies any air or sea freight consignments of personal effects from outside the EU). It is signed by the owner and is confirmation of what is in the load. Videos were listed on the C3 but not the content.'

The videos were brought to my office and given the horrific content I gave careful consideration as to who I would nominate to investigate the case. Norman Trew was a family man who was level headed and I was confident he would be able to keep his emotions in check and conduct a watertight case.

Investigating paedophile material can be challenging. Investigators must be experienced, sober and resilient enough to professionally put aside any personal revulsion.

It came to me to take a look at the video material to validate the subject matter before planning our investigation. The owner of the personal effects was identified as Robert Coghlan, a high ranking (First Secretary) fluent linguist with 33 years in the Diplomatic Service. He had accompanied Diana, Princess of Wales on her visit to Japan in February 1995.

We found out that Coghlan's next posting was to be in Madrid. His status in the Diplomatic Corp was high so I decided to advise Head of Security at the Foreign Office in King Charles Street Whitehall.

I met senior officials there, explained the circumstances and that it was our intention to visit Woods at his home the following day where he would be arrested and interviewed under caution.

One of the officials said. 'We shall be wary of where we send him next time as a posting.'

I asked him what he meant.

'Another country. A posting in another country'

'You do realise,' I said, 'that if he goes to Court and found guilty, he will go to prison.'

To my surprise the officials were taken aback.

'We do have a precedent,' one said. 'We had an individual who we suspected of having unusual sexual preferences. We solved the problem by restricting his movements. We arranged a post in London for a few years and then sent him off to the Philippines.'

I seemed to remember I swore. 'He must have thought he died and gone to heaven. Sex trafficking is rampant in the Philippines; women, men, girls and boys.'

Not much was said during the rest of our meeting. They hadn't given me the green light to arrest Coghlan, (I didn't need their green light) but they said nothing to prevent me going ahead.

The next day at 6 am the team knocked on Woods' door. It was an age before a young boy answered the door.

'Is Mr Coghlan here? Norman asked.

'That's my dad,' the boy said.

'Is he here?'

'He's in the bedroom.'

Gary Bishop one of my officers, found Coghlan and told him he was being arrested and the charges against him.'

Coghlan was brought back to the custody suite in Customs House, London that had all the hallmarks of a police station with a secure cell and custody procedures.

His rights were read and shortly after he made a phone call to his solicitor.

I sat in on one of the interviews and was appalled at how arrogant Coghlan was.

'I committed no offence here,' he said. 'The shipment was in transit to be sent on to Spain. I'm a diplomat.'

'In Japan you were a diplomat,' I said. 'In Spain, if you get there, you'll be a diplomat. Here you are just another Joe Bloggs.'

'You should have called me. We could have smoothed over the whole affair.'

I don't think we bothered with a reply.

When interviewed, he admitted knowing the tapes were indecent but claimed he did not know they contained paedophile material and insisted that he always fast- forwarded past scenes involving juveniles.

He later told the jury that he considered disposing of the tapes but feared he was being followed by Japanese police whenever he left the Embassy. He never thought to erase the tapes.

After consulting the Customs solicitors Coghlan was charged. All the Customs documents had been signed by Coghlan providing us with all the evidence we needed. And, we discovered, the container was not in transit. Its destination was in the UK.

Coghlan was remanded in custody until his trial in August 1996 at Southwark Crown Court.

Coghlan's defence tactic was that he did not intend to commit an offence in the UK and that the material in question was in transit only. The shipment was sent from Japan directly to Spain.

As the trial progressed it was agreed that the jury would view two of the videos.

I found it difficult to accept that the jury made up of ordinary folk would be obliged to watch what was the most repellent of material. I couldn't imagine what went on in the jury room where the viewing had been arranged. I had seen what they were seeing so my sympathies were with every one of them.

When they emerged into the Courtroom their faces were white with horror.

Sensing that things were not going the defendant's way his barrister asked if the jury could be dismissed so a point of order could be made.

I couldn't guess what this point of order could be so when he addressed the judge I was as surprised as everyone else.

'My client,' the barrister said,' has complained that two of the jury are constantly and aggressively staring at him. This I suggest, is prejudicial against my client.'

The Judge was not moved by this appeal and promptly dismissed it.

A question arose from the jury; 'If the shipment was destined for Spain why wasn't a C3 form completed in Spanish?'

Coghlan and his barrister had no answer to that and it confirmed his personal effects were not in transit to Spain and were imported into the UK.

The prosecution dismissed his claim not to have known what he was buying, pointing out that he was a trained linguist who spoke Japanese, French, German, Portuguese and Serbo-Croat.

Nigel Lithman, for the prosecution, said Coghlan spent four years painstakingly building up his collection at the expense of young children exploited and abused by the film-makers. 'In Japan it would seem that Coghlan had something of a dual existence. He was something of a Jekyll and Hyde character'.

The trial at Southwark lasted a week after which the jury unanimously found him guilty.

His sentence was four years in a prison and was sent to the secure Brixton prison. All prisoners when convicted are sent to a category A maximum security prison until they have been assessed. Paedophiles are segregated from other prisoners as the majority of criminals abhor child abuse.

I was outside the court with one of my Deputy Chiefs, Jim MacGregor, when he was interviewed by television reporters. Jim was asked if the accused was part of a large paedophile group.

'It's generally the case the paedophiles do belong to groups but in this case, we have no evidence that the accused belonged to any such group.'

A few months later Coghlan appealed against the sentence and the judge's summing up and his sentence was reduced to 3 years.

A year later, when I was about to be posted to Brazil as a Liaison Officer, I attended training courses at the Foreign Office in Whitehall. Coghlan's name came up in conversation with some FCO officials who were also being posted out to various embassies throughout the world. I was told that Coghlan had been in Brazil and was well thought of and liked in the consulate in Sao Paulo and he had been carrying out important duties around Princess Diana's visit to Japan in February 1995.

'Jim, If the Sao Paulo staff find out about your involvement with Coghlan case you won't be popular.'

I angrily bit back. 'If they want me to be popular, I'll explain, in detail, what I had to watch on his videos and what the poor boys were put through. I have no fear about telling people what's right and what's wrong.'

Mercifully, Coghlan's name never came up again.

About 90% of my team's work was taken up with the Hare brothers. Their consignments driven by Windsor's lorries were observed leaving ports and coming back in with the same load 24 hours later. If they were stopped by Customs on the way in, they would explain the load had been incorrectly ordered and had to return to the Hare's cash and carry where, of course, the tax would be paid. Many loads were driven straight to a UK outlet. One member of the gang, an Italian Giselli, had false Customs stamps for most EU countries and would prepare the document as if it had been exported and duty and tax had been collected abroad. He was responsible for ensuring the paperwork, although fabricated, would pass a cursory inspection.

Observations by the team, logging of the dates, times and vehicle registration numbers ensured the evidence against all the suspects were strong. The French Customs had given us permission to travel over to France to observe suspect vehicle movements. We were able to take photographs of lorries arriving in France and almost immediately turning around and driving back to the UK. Invariably, the lorries would leave via Folkestone and return via Dover before delivering the alcohol in the UK.

The team spent all of their time working on Operation Fluke but occasionally a new fraud of prohibited importation case would be referred from Customs staff at a port or airport.

One such case involving obscene material was referred to me by staff at Heathrow freight team. Pornography was always a tricky area as we were not exclusively employed to judge what was obscene or indecent but to interpret current thinking on what was obscene or indecent, as best we could. We then had to assess if the material should be presented in Court for a jury to judge. I would discuss any importation with my Assistant Chief, Cedric Andrew and decide whether the importation should be adopted and investigated.

In 1960 the trial of D.H. Lawrence's book "Lady Chatterley's Lover" captured the public attention and set off a long-ranging debate on the levels of acceptability of "sexual" material. The Arts Minister of the time, Michael Ellis, said, 'It was a watershed moment in cultural history, when Victorian ideals were overtaken by a more modern attitude.'

The publication may have been a liberalising moment on the cusp of the Swinging Sixties but twenty years later views on moral issues still divided opinion.

A consignment of "Hustler" magazines had arrived from South Africa. There were a few similar "men's" magazines published in the UK but this publication' contents, it seemed to us, went far beyond current decency lines. Hard core images of women being subjected to extreme bondage and degrading abuse, in my eyes, crossed the line.

I appointed Pete Harvey as the case officer and the consignment was seized much to the annoyance of the distributors in the UK. They were formally interviewed and appeared at Middlesex Crown in Court September 1995. It was a fairly straight forward case where the jury had to decide if the publication exceeded what is deemed acceptable pornography.

In our view the visual physically extreme exploitation of women contained in the photographs were both obscene and indecent.

The jury thought otherwise. "Hustler" magazine and the UK distributor were found not guilty.

For his pains Pete Harvey was featured in a later edition of the magazine under the heading "Wanker of the week".

The whole question of obscenity and decency went on for a long time, most famously challenged by Mary Whitehouse CBE, an English social activist who opposed social liberalism and accused the mainstream British media of encouraging a more permissive society. She set up the "Clean up National TV" campaign. The "Adult" magazine hit back by publishing The Mary Whitehouse Magazine.

On Saturday 19 August I was shopping with Pauline and my sons in Sainsburys in Croydon when I received a pager message asking me to ring the office urgently.

I rang Ian Donald, one of the case officers (Paul Roden was the other one). What had transpired was, on the Friday, the day before, one of suspect transport companies run by Alex Windsor had one of his lorries hi-jacked in East London. The driver had been shot in the leg and dumped on Hackney Marshes. He wasn't dead but injured and a consignment owned by the Hare brothers had been stolen.

By that time, we had accumulated sufficient evidence against the Hare brothers, Tofail, Windsor and Giselli and a massive "knock" had been planned for Tuesday 22 August which would require 300 or so officers and over 60 suspect addresses, including homes and warehouses. Officers were to be assembled on the Monday ready to knock all the addresses the following day.

The hi-jacking brought matters to a head and we had to quickly change our plan of action. I abandoned the Saturday shopping and drove into my office. Ian Donald and Paul Roden, the joint case officers were already in the Custom House and together we set out our new game plan.

What we knew was that suspicion around the shot driver was high and it was thought by some he was probably part of the hi-jack team. We had to deal with the fall out of the hijacking first and foremost and we had to ensure the shot driver was not harmed further. Information from the police suggested that Windsor was unhappy with the driver and was looking to "deal with him". He was overheard saying he wanted to go round to the driver's house once he had obtained, "something not just to wave but to have something up it". This was interpreted as he intended to obtain and potentially use a firearm.

Giving such short notice, we couldn't bring the "Knock" forward but on the advice of our lawyers I decided to have officers visit the driver and place him into protective custody. It was a high-risk strategy and I deployed the team to watch Windsor's home address to ensure he was not on the loose. If it worked, this strategy would give us the time we needed to organise the "Knock".

The home of the driver was being watched at 10pm when a car drew up. The driver hobbled out of his home with a suitcase and got into the waiting car which quickly drove off.

I was faced with another difficult decision but in consultation with Ian and Paul it was decided to let the driver go, hoping that he was no longer at risk and that he would simply disappear off the radar. Our minds quickly turned to organising the search of addresses and arrest of all the suspects identified on Operation Fluke.

231

I phoned Pauline to say I wasn't sure when I would get home.

My colleagues and I manned the phones and spoke to many of the Investigation teams across mainland UK and Northern Ireland. We asked them to travel to London for a briefing in the afternoon. It was the ID at its best. Not one officer complained and some cancelled their days off. None of the trivial questions such as where do we stay and how do we get to London. I think of the fantastic response with nothing but absolute pride. The phones were red hot and we decided to sleep in the office. We managed to find three camp beds which we set up next to the phones. Probably not the best night's sleep I have ever had as my mind was spinning as to what had happened in the past 24 hours, but more importantly what was to come.

The hijacking and the access to firearms by the suspects meant that nine addresses would have to be visited with firearms support. On the Sunday morning I drove to the headquarters of the Met's firearms command SO19 to discuss our requirements. Despite this being dropped on their toes at short notice SO19 were really supportive. Armed Response Units would go to some of the addresses with a full armed arrest team going to Windsor's home address.

On the Sunday afternoon we held the briefing in the Customs House canteen – about 300 officers – packed out.

All were assigned to different roles for the Monday morning "knock", set for 06.00.

At least six officers were nominated to accompany each firearm team. I returned to SO19 and briefed the firearms team and the nominated lead arrest officers. One of the nominated officers came up to me and said he wasn't happy about his role.

'What do you mean, not very happy?'

'I'm not comfortable going out with a firearms unit. It might be dangerous.'

'I've been in the office since Saturday morning. I'm going to be here for the next two days sleeping on the floor. I'll swap roles with you. I'd love to go out with the firearms team and be involved in the arrest.'

For me accompanying the firearms team was a great privilege. They were always dedicated, professional and brave.

He wasn't happy but he agreed to go out.

In all of my investigation career it was one of the few occasions I have encountered a colleague close to bottling it.

I returned to the Custom House and at 17.00 the briefing was held in the two- storey canteen area. It was packed as 300 officers listened intently to the briefing. The arrest team leaders then further briefed their teams in offices in the Custom House.

At six in the following morning was the start time so we arranged to raid the addresses and the arrest teams were to meet up at 4am. I was in the office so I didn't have any transport problems. Nobody complained. A few technical issues were discussed and the correct paperwork was distributed.

All Customs "F" operations began with a "F". We called the current operation "Fluke". (a liver fluke, is a parasite that tends to live in cattle or other grazing mammals). Its other usage is an unlikely chance occurrence. Perhaps not the best name for a detailed, well thought out plan.

We didn't get a lot of sleep on the Sunday night, my second disturbed night. I had a good idea of what was ahead of us and periods of rest were not included.

At 4am Ian, Paul and myself sat in the office. I made sure that all the teams knew that I had to immediately know as soon as they had entered their target premises and made it secure. My greatest fear was that behind any of the doors were people with firearms ready to use them.

The "Knock" was called at 6am. All teams were told to move at that moment.

Over the next hour the team leaders telephoned me to say that all officers were safe, the suspects had been arrested and were being taken to a designated police station for questioning.

One firearm team hadn't called in, so concern grew. What seemed to be a successful operation could be turned upside down by bad or tragic news.

After 20 minutes they called in. My anxiety had got the better of me when I tore them off a strip for not calling earlier. I quietened down when they explained the complications of the knock – many locked rooms and lots of people, some of whom were just visiting. Each room, each person had to be restrained fearing that anyone of them may pull out a gun.

I did sympathise. I would have done exactly the same in their position. Niceties over the telephone come a distant second to operational demands.

In the middle of the knock my phone rang. I thought it was an update from one of the house searches.

The voice at the other end said, 'Hi, Trapper. It's Jake McManus. I need some statistics on Excise smuggling for a report I am preparing'.

Jake had moved from Investigation on promotion to HQ Excise policy group.

I was really diplomatic and replied 'Jake I am a bit tucked up at the moment can I speak to you in a couple of days?'

He had no idea the scale of the operation that was unfolding and much later we joked about how diplomatic I was. He was surprised I didn't just tell him to 'F' off.

All the addresses were searched. The Hare brothers, Tofail, Windsor and Giselli the main suspects were all arrested with others further down the chain of the crime group. Some were taken to the Customs House and others taken to police stations, Limehouse, Kings Cross and Snowhill for interviews.

The raids on warehouses revealed huge quantities of wine, beer and spirits owned by the crime group. Over 190 lorry loads of alcohol were seized and removed to a large storage facility in North London. On paper these had been sent abroad but sat there, waiting to be delivered to outlets in the UK. With the seized loads and those previously sold on we reckoned the tax loss was nearly £100 million. Such were the quantities of goods that we had to employ a logistics company with sufficient vehicles and manpower to move quickly. It took them nearly a week to remove all the alcohol.

It was impossible that the seized alcoholic drinks could be sold on through the Department's auction service – differing from cars, electrical or domestic items that could. There was no way we could guarantee the provenance of the produce giving health and safety concerns. A successful outcome of the trial would see the goods destroyed.

Some of the minor players were bailed to appear at a later date but the main principals charged with evading excise duty and VAT.

They were all remanded in custody after appearing at the Guildhall Magistrates Court and remanded in custody.

The case was transferred from the magistrate's court to Southwark Crown Court. Richard Kramer, a senior QC was the lead Counsel for Customs and David Howker, a tenacious barrister, did the legal ground work. Kramer and Howker had been involved very early on in the investigation so we could present our case in the best possible way and to take in our duty of care for the driver.

The defendants applied for bail but because the sheer size of the fraud estimated at 300 million pounds it was turned down.

At the bail hearing the defendant's barrister accused us of exaggerating the amount of money.

'I've looked at the paperwork,' he said. 'I can see only 15 million pounds.'

We knew it was far more than 15 million.

I commented to the team that even this low amount was six times greater than the Great Train Robbery which netted the villains £2.6 million.

Whenever Ian Donald and Paul Roden spoke about amounts of money, they referred to them as "GTRs" i.e. Great Train Robbery equivalents. Enquires with their banks revealed the Hares paid in over £400,000 in cash.

The trial took place in Southwark Crown Court in front of Judge Jeffrey Rucker QC in September 1997. Windsor pleaded guilty and received three years in prison. Tofail 6 years, Avtar Hare 5 and a half, Kulwant and Sohan three and a half years. In addition to £1.8 million seized at the time off arrest, Tofail and the Hare brothers were ordered to pay £1.4 million each. The amount was not a problem for any of them.

In December 1995 our team had an overnight stay at a hotel in Bournemouth to celebrate Christmas and reflect, with some pride, on the past year's achievements. Long hours had been spent on surveillance leading up to the Operation Fluke arrests. This followed a day of planned surveillance on route. I was to drive ahead as the target. We all met off the M25 and I was taken aback as the team emerged from their cars. Some had wigs, funny hats and outlandish clothes. All had a silly look on their faces. Over the top, I thought, and a bit stupid. I made an announcement over the radio for the cars to pull into the next layby.

I was angry and wanted to read them the riot act. 'Unless you all take this exercise seriously, we're going to turn around and go home. This is not a stag do. No messing around.'

They got the message. We carried out the drill as planned lasting from mid-morning to early evening and the team took the surveillance operation seriously. I was the person they were following so I stopped at various locations and left written notes which if collected would provide crucial evidence as if it was a real live operation.

In April 1996 I received a phone call from Roy Brisley, my first SIO on the Deltas. He was working for Crown Agents who arranged detail for Government Employees being seconded abroad helping them with tax, customs and other services.

Roy wanted to see me so I popped over to his office in South London.

After a few niceties he asked me if I was interested in going to Mozambique.

'To do what?' I asked.

'To be Chief Investigation Officer in Mozambique.'

'Mozambique!'

'Chief Investigation Officer.'

It would have been a major promotion for me.

'I'll have to think about it, Roy. There's Pauline and the boys to consider. It's a big step for them right now.'

I knew Pauline would be apprehensive as indeed, was I. News of recent bloody events in Mozambique were hardly an attraction for a young family even for a short time. It seemed that it was still a dangerous place to live and work.

For a few decades Mozambique was the playground for wealthy South Africans. Miles of golden beaches, cheap living and wall to wall sunshine. Then the Mozambican Civil War came which lasted from 1977 to 1992. Like many regional African conflicts during the late twentieth century local factions fought each other backed by leading world countries eager to establish influence in the region. The Marxist Front for the Liberation of Mozambique (FRELIMO) ruled the country and were opposed by anti-communist insurgent forces of the Mozambican National Resistance (RENAMO).

Dick Kellaway was my incumbent Chief Investigation Office so I spoke to his assistant to request a chat.

Twenty minutes later I spoke to Dick; 'I've got to be honest Dick. Roy Brisley has asked me to consider being the Chief Investigation Officer for customs in Mozambique. I've got reservations.'

'It's not a bad place to be nowadays,' said Dick. 'But if I'm on a beach running my hand through the sand I wouldn't like to come across a landmine.'

Dick hesitated but eventually said, 'No, Jim. If I were you, I wouldn't go.'

'That's what I'm thinking,' I said, 'but I just wanted to run it past you.'

'So, what is ahead of you?'

'Brazil,' I said without thinking. 'I heard there's drugs liaison officer job going in June 1997 when Teresa Lee comes back to the UK.'

In those days we had to spend two years back in a UK work place after an overseas posting to ensure DLOs were up to speed with changes in legislation and investigation techniques. There was always a fear officers could go "native".

'You've been back for eighteen months, said Dick. If you're keen, I'll delay the posting. If not, I'll change the rules. You've done a good job overseas before. Ideal person for this posting.'

The post for Brazil was advertised – rules demanded it was so I applied.

I soon discovered I was the only candidate so I spoke to Graham Honey, the SIO who managed DLOs in the Western Hemisphere.

'It's just you,' said Graham. 'No-one else has applied. You'll have to be interviewed.'

'Why?'

'To establish if you're up to the job. What qualifications, what experience you have.'

'I was a Liaison Officer in Portugal for three years. Are you saying I didn't do a good job?'

'Oh, no. I'm not saying that.'

'I'm uncomfortable with that. I think I might withdraw my application,'

'No! Don't do that.'

I didn't and, in the end, I didn't have to attend an interview.

The new posting was at the FCO First Secretary grade. It was a level transfer at my current grade SIO/Team Leader.

Pauline and I talked endlessly about the prospect of moving abroad again. Alex was 10, Alistair was 8 and Jimmy, 5. Their needs were uppermost in our thinking.

If we made the move, it would be in June 1997. We both agreed life is too short and we should up sticks, and go to Brazil.

Although Portuguese is the fifth major language in the world it is not spoken by many countries. Portugal, of course, Brazil, Cape Verde, Guinea-Bissau, Mozambique and a few others. Brazilian Portuguese is not the Portuguese I battled to learn. My nasal pronunciation of the language is absent in the lyrical nature of spoken Brazilian.

As few people spoke English in Brazil it was decided I would have a short intensive language session.

Leaving Pauline at home in April 1997 I flew to Florianopolis, a city in the Santa Catarina State, to live with a Brazilian family for three weeks. We spoke only Portuguese – Portuguese as they spoke it – never any English. This was all arranged through the Embassy who used a company called Cultura Inglese. I just had to turn up.

The son was nineteen and spoke some English. His parents had none. During the day I went to language school organised by Cultura Inglese. Classes were run by English people who spoke only Portuguese. Throughout the three weeks I never spoke a word of English. We managed to small talk through the family meals in the evening and at weekends we would go out to markets. I would never have imagined how tiring this would be. Only when I telephoned Pauline at home could I express myself clearly but these calls lasted only for a few minutes. I would phone home a couple of times a week using a call box that took phone cards. Not surprisingly, I was really home sick and really missed Pauline and the boys.

On my way back to London after the language training I called into the British Embassy in Brasilia and met the Head of Chancery who effectively would be my Foreign Office boss. Sarah Gillett was a charming FCO career diplomat who turned out to be incredibly supportive. I thought she was the best example of how a diplomat should be and wasn't surprised to see a few years later she was appointed as the UK's Ambassador to Norway.

The ID allowed DLOs and their wives to have a preliminary visit to the countries they are being posted to. In May of 1997 Pauline and I flew over to Brasilia where we spent a week being taken around looking for a house that would be home for three years. We visited the Mackenzie school that we hoped our boys would attend. The school had a fantastic reputation although none of the embassy staff sent their children there. We had seen the school advertised in an English magazine issued in Brasilia. The impressive Head pointed out that our eldest, Alex, would find it initially testing having no Portuguese.

'It's a difficult age. Two years younger and he would have found the integration easier.'

So, we decided to send the boys to the American School in Brasilia, a cosmopolitan school, mostly American and Brazilian but a smattering of other nationalities. It had a relaxed atmosphere, no uniform – shorts, baseball caps.

The school fees, on a par with a minor public school in the UK, were being met by the Embassy so this school was chosen.

The house finding proved more challenging. Brasilia is built on the shores of a lake, formed when they dammed a valley to establish the country's new Capital.

Curiously the city was organised in a sanitised way that reminded me of Milton Keynes in the UK.

My parents were distraught by the news we were going to Brazil. I tried to assure them that what they had read in the newspapers and seen on television was not the Brazil we were going to. A world away from the Favelas, the shanty towns of Rio. Pauline stayed for a week and we looked at a number of houses.

The Embassy had a block of six houses with a swimming pool area. Because I was not Foreign Office, it didn't matter where I lived. Although we needed to be near the school and not to be too remote for Pauline.

We saw an advertised house and turned up with the Admin Officer. According with FO regulations we could only have a house a certain size with a limited number of bedrooms. When we parked outside this house Pauline and I burst out laughing. It looked like the White House in Washington.

I addressed the agent who had joined us. 'I've got to be honest this will be way out of our price range.'

'$8000 a month. What is your limit?'

'$2000 a month.'

We did have a look around. It was nothing short of palatial, a number of massive rooms that were more suitable for other purposes. It later became the Indian Embassy.

As we were due to fly back to the UK, I told the Admin Officer I would move into Theresa Lee's house. Theresa was the DLO I was replacing. The house in North Pen was close to the other families. Pauline returned to the UK and I remained in Brazil.

The Embassy Admin Officer, Alan Gee called me in to Theresa's office to ask me for a favour.

'We would like the house you've looked at for one of our 3rd Secretaries.'

3rd Secretary was two rungs down the ranking level to me.

The Admin Officer continued. 'He's arriving soon with his family of three children.'

'Where does this leave me and my family?'

'We've found a suitable house a half mile away from the North Pen and closer to the Embassy. Would you like to have a look at it?'

Later that day, accompanied by the Admin Officer, I drove to see the house.

It was stunning from the outside with a covered bar-b-que area and a swimming pool in a well set out garden. The interior matched the exterior. Four bedrooms, large living rooms and kitchen. It also had uninterrupted views of the lake.

'I like it very much,' I said. 'But I'll need to speak to my wife.'

I phoned Pauline. She listened as I enthusiastically described the house and garden.'

'Does it have a double sink in the kitchen?' she asked.

'I can't recall.'

Pauline asked a number of questions that I couldn't answer.

'I've taken photographs inside and outside,' I said. 'You can see them when I get back.' I returned back to the UK after a few days but had already agreed to take the house I had been offered.

Photographic evidence was good enough. Pauline said yes so, I called the Admin Officer to confirm we would take the house.

He undertook to furnish the house throughout. A brochure from an American supplier arrived listing a great choice of furnishing. Everything was included, tables, chairs, sofas, beds, lampshades.

A new home was being created for us from a brochure.

We sold our house rather than renting it as previous tenants had been troublesome when we away living in Brussels. When we returned from Brussels and had settled back into work and domestic life. I answered a knock at the door and was confronted by a strapping man with a clipboard. He turned out to be a bailiff and was looking for the tenant who had previously rented our house.

'He's moved on,' I said. 'What's the problem?'

'He owes money. He sold second hand cars from this address.'

The other factor in selling was the distance between the UK and Brazil. We couldn't pop home anytime without costing a lot of money.

Our house was put onto the market and we hoped for a quick sale.

CHAPTER 21
BRAZIL

In June 1997, the family Jarvie flew to Brazil after saying a tearful goodbye to my mum and dad. Pauline's parents had passed away a few years before but she was close to her brothers and sisters. She also was close to my parents so it was with mixed emotions we flew from the UK.

The sky was blue that day, the air felt dry and a little chilly. Brazilian summers are like that. We arrived early afternoon with four suitcases containing nearly all our clothes. We were dressed in summer clothes but noticed the locals were dressed in jackets and some wore gloves.

There was an Embassy uniformed security guard outside the house wearing gloves and hats.

I said hello to the guard, as did Pauline and the boys. I had always taught the boys to be polite to all people they met and I was really proud they never let me down.

The boys ran around to the swimming pool and were jumping up and down with excitement, pulled on shorts and jumped into the pool. The guards were aghast. To them it was far too cold to take a dip.

That move by the boys meant everything to us. They had adjusted to a new country very quickly. My police colleagues later on asked me how long it took for my family to settle into life in Brazil. I always replied (in Portuguese) 'about 5 minutes.' I then related the story of the boy's first encounter with the pool.

I took a few days off before I started my work for real, armed with a mobile phone which would keep me in touch with HQ.

We attended a number of arrival parties, many of them during the day when the boys could come along as well. The ambassador Keith Haskell also hosted a reception for us to be introduced officially to the Brazilian authorities and staff from other embassies. Embassy staff usually have a three-year posting.

Our new home had been rapidly furnished with odds and ends from the embassy's housing section which was fairly basic but functional. Not to our taste at all, but the basics were there, beds, sofa and chairs, tables and kitchen utensils.

As the school years differed between the UK and Brazil the boys had June and July to enjoy themselves before starting the first term.

Although the boy's bikes and toys, and all our personal effects, were on the high seas, they found plenty of things to amuse themselves. Most of it revolved around the swimming pool. At the end of July, it was time for the boys to start school.

At the time, Alex, our eldest, was ten years old and was rather anxious and his first few days were a bit of a trauma for him. He had left his school friends and a football team at home and he was old enough to understand the challenges of the move we had made. The younger two seemed more relaxed and comfortable taking in the new system of teaching methods and the environment. Thankfully, over a week or so, Alex began to lose his unease and, with the help of his peers and teachers, participated more and more in school activities.

It was a bit of a culture shock for us as there was no school uniform and students could dress as they liked. Football shirts, shorts and baseball caps were generally the dress code which I assumed was an American thing.

A mini bus picked the boys up from home at 7am and dropped them back later at 4pm. Their fellow passengers, 10 or so, were the children of Embassy staff. Luckily, the new Military Attaché, Mike Bowles and his wife Ros had recently arrived and their two children John and Kathy went to the American school. Kathy was the sensible one and the four boys were generally being boys. They became really close friends as we did with Ros and Mike.

Having assured my parents that Brasilia was similar to the town of Milton Keynes in Buckinghamshire an event brought us back to reality. It was the third week at school for the boys and our second month in Brazil. We had read about the violence in Brazil, particularly in the shanty towns (favelas) in Rio.

When the boy's minibus arrived at school one morning they were met by a distressed headmaster, who along with some other teachers were running around half crouched with their hands over their heads.

'Hit the dirt!' the headmaster shouted.

My sons weren't sure what that meant but immediately followed the other children by lying on the floor in the school's car park.

Less than fifty yards away an eleven-year-old girl from the school was being kidnapped. The driver of her car was held at gunpoint and had been shot in the arm. Bullets were shot in the air so everyone took cover.

The kidnappers then sped away in two cars. Surprisingly, the students were ushered into the school and after an impromptu assembly, went to their classrooms as if nothing had happened.

The kidnapped girl was the eleven-year-old daughter of a local Brazilian politician who was candidate for the City Senate. (Similar to a UK mayor, but with a lot more political power). Her driver had been shot in the arm but although several bullets were fired no other person was injured.

Due to the serious nature of the crime the Federal Police took over the investigation. Kidnapping was rife in Brazil and the police had their own teams dealing with the threat.

When the boys got home, we talked about it and I insisted that when we next telephoned my parents the kidnapping must not be mentioned. 'We don't want to worry them,' I said.

Of course, when the next call to the UK happened the whole episode was blurted out.

'You'll never guess what happened at school Grandma.'

'Did you go on a school trip? Was it exciting?'

'No! No! They kidnapped a girl from school. They were firing guns. They shot the driver. They were bullets everywhere. The teacher told us to "hit the dirt"'.

There was silence until my mum asked to speak to me.

She didn't wait for me to speak. 'What have you done? You've taken our grandchildren away and put them in danger.'

'It's not normally like this,' I said. 'The boys are fine. It's a local matter, a local family, nothing to do with us or the school.'

I don't think I came anywhere near convincing my mother that the chance of anything bad happening to her family was no more than being in a number of cities in the UK.

Pauline and I discussed the situation and concluded that problems could happen anywhere in the world, including the UK. We were advised by the Embassy to keep out of the poorer areas and to stick to the larger shopping malls.

As part of my official duties, I liaised with the Federal Police Drug Teams on a daily basis. I was given an update on the progress of the kidnapping investigation. After about a week the kidnappers made contact with the girl's father and made the mistake of using a traceable landline. If a landline is used it can be traced within a few minutes.

The police, like most forces throughout the world, were able to locate the address where the call was coming from.

A week after the kidnapping, which must have seemed like a lifetime for the girl's family, the police raided the house and rescued the girl but only after a shoot-out. Three kidnappers were shot dead and two arrested. Thankfully, the victim was rescued unharmed.

To everyone's shock but probably not the Federal Police the kidnappers turned out to be members of the Military Police.

Brazil had three police forces. The Federal Police (the people I dealt with) were the main force better trained, better educated, better paid. They covered cross-border, serious and international crime. Then there were the Civil Police who carried out investigations in their locality.

The Military Police patrolled the streets, transport and first responders to robberies. They, I was told, were paid peanuts. The saying goes, "if you pay peanuts, you're going to get monkeys." I was also told that their monthly pay of about $150 was not enough to feed and support a family. As such, corruption, particularly the taking of bribes, was rife.

I had no dealings with the Military Police and rarely rubbed shoulders with the Civil Police.

The Federal Police were my contacts in Brasilia. Everything had to go through them, particularly if I wanted to go to other regions of the country.

I was the third British Drug Liaison Officer to be posted to Brazil. Martin Crago had originally set up the office as I had done in Portugal. He was replaced by Teresa Lee who I was replacing. Teresa had been there for four years and fed me all of her contacts.

Normally the handover period lasts a couple of weeks. Theresa stayed well beyond that period. It was a relief when she finally left after a few weeks and returned to the UK. It is always difficult at handover time and I wanted to stamp my mark on the role. During the handover I travelled a lot with Theresa and I was conscious that Pauline was at home looking after the boys whilst I was visiting glamorous locations such as Rio, Manaus and Recife. As always Pauline accepted this was all part of my job.

Thankfully Pauline, being a sociable person, didn't take long to make friends with wives of the embassy staff, particularly Ros Bowles. Parks and beauty spots were nearby and there were plenty of modern shopping centres, supermarkets, cafes and restaurants where friends and family would meet up.

In addition to the families from the Embassy we met up with friends from commerce. International companies had offices there including the De Beers Group, the world-wide corporation that specialised in diamonds.

The ex-pat community was small but had created strong bonds which we quickly joined in with.

For the first time in our lives, we had a maid, Teresina, who came every day. At first Pauline used to tidy up and clean before she came but after a few weeks got used to it. Pauline still cooked at home and the five of us would regularly go out to eat.

The boys loved the Churrascarias where the waiters came around with skewers of meat and would only stop when a small block of wood on each table was placed red side up.

Brasilia is futuristic and divided into distinct areas; the banking section, the hospital section, the school section. Built in the 1960s, it is a planned city with its white, modern architecture, and set out in the shape of an airplane, its "fuselage" is the Monumental Axis, two wide avenues flanking a massive park. In the "cockpit" is Praça dos Três Poderes, named for the three branches of government surrounding it. Two "wings" spread out East and West of the fuselage.

Most of the social clubs were on the lake but there was one on the North Peninsular.

The social life for the Brazilians was also done on a sector basis. The military would have their own social clubs as did the banks, hospitals and government agencies. At the end of the peninsular, close to our home was a social club on the lake. It had two swimming pools, tennis courts, and over 30 bar-b-que areas. (next to Samba, dancing bar-b-cueing was the most popular pastime for Brazilians).

So, we thought it would be a good idea for the whole family to join this club.

I called into the club and approached the receptionist.

Speaking in Portuguese, I said, 'Would it be possible to become a member here?'

'This is the Club Congresso. It is for Parliament employees only.'

'I live a mile away. There are five in our family. It would be wonderful to join a club so close to where we live.'

'Leave it with me,' he said. 'We have never had a foreigner ask to be a member. Come back next week.'

I drove up in my diplomatic car the next week.

'Ah, Senhor Jarvie. We have two sponsors for you. You are welcome as members.'

It didn't take long for Mike and family to become members and they were joined by Andy and Sandy Belfitt with their children, Samantha and Nick.

Saturdays were the days we would meet up for a bar-b-que and often be invited to join Brazilian families. These new friendships opened up new opportunities. The boys were invited to play 5 a side football and take part in different games. The club turned out to be a fantastic facility for us.

On the 29th July I had a visit by Alexander Russell, a senior Commissioner of Customs and Excise. Known as Sandy, he was a high-ranking officer although not connected to Customs Investigation. He was in Brazil to meet up with the Receita Federal, a department that covered Customs and Inland Revenue.

I accompanied Sandy to the Ministry and introduced him to the Head of the Receita Federal who spoke reasonable English. That evening Sandy came to our home for dinner. It was a lovely evening and prior to dinner Sandy played football with the boys in the garden.

'Pass the ball Sandy,' I shouted. 'Go on. Head it!'

This was something I never expected, to direct such a senior official.

The day after I received a call from Sandy's personal assistant in London to say that she had an urgent phone call telling her that Sandy's brother had died in the UK. She had tried to contact him but failed. She wanted me to get a message to Sandy.

I drove over to the Receita Federal and asked if Sandy could be brought out of meeting and meet me in reception.

When he did arrive, I suggested he sat down.

'What's the problem?'

'I'm sorry to be the bearer of bad news but I have had a phone call from your secretary to tell me your brother had died back home.'

'Jim, I haven't got a brother.'

'I'm really pleased you haven't,' I replied.

I was immediately relieved but confused. Neither of us could guess why this message had got through to us.

It transpired that there was another Alexander Russell in the department whose brother had indeed died.

At the beginning of August, I was joined in the office by Rebecca Brown who was going to be my assistant. Rebecca was from Bolton in Lancashire started as an administrative assistant in the radio section of Customs and Excise. This department organised the distribution of official radio hand-sets. "Beccs" had a degree in Spanish and was also fluent in Portuguese. She had also studied and worked in Bogota so living in south America didn't challenge her. We hit it off straight away.

I soon found out that Rebecca was more than capable of running the office while I was away. She would deal with communications, phone calls from London and informants who would ring the embassy.

A good sense of humour was essential and Rebecca had a lively one often calling senior diplomats, including the ambassador "Chicken". The public often have a perception of diplomats but in reality, most are genuine and lead normal lives.

After about three months, the Admin section advised me my personal effects, my official cars, a Chrysler Jeep and the family car a 7-seater Chrysler Voyager had arrived at the Embassy. I wasn't sure what I expected but was a little surprised to be told a forty-foot container was waiting for me outside the Embassy. I also didn't expect to have to unload the vehicles myself.

There was just enough room to get into the cars. Two makeshift metal ramps were placed at the exit. With the Embassy staff watching on I reversed the first car gingerly down the ramp. I breathed a sigh of relief when both cars were on the road. Pauline, who had been driving an embassy car took the keys of the voyager and happily drove off home.

I had been used to driving surveillance cars but a Chrysler Jeep was something else. It was a bit ironic but the only car I ever had with heated seats was in Brazil where I never used it. More importantly the boy's toys and bikes were in the container and were delivered to the house. It was like Christmas day when they opened the boxes.

We acquired for Rebecca an older jeep, a heavy armour plated, bullet-proofed windows one, which we nick-named "the wardrobe". It drove like one. It had been in Colombia where the threat of an armed attack was a lot higher.

When it first arrived, I drove it for a couple of days and on one occasion I was driving with Pauline. I wound the window down only to realise I had triggered an emergency locking system. Massive bolts in the door had moved into the chassis. I didn't realise that the window winder released the bolts and I ended up crawling out the back window.

The Head of the Federal Police drug squad was called Cavaleiro, an experienced but difficult character. He was outspoken and feisty, irritated by the demands made on him. On a daily basis one or more foreign liaison officer would make a request for help. We were often asked for surveillance teams or to make some enquiries, mostly in Rio and Sao Paulo.

He was from Fortaleza in the north of Brazil and had a strong dialect which was difficult to understand and at times words or phrases were lost. He was very close to the Dutch Police Liaison Officer, Aart Modderkolk, who had helped me immensely in the early days. Because he was Dutch, Cavaleiro called Aart a "second-hand German", the Americans, Gringos and me, "the original Gringo!"

Most of my work was in San Paolo, the city of over 20 million. The port of Santos is a two- hour drive from San Paolo. This port handled containers going to Europe and the UK.

I visited the customs and police in Santos who offered help in any identification of ships and cargo. I also visited shipping agents who were able to identify specific containers or shipments that looked out of the ordinary. I was passed details of one such shipment which was a forty-foot container of five litre tins of paint. The company supplying the paint was suspect as it had been linked to a previous consignment intercepted in Rotterdam. Details of the shipment was passed to London and the container searched at Tilbury. Approximately 100 kilos of cocaine were discovered in sealed bags within the paint.

Rob Noble was a vice consul in the Consulate in Rio. Rob and I worked together at the embassy in Lisbon. I was pleased to have a friend in the office.

Unlike Lisbon I didn't have direct access to ports and airports. I had to go through the Federal Police to approach airports or docks. I was also fully aware of the potential corruption of local law enforcement and port and airport officials.

It was against the law to run informants so we had to tread carefully if we sought information from anybody. However, there were people in the airline and shipping businesses willing to help me, not as informants but on general intelligence. A chap in Rio, called David Lloyd, had access to lots of data on containers and was able to help us identify routes and sailing times. I would speak to him almost on a daily basis.

Although I dealt with the Federal Police, I did have a relationship with

George Henry Millard, who worked for the Civil Police as a senior manager. George was a real Anglophile and was respected throughout the world. He was often invited to Cambridge university to speak on corruption in South America. As well as working for the Civil Police George ran a security company and he also had access to the shipping world.

Rio, Sao Paulo and the north of Brazil were the most important areas for drugs transiting from Colombia and Bolivia. Given the vast distances involved I found myself on flights at least twice a week. I would stay over at hotels, usually recommended by the embassy or the local police.

After a while flying became a bit of a bore. On one flight from Brasilia to Manaus we encountered a thunderstorm. We were flying over the vast Amazon jungle and it shook violently flying through a storm. It crossed my mind if the plane were to crash in such a remote area I would never be found. As the plane dropped, twisted, rose and twisted again I thought about writing a farewell letter to Pauline and the boys.

Over time, with the help of the Federal Police office in Brasilia, I was able to build up Police contacts throughout the country.

I met with the head of the Drugs Squad in his office in central Sao Paulo. His name was Marcelo Itagiba and we chatted in Portuguese when three American DEA agents came into his office. The Drugs Enforcement Administration had a large presence in Brasilia but also had a team of three officers in Sao Paulo.

I wore a suit and tie and they wore jeans and t-shirts and cowboy boots.

The Americans, it seemed, insisted anyone they had to work with be vetted by their security department. Officers from the Brazilian Federal Police would be funded to travel to Miami and to be polygraphed to establish if any were corrupt.

'Last month,' a DEA agent told me that a question was asked, 'Have you ever taken a bribe over $20,000?'

A Brazilian officer replied. 'All in one go or in part payments?'

That officer was not selected.

Out of the blue, in immaculate Oxford English, Marcelo said, 'This is my country. I do not see why my officers should be polygraphed to see if they could work in their own country.'

He really tore them off a strip.

Three DEA agents left the office with their tails between their legs.

I said to Marcelo, 'I didn't know you spoke such good English.'

'My children go to English School in Sao Paulo and I am one of the school governors and I have to speak English.'

It turned out that Marcelo was highly educated and a passionate anglophile. Initially he jokingly accused me of being a spy for the embassy, calling me James Bond but latterly as our relationship grew, he called me "Jungle Jim".

I don't think I ever persuaded him that I was not a spy for the British Embassy but that didn't stop us getting close. He was increasingly helpful to me and when he went on secondment to the Health Ministry, I helped him forge links to the medicines control agencies in the UK and other parts of Europe.

In the British Embassy, Foreign Office officials (the diplomats) would take it in turns to be on call, out of hours and at weekends. So, any emergency calls would go straight to that official via the on-call mobile phone. This included British nationals in trouble, car crashes, lost passports, local disputes.

I saw the Deputy Head of Missions who advised me I was on call for the Embassy the following week.

'I can't be on call for the embassy. I'm on call for my own job. I thought there was an agreement with my people in London.'

'You'd better talk to them,' he said. 'We've got you down for cover.'

I telephoned Michelle Rice- Wilson at HQ who put me through to Phil Byrne my ACIO (Assistant Chief Investigation Officer).

He told me that a colleague based in Peru had volunteered to be on UK Embassy call a year before. This, in the Embassy's mind, changed the rules for Customs staff to be included.

So, I was given an Embassy phone and went home. At 3am on the Sunday morning I got a call from the Foreign Office in London to say that a party of students were lost in the Amazon area. They didn't know if they were in Brazil or Peru. They had sent off a distress beacon which failed to identify their location.

'Could you send out an aircraft to search for them?'

'You do realise that the area we are talking about is larger than Europe. It'll be like looking for a needle in a haystack.'

'We don't yet know if the beacon was let off by mistake.'

'I can't scramble a military aircraft without a degree of certainty. Even then it might take days to find them. If you get more information, come back to me.'

As soon as I could I rang the Consul, Alan Gee, who took on the problem saying he would make contact with London.

The students were fine and the beacon had been let off by mistake.

Other calls were mostly people who had lost their travel documents. Details were passed to the Consulate who would sort it.

The majority of calls I answered were ones I couldn't act on as I had received no consular training. The initial call set off the consular process and the majority of problems were resolved quickly.

I worked in the "confidential" area of the embassy which was off limits to the public and the locally employed staff. All the military, communication and political staff were located in this area. I partook in the rota of "cleaner-sitting". Cleaners were not allowed to be in certain rooms unaccompanied. The cleaners came to the embassy at 06.00 and had to be let into the secure area.

I was on call approximately every six weeks. If I was away, I had to get another diplomat to cover my duties.

In August 1998, I had a phone call from my desk officer in the UK, Michelle, regarding a major investigation by the Customs Investigation team in Leeds "Operation Table Cut".

The Leeds team had identified two Land Rovers from the local area that had crossed into Europe and driven to Genoa in Italy where they were put on a cargo ship to a ferry bound for Buenos Aires in Argentina. Two suspects, Alan Barker from Cleckheaton and Michael Ackroyd from Batley flew out to Buenos Aires to collect the vehicles. They were joined by Anthony Hill from Dewsbury and Phillip Riach, also from Batley. They were stopped by Argentinian immigration officials and told them they were all on a wildlife expedition in South America.

It was thought initially that they were going to collect drugs in Argentina but they actually drove north to Brazil. The Land Rovers were spotted driving along Brazil's coastline to Recife and Belem which is at the mouth of the vast Amazon River. The vehicles were loaded onto a cargo vessel destined for Manaus, a journey of five days. The four suspects then flew from Belem to Manaus to await the vehicle's arrival. They had already driven an incredible 7000 kilometres so far. I received the occasional update on the vehicle's movements as they drove from Manaus to Caracas, to Bogota then on to Cali in Colombia where it was believed they collected the drugs.

Unbelievably, the two Land Rovers drove through Colombia, Ecuador, Peru, Chile and Argentina eventually arriving in Rio around the 23 December. A port contact of mine confirmed both vehicles were booked on the cargo ferry "The Republica de Venezia" destined for Genoa in Italy.

I phoned Michelle who advised me that the vehicles would be stopped and searched in Italy.

To our surprise the Italian Customs found nothing in the Land Rovers when they arrived in Genoa on 7 January 1999 and they were allowed to continue their journey back to the UK.

At Coquelles in Northern France, the terminal for the Channel Tunnel one of the suspect Land Rovers was stopped by UK Customs (UK Customs had officers based in France) who, after searching the vehicle, removed the four wheels from the car. Alarm bells started to ring when it took three officers to carry one wheel. When the tyres were prised off the wheel rim 35 kilos of cocaine in each of them. They arrested Barker and Hill.

The second car had disappeared from our radar and was never found.

This find led to the arrest of the traffickers in Leeds. Those found guilty received prison sentences between 10 and 20 years in prison.

I found it incredible that the Land Rover could drive a distance of over 10,000 kilometres from Cali in Colombia to the Channel Tunnel with 120 kilos of cocaine in the four wheels.

Many politicians came over from the UK and visited the Embassy. One was John Battle, a Foreign Office minister and MP for Leeds. The Ambassador's secretary called me to arrange that I meet him.

At the Ambassador's residence I sat between Battle, a blunt, outspoken Yorkshireman and the Ambassador.

'I don't understand,' he said, 'why the government pays for you to live and work here. Can you explain to me what do you do for my constituents in Leeds?'

I am sure he thought he had me on the back foot. I was simply going to say that I was there to stop drugs coming to the UK.

'I can tell you exactly what I and my team do for the people of Leeds,' I said.

'What's that?'

I took a deep breath and with real relish explained "Operation Table Cut", the day two Land Rovers left Leeds, their voyage to Columbia and back and their eventual arrest and the seizure of 120 kilos of cocaine.

John Battle was silent for quite a while. When he did speak again his tone was conciliatory. Wonderful timing, I know. Had Battle been MP for other constituencies, I may have had nothing significant to say.

Terry Byrne who had risen though the ranks to become the Director General of Law Enforcement (he managed over 9000 staff including all the uniformed, investigation and intelligence teams) phoned me the following week to say that John Battle had been on to him insisting to be kept up to date on the Leeds drugs case. I was almost apologetic to Terry but we both knew the case was good news for the department.

After several months of lobbying the Justice Ministry and Federal Police we finally got permission to open a sub office in Sao Paulo. The American DEA were uncomfortable with sharing a territory with their British counter-parts but were in no position to resist. Dave Sterling, an experienced cocaine investigator was appointed to the role and with his wife Helen, moved to Sao Paulo.

I introduced Dave to Marcelo and his newly appointed deputy Roberto Troncon. He was a young police officer who I immediately liked and saw him as someone who could rise through the ranks. The fact Marcelo thought so much of him was enough for me.

At that time Roberto didn't speak English so myself and Dave discussed how we could sponsor him to learn. Dave arranged a suitable course for him to attend with the Cultura Inglese in Sao Paulo. Each time we met up he loved to demonstrate how his English was improving. Roberto was well respected by the Federal Police and successfully moved into Marcelo's shoes when he moved on to the Health Ministry.

He quickly became fluent in English. So much so that a year later, he was appointed as the Federal Police liaison officer in London.

The initial funding of Roberto's language training turned out to be a great investment. He could not do enough for myself and Dave and Frank Dick who would replace me in Brazil. He would provide surveillance teams on British suspects at a drop of a hat. He would also handle the deployment of tracking beacons on suspects vessels if required. Everything would have to be cleared by Brasilia but he would oil the wheels for us.

The sheer size of Brazil meant we were thinly spread. We relied on the network of Honorary Consuls in all the major cities to be our eyes and ears.

Very similar to Richard Blandy in Madeira, the Consuls would provide me with details of drug arrests in their area. Ideally many of them worked in the shipping or export industry. I often visited them and spoke to them on a regular basis to keep them focussed on identifying unusual shipping movements.

Although it was against Brazilian law, we did recruit a limited number of informants. The majority of them rang into the embassy or Dave's office in the consulate. One was recruited by Dave and despite our initial reservations (we thought he was a bit of a Walter Mitty), he did provide the name of two couriers who were flying to the UK with cocaine. He was paid about £2000 for the information but he made some strange requests. He asked if we could get military memorabilia from Scottish regiments. Dave suggested we give him the code name "Jock".

Lou Reade and Kay McClelland, our new desk officers (they job shared the role), must have thought we were mad when we asked them to go to a military surplus market stalls to buy various items. They managed to get hold of military berets and badges. I did draw the line when "Jock" asked us to get hold of a Ghurka kukri, the traditional knife with a recurve blade.

After about a year in Brazil I was advised by Head Office in London that the new emphasis of our overseas work was to help stop drugs leaving source and transit countries. The tactic of "upstream disruption" meant I had to approach the Federal police to see how we could help them intercept commercial consignments of drugs transiting Brazil. My colleagues in other South American countries focussed their activities on "upstream disruption".

Myself and Dave were visiting the Federal Police in Sao Paulo and Marcelo told us they have major difficulties in intercepting mobile phone communications when they were being used in remote locations. I agreed to explore how we could support them. When I returned to the embassy, I spoke to the ambassador to see if he would support an application for funding by the Foreign Office. He said he would and I then spoke to my office in London. After a few days, they came back to me and told me interception kits contained in a small suitcase is available. With the funding agreed the kit arrived a month later and it was handed over to Marcelo and his team.

Following a seizure of 200 kilos of cocaine in a remote area on the border with Bolivia I was advised by Marcelo the kit provided by us provided a major help to identifying the light aircraft and the landing strip. I was really pleased and would notify the office, the ambassador and London. I asked Marcelo how many people were arrested.

He replied, 'The light aircraft pilot'.

'Nobody else?' I asked.

'No. The other three suspects were shot and killed by gun fire with my agents'.

Perhaps it was the way he said it. It was not the most important issue to him. My report back to London and the ambassador was a little economical with the truth. We managed to fund and provide a second piece of kit for Brasilia.

The first few months went very quickly. My daily visits to the Federal Police meant that trust as well as friendship was developed. Any intelligence they had relevant to the UK would be passed over only when they saw it appropriate. Their priority was on Brazilian matters so other country's concerns took second place. So, second place that it seemed, at times, as painful as drawing teeth.

Names and telephone numbers were passed on, but rarely did that happen even though I would do the same with any information I or, HQ, had gathered on Brazilian matters.

Cavaleiro continued to be a crusty character. My relationship was helped by the Dutch Police officer Aart, who had been a close friend to Cavaleiro. I visited the Federal police daily and would initially speak to the managers but would spend most of my time with the operational officers. Officers Renaldo, Carlos and Lima were more than accommodating, helping out whenever they could. They had hands-on experience and would give me information on Brazilian smuggling gangs targeting other countries apart from the UK. Nigerian crime groups were heavily involved in drug smuggling and had a major presence in Brazil. They would give me details of telephone numbers in West Africa and show me transcripts of telephone intercepts.

In return, I was able to get a Customs officer based at Heathrow to come over to Sao Paulo. He was a Yoruba speaker and could understand the dozen or so local dialects that make up the Yoruba language. He proved invaluable in helping the police with the intercepts. He stayed in Sao Paulo for two weeks but his input was a real help and it won me a few Brownie points.

As well as the officers the two girls, Regina and Anna, who were the office managers made sure all my requests were dealt with quickly.

As December arrived the family and I realised we would be spending our first Christmas in Brazil. Sunny, warm, blue skies in sharp contrast to dark clouds, rain, snow and cold. Brasilia did, however, have its share of furious storms, thunder, lightning and stair-rod rain.

We soon discovered that the traditional Christmas we knew back in the UK was replicated in Brazil; twinkling lights, Santa Claus on a sled pulled by reindeers. All the decorations were the same as we had at home although there, at 28 degrees, the snow was fake.

The shopping centres had gone overboard on the trimmings with white bearded Santa in elaborate grottos. Our sons were transfixed at what was going on. What was different was that after a shopping trip they would jump into the swimming pool. Some of the shopping malls even had ice rinks for the locals. Unlike the UK, the rinks were often very wet as the hot weather melted the ice.

There were modern shops in Brasilia catering for all ages and styles but we were thrown by our sons request for a home computer.

We discovered Peter Justesen, a Danish company who offered duty-free shopping for diplomats. They supplied a catalogue and would order one for us. It arrived two weeks before Christmas and was promptly hidden from prying eyes.

Close to where we lived the roads had gone to town on the lights and decorations. Every house was festooned with colour and a garlanded vehicle in centre stage. Streets competed with each other for the Christmas Cup – whose street was the most dazzling.

Pauline and I and two friends took a short walk along these streets and found out how warm and hospitable the locals were. After their amazement at seeing four Brits waving and smiling at them, we were invited in for drinks. It confirmed something we already knew; the Brazilians are friendly, generous and unashamedly Anglo-files.

Pauline and Embassy staff organised a Christmas party for an orphanage set up by a Craig Alden, a British guy who worked for BT.

While in Rio he had witnessed two boys being shot by the police. This was then a policy to rid the streets of urchins.

At the Embassy party thirty children were bussed from the orphanage in north Brasilia.

They were delighted, eating the special food that had been prepared, accepting small wrapped presents and some even risked a dip in the swimming pool, for some the first time.

One little boy humbled us all by relishing his unwrapped gift as it was, not realising there was something inside. He was delighted to just receive a bright coloured parcel.

We heard stories of the children's desperate state before they entered the security of the orphanage. One boy, eager to escape the abuse of drug addict parents, clung to the underside of a lorry for over two hundred miles before finding a degree of comfort in the company of kind strangers.

A handicapped boy had been thrown in a rubbish skip by his parents but was found and taken in by the orphanage.

Family and friends from the UK sent over gifts and I was able to record my sons tearing open the boxes. Their excitement went up a few notches when the computer was unwrapped.

At that point panic ensued. The computer had to be plugged in to the power, be switched on and sense be made of whatever appeared on the screen. I was forever grateful to IBM who supplied an idiot proof set of instructions; press this, then that, pause, choose this, then that, wait and there it was; a menu of options you could choose from. I clicked on the internet connection then, within minutes, the boys were playing simple games on it.

Mike and Ros Boles invited us and thirty or so of the Embassy staff who were obliged or chose to spend Christmas in Brasilia to lunch. It turned out a feast with each family supplying cooked ingredients, multiple turkeys, potatoes and vegetables.

New Year celebrations were held at the Embassy. We telephoned home who had passed midnight hours before us.

Like most cities in the world Brasilia set off a vast display of fireworks as the clock struck twelve.

1998 arrived. It was both strange and wonderful to be in such an exotic country, miles from home sharing the event with people we had only recently met.

Steve Read was an assistant to the Military Commission being seconded from the RAF. He was married to Suzanne from Sweden. They had three daughters, Sarah, Sophie and Victoria.

The Reads had been so kind to us when we arrived, hosting parties, making sure we met up with people. It was quite a shock to hear that they were coming to the end of their tour. Steve would re-join the Force.

Andy Belfitt filled Steve's role at the Embassy. His wife Sandy also worked in the communications department of the Embassy. This department, under the Foreign Office umbrella, would transmit telexes and the like to London for onward transmission to my HQ.

Sandy had worked for Customs before joining the Foreign Office.

The Belfitts had two children, Sam and Nick, a bit younger than our boys.

As I prepared to leave home one April morning my mobile phone rang.

The female voice over the phone was strained. 'Jim, would you come and help us. We've had a serious crash. A road accident.'

'Who is this?' I asked.

'It's Sandy.'

I didn't hesitate. The anxiety in her voice was enough. She managed to tell me where she was so I drove along the back road leading to the city bordering the lake. From quite a distance I could see Andy's Land Rover almost curled around a tree. My heart sank. For a moment I feared the worse for Andy and his family.

The ambulance and local fire brigade had just arrived, the officer's total attention on the car's occupants. The middle son, Nick, was being carried out of the crumpled car as I spotted Andy and Sandy close by. I stood back a little but was able to speak to the support people in Portuguese telling them who I was and the names of the Belfitt family. There were special worries about Nick's condition but they were all taken to the local hospital.

I told Sandy and Andy that the medics wanted to check Nick out and take x-rays and that I would follow and translate as we went through the procedure of admitting Nick.

I phoned the Defence section of the Embassy explaining what had happened and what was going to happen.

The public hospital was in the centre of Brasilia, not exactly run down but didn't stand in comparison with the many private hospitals ex-pats would normally have access to.

Some of the doctors and staff spoke broken English but most did not. My linguistic skills were tested when I was required to translate complicated medical terms to Sandy and Andy.

Nick had hit his head and his body was badly bruised but the radiographer announced there were no broken bones, no serious injury that would suggest permanent damage.

Spirits were lifted when we were advised that the family could go home.

A colleague from the Embassy picked them up and took them home. I returned to the Embassy as Andy's car was being delivered on the back of a trailer. Such was the impact of the crash that the sturdiness of a Land Rover was breached and almost split in half.

Later Andy told me what happened. 'I headed down the Lake Road toward the City when a car coming in the opposite way lost control and knocked me off the road. The next thing I knew we had already hit the tree.'

In 1998 my work was more focused on the north of the country traveling up there at least once a week, usually by aeroplane. The airlines were very modern and although the planes were small, they were very modern jets. Road or rail systems were not in place.

It was fun travelling with a company call TAM.

Just before the plane was due to take off the captain would make an announcement. 'If you look under your seat one of you will win a small prize.' (Often a travel voucher for the airline).

When serving meals and drinks they would provide napkins with small pegs to attach them to your lapels. When booking my flights, Rebecca would often ask, 'Do you want to fly with the bib and bingo flight?'

I received information from the Customs Maritime Intelligence team in the UK that a yacht had been identified through a UK based informant who had been told the yacht was suspect. This vessel had been overhauled in preparation for a trip from somewhere in Europe across the Atlantic. It was thought that it was about to be used to smuggle cocaine on its return voyage. I was asked to go up to Ilha de Itaparica, a small island opposite Salvador in the North-east.

Once the nation's capital, Salvador was the largest city in the state of Bahia. It is known for its Portuguese colonial architecture, Afro-Brazilian culture and a tropical coastline with a population of over two and half million.

From 1501 to 1886 an estimated 4.9 million slaves were transported from Africa to Brazil to work in the rubber, sugar cane plantations and the newly discovered diamond and gold mines.

In 1888 Brazil was the last country in the Western world to abolish slavery.

This influx eventually contributed to a diverse and vibrant community noted for its cuisine, music, and dance. Part of all this were its shady and violent gangs of criminals. This state of affairs would eventually lead to

Salvador's having 60 homicides for every 100,000 people, more than double that of Rio de Janeiro's, at 21.5 per 100,000, and four times that of Sao Paulo, at about 15 per 100,000. Compared to other cities Brasilia was considered a safe city, helped, I think, by its relative affluence.

I met up with a Federal Police officer who took me around the City of Salvador (it means Saviour in Portuguese) stopping in a square for coffee. There were African descendants playing the berimbau, a single-string percussion instrument, a musical bow. This had been incorporated into the practice of the Afro-Brazilian martial art, capoeira.

The capoeira combined elements of dance, acrobatics, and music and dates back to the beginning of the 16th century. It is celebrated for its acrobatic and complex manoeuvres, involving hands on the ground and inverted kicks. It was encouraged by slave owners who were against any contact sport likely to cause injury and debilitate their investment.

The policeman and I parked near the marina getting as close as we could to the vessel that was of interest. It was a racing yacht 80ft long with a few workmen fixing it up. Through binoculars we could see clearly what was happening but a hundred yards away proved difficult on detail. We were able to take photographs which I would send back to the UK. The mast was yet to be fitted so we knew we were at a very early stage of the investigation if indeed it required an investigation. The yacht was obviously being prepared for sea racing not for transporting drugs across the Atlantic.

Although we did not follow up on this case it had provided me with valuable contact in this northern city.

Although Rio's annual carnival is the most famous, carnivals are held throughout Brazil although, in most cases, were held for the benefit for tourists. Many locals, I was told, would move out for the duration.

We had two days holiday in February that covered carnival time in Brasilia so I took extra days off work so the family could visit the beach.

One of my embassy colleagues, Neil Storey asked me if we fancied joining him in and his family for carnival in Ilheus. I looked at the map and it was the nearest beach area to Brasilia. Couldn't be that difficult to drive to, I thought.

We set off on the Thursday prior to the start of carnival in February 1988. I had a basic road map and directions to the villa. We decided to take our maid Teresinha who was so excited as she had never seen the sea before.

After 20 minutes the boys enquired, 'Are we there yet?'.

Little did we realise that it would take us 17 hours to drive to the nearest beach. We stopped to fill up with petrol and a sign at the garage stated that this was the last petrol station for 200 kilometres. The "A" roads were a nightmare, often just dirt tracks and giant potholes. Lorries would be driving on the wrong side of the road to avoid the potholes and we often had to drive off the road to avoid being hit.

When we arrived Tereshina and the boys ran down the track from the villa to the beach.

Despite the ordeal of getting there it was a great trip and the locals welcomed us Brits with open arms. We attended their parties and barbeques.

I was dreading the drive home but at least this time we travelled in convoy with Neil and his family. We also stopped overnight in the small town of Barreiras. The hotel staff were really friendly but often looked at the "Brits on tour" as a bit crazy.

When I discussed the trip with the Federal police the following week, they were amazed I had driven this distance in one day. They also told me the road was notorious for kidnappings. It was a relief for me we all survived the trip unscathed.

In June 1998 Brazil hosted the football World Cup. The opening game on 10 June was Brazil versus Scotland. The Press were having a field day and the embassy became a focal point for journalists.

The day before the game news journalists and a couple of film crews were stationed outside the embassy complex. As we were considered diplomats the Ambassador asked us not to comment to the press but refer them to the press officers.

My boys and a couple of the younger children were playing football on the tennis court inside the complex. One of the television reporters shouted to the boys, 'Who is going to win the game?'

The reply game back when the boys chanted, 'Scotland, Scotland'.

They actually appeared on the local news and thankfully the Ambassador saw the funny side and our boys had not caused a diplomatic crisis.

The morning of the game I donned my kilt and headed to the Federal Police office. What a reception I received not just by the police but the locals when I walked through the streets.

Cavaleiro and his colleagues wore Brazilian football shirts and they cracked open a bottle of beer. All we talked about that day was football. Scotland were the underdogs but I kept saying to the Brazilians have you seen the film, "Coracao Valente." (Braveheart.)

A large TV screen was set up in the meeting area and a loud cheer went up when John Collins equalised for Scotland. The final score was 2-1 to Brazil but it was a "braveheart" performance.

Before the actual final took place, we all flew back home for a scheduled annual break so watched the game, Brazil against France, from an armchair in my parent's house.

On return to Brazil, we found the locals were amazed that all we Brits had supported their team and not France in the final. I did explain it was like them supporting their neighbours Argentina and the penny dropped.

I spent a short time explaining that the history of Britain and France had not always been "entente cordiale."

In November 1998 I received a call from Michelle who passed me some Brazilian telephone numbers and details of a suspect yacht. Through the Federal Police I was able to confirm the yacht had been in a number of marinas in the north of Brazil including Fortaleza and Belem. One of the crewmen, a Dutchman called Godfreied Hoppenbrouwers, was a key suspect and had access to numerous yachts and boats. He lived part of his time in Brazil.

The suspect gang was headed by Brian Brendon Wright (nick-named "The Milkman" because he always delivered). Wright was suspected to be behind an importation of over a ton of cocaine concealed in the dumb waiter of a yacht called "Sea Mist". Although destined for the UK the cocaine was seized by the Irish law enforcement agencies. Operation Extend was commenced and Wright's movements monitored.

We discovered that one of the telephone numbers in Brazil had contacted an address in the Southend area.

At three in the morning my mobile rang and it was Barry Clarke from the Customs ID cocaine target teams (Romeos and Sierras). 'Sorry to wake you up but in a couple of hours we are about to bust the address in Southend where we suspect there is a large stash of cocaine'.

My role in Operation Extend was minimal and Barry and his teams had done a lot of work over several months to get to this point. I was really chuffed Barry had taken the time at what must have been a hectic pre arrest period.

Nearly 500 kilos of cocaine were seized and numerous arrests made, including Brian Wright's son. On hearing about the bust the "Milkman" hired a light aircraft and flew to Northern Cyprus where there was no extradition treaty with the UK.

He remained at large for several years until he was arrested in Malaga by the Spanish police and in April 2007 was sentenced to 30 years in prison. Hoppenbrouwers was arrested and imprisoned in the USA. Ronaldo Soares, the Brazilian principal, received 24 years.

My support office in London had been asked by the Maritime Intelligence Team requesting me to travel to Macapá, the capital of Amapá state in the country's North Region. A suspect yacht was thought to be in the area as one of the crew had phoned an informant in Belgium. According to the Belgian police the crew were paranoid that they were going to be kidnapped by pirates.

Macapá is located on the northern channel of the Amazon River near its mouth on the Atlantic and not far from the borders of Guyana and Suriname.

A local policeman met me at the airport and took me to his HQ to meet his boss. It was a small office with twenty or so agents.

As I stood in front of the boss whose feet were firmly planted on the table, a machine gun to his side I was reminded of a "spaghetti western" movie. He was welcoming but showed little interest in my work in his city.

The people hanging around my hotel continued the "spaghetti western" theme. It wasn't the most well-appointed area but I doubted if there was another safe hotel in Macapá.

I must have been more concerned that usual for after a meal at the nearby restaurant I went back to my room and dragged a heavy chest of drawers across the door. I slept little and dawn brought a welcome relief.

The next day I joined up with the agent who was keen to show me the sights of the city. I was fascinated to realise we were criss-crossing from the Southern to the Northern hemisphere.

We went to the "Zerao" football stadium. Zerao in Portuguese means "the big zero" in reference to the 0 degrees latitude of the Equator.

Inside the stadium where the Macapá team played I was shown the white painted halfway line that ran left to right on the Equators track. I was quite tickled to realise that a team would defend from the Southern Hemisphere in the first half of the game and defend from the Northern hemisphere in the second half.

After a while I said to the agent that we had to locate the yacht. A few miles from the city, boats were moored on the Amazon River. It didn't take long to find the Belgian registered yacht flying the Belgian flag. From quite a distance we could see that there were Europeans on board.

We found out from the Port Authority that two dutchmen and one Spaniard made up the crew.

The border area was indeed bandit country and there were many reports of boats being seized at sea, the boat itself and occupants held for ransom payment.

Between Guyana and Suriname there was a disputed zone, a no-man's land known to all as a seriously lawless region. I could understand any foreigner being obsessed with their own safety.

All the signs were that the yacht was going to set sail within days. With so few Europeans around it could be counter-productive if I hung around the marina so I asked if someone could monitor the movements.

The agent said it could be arranged so we drove off into a shanty town stopping at a run-down looking bar. A guy came out, climbed into the car, and we all drove back to a forest near the marina.

'You watch boat, okay?' said the agent.

'Okay,' said the man.

'You call me as soon as something happens.'

'Okay.'

Money was passed over but I suspected no more than would buy a coco-cola and a sandwich.

We were not sure if he stayed overnight but the next morning, we got a phone call to say the yacht was leaving.

We arrived in time to see a dot disappearing over the horizon heading along the Amazon River toward Columbia.

Several months later the yacht arrived in Holland. It was stopped and searched, the Dutch Customs finding 60 kilos of cocaine aboard. So, although weeks had gone by, my report of the yacht's departure from Brazil assisted in the estimated time of arrival in Dutch waters.

A few weeks later I flew to Manaus, on the banks of the Negro River. Manaus is the capital of the vast state of Amazonas. It's a major departure point for the surrounding Amazon Rainforest.

During the lengthy discussion the senior officer of the Federal Police Force asked me if I would like to visit his village and have supper with his family.

We were to travel in a motorised canoe along the Amazon River passing hundreds of small one-man boats and larger vessels that reminded me of "The African Queen" a 100-year-old steam boat famed for its role in the 1951 movie of the same name. In the absence of roads or rail the river and craft that sailed on her was the highway and railway of the region.

The steam boats had hammocks on the deck for sleeping rather than inside cabins.

Alas, it wasn't to be. A phone call from Rebecca in Brasilia told me Pauline had had an accident and been taken to hospital.

I immediately apologised to my host and made my way to the airport to catch the next available flight. It would be a 4- hour journey.

On arrival in Brasilia, I went straight to the hospital.

On occasions Pauline would volunteer at the Embassy preparing lunch or sandwiches. In the corner of the kitchen was a refrigerator crammed with bottles of beer or cola. Unbeknown to Pauline, workers had moved the fridge and its contents, dislodging the bottles. When Pauline opened the fridge door the bottles cascaded out, bouncing and braking on the stone floor. One bottle bounced, broke and seriously lacerated Pauline's foot. She was rushed to the hospital receiving ten stiches on the skin and three on a tendon. She had lost a lot of blood. She had an epidural to undertake the surgery and her foot put into a plaster cast for a few weeks. It is an injury that continues to be troublesome years later.

I restricted my movements for a while, needing to be on hand to cover, with back up from the maid, domestic duties.

Another medical emergency occurred when our middle son, Alistair, had fallen over at school and dislocated his elbow. I was telephoned with the news by a teacher.

'What hospital is he in?' I asked.

'He's not. He's still at school. We can't take him to hospital.'

'Why not?'

'It's a legal matter. If something goes wrong you could have grounds to sue the school.'

I had forgotten that an American school would follow American culture. Litigation was as much a threat as it was an opportunity.

I was twenty minutes away from the school so drove straight there.

I collected an ashen-faced Alistair, obviously in pain, and took him to a private hospital.

By then Rebecca had called Pauline so they met us in reception. Alistair was admitted but only after they swiped our credit card.

The doctor spoke English as he examined Alistair's arm. 'Would you look toward the window,' he said calmly as he pulled down on Alistair's wrist and levered his elbow back into place.

This is very painful procedure. Alistair winced but soon recovered.

His arm was bandaged and we were able to go home.

At carnival time in February 1999 the Consulate in San Paulo rented us an apartment in Juquei not far from Santos.

There were beautiful sandy beaches a stone's throw away from the apartment block that had its own swimming pool.

Our friends, Sue and Martin Doyle and their children, came with us.

All went well until Alex, my son, ran into the sea and trod on a discarded broken bottle.

Hearing his painful screams, I rushed into the water and quickly wrapped his bleeding foot in a towel.

There were no medical centres around so I asked a local for help. He immediately offered to drive us to the local hospital.

The facilities at this hospital were third world, very basic. The doctor examined the wound which was on the soft part of sole.

'He will have to have stitches,' he said.

'Can you give him something to null the pain?' I asked.

'Not really. I can spray. That will help a little. You will have to hold him down.'

The pain was excruciating as the stiches were inserted. Alex screamed, 'Dad, is it going to stop?'

Minutes later it was over. Alex was still in a lot of pain but somehow was coping with it.

The local man was waiting outside and took us back to the apartment.

It took a little time for Alex to completely recover.

These were times one wished the UK's National Health Service serviced the world.

On another trip to Manaus, I discovered Mike Bowles was staying at the same five-star hotel situated on the bank of the Amazon River. We had received an invitation by the Federal Police to visit the jungle training school. This had been set up to train officers to protect the environment. This would involve policing the Amazon, preventing illegal mining, illegal logging and protecting the many "tribes" of indigenous Indians. The traditional way of life of these people is, thankfully, protected as much as possible.

As part of this "jungle brigade" officers would live and operate in unpopulated, wild landscapes using boats and helicopters.

We were met at the pontoon by two Federal agents and we clambered aboard a rigid inflatable boat.

At this geographical point the Amazon is twenty miles wide, almost the width of the English Channel. Their lengths dramatically differ, 150 miles for the Channel, nearly 4000 miles for the Amazon.

Because of the unpolluted nature of the air, you could sometimes see the other side of the river.

After two hours we turned into one of the hundreds of tributaries, heading for the jungle training school.

Thirty minutes later the driver turned in confusion.

'Is everything okay?' I asked.

'I'm not sure. I've been here a few times but there's something different. It's not the same.'

At the side of the river there were Amazon Indians washing clothes.

A few greetings were passed and then the driver asked, 'Jungle training school. This way?'

'Not this way. Next river on left.'

Half an hour later we were on the correct tributary and approaching the jungle school.

Far from a fortified substantial building, there was a large flat roof resting on stout wooden posts. Instead of bedrooms there were hammocks tied to the posts. There was a cooking area with stoves and toilet facilities were somewhere in the bush. The humidity in the Amazon region is often unbearable and sometimes it is like somebody has thrown a bucket of hot water over you.

A career civil servant from the Ministry of Defence was there. He obviously had not been briefed on the lack of facilities, the discomfort, the heat and humidity, and the flying insects. He made his feelings known and stayed miserable as we were offered lunch.

The Federal Police officers thanked our hosts who dispatched two men down to the river's edge. Twenty minutes later they returned carrying a very large fish. There are hundreds of fish species in the river. Some, like the piranha, are not eaten but this catch was simply thrown onto a bar-b-que and cooked.

Cachaca, a spirit made from distilled sugar cane contains 40% alcohol. It was served with some crushed ice and limes.

The head of the battalion got out a map and described the vast area he and his men covered. A staggering achievement when you saw how limited their resources were.

Shortly after lunch we were asked if we would like to trek through the jungle. Mike and I enthusiastically agreed. The Ministry man grunted his assent.

We walked slowly for a mile or so until we found a clearing.

A patrol officer handed me his Mekanika machine gun. 'Would you like to shoot?'

Mike and I took up the offer and spent twenty minutes playing at big game hunters, though our targets were fallen trees. The Ministry man declined.

As we walked back to camp Mike picked up a pistol lying in the undergrowth.

'Has anyone dropped their gun?' Mike asked.

A Patrol Officer without any embarrassment looked into his empty holster and took the pistol off Mike with a simple shrug.

We were taken back to the jungle camp then onward, by boat, back to our hotel. No-one was happier than the Ministry man.

A few months later I was invited to a drugs conference in Cartagena, a port city on Colombia's Caribbean coast. Caveliero also attended.

We flew from Brasilia to San Paulo then on to Panama. From there, it was an hour or so flight to Cartagena.

The flying time for the whole journey was ten hours which Caveliero and I spent chatting away. We had time to share family history and early experiences with the space not normally afforded in our official meetings.

For the last leg we flew business class with Copa Airlines, the largest air carrier in Panama. It was certainly a first-rate class, so much better than others I've flown on.

The conference, funded by the USA's Drug Enforcement Administration, was attended by delegates from all over South America.

We had a briefing about local security and an update on the Colombian conflict that began in the mid-1960s between the government of Colombia and FARC, (Fuerzas Armadas Revolucionarias de Colombia) the communist guerrillas.

Political parties, left and right, small and large were being funded by drug smuggling cartels.

The message got through – be wary.

I recall walking out of the conference with an American with a "DEA. Bogota Office" emblazoned on his t-shirt. For a while I wondered if it was a good idea walking side by side with him. A drugs liaison officer would be a target for kidnapping or worse.

A local offered a tour of the city. We declined but not until after he announced that he knew we were all drugs enforcement officers. You could understand why Cartagena was chosen as a venue for a conference, it is a beautiful city, but without the most rudimentary security.

Like many of meetings it was of little value apart from getting to know law enforcement colleagues in the region.

Cavaleiro enjoyed winding up the colleague from Portugal who I knew when I was posted there. The pronunciation of Portuguese and Brazilian Portuguese differs a lot and Cavaliero at one point asked Paulo to speak English as he was having trouble understanding his Portuguese. It was a bit rich as Cavaliero spoke only a few words of English.

I planned a meeting with Reg Low, a colleague who was based in Bolivia on the border between Bolivia and Brazil. He was based in La Paz the Capital but, like me, had to cover a vast area.

I flew into Corumba, a coastal town near the Pantanal wetlands (an area two thirds the size of the UK), on a Sunday morning and met by a Federal policeman, Jose, who took me home to his ranch for a family meal. He was married with two children. It was one of the job's many benefits, to experience a local's daily life, their habitat, their food and their sense of humour. It may have been a simple bar-b-que, eaten with fingers, but it was all the more delicious because of it.

Acres of cattle land surrounded their home.

The next day we drove along dirt tracks to the border with Bolivia. At one point I asked the driver how far the border crossing was.

'We've passed it already,' he said. 'See the signs.'

I realised that the signs were in Spanish not Portuguese.

My meeting took place with Reg, the Brazilian Federal Police representative and a Bolivian Drugs Enforcement Officer. It was the first official meeting between the two countries concentrating on smuggling issues. Over lunch we talked about drug smuggling and money laundering.

We stayed in the border area for two nights and discussed the local crime groups that were smuggling drugs and laundering dirty money.

Back in Brasilia I was approached by the American School to become a school governor. I was reluctant to commit to even a limited role. I could not ignore demands of the job to attend school meetings. Eventually I was persuaded.

Most of the school pupils were Brazilian, some American and the rest, were referred to as third country nationals.

My joke was, 'I'm Jim Jarvie. I'm from the third world.'

At least, I thought it was a joke. No-one else did.

At one meeting I was asked by the headmaster, Phillip Loak, to circulate a request that should any family host a party where school pupils were present no alcohol should be available.

I pointed out that some of the older pupils were nearly twenty years old. 'How old do you have to be to drink alcohol?'

'Twenty-one in the USA,' said an American parent.

'How old to buy a gun?' I asked.

'In some States, thirteen.'

I had to bite my lip. The incongruity of it and the dangerous set of values.

We got a little concerned when a welcoming party was organised employing a chef and waiters in white jackets. A very expensive do and one that prompted me to ask at the next Governor's meeting, 'Who paid for it?'

'The school paid for it.'

'Why did the school have to pay for a party?'

A governor spoke. 'We wanted to give the new Head a warm welcome. The opportunity to meet everyone socially.'

'I think it was a complete waste of money.'

Others on the Board agreed with me.

The Head's wife was a Brazilian and like others I suspected she used her husband's position and this party to promote their (mainly her) position in Brazilian society.

He left the school after a couple of years.

We often received phone calls from the school if the boys were feeling under the weather. Pauline received a phone call from Jimmy's class tutor to say how sorry to hear Pauline's mum had passed away.

'What do you mean she died five years ago.'

'Oh! Jimmy said he couldn't do his homework because his granny had died'.

Technically he was right but when the school threatened to send flowers, Pauline had to come clean. 'Jimmy is a charmer,' said Pauline. 'Although he is only seven, he has the makings of a con man!'

I had to stop myself laughing when I told him off that evening.

In November 2000 I was in Fortaleza in the north of Brazil I was to meet up with the Honorary Consul, a successful female business woman whose job was shipping Brazil nuts, known locally as 'castanhas-do-para' (chestnuts from Para, the name of the state).

An evening meal was planned but at lunch time I was called by the Federal police to help them out on a case. They wanted a foreigner who was likely not to speak Portuguese to pretend he wanted to buy 6 kilos of cocaine.

'We have trained undercover officers in the UK. They work as go-betweens all the time. I'll arrange for someone to come over.'

'There is no time,' he said. 'We must do this now. You must meet this person and negotiate the deal.'

I would normally seek permission from my bosses in London to do this but that would take time so I agreed.

I put my casual clothes on and waited in the reception of the hotel.

A few minutes later a man came up to me and in broken English said, 'are you interested in business?' (a code for - are you in the market to purchase drugs.)

He showed me a small wrap of white powder which was obviously cocaine. I examined the drug wrap but unlike on the television I did not put some on my finger and rub it on my gums. I did feel the texture and sniffed the powder but not enough to snort it up my nose. This was all done in a quiet area of the reception but I knew I was being watched by Federal Police officers who pretended to be hotel staff.

He told me the purity of the cocaine was over 90% We agreed a wholesale price of $5000 a kilo.

I agreed with the dealer I would buy 6 kilos and would have the cash when he returned.

He was observed by the Federal Police who had followed the suspect from the hotel to a house on the outskirts of Fortaleza to collect a hold-all.

Although I was waiting in reception, I played no further part. As soon as he set foot in the hotel he was pounced upon by Federal agents.

I was relieved. There was no time to arrange for $30,000 to be brought to the hotel where I would give the supplier a "show" of the money before we did business.

He was charged with distribution of drugs and 10 kilos of cocaine was found at his address.

Although I knew that UK permission on such a scheme would never have been granted, I was, nevertheless, pleased that one half hour of my day had such a successful outcome.

Because of Brazil's buoyant economy the Embassy hosted a number of high- profile visitors, hoping to do business. Politicians, in particular wanted to promote the UK and British interests.

In September 2000 the popular former Northern Ireland Secretary, Mo Mowlam, head of the UK Government's anti-drugs campaign, visited Brazil and Colombia.

She arrived in Brasilia and was brought to the embassy where diplomats and locally employed staff were gathered to celebrate Brazil's National day (7 September). Mo Mowlam did not stand on ceremony so it was a casual affair. I was asked to brief her regarding the drugs situation in the region. Although a senior government minister, she was very approachable which made me feel relaxed.

In the centre of Brasilia, a spectacular firework display started.

'What are the fireworks for' she asked.

'They are for your arrival in Brazil,' I quipped.

She jokingly clipped me around the ear, burst out laughing. 'Don't be so **** stupid.'

Pauline had cooked a chilli for lunch and typically Mo thanked Pauline for all her efforts. I can understand how she managed to get Gerry Adams and Ian Paisley to sit down together when she was the Northern Ireland Secretary. She oozed charisma and charm which, to me, was how a politician should behave.

The next day I went with Mo Mowlam and Sarah Gillett, the Deputy Mission Head, to meet the Head of the Casa who was second only to the President. Sarah played the diplomat whilst Mo joked with the minister.

He gave her a very impressive ornate plaque and Mo brought out a package wrapped in tatty brown paper.

'I have brought this from London for you'.

The Minister opened up the parcel to reveal a small plastic snow scene of London in a globe.

He shook it and said, 'Very nice. I will give it to my children'.

I am sure Sarah wanted the ground to open up and swallow us all up.

That said, Mo had a really constructive meeting discussing not just drugs but Brazilian UK relations.

The Millennium Bug was seen as a real threat to Brazil as it was to the rest of the world. As the date approached the embassy started to plan for every eventuality, including the failure of computers.

On 31 December 1999 the embassy staff gathered to see in the New Year. At 10pm I rang my parents in the UK to wish them a happy new year. At a minute past mid-night the phones at least were working.

As the capital Brasilia wanted to have the biggest firework display in South America but more importantly beat, Rio, a fantastic display started.

As the fireworks were going off Sarah Gillett drove into the Embassy and complained that the traffic lights had been affected by the millennium bug and were just flashing yellow. I explained that at night the lights are set on orange, and they don't change until 06.00 in the morning.

I then rang Dave Sterling in Sao Paulo to wish him and his wife Helen a happy new year.

Sarah was surprised he answered the phone. 'The mobile phones are working? OK?' she asked.

'They are working OK and I've already called my parents in England.'

No-one was more relieved than Sarah that all the fears of catastrophic collapse were unfounded.

As 2000 started I realised I had only a few months left in Brazil so Pauline and I had to make a few plans as to where we were going to live back in the UK.

My father was about to be admitted to hospital in February to have a triple bypass operation. It was news like this that made you feel a long way from home. I decided I would try to get home when he was in hospital.

I flew from Rio at 38 degrees. At Stansted Airport waiting to get the train to Cambridge it was minus 8 degrees.

I did arrive at Addenbrookes hospital near Cambridge, met my mum and we visited my dad in the recovery ward.

My father, who seemed to have wires and tubes attached to every part of his body, was just coming around from the anaesthetic, recognised me,

'What are you doing here?' he asked

'I've just flown in from Brazil to see you. Can I get you anything?'

'I fancy a slice of toast.'

I stayed with my mother for a few days seeing dad every day. He was on the mend.

The day after his operation he was walking along the corridor trailing a drip stand. After three days he came home.

I then flew back to Brasilia.

Returning Drug Liaison Officers were then given a choice as to where they wished to work in the UK.

Pauline and I decided to pursue Nottingham as an area to settle. The city had a small Customs Investigation office and it was quite close to where my parents lived.

On the computer we looked at properties between Nottingham and Melton Mowbray the Vale of Belvoir. The prices of houses there were a lot less than in the south east of London where we had sold our home. We couldn't believe the size of the property we could buy.

Later on, in February, I had a call from Euan Stewart, a Senior Manager, a Deputy Director in charge of the Investigation region covering the east of England. Nationally, the number of investigators had increased dramatically over the previous three years. Some of the smaller units spread throughout the UK had amalgamated into the National Investigation Service.

'Jim,' said Euan. 'Would you consider joining the investigation office in Ipswich? It covers Harwich, Felixstowe and Stansted and Norwich Airports. You'll have to stay on your current grade, Senior Investigation Officer, but the current Assistant Chief is retiring in a couple of months. I would like you to take on that role on a temporary basis.'

I told Euan I would get back to him quickly. Although I had started my Customs career in Norwich, I didn't know Ipswich well. I sounded out Pauline on the prospect of moving to East Anglia.

Our priority again was to find good schools for the boys as well as suitable properties.

Pauline flew home to check these things out and somehow the boys and I muddled through for the three weeks she was away. The boys now joke saying we went to McDonalds every day but the truth was the close-knit embassy "family" ensured we were not going to starve.

Pauline and my Mum drove daily from Lincolnshire to Suffolk and visited a number of schools. One school in Framlingham stood out. Framlingham was situated a small market town north of Ipswich.

Our two eldest, Alex and Alistair, would go straight into secondary school. The fact that both boys had a foreign language and had travelled helped their qualification to join the school as much as their academic levels. The offer of a school place was a great weight off our minds.

Jimmy, now six years old, would join a nearby primary school.

We decided that we would rent a house on our return and take our time finding a new home. The months of April and May were busy for me.

My replacement, Frank Dick, was to arrive at the end of June. He was already in Brazil undergoing language training and to meet up with the contacts I had made in the Federal Police, the Customs, the Consulates in Rio and San Paulo and the Honorary Consulates. This took longer than I hoped as Frank's Portuguese was slow getting up to speed.

Nevertheless, I had every confidence that the good work we had already achieved would be continued in Frank's hands.

My parents came over in June for three weeks. I took them to Manaus and the Foz do Iguazú Falls, the famous waterfalls on borders of Brazil, Paraguay and Argentina.

Although spectacular, none of us expected it to be so cold. We were high up in exposed country and in the middle of winter.

The hotel we stayed at, The Cataratas, was built on the side of the waterfalls.

In Manaus we stayed at the Hotel Tropical on the Amazon River. We took a boat trip to see the "Meeting of Waters", the confluence of the dark Rio Negro with the sandy coloured upper Amazon River, or Solimões.

We saw pink dolphins in the dark coloured waters and stopped off to visit a small village habited by indigenous Indians. It was a real eyeopener for my boys and particularly my parents. To get so close to the vast River and the people who live there was truly memorable.

The boys took a brief swim in the water but we pulled them out when the boatman spoke of piranhas.

The boys accompanied my parents back to the UK. They immediately visited Butlins in Skegness and when asked about the best thing of living in Brazil they would move the conversation on to the virtues of Butlins.

Pauline and I packed up our personal belongings ready to ship home.

The Ambassador arranged a reception as a cheerio to us and a welcome to Frank and his wife, Cay and their teenage son, James. We had a series of farewell parties thrown by our friends and embassy colleagues.

Frank took on my office, mobile phone and jeep and prepared to move into our house.

To break up the long journey to the UK we stopped off in Rome where a colleague based there booked us into a hotel. We arrived carrying two giant suitcases requiring an upgrade to a larger room. We did all the tourist bit but it was one of the hottest Julys for years and the heat was unbearable although the humidity was a lot lower than Brazil.

Arriving back into the UK after 4 years in Brazil was a real shock but at least we were back enjoying the seasons and the long summer evenings.

From Rome we flew to Gatwick, hired a car and drove to my parent's house in Stamford. After four years living and working in Brazil it was strange feeling being back at home. My parents lived in a three bedroomed semi so there was not a lot of space for me Pauline and the boys. We then arranged a short holiday and rented a lodge near Fintry in the Trossachs, which although small gave us a bit more independence. It gave us an opportunity to meet up with Scottish family members.

Two of my Scot's uncles, George and Willie had passed away whilst I was in Brazil. I was close to them both, particularly George who took me and my brother Ian to see Glasgow Rangers. He also knew the hills near Kilsyth (my dad's home town) and we would go out for hours hill walking in the Campsie Hills. We also stayed in a mobile home on a complex run by Haven Holidays where we could, as a family, have our own space. The boys joined in the various activities and the football coach was amazed they were happy to take penalties with their bare feet on an astro turf pitch (a skill picked up playing with their friends in Brazil).

Returning south, Pauline and I surveyed maps covering the Suffolk countryside around Lowestoft and Aldeburgh. Both towns were less than an hour's drive from Thomas Mills High School in Framlingham, the school we chose for our two eldest boys. Nearby was the Robert Hitcham School, ideal for Jimmy, our youngest, and a feeder school for Thomas Mills.

We chose Halesworth in the north of Suffolk to rent a four bedroomed house, 13 miles from the school.

Our personal effects, from lampshades to bicycles, were en route so we had to cope with what was available. Thankfully the house was fully furnished and we were able to release the goods we had put into store in Croydon prior to going to Brazil. It was the bikes and toys the boys really missed.

I was dealing with a shipping agent who kept telling me our container was still on the high seas. I knew Customs staff at Tilbury and spoke to Martin Ludlow, the Senior officer in charge of the uniformed teams. He was able to trace my container on the ports computer and told me exactly where it was.

I rang the agent who said, 'Sorry, it hasn't docked yet.'

'I think you will find it has. It's actually at Tilbury Dock, row ten and fifth in the stack.'

'I will get back to you,' he nervously replied.

Not surprisingly he rang me a few minutes later to confirm the container had indeed arrived. It was delivered to our rented home in Halesworth the following week.

The boys, still mindful of safety restrictions after Brazil, were delighted to stroll along to play football in the local park without adults to look out for them. They had June, July and August before they started the school term.

When term eventually arrived, the school arranged for mentors to assist our two eldest in settling in at school. This one-on-one relationship developed into friendships that lasted into adulthood. The boys football talents saw them straight into school teams.

It took the family a little time to settle back into the rural life of England.

Once the boys were content, Pauline, never an idle person, found a job at a local housing association in Framlingham.

My Branch took on investigations throughout the eastern region, particular Felixstowe, Harwich and Tilbury. In addition, we were expected to investigate criminals living in the region but smuggling in other parts of the UK and abroad.

I arrived at my Ipswich office at the beginning of September. On my first day I was taken from the Investigation Dept down to the Customs Office in Haven House. As I entered the building, I saw that all the staff were watching a television screen.

'There's been a plane crash in New York,' one said. 'It's hit a sky-scraper.'

Like millions across the world, I watched 9/11 unfold.

The horror was such that it seemed unreal. The actual footage of the plane crashing, the fires and the pandemonium that followed. Little did we know the scale of the tragedy or the desperate aftermath.

Initially I took over as a team leader (Senior Investigating Officer) on one of the drugs teams based in Ipswich. To my delight I knew a number of officers within the Branch. An old colleague from my Delta days was a team leader, Peter Finch and Chris Webb, who I had met in Birmingham in 1982. He ran the VAT and money laundering Investigations. Another ex-Delta, John Philips headed the tobacco smuggling section and Port Crime Team. Liz Haines had been on the Bravos and Charlies during my second stint on the Charlies. A lot of experience in the Branch combined with younger members who were as enthusiastic as I was when I became an investigator.

At my first staff meeting a male member said, 'You've come here to close the office, haven't you?'

'What do you mean by that?'

'Well. There's a rumour going around that a number of provincial offices close to London are being disbanded.'

'I haven't heard that rumour. I can assure you that I would not be moving my family lock, stock and barrel and putting my sons into a school in Framlingham if I thought there was even a hint of this office closing.'

I believed I convinced them that closure was not about to happen although when a rumour like that happens it almost impossible to eradicate all traces.

The recently appointed Chief Investigation Officer, Paul Evans, had the habit of visiting offices and threatening them with closure if they did not deliver on his targets, particularly in relation to criminal cash seizures and proceeds of crime (money laundering).

Evans, an ex-I6 officer had transferred to Customs as Chief. In his previous role he had been the link between MI6 and the Investigation Division. He had many supporters in Customs but other were more wary.

His management style was not liked by many and the newly named National Investigation Service had undergone a monumental shift in culture.

Throughout my career I had been able to speak to senior managers and offer operational suggestions without fear of retribution. Indeed, the likes of Terry Byrne encouraged that culture which made the ID such a unique investigation service envied throughout the world.

One colleague quipped Evans didn't like "yes men". If he said no, they would have to say no as well.

Evans didn't cause me any problems, possibly due to the fact I was based in Ipswich rather than the Custom House in London.

I am not sure if the two were related but long-standing colleague and friend, Terry Byrne, had risen to the rank of Director of Law Enforcement and was, effectively, Evans' boss.

After three months, Ipswich's Assistant Chief Investigation Officer retired, Euan Stewart, the Regional Director then asked me to take over as Assistant Chief for East Anglia. Initially it was on a temporary basis and if it was to be permanent, I would be required to attend a civil service assessment board to secure a substantive position. In fact, I never attended a civil service assessment board and was one of a handful SIOs that received a "battle field" promotion.

So, from that day I was managing four teams of investigators with 12 in each team. John Brindle was my Support Officer who ran the support team of three who dealt with most of the backroom work such as arranging travel, managing the fleet of vehicles and preparing documents for court.

Our branch was multi-disciplined and tasked with investigating drug, tobacco smuggling, VAT fraud and money laundering. Although I had some VAT and tobacco smuggling experience it was never on the investigation side so I was reliant on Peter Finch, Chris Webb and their knowledgeable teams. It was another transformation for me from being a team leader to managing a regional branch.

I did not deal with the nitty gritty of day-to-day operational meetings and it was my role to lead and manage the Branch. I am sure it was the same throughout the Civil Service but the number of management meetings I had to attend had increased dramatically.

At most of the meetings we discussed health and safety, human rights, gender equality and performance. I attended one meeting which was mind numbingly boring. Nick Burriss, one of my fellow ACIOs commented, 'Can somebody direct me to the wardrobe so I can return to my world'.

In addition to drugs, tobacco and VAT we took on board the 2001 implementation of money laundering legislation.

Banks, mortgage companies, any organisation that eased the flow of money, were required to comply with this new letter of the law.

A report in the Guardian newspaper two years earlier stated that, "Hundreds of billions of pounds could be being laundered through the UK every year, but the government is unable to give a precise figure of the scale of the problem, MPs have found."

Estimates ranged from tens of billions of pounds upwards.

International "dirty money" was being channelled into the UK and used to pay for everything from luxury properties and cars to school fees.

Intelligence from investigation agencies identified a number of individuals who appeared to have no legitimate source of income but had rock star lifestyles.

To support of the Proceeds of Crime Act, law agencies were asked, when involved in a drugs operation, to "follow the money not the powder".

The Minister of State for Security at the Home Office, Ben Wallace, said it was wrong to think of money laundering as a victimless crime. 'Those with dirty cash to clean don't just sit on it,' he said. 'They reinvest it in serious organised crime, from drug importation to child sexual exploitation, human trafficking and even terrorism.'

After the crime had been discovered we, at Customs, had to ascertain the "ill-gotten goods", the assets acquired as a result of the illegal movement of money. This was channelled to us through the National Intelligence Service at Scotland Yard. This Unit would handle all reports or suspicions of illegal activity. They would decide who the information would go, to Customs or, if it was general crime, the relevant police. If it was terrorist related Special Branch would be informed and they would process the inquiry.

In March 2003 I was informed by the Customs money laundering intelligence team that a large movement of money from pounds sterling to euros. A suspicious cash movement report identified a suspect, Paul Ellingham. He, we learned, had made an appointment to visit a branch of Barclays Bank in Bishops Stortford to collect three quarters of a million euros.

It was suspected that this money had come from illegitimate sources and therefore being "laundered". Although at that stage no specific crime had been identified Ellingham was known to have links to tobacco smugglers.

Our job was to set up surveillance and observe the handover of money and to arrest whoever was carrying out the potential offence. We would seize the money as possible proceeds of crime and then attempt to link this transaction to other criminals. The cash would then be detained under the Proceeds of Crime Act pending a money laundering investigation.

The fact that this operation came through an alert from the bank and was the first case to be handed to Customs, it was essential we got everything right.

An office briefing took place in Ipswich and a Senior Higher Investigation Officer Gareth Griffiths was operational lead. Ten other officers were to be deployed around the bank to observe if Ellingham was with anybody else and to assist in arresting him.

It was so important that we were 100% sure the cash had been collected.

I addressed them. 'We are going to put someone inside the bank. That person must be able to see clearly the money changing hands.'

'How do we do that?' an officer asked.

'You've got to think on your feet. If you see the suspect walk up to a teller, you approach the next teller up. Pretend you have lost your bank details and need money urgently. Say anything that keeps you close to the target. Play an idiot if you like but don't lose your line of sight. Remember, we can't arrest anyone if they don't have the money in their possession.'

Gareth said he would go to the teller's booth next to him to see the cash physically being handed over. As we were going to arrest the person after he had left the bank (Barclays bank insisted no arrests were to be made in the bank) a number of safety issues had to be in place. We did not want the suspect to think he was being robbed, so all staff carried a Customs and Excise baseball cap which would be put on just prior to the arrest.

Using his intuition and nous Gareth walked into the bank behind our suspect and followed him to a teller, taking up a position next door.

While he engaged the bank official with questions about opening an account, he would hear the responses but his gaze took in the money being counted out and the eventual transfer.

Ellingham left the bank and within seconds he was arrested by the surveillance waiting outside. The 700,000 Euros were in large denominations which incredibly fitted into the pockets of the suspect's coat.

I remained in the office waiting for an update. I was desperate to be out on the ground in Bishop Stortford but as Branch Manager I reluctantly knew my place.

Back in our office in Ipswich, Ellingham was interviewed and his home was searched, the 700 thousand euros, in 500 and 300 denominations was placed in our secure safe and eventually paid into a high interest-bearing bank account.

Some years later, after Europe wide pressure from law enforcement agencies, the European Central Bank stopped issuing the 500 euro note.

Rebecca McDougall, one of our new recruits, was nominated as the case officer. She investigated the background of the suspects and discovered links to a significant illegal tobacco smuggling organisation. Although relatively new to investigation, Rebecca left no stone unturned which led to the arrest of a further suspect from Harlow, Shane Valaitis.

Documents found at Valaitis' house revealed details of shipping and transportation of millions of cigarettes into Felixstowe. In addition, over £6 million had been laundered through various banks throughout Essex and Hertfordshire.

In November 2003 at the Royal Courts of Justice in London, Ellingham pleaded guilty to tobacco smuggling for which he was sentenced to two and a half years in prison. He also pleaded guilty to money laundering for which he received a further eighteen months in prison. Valaitis had previously been found guilty of tobacco smuggling for which he received three and a half years.

The 700,000 Euros were forfeited to the Crown (the Treasury) to be used to fund law enforcement efforts.

In my experience criminals are always realistic about being caught and doing time in prison. It was a hazard of the job that would, however reluctantly, be accepted. What criminals hated was when they lost all their worldly goods with no prospect of appeal.

In a way, being the first of such cases, put the Ipswich office on the map.

Paul Evans and other senior managers throughout the wider department took an interest in this case It did highlight how early notification of suspect money transactions through compliant banks and financial institutions, can result in dirty money being taken off the bad guys.

Paul Evans, our Chief Investigation Officer in London, was keen to know all there was to know about how we carried out this operation.

Its success did no harm to my new role as a manager.

Such were the positive feedback our office received that it squashed all fears of an office closure.

Much of my work as manager was keeping an eye on how investigations were developing, authorizing human and monetary resources. This role dramatically contrasted with previous roles where hands on skills were required. Leaving my office for a regular stroll around the officer's open plan room would, I suspected, be treated with a small degree of unease and a large degree of grudge.

I did try to explain that I was not interfering with their work; I was very interested and still had a buzz on hearing detail of their efforts.

If there was an opportunity to go out with a team I would jump at the chance.

After a year renting a house, we finally bought a property closer to Ipswich. I was at work so once again Pauline was left to deal with all the home issues. We moved into a small village near Woodbridge and next door to a freehold Suffolk pub. We immediately felt at home in the house and the village. Although I was working long hours, when I was free, I would participate in the village events.

There were times I could escape the office an participate in an operation. An illegal tobacco importation arrived at Felixstowe Docks. A container was discovered full of cigarettes and was destined for an address in Birmingham.

I joined the surveillance team of six cars, a motorbike and thirteen surveillance officers as they followed the container lorry for four hours until it turned into the entrance of a big warehouse on the outskirts of Birmingham.

Plans were made for a "Knock" in the Birmingham area so I said, 'I'd love to be part of this but I don't want any involvement that would result in me going to court. I've spent weeks/months in a courtroom. No more. I'll be an observer.'

'No problem, Jim,' Andy, the case officer said. 'I'm the arresting officer. If hands get dirty, they'll be mine. If more arrests are needed others will assist.'

As we ran from our position towards the lorry which had parked up next to a white van, Andy slipped and fell. I had spotted the driver so ran on and carried out the arrest myself, cautioning him and clamping on handcuffs.

'Thanks a lot Andy,' I said. 'I'll now have to write a report and make a statement.'

Thankfully, the gang all pleaded guilty at Chelmsford Crown Court six months later and were sentenced to between 18 months and three years in prison. I did not have to attend court I merely supplied a written statement.

In my time in Brazil, some laws in the UK had been enacted to accommodate changing criminal investigation procedures.

Two Acts came into law. In 1996 The Criminal Procedure and Investigation Act came into force as I was preparing to leave the UK. It reformed the way prosecutions were presented in court. This demanded that any evidence or disclosures that would help the defence must be given to the defence. This required us to hand over any data we had that previously we may have chosen not to submit as we didn't think it was relevant. Initially many of the judges did not have a full understanding of this new law. The test of relevance of each case went far beyond what was envisaged and it was used as a tactic by criminals to identify informants. Several cases were dropped if an informant would have been outed.

Some judges insisted that all background information be disclosed so we had to decide whether or not to proceed. That almost definitely meant that guilty people walked free.

It took years before the system absorbed the full implications of "disclosure" and led to a degree of flexibility in the behaviour of judges.

By 2001 the Criminal Procedure and Investigation Act had been embedded in the Customs Service. I had a bit of catching up to do.

Unlike the old days when we had one officer reporting a large operation, now there could be three on a relatively small case. A reporting officer, a disclosure officer and a financial officer.

Throughout my career if a person or premises was of particular interest the decision to carry out a surveillance operation was a straightforward one. Authority was sought from a senior officer, given and off we went.

An official record of this arrangement was not required. The active case officer's notebook would be the only written record.

A regular update of progress (or otherwise) would be passed on to colleagues as necessary.

A Higher Investigation Officer, Paul Palmer, had arrived from the fraud unit in Luton and joined the Ipswich office bringing his family to live in the area. He was a very keen officer.

'I've had a phone call,' he told me. 'A packet of 3000 ecstasy tablets were discovered in a local post office about to leave the UK for Hawaii. They've already been tested.'

Drugs sent to Hawaii was unusual so we took a special interest in it.

I called the Drugs Enforcement Administration office in London who were really eager that we allowed the package to travel to Hawaii where a controlled delivery would take place using the local postal service.

It was decided that the package be taken directly to the airline and flown on via Los Angeles. The relevant enforcement authorities would be advised of its journey so each stage could be monitored.

Paul took the package to Heathrow Airport and under escort placed it into the aircraft's cargo space. He then had the evidence he needed to verify the first part of the passage. It was vital that the package remained in a controlled and co-ordinated manner.

The American DEA intercepted the package in Los Angeles who put it on an aircraft destined for Honolulu where it was collected by local officers.

An operation was set up that included a delivery by a "postman". The recipient signed for the package. Allowing a short time for the suspect to make his move, the local officers raided his house, seized the tablets and made an arrest. Two other suspects were arrested at the airport. It soon became clear that this was not the first illegal importation to take place.

Paul wrote up his report and I made a statement on my involvement.

A few months later Paul was summoned to Hawaii to give evidence at the trial.

I tried and failed to convince Paul that as the team leader who authorised the operation, I should be the one to give evidence.

'I can find a space in my diary', I said.

Paul smiled. 'They don't want you, Jim. They've accepted your authorisation. The Americans want me as I was the operational officer.'

So, Paul spent ten days in Hawaii and it turned out to be a trip of a lifetime for him and although I didn't say it at the time, I was pleased he went (I had had my fair share of overseas trips to exotic locations).

John Phillips managed one of our teams; "Port Crimes". This looked at criminality within the port of Felixstowe and Harwich. It was known that a small number of port employees were crooked, abusing and by-passing the security systems in place, encouraged and paid by criminals.

We had four officers working at Felixstowe. They would liaise with uniformed Customs officials, carry out night and day surveillance and cross-checking cargo with paperwork.

John and I were chatting and we decided to have an exercise looking at the cars being driven by port workers. If they were driving a small, aging Ford they could probably be discounted. If they drove a top-range Mercedes, Porches or BMW it was possible they were financing the purchase from sources other than a wage packet.

Although incomes are legitimately supplemented by extra work, family and inherited money, it was often the case that villains wanted to flaunt their success. What better than a flash, gas-guzzling motor-car costing twice the amount a year's earnings would bring in. Throughout my career it was always so. The most profitable of crimes resulted in rocketing egos that demanded adulation.

Thankfully, this audacious display often led to their downfall. The bigger the splash the more likelihood of drowning.

At Harwich we had significant seizures of heroin and cocaine arriving from Amsterdam. This Dutch port was a thorn in our side as the liberal nature of its society tolerated drug use. Those caught trafficking cannabis could expect no more than a slap on the wrist as punishment.

This freedom allowed drugs to flow easily in and out of the country, the Hook of Holland ferry to Harwich was a well-used route for all drug smugglers.

Drugs were often hidden in the depths of lorries, sealed and fixed into the inside of petrol tanks, the innards of spare wheels that are used only to carry heavy loads. Door panels would be taken off and carefully re-fixed. The metal hollow cross members of trailers would be opened up, stashed with drugs the welded back up. Grease and grime would be applied to cover up the ingress. Containers would be loaded onto the trailer completely hiding any tampering of members.

Innocent looking motor cars driven by unremarkable drivers with passengers would arrive in these ports as if returning from a motoring holiday. Most would not be stopped and searched. There is no doubt, a huge amount of drugs were smuggled through. Anyone caught with drugs denied any knowledge and often forensic evidence was needed to convict them. We often found telephone records that linked them with the source countries, Holland, Spain, Morocco and South America.

Tachometers, carried by most lorries, reveal a lot of detail; miles on the road, breaks taken for a much longer time than usual. Homes or company addresses would be visited.

Every interception of an airline courier, accompanied lorry, van or car not only looking for incriminating evidence but also any documents that may indicate the driver was innocent.

If there were records on paper or phone that directly connected to other individuals there were arrested.

Thankfully, for all the officers involved, sentences for drivers found guilty, were significant. Ten years imprisonment was the norm, a fitting deterrent for would-be smugglers.

It took me some time to adjust to the job as "manager" rather than be on the active edge of operations. I carefully developed a situation where the teams found it easy to consult, knowing that any contribution I made would be designed to be of assistance rather than imposition.

Peter Finch and Liz Haines managed the double-headed "target" teams that looked into the activities of known criminals, steadily building up a case against them which hopefully would lead to the identification of a drug importation.

Early one morning in March 2002 I had a telephone call from Liz.

'I need to speak with you urgently, Jim.'

'I'm in the office later on,' I replied.

'No, Jim. I've got to go to London. Can you meet me at Ipswich railway station?'

I agreed, but during my journey I got increasingly concerned fearing she was seriously ill or had a break-up with her long-term partner who was also an investigator.

It was 8am when I met up with her.

On the platform awaiting the arrival of her train she said, 'Jim, I wanted to tell you first. I'm resigning from Customs.'

My heart sank. I think it showed.

'It's nothing to do with the job,' she said. 'Arthur and I have discussed it for weeks. We've decided to take over a pub. I want a clean break from Customs and take on a new phase in our lives.'

'Please don't rush,' I said. 'Don't make this sort of decision in a hurry.'

'Jim, we've spent months thinking about it. The decision has been made.'

It took a little while for me to collect myself. 'All right but if you change your mind.'

As the train to London arrived, we continued the conversation.

'Take a career break,' I said.

Liz didn't answer. She climbed aboard, closed the door and pulled down the window. 'We've discussed it over and over,' she said.

We were still talking as the train began to move. It must have looked like a forties black and white film of a couple, faced with certain parting, sobbed their final farewells.

I found myself at the end of the platform as Liz sped off.

Filling Liz's shoes was going to be a mighty task. She was outstanding at her job, well respected in Ipswich and throughout the service. I knew that there were a few officers who could step in on a temporary basis until the position was advertised but this didn't abate the apprehension I was experiencing.

Liz was required to give a month's notice and I knew she would not leave her post with any loose ends, any actions not accounted for, all on going plans justified and crystal clear.

For most of my time in Ipswich one operation had dominated for 18 months. It was a joint operation with ourselves and the Police National Crime Squad. It was called operation "Homespun" and Jeff Laidlaw was appointed as case officer.

The NCS covered the whole of the UK with nine commands that looked at serious cross-county border crimes. Some of their drug smuggling operations over-lapped with one of ours.

At the time the principal targets for the police National Crime Squad were gang members whose cover were flowers imported from Holland.

Trevor Long, a market trader in the Romford area, was on their watch list.

My Branch was targeting a Turkish national based in Sidcup, Hamin Soylu who worked alongside two of his countrymen, Saskip Gundoglu from Buckinghamshire and Muzaff Arslanoglo, based in London. They were involved in trafficking heroin from the Golden Crescent Area covering Turkey, Iran, Iraq and Afghanistan, prolific producers of the opium poppy.

A 57-year-old from Pembury in South Wales, John Dalgleish, was responsible for the transportation and storage of drugs for Soylu's gang. They engaged Dalgleish to find warehouses to store the importations.

At that stage we did not know where or how the drugs were coming into the country. An associate of Dalgleish, 47-year-old Grant Connors, was responsible for providing the transport.

We had established observation posts and were able to follow their movements by deploying tracking devices on their vehicles. All the procedural requirements were adhered to. It often came down to us to prove that while we were following the suspects vehicles, we were not about to follow wives or family on school runs or out shopping. There would be no "collateral intrusion".

The employment of tracking beacons is a risky job. Especially placing such devices under suspects cars when parked in their drive. You have to avoid guard dogs, security lights, alarms and cameras.

It was always easier if they were out shopping or at a restaurant. We waited until they were out of sight then pretend to be attending to a loose exhaust pipe when a magnetic beacon was placed underneath the chassis.

The active "life" of these beacons was limited to a few days by the capacity of the battery that powered them. We then had to change the battery or replace the beacon.

As a junior investigator I had deployed numerous tracking beacons on suspect cars and yachts. It was always nerve- wracking time when lying under a vehicle in a criminal's drive trying to place the beacon in a place under the chassis where it couldn't be seen. The fear of being spotted by a suspect or a neighbour never left you, no matter how many times you had done it.

On the downside, a constant worry was if they took the vehicle to a garage where it was raised on a ramp – exposing this device that had nothing to do with the car.

It could be dangerous. We knew these people were open to violent reaction when threatened so we had to ensure our officer's safety.

We were also aware that we had a duty of care to the public at large so if the suspect had spent a long time in a pub and was observed to be well over the drink/drive limit we had to call the local police reporting the driver but not saying who we were.

Intelligence teams in London had put a lot of work into operation "Homespun". We had to match their efforts, a task demanded by Kevin Byrne, my Regional Director.

'I'm under pressure,' said Kevin. 'London had committed a lot of time and intelligence recourses. They need to commit to other cases.'

'There's a job there,' I said. 'I'm 100% sure.'

I then received a telephone call from Kevin's brother, Terry, asking me if I was convinced a successful outcome was possible.

My reply was short. 'I guarantee it.'

'You've got the evidence?'

'I've got the evidence.'

In May 2003 on the Bank Holiday Monday, we discovered that 11 forty-foot containers, destined for Dalgleish's transport company had arrived at Felixstowe dock over the preceding few days.

All contained vast quantities of one-ton sacks of cat litter from Turkey. This material was made from clay, a binding agent, baking soda and some sort of fragrance, made examination very difficult. Some appeared to contain only litter but we were convinced illegal drugs were hidden inside. In total there were 18 tons of cat litter.

It was thought that if 4 or 5 legitimate loads were looked at it would deter Customs searching those that followed. A well-used attempt to foil Customs.

The one advantage we had was that organic material in sacks could be X-rayed.

The container arrived, x-rayed, and revealed packages inside.

At the time I was home, barbecuing for the family and receiving regular updates from Geoff Laidlaw, the Homespun case officer. In his first call he said the initial estimate was 200 kilos. I was delighted but a call from Geoff an hour later the estimated amount was 70 kilos. It was a bitter sweet feeling as 70 kilos was still a massive seizure but 200 would have been better.

After an hour I got an excited phone call from Geoff Laidlaw.

'We've taken all the packages out,' he said. 'We've weighed it. 400 kilos of heroin. 30 million pounds worth.'

400 kilos of heroin! The largest heroin seizure in the UK up to that time.

The barbecuing became a concerto, arms flailing, sausages and steak, sizzling, smoke billowing. I could have been mistaken for a child with a brand new, much wanted, toy.

I received a phone call from Terry Byrne, who was on holiday in the Algarve.

'We done it, Trapper,' he said. 'Congratulations.'

'I told you there was a job there,' I joked.

We joked afterwards that we had enough cat litter to supply most of the UK's feline population with some left over for London Zoo.

It was decided to allow the consignment of cat litter to go on to its final destination which would require 24-hour surveillance on the container by ourselves and the National Crime Squad.

The onward address was a warehouse in Pembury, South Wales but we knew it could well be diverted along the route.

Packets of self-raising flour replaced the heroin which, on a cursory glance, would appear to be powdered drugs.

It took two days for the paperwork to be completed, charges paid and the load released ready for collection.

Once it had been cleared, we had to wait. It was their move. They could turn up at any stage. Surveillance teams were on stand-by twenty- four hours a day. Had we, for operational reasons, not been ready, we could have delayed matters through the uniformed Customs team. The experienced officers could build in a delay if required.

On the following Friday we were informed that a lorry was on its way to the docks. Fridays were always busy at UK ports as consignments needed to be delivered prior to the weekend.

On a completely separate operation the Romeos and Sierras, the cocaine target teams, had information that 200 kilos had been discovered in a container from South America and it was also due to leave the docks on the same day and was also destined for Wales. Not far along the docks, the tobacco team had located 8 million cigarettes in a container. This team was arranging a controlled delivery. The two other operations had surveillance teams waiting for their movement.

No surveillance team would want to carry out their work side by side with another. They certainly would avoid the scenario where three teams were working alongside. Potentially a logistical nightmare but on this occasion it did work.

The respective lorries left at different times. The cigarettes headed toward South Wales, as was the cocaine. All this, of course, would be divided up and circulated around the country by gangs and dealers.

The driver of Dalgleish's lorry complied with all regulations, speed limits, rest periods and non-deviation of his route that would have shown on the vehicle's tachograph.

So, when the driver took a four-hour-break in a service area on the M25 we had to find a place to park up and continue looking for movement. The driver may have had forty winks but we couldn't. It has been known for such a lorry be hi-jacked by another crime group. Cargo may be off-loaded to another vehicle.

The lorry entered a goods yard in Berkshire and stayed there overnight. Extra officers were brought in to watch during the dark hours.

The following day it drove to Pembury and into a warehouse we had previously identified. A few days before we had been able to place audio equipment and video cameras inside the warehouse. Officers from the National Crime Squad and Customs broke into the warehouse and placed cameras to cover all the entrances and storage area. We knew that once the consignment had been breached, we would have to make the arrest. It wouldn't take long for the villains to realise the packages had been switched.

We found out later that Dalgleish's unsuspecting wife was asked to carefully number the sacks as they were unloaded from containers.

We watched as Dalgleish and Connors push metal rods into the sacks to try and find where the drugs were. After several false starts they hit something. Someone shouted with delight. They could see a very wealthy future in front of them.

As Dalgleish was arrested in the warehouse other officers were following Soylu in the Sidcup area.

Dave Cater of the Crime Squad wanted us to lay off Soylu as their main target, Trevor Long was then at a flower market in Holland and was due to fly back to Luton the following day.

'Soylu is the main target in our operation,' I said. 'He arranged the importation. We're going to arrest him.'

Cater eventually agreed.

Soylu was in his car approaching the Dartford Crossing and as he joined the queue for the tunnel he was stopped and detained.

Trevor Long returned to the UK where he was arrested at the airport by Crime Squad officers.

The trial was held a Harrow Crown Court where the Turkish nationals all pleaded guilty.

Dalgleish and Connors pleaded not guilty claiming they were not involved in the crime. At his trial Dalgleish had claimed he thought the drugs were cannabis but this was rejected.

Both of them were found guilty 11 to one by the jury.

Soylu was sentenced to 16 years in prison. Muzaffer Arslanoglu, a 45-year-old taxi driver from Edmonton, north London, admitted conspiracy and was jailed for 5 years.

Later on, Dalgleish got 18 years and Connors 20 years. None showed reaction when jailed by Judge David Mole QC.

The judge told Dalgleish: 'Heroin, being seriously addictive, reduces the people who use it to degradation. The courts have long made it plain that this is such an evil that very serious deterrent sentences must be imposed. The evidence clearly demonstrated that you had played a "vital role" in an operation that was at the "top of any scale.'

Trevor Long's defence that he was no more than a flower trader and that any sightings of him in the company of the drug gang was only to do with flowers. He was acquitted much to the disappointment and fury of the Crime Squad.

In 2004 I heard from Teresa Lee who had been my predecessor in Brazil. She was working on the cocaine intelligence team in London that were running a joint operation with the Spanish National Police. This was concentrating on rigid hull inflatable boats, being supplied to Spanish smugglers by a company in Lowestoft.

'We want to put tracking beacons on boats in this yard,' Teresa said. 'Ones destined for Spain.'

'We'll have to prioritise,' I said. 'We'll never get way with a blanket cover. There's also a limit on equipment available.'

Neil Davidson owned the company, Crompton Marine Ltd. He lived with Ellen George in Lowestoft.

Officers were dispatched to observe the boatyard as best they could. The inflatable boat being built was massive, 18 feet long, and nearing completion. We checked our records and those of other agencies. No-one had heard of a RIB that size.

Our Spanish colleagues confirmed that the boat was to be delivered to Galicia, in northern Spain and it was thought its purpose was to meet up at sea with larger boats smuggling cocaine. The drugs would then be transferred back to land and distributed in Spain and the rest of Europe.

This operation was instigated by the Spanish, intent on protecting its borders. The position of Gibraltar, geographically had for decades been a bone of contention for the Spanish. The Spanish authorities always considered Gibraltar was being used as a conduit for drugs and cigarettes being smuggled from Africa to Europe.

Neil Davidson and 43-year-old, Ellen George, became the focus of our attention and investigations began on their background.

The 18-foot RIB left the yard and put to sea for trials. Even from our distant observation points we were taken aback with the speed of this boat, the deep V hulls slicing through the water reaching, we thought, speeds up to 50 mph. There were 8 outboard motors powering it. At that time even the boats of the UK Special Boat Service wouldn't keep up.

There was no question that should such a vessel fall into the hands of smugglers it would prove uncatchable.

In 2004 the Spanish arrested Davison as he came out of his flat overlooking the beach at Estepona on the Costa del Sol, east of Gibraltar.

16 others involved in the trafficking operation were held as 70 Spanish officers carried out raids to round up the suspects.

(At the time of Davison's arrest Chief Amparo Estrada, of Spanish customs, said it was estimated 141 tonnes of cannabis valued at £546m had been moved on Crompton Marine boats. 'This boat was tested in the sea off Lowestoft. The gentleman who took it out loaded it with six tonnes of shingle, it had five people on board and it was still able to travel at 50mph.')

Davison is believed to have taken more than 150 RHIBS over to Spain, before selling each of them for an average of 60,000 euros. Although he was not accused of carrying the drugs on the boats himself, the authorities alleged he knew what they were to be used for.

Officers went along to the magistrate's court to obtain a search warrant for Compton Marina and to arrest Ellen George. Within an office cupboard they found a holdall containing 250 thousand pounds, mainly Scottish notes that were difficult to trace. Scottish notes were a first-choice currency for the drug smuggling community.

The holdall was obviously placed ready for a quick getaway. We've seen them many times. The go to/future bag on hand to escape with. As well as money they would contain passports, jewellery, anything small and valuable. 250 thousand would last quite a long time.

There was also a locked safe. Ellen George pleaded ignorance of that as she had everything else. So, a locksmith was called in and successfully opened it. It contained over one million pounds, mostly in Scottish notes.

The money was bagged up and taken to my office. Few of us had ever seen that amount of money before. The money had to be forensically examined for traces of drugs and for fingerprints and was then taken to a secure office in London.

The defence counsel refused us permission to count the money insisting it must be done by an independent party.

The money was examined by our chemist and it was decided that as it was so heavily impregnated with Class A drugs that it could never be allowed to go back into circulation. They would have to be destroyed. It was pointed out that most notes used by the public was likely to be contaminated with something illegal. But they would not pose any danger.

The currency was taken to The Bank of England and counted by their staff. It was 1.2 million pounds. As they destroyed the notes, they issued new currency that was paid into the Government coffers to be used as "proceeds of crime."

Davison was then in custody in Malaga, Spain.

We charged Ellen George with money laundering.

Cathy Pryn was nominated as the case officer. Little did she know this case would require years of work identifying and tracing overseas cash and assets owned by Davison and George.

George was found guilty at her trial. She was given a confiscation order of 1 million nine hundred pounds – a figure calculated to have been the profit she made. She fought this order through the courts and it was not until 2011 that it was resolved.

Bank records over a number of years revealed over 6 million was paid in cash out of a 21million income.

A five-year investigation involving thousands of hours work by our officers culminated in Ellen George receiving a two-year suspended sentence at Ipswich Crown Court.

Davison and George had bought over forty properties with their ill-gotten gains

She had also admitted five charges of evading £394,000 in tax relating to her partner's property business.

A Spanish customs officer involved in the case said: "This was a very interesting operation. The type of boats used put in danger customs officers out at sea who had to follow these vessels, so it was very important to catch the people responsible. This would not have been so easy without help from English customs officers. As we continued to investigate, the money laundering also became more and more important as well. It was vital to have stopped that 18-metre boat, because nothing could have followed it."

Given bail by a Spanish court after his arrest, Davison then went on the run. He was at large until recaptured in February 2008.

However, he was given bail in Spain for a second time, only to flee again. Davison has been a wanted man ever since. At one stage he was suspected of having fled to South America. In 2016 The East Anglian Daily Times wrote, "Anyone with information about Davison's whereabouts should telephone HM Customs and Revenue hotline.".

In September 2004 I received the terrible news that my friend, my colleague, my boss, Terry Byrne, had been suspended, accused of withholding information from the defence in a number of fraud cases. One case had collapsed as a result of "outing" of an informant, Alf Allington, who worked for London City Bond.

London City Bond advertised themselves as, "From London's oldest bonded warehouse to the UK's leading tax warehousing company. LCB has an impeccable reputation with renowned drinks trade customers. Fine wine merchants and global investors entrust us with their storage in the ideal conditions of Vinothèque, Melksham and Dinton."

Allington had given information about suspect excise goods, a scheme similar to those used by fraudsters in the "Fluke" operation. They had used London City Bond in their conspiracy.

The scam was based on exploiting tax rules whereby alcohol held in a government licensed tax-free warehouses can be transported to other similar warehouses without paying tax. Forged documentation "proved" that goods had gone abroad, while in reality they ended up being sold on to the UK market.

Alf Allington, managing director of LCB, who gave evidence in numerous trials in which he was presented as a "trade source" - a straightforward businessman doing only what he was obliged to do by law.

Under oath he denied he was an informant or had any knowledge that fraud was taking place. Customs knew at the time that both these statements were lies. In fact, as he later confessed, he was a participating informant facilitating the fraud with the knowledge and encouragement of Customs.

Customs and Excise were accused of failing to register Allington as a participating informant. Crime groups would go to him. Informants would usually play a minor role. The part Allington played was a major one. By inviting villains to use his company his profits multiplied. He thought that by passing on a limited amount of information he would not be suspected of seeking richer pickings.

Terry Byrne was based in Custom's House London. He was approached by a fellow Commissioner, Mike Hanson, who advised that he was to be suspended and to hand over all the trappings of office; mobile phone, ID card, keys and various passes.

He was then marched out of the building.

He was treated disgracefully.

Other investigators had also been suspended because of their involvement in the case. They were investigated over several months by the Metropolitan Police in "Operation Gestalt."

I thought at the time that it was ironic that the Met, with so many corruption scandals, should be asked to conduct an investigation of corruption in another security service.

A headline in The Guardian Newspaper on 30 Sep 2004 read – "Customs suspends two leading officials. Whistle-blower claim as Yard inquiry identifies 20 officers"

"Two of the most senior customs officials have been suspended after it was revealed that they are under investigation by a Scotland Yard squad investigating allegations of perjury and perverting the course of justice.

Terry Byrne, customs commissioner and its director of law enforcement - in effect number three in the organisation - was ordered to leave his desk yesterday at the Thames-side headquarters of Britain's oldest law enforcement agency."

David Pickup, head of the customs solicitors' and prosecutions department, was also suspended.

Both men, close colleagues for a number of years, were suspended on full pay by the customs chairman, David Varney, because the "seniority of their positions and broad scope of their responsibilities make it impossible for them to remain in their posts pending investigation".

He added, "The investigation was at an early stage and charges would not necessarily follow. Allegations relating to the two men are in connection with non-disclosure."

The dramatic decision to suspend Terry and David followed discussions with the attorney general, Lord Goldsmith, and a personal briefing for Tony Blair.

Norman Lamb, Liberal Democrat MP for North Norfolk, said, 'The customs investigation is a can of worms that appears to go right to the top of the organisation.'

After a six-month inquiry, Mr Justice Butterfield concluded he could find no evidence of criminality by Customs.

It was quite a shock to us all. Terry was held in high esteem by all of us and the wider law enforcement community.

As time went on it was established that he had not prevented disclosure detail and had not broken any rules. He was exonerated but by then damage had been done.

Terry was due to retire a few months after suspension so he left the service on a sour note. He had given forty years to the service and had been instrumental in so many successful operations as well as playing a huge part in the modernisation of the service.

As with other vindictive investigations like this, Terry had his close supporters and his distant critics. Having colleagues blank you must have hurt.

Paul Evans was the Chief Investigating Officer at the time and because of their difficult history was probably delighted to see Terry leave.

We were all outraged that such an event took place. Everyone's house was searched, causing family distress.

It was sad that certain people took such pleasure out of this calamity that severely tested our reputation as a force.

It was also ironic that Terry Byrne was instrumental in creating The Serious and Organised Crime Agency (SOCA) seen as the UK's FBI. So, he found himself out in the cold as this Agency took off.

There were major changes at the time with Gordon Brown. Accompanying the budget of 2005 there would be a merger between the Inland Revenue and Customs and Excise. The Tax element would go into HMRC. They wanted the direct taxation departments to work alongside those with experience of fraud and organised crime. This would give them the capability to investigate all tax affairs and see through prosecutions if required. It was seen as bolstering the tax collection service.

It didn't turn out as hoped. HMRC were not interested in tobacco smuggling. Dirty hands were to be avoided.

I knew the double whammy of the merger with HMRC and the Crime Agency (SOCA) would be game changing for all in investigation teams.

As a manager I had to cope with those staff who wanted to be part of the Agency but couldn't, through lack of vacancies or unsuitableness. I was keen for all the staff to feel they were valued whether or not they moved or stayed. It was sometimes seen as a two-tier system, first class and second class even though this was never the case.

All the time this was going on we had work to do. Villains did not hold off until 2006 when we will have rearranged our company structures.

A number of senior officers joined the Serious and Organised Crime Agency and assisted some sort of continuity regarding practical and legislative regulations. They became SOCA agents working for a brand-new organisation that had its own rules and practices. Even the terminology was changed.

I decided not to join SOCA. Throughout my career I had nothing but respect for my senior managers. I did not rate SOCA's senior management team with one exception, a Crime Squad police officer, Trevor Pierce.

I remained with HMRC and we continued to pick up major smugglers and significant drug consignments.

SOCA were given the opportunity to adopt any of the seizures but they appeared just to want the intelligence but didn't want the "grubby" side; carrying out arrests and prosecutions.

A number of significant seizures were left with HMRC to deal with.

I spoke to Andy Sellars of SOCA. 'If we find 300 kilos of heroin at Felixstowe where does that fit into your list of priorities?'

'It depends if we have prior information about it, if its international.'

'All drugs are international,' I pointed out.

'If we've got sensitive information we've got to act on. A straight forward interception would be top of our list.'

'I can't believe that, Andy. With 300 kilos imported by "clean skins"! Surely, they'll be top drawer criminals!'

This arrangement, although unsatisfactory, gave us licence to do our job; seize illegal consignments, catch the people behind it and take them to court.

HMRC press office was keen to keep our successes in the public eye. We were finding the baddies, confiscating drugs that seriously harmed young and old people and we wanted everyone to know what was being achieved.

The press office and I had a really good relationship and I was quietly pleased that our good reputation had not suffered by organisational changes. We were busy people and, because of the publicity we got, the general public knew what we were up to.

At this time a number of ex-colleagues who had joined the Serious Crime Agency complained at the lack of activity. Disillusionment was rife. In their words, SOCA was an unmitigated disaster.

I resisted saying – I told you so.

On a Friday evening I had a call to say there was 200 kilos of cannabis at Harwich docks and a number of SOCA officers had arrived.

'Cannabis is not their brief,' the caller said.

'You know why they're there on a Friday evening,' I said.

'No.'

'They're ex police officers and they never change their spots. They're going to claim overtime payments. It'll be a good earner. Friday evening, Saturday and Sunday. Double time at least.'

CHAPTER 23
ALLEGATIONS, SUSPENSIONS, PROMOTIONS, (and Chinese liquor).

The top management in Customs and Excise was changing. A former merchant banker Richard Broadbent became the Chairman of the Board for Customs and Excise. A few rungs down the ladder, Dick Kellaway was coming to the end of his time as the Chief Investigator. Paul Evans was brought in to replace him.

It was the first time our Chief Investigator was appointed from outside. Paul Evans had been a MI6 man for 18 years,

Many of my colleagues thought this a fantastic move. A person from the security service, former head of the Vienna Station, would add an effective dimension to our department.

Paul brought with him an extensive knowledge of international security issues and with it came a contact list previously out of the Customs and Excise reach. MI6, like other enforcement groups, would have experienced drug smuggling and smugglers at first hand.

Russian or Chinese criminality had not materialised as a threat in the UK as it had in other parts of Europe. Problems with Islamic fundamentalists were some time off.

But there were some in Customs Investigation who thought Evans' appointment was a bad move. There was a deep suspicion, particularly by some of the old school senior managers that this move would result in the watering down of the Investigation Division's standing in the law enforcement community.

There was always a move by security departments to establish a bigger role in drug smuggling, to be top dog. MI6 and others had vast resources for a worldwide role that lent itself to the fight against international gangs. The police, particularly the Met, were also keen to take precedence.

Previous governments had rejected any "land grabs" by the police (or others) and had considered Customs the most competent department to deal with international drug smuggling.

A number of government enquiries on the working practices of the Customs Investigation Division had taken place over the years.

In January 1995 over 100 Customs investigators were involved in the search of a catamaran, "Frugal" owned by Louis Dobbels. Although all the suspects had long gone, 309 kilos of cocaine and four passports with Dobbels' image was discovered on a beach in Sussex. Dobbels was subsequently arrested and pleaded guilty. Two well known drug smugglers Brian Doran and Kenneth Togher, were also charged and found guilty at the original trial. It went to appeal where Customs were accused of illegally searching and bugging a hotel room occupied by Doran. During the covert search a wad of cash and details of a trip to Panama was seen.

Despite having permission from the hotel management, Mr Justice Turner ruled the hotel room should have been treated as a private house and any bugging and search was illegal.

Doran and Togher were found not guilty and their 25-year prison sentence quashed. Customs were ordered to pay costs and compensation.

This bombshell led to a review of Customs which was conducted by Judge Butler. Although highly critical of the investigators it was suggested that they had been poorly advised by their own solicitors. This turned out to be the death knell for directly employed solicitors by Customs and Excise. Distance was required between the operatives and the law advisors.

(The Customs solicitors office was eventually merged with the Crown Prosecuting Service.)

This was followed by Operation Branfield, that involved heroin from Pakistan that had (allegedly) been allowed to go on the streets to facilitate the progress of a case. It was rare, but occasionally there were circumstances where a drug could be released into the public domain. Additional guidelines were put in place for the recruitment, handling and rewarding of informants

Three experienced officers in our Manchester and Leeds office, had been working with an informer who supplied detail on an importation of heroin from Pakistan. The West Midland police sought to establish if all actions were strictly legal. All three officers were suspended.

Again, I thought it was somewhat ironic as it was the West Midlands police mistreatment of the Birmingham Six that led to the introduction of the Police and Criminal Evidence Act that governed all law enforcement activity.

As a potential witness to an event, years earlier in Portugal, and in company with Mike Stephenson, I was interviewed in Ipswich by officers from the West Midlands. Mike had worked with an informant, known as "Jimmy", in Madrid. I had been a back-up for Mike as he dealt with the arrangements. I briefly met the informant in a hotel. He was to meet up with a Columbian crime group. We had no help from the Spanish police and no surveillance could be set up. The UK Drugs Liaison Officer, Cliff Craig, was aware of this visit but he was unhappy we were not telling the Spanish police.

As Mike did all the handling, my input was limited. I had nothing to do with the Columbians and didn't witness the meetings.

Peter had telephoned me when I was in Brazil to ask me if it was possible for his informant to visit Brazil to "dig around" the local drug trafficking gangs. My notebook of the time confirmed I was not happy about the idea.

'There were two investigation departments in Brazil,' I said, 'and four police forces, none of whom talked to each other. Each of them would relish the prospect of catching others out. There's no cast iron guarantee that the informant could operate there without a major calamity occurring.'

It was later authorised by Mike Newsom, the Deputy Chief Investigation Officer in London but thankfully this deployment did not happen.

An Assistant Chief Investigation Officer, Pat Cadogan, was also suspended from operational duties. Amjad Bashir, an Asian Officer, took suspension so badly he began to lose weight. Over time he had suffered shameful prejudice. Now, under suspicion was too much to bear. He sadly took his own life. Amjad was never charged with any offence or even disciplined internally for his actions. He paid the ultimate price for being a frontline officer.

There was no corruption, no financial incentive. The manner in which the officers carried out their responsibilities was guided by the advice they had received. Hindsight suggests that the informant was allowed too much free will, but in many eyes, this came nowhere near as a calculated negligence of duty. If this had happened within the police it would have been dealt with as a disciplinary issue. They felt Senior Officers just rolled over. The West Midlands Police described Paul Evans as being "very supportive of the investigation".

Sadly, three officers were found guilty of malfeasance in public office for the way the informant was managed and given six month suspended prison sentences. All lost their jobs and faced carrying the yoke of culpability around for the rest of their lives.

Many police forces throughout the UK had been criticised on how they handled informants. A number of cases had collapsed because on non-disclosure of information to defence teams. It seemed to us that Customs were being scrutinised at an intensity that escaped other security forces, certainly, police forces.

This period, this level of allegations, had not occurred before. Customs had always been deemed whiter that white. We had a habit of looking down our noses at those who hadn't followed correct procedures. Customs had been involved in arresting police officers caught in corruption scandals.

The whole team of investigators were in shock and there was a feeling in the rank and file that Evans didn't like operations, didn't like arrests, didn't like informants. In his mind each of these things meant trouble.

Being stationed in Ipswich gave me an advantage. My teams were achieving very good results with no suspicion of bending any rules although, with events going on elsewhere, my scrutiny became razor sharp. Our office was a few miles away from Felixstowe and Harwich and we had first refusal on some large seizures of heroin and cocaine. I intended there would be no dire consequences to our actions.

A lot of changes work wise but much to my relief Pauline and the boys quickly settled back in the UK. The boys continued their schooling in Framlingham and joined local football and rugby teams. Pauline's part time job with the housing association was on-going.

My youngest Jimmy came home from school one day. 'There is a boy at school who writes his own tunes and is a great singer'.

'Don't be silly,' I said. 'Every kid says that. He should concentrate on his studies. What was his name?'

'Ed Sheeran.'

Sometimes parents do get it so wrong!

We initially rented a house on the Suffolk/ Norfolk border whilst we decided where we would eventually settle. For nine months we looked at a number of houses and eventually found one in a small Suffolk village. It seemed and looked ideal.

After visiting the property with the estate agent, I put an offer in slightly below the asking price. Within a few minutes he rang me to say the owner would only accept the asking price. After a quick discussion we agreed to pay the full amount. A few minutes later the agent rang me to say if we agreed to pay another £3,000, they would not advertise it.

I was taken aback and said, 'We agreed to pay the asking price and if the owner wants more money we will pull out.'

I received another call to say my offer had been accepted.

Still reeling at the audacity, I said, 'If the house was the best I have seen, I wouldn't buy it as the owner was trying to get more money out of us.'

We eventually found a better home in a really good area.

Although times at work were difficult with all the investigations into the department's working practices and informant handling, it wasn't all doom and gloom.

As Branch Commander I attended Crime Group meetings that included the regional police forces. The whole gambit of crime would be discussed including Customs and willingness to co-operate would be encouraged and confirmed.

Fortunately, I had a good relationship with Peter Warobec, the Head of Crime for Suffolk Police. Peter's concern was that as The Home Office had a league table of cash seizures as proceeds of crime, his force had no money-laundering case, no proceeds of crime cash seizures.

News came in that Suffolk police had received intelligence on a suspect, a Turkish male, was due to fly out of Stansted Airport but they didn't know when. My officers put the name on the warning lists and they monitored the bookings and passenger lists for flights to Turkey.

We were then alerted and gave Peter the nod. He sent some of his officers to Stansted Airport and they successfully intercepted the suspect who was carrying £20,000 in cash as he booked in for a flight to Turkey.

Customs would normally have prosecuted the courier but he was dealt with by the Suffolk police.

Much to his relief, Peter and his office appeared on the league of a successful arrest of a money launderer.

In June 2004 I was invited St Katherines Dock to witness the launch of "The Valiant", a Custom cutter. A number of colleagues from the Maritime Branch and Investigation were there. Dave (the Admiral) Hewer was the Assistant Chief investigation Officer managed the ID's Maritime intelligence teams. He was also involved in the Territorial Army and was able to acquire the Royal Marine band to play at the event. Pamela Byrne, Terry's wife, performed the launching ceremony. The Marine band played, adding to the special nature of the observance that everyone present found joyful and moving.

My son, Alistair, who has worked on the Customs fleet for many years has a little chuckle when he sees the Cutter's plaque, naming Mrs Byrne. He first met Pam when he was 6 months old attending the Investigation division children's Xmas party.

I was asked to do some role playing for the recruitment of drug liaison officers about to be posted overseas. I decided on a management scenario rather than an investigation topic as I wanted them to think outside the box. One of the candidates had applied for a position in Colombia. I asked him to be a team leader at an airport with an officer fanatical about "CITES" (the Convention on International Trade in Endangered Species). It is a multilateral treaty to protect endangered plants and animals, covering 5,800 species of animals and 30,000 species of plants. This assistant's daily mission was not to discover drugs but to find samples of endangered species being illegally exported or imported.

The question put was, 'How would you deal with that scenario?'

The officer looked at me and rapidly turned ashen.

'What's the problem?' I asked.

'CITES? I don't know what CITES is.'

I could have hung the young fellow out to dry but instead explained the purpose and scale that CITES aspired to.

For him it didn't matter. He was by far the most suitable candidate for the job so he got it.

As senior managers (Assistant Chief up to the Chief), we would meet quartelyS, normally in hotels with conference facilities. Our Chief Investigation Officer, Paul Evans would host the meetings.

Every time he would open the proceedings by saying, 'Turn your phones off. There's nothing so important that it can't wait.'

Of course, someone forgot and twenty minutes into a discussion his phone rang the theme from "Captain Pugwash". (Captain Pugwash is a fictional pirate in a series of British children's comic strips and books.)

All eyes focused on "The Admiral", Dave Hewer, the Assistant Chief of our Maritime Branch. Dave's face turned an alarming shade of crimson as we all fell about laughing.

Paul Evans was far from pleased particularly as it took an age before Dave found the mute button.

Terry Byrne had been a major supporter on the creation on the Serious and Organised Crime Agency but he was keen it wouldn't just be an extension of the current police National Crime Squads. UK Customs were recognised as world leaders in tackling drug smuggling and our reputation was at an all-time high. His ideas were accepted and fully supported by the Chairman of the Board of Customs and Excise, Richard Broadbent.

In the March budget of 2004 the Chancellor of the Exchequer, Gordon Brown announced the merger of Custom and Excise with the Inland Revenue which is now HMRC (Her Majesty's Revenue and Customs). This would be enacted in April 2005.

Long term, dedicated Customs officials were not included at the top level. SOCA seemed destined to abandon "investigation" and concentrate on gathering intelligence to off load to other security and police forces. Much frustration was felt by officers who joined SOCA believing it would be a pro-active organisation, not a collection point for information.

In October 2005 I was called by Mike Norgrove who was Director of Intelligence for HRMC to head up the CHIS operations (the Covert Human Intelligence Sources) that managed human sources of intelligence or informants as I knew them.

Although a temporary promotion as Deputy Director of CHIS, I could not refuse it. There would be an increase in pay and, as I was to be based in London, an additional supplement would also be granted.

'You'll be head of CHIS operations,' said Mike. 'You've got the background and experience for the job.'

I nodded with no expectation of the bombshell to come.

'In a month's time,' said Mike. 'Her Majesty's Inspector of Constabulary will be conducting a review of CHIS within the umbrella of Customs and Excise to see if we are fit for purpose.'

In October 2005 I took on the responsibility of what might become a poisoned chalice.

So, I left "Investigation" for "Intelligence."

John McManus was the Director and a long-term friend so I knew they would provide a change that would be as painless as possible.

It meant, of course, getting up at 5am to catch the 6.15 train from Suffolk to arrive in London, Liverpool Street and walk to the Custom House, near the Tower of London.

It was long working day, often arriving home after 8pm.

I also managed the National Humint (Humane Intelligence) Centre which was located in Ipswich. This office kept a record of all persons that had contacted Customs and Excise whether they were reporting suspicious activity or suspect importation documents. Many agents from the UK importation world were registered.

Humints were not involved in any criminality but if we required them to take on a more active role, they would become a Covert Human Intelligence Source and would be managed accordingly. I was also head of the National Coordination Unit for Customs and Excise which received suspect reports and phone calls, often anonymous which would be researched and passed out to operational teams to investigate. This office was manned 24 x 7, 365 days of the year. It was the envy of the police forces that had their own intelligence hubs but they did not cover the whole of the UK.

As my new command was being inspected by HM Inspector of Constabulary, we were well and truly under the microscope. If HMIC found informant recruiting, management and oversight was not up to the highest of standards they could recommend we were no longer able to have CHIS. This would have meant our standing in the law enforcement community would have plummeted. I was ultimately responsible for my command, albeit I had been in place only for a few weeks. Thankfully, I had a great team of professionals around me. Two of my senior Assistant Chief Investigation Officers, Dave Fairclough and Chris Martin had a vast amount of experience in informant management. They ensured that the visit by the HMIC inspectors to our offices throughout the UK went smoothly. Inspection team also visited our overseas offices in Colombia, Pakistan, Turkey and Holland to ensure our handling of overseas informants was at the required standard.

Management of informants in Colombia was fraught with difficulties. Those giving information to law enforcement were constantly in danger of being exposed to dangerous and ruthless drug trafficking groups.

At the time of the creation of SOCA we had over 400 informants throughout the UK and overseas. When they were transferred over to SOCA, the vast majority of them were de-registered leaving just a handful. It was obvious from day one the management of SOCA were risk adverse to recruiting and managing informants. A valuable source of intelligence was turned off overnight. I had more dealings with informants than SOCA had on their books.

The HMIC inspection lasted nine months which took me up to a year in the post when, under Civil Service rules, my job had to be advertised. This time it would be a substantive position, not a temporary one.

Unfortunately, I was "gazumped" by a colleague who was already a substantive Deputy Director grade so my only course of action was to head back to Ipswich as Assistant Chief Investigation Officer (as Branch Head). It was not an unhappy move for I still lived in the area and felt comfortable with my responsibilities at work.

Back in Ipswich I had a phone call from Mike Norgrove, Head of Intelligence for Customs and Excise who asked if I would go with him on an official visit to Hong Kong and mainland China. As Head of Intelligence, he wanted to meet with Chinese Customs but also build stronger relationship with China Shipping, the largest importer into the UK. Counterfeit tobacco smuggling was becoming a big problem and the majority of consignments originated in China so any help from the Chinese authorities and companies would be welcome. I had never been to China and I jumped at the chance. I knew Mike well and though he was a Senior Commissioner of Customs and Excise, he was great company.

A requirement was that I had to have at least six months on my passport. I didn't, so I had to queue in the Passport Office in London to obtain a new emergency passport. As soon as it was issued it had to be sent on to the Chinese Embassy to be granted a visa.

The direct flight to Beijing took 22 hours.

We were met by Andy Lawson, the Fiscal Liaison Officer (FLO) who looked into money fraud through VAT, tobacco smuggling, anything that affected tax coming into the UK. He was based in Hong Kong but covered mainland China as well.

The trip was scheduled for a week and we had three locations to visit, Beijing, Shanghai and Hong Kong so our days were hectic.

The first morning Andy took us to see the Head of Chinese Customs. As we arrived at the modern impressive building, we were met by two immaculately uniformed officers who welcomed us in English. We sat in the reception area and served Chinese tea. A few minutes later we were beckoned into an adjoining office.

The head of Customs sat at a large table with the Directors of Intelligence, Operations, Investigation, ports and airports. After the usual introductions we were again served with more tea and glasses of water.

Mike stated he was pleased with the co-operation and relationship with the Chinese authorities and in particular with their working relationship with Andy. After a couple of hours of presentations and discussions we left the office and taken to a hotel owned and run by the Customs. We went into an impressively large private room and we sat at a table of about twenty. There was four of us, Mike, Andy, Alex our interpreter from the Embassy, and me.

The banquet lasted most of the afternoon and it must have been at least fifteen courses. I was told it was considered an insult not to eat the dishes put in front of you. Some of the dishes looked and tasted like raw offal and it took all of my willpower to actually eat it. I decided not to ask what it was and I was happy to remain ignorant. Although I was happy to experiment with local cuisine this was particularly challenging for a Brit used to English takeaways. Moutai was served, a strong distilled Chinese liquor, made from fermented sorghum grain, throughout the meal.

Every 15 minutes a toast was made. Mostly in Chinese with it being translated into English and vice versa. We all had to stand, acknowledge the speaker and take a swig. Lager was also available to help counter the taste of the strong spirit and the overseas contingent began to sway and slur a little.

I did suspect that our hosts drinks had been watered down and they were relishing the gullibility of their western guests.

I had no difficulty sleeping that night but woke up with a hangover.

We recovered quickly as the visit to the Chinese Customs required us to be focussed and in fine fettle, and not to be seen the worse for wear. We visited the Investigation Service and again given Chinese tea most of the morning. I cannot say it was an ideal hangover cure but it helped a bit.

We were given a choice for leisure time – to visit the Great Wall or to tour the kennels that housed the Custom's dog handling section. There was a strong perception that our hosts wanted us to observe the dogs undergoing training, so the exciting prospect of walking along the Great Wall was eased out of our thinking (a big regret to both of us but we were in China to work).

The dog handling establishment was a modern office block with about thirty kennels and about ten miles outside of Beijing. More Chinese tea and water was served and conversation level remained on the smallest of small talk. This led seamlessly into a light lunch, thankfully not with seventeen courses but just rice, meat and bean sprouts.

We were expecting to see the sniffer dogs in action and after lunch Mike asked if we could see some dogs in active training.

A few minutes later a bedraggled springer spaniel was brought in to "sniff out" some kind of drugs secreted away in the room. When we asked if we could see the training stable, we were told that an outbreak of canine flu had taken over so visitors were kept away.

'All kennels are isolated,' someone said.

We could have had wonderful experience visiting the Great wall of China but instead we saw bedraggled springer spaniel with flu! We went over the day's events, impossible to do so without hearty laughs.

My lasting memory of Beijing is the air pollution and the grey high-rise buildings. Shops and restaurants were few and far between and tended to be in the tourist areas. The population seemed to be all dressed the same and their clothes tended to lack colour.

We were to meet up with the British Ambassador Sir Christopher Hum in a shared office bock in the finance sector.

As we drove there the roads were choking with cars, lorries and buses but the number of people riding bicycles really made an impression on me.

A song by Katie Melua came out years later with the lyrics.
"There are nine-million bicycles in Beijing.
  That's a fact,
  It's a thing we can't deny,
  Like that fact that I will love you 'til I die.
  And there are nine-million bicycles in Beijing."

Every set of traffic-lights would have confirmed the numbers. Hundreds, perhaps thousands of cyclists lined up determined to beat the car drivers as the lights turned green.

The Embassy meeting with the Ambassador was convened to thank the staff for the help and support given to Andy. Thankfully, we were served coffee.

We did manage a couple of hours sightseeing and we went on a very clean and efficient metro to Tiananmen Square. With both of us being over six foot we stood out amongst the Chinese tourists. One delightful family approached us and their ten-year-old daughter asked very politely if she could practise her English. We were both impressed and spent a very enjoyable 20 minutes chatting with the charming family. We also visited the accessible parts of the Forbidden City.

The following day we flew to Shanghai for only one day but it was important that we improve the information we received on China Shipping, one of the biggest containerized marine, shipping company in the world. It was founded in 1997 it just grew and grew.

Andy and Alex accompanied Mike and I to meet up with seven Directors of China Shipping all in their late twenties. A young company with young dynamic people running it. As with many modern companies the offices were open plan, large, light and airy.

Shanghai, on China's central coast, was the country's biggest city and a global financial hub. Its heart is the Bund, a famed waterfront promenade lined with colonial-era buildings. Across the Huangpu River is the Pudong district's futuristic skyline.

The meetings went well with a promise to boost the flow of information on shipping data to our teams stationed there.

The never-ending flow of goods from China to Felixstowe required as much "live" data as possible. Up to date activities of Chinese companies exporting to the UK was vital so that any suspect shipments could be monitored, checked, searched if necessary. China Shipping later merged with COSCO, the Chinese Government owned shipping company and have 2 million containers making them the third largest container company in the world.

Although it was a flying visit it was a successful one. UK Customs had enhanced the relationship with the Chinese authorities and Andy's standing had been strengthened.

We took a three-hour flight to Hong Kong where Andy had arranged a car to meet us.

It was a Wednesday and Mike was very keen to go to Happy Valley Racecourse in the centre of the city. We left the airport at six in the evening and drove straight to the racecourse.

Happy Valley was built on reclaimed swampland with races dating back to 1846. The course itself was surrounded by seven-storey stands. There must have been tens of thousands of spectators, some already leaving as there were only 3 races left. We simply walked in through open gates.

It was quite a spectacle of colour and atmosphere, all under floodlights. Mike bet and lost a few Hong Kong dollars.

The next day Andy collected us from our hotel.

Andy's wife Janette and three children lived in Hong Kong and we were able to meet up with them at their home. Although Janette was on a career break, she was an experienced and respected investigator. We had worked together in the mid- eighties.

The next day we drove to the border between Hong Kong and mainland China. I wasn't sure what to expect. As Hong Kong's "independence" ended in 1996 after 156 years of British rule and became the "Hong Kong Special Administrative Region of the People's Republic of China", I thought that no border restrictions would apply. Instead, I found one of the tightest, secure borders I had come across anywhere in the world. Barbed wire fences patrolled by armed guards and the scrutiny of paperwork and visual as well as technological examination of goods had to be seen to be believed. No-one and nothing were going to cross the border in and out if there was the slightest hint of something amiss. With different rates of duty and tax any border crossing was open to fraud. Every vehicle, container and person were stopped and the paperwork thoroughly examined.

The smuggling of oil from mainland China was worth millions of dollars as Hong Kong duties were much higher.

From the top of one building, we stared out to the mainland.

In the distance we could see the huge and modern city of Shenzhen built over a period of 15 years and housing nearly 12 million people. A small village in the fifties Shenzhen was considered to be the fastest growing city in the world. Because of its close proximity to Hong Kong, it was designated as an economic zone with high tech development and manufacture to rival places such as Silicon Valley in California.

The new facilities were to take advantage of Hong Kong's wealth and act as a gateway from China to the rest of the world.

We were shown around the Control Area although the red and green channels were made redundant by the fact that every movement over the border was stopped and checked by Hong Kong officials. All traffic from the opposite side of the border was treated in the same way.

The next day Andy took us to the ferry terminal where we took a short trip across the bay to the island of Lamma. There are no cars allowed on Lamma, a sharp contrast to the streets of the city only a few miles away. It was the home to hippies, artists and creative beings and nicknamed Hong Kong's "Cornwall."

Buildings higher than three storeys are prohibited and there are no automobiles allowed except for small fire trucks, ambulances and light goods vehicles.

We walked past boutiques, craft stores and art galleries before we found a fantastic seafood restaurant. The thirty-minute journey from non-stop bustle into a different world.

The next day we boarded the flight home armed with gifts for the family. Hong Kong Sevens rugby shirts for the boys and a silk dress for Pauline. It was an enjoyable week and my swan song as a temporary Deputy Director.

The next step in my career was pre-occupying my thoughts. To return as a Branch Commander or look further afield.

A post was advertised in "Detection" the uniformed side of Customs. It was for Head of Operations, a Deputy Director level and a promotion for me. It covered the central region of the country. Anglesey in North Wales, west to Norwich Airport, south to Felixstowe and Tilbury Docks. Birmingham and East Midlands Airport was included. Other Regions were Scotland and the North, London Airports, South and European Operation. Pembroke to Fishguard.

Another career change and new challenges to consider.

CHAPTER 24
COUNTERFEIT VIAGRA, RHINO HORNS, SHAM MARRIAGES AND BAGPIPES.

Most people picture "Customs" as uniformed staff at ports and airports, those checking luggage and passports but the true scale of their modern-day undertakings was as varied as they were complex.

The Customs Detection teams, numbering four and a half thousand were based at ports and airports throughout the UK. Officers were also based at the Channel Tunnel terminal in Coquelles, near Calais and Jamaica and Nigeria as part of an initiative to identify and arrest drug couriers before they travel to the UK.

Four "Detection" regions had been created in England, North, Central, London airports and South/Eurotunnel. Although I had never worked in Detection, I was very interested in applying for the advertised role as Head of Operations, Detection. For me this would be a permanent promotion, working at the HQ based in Ipswich.

I applied for the job and was interviewed by Bob Skinner, the Director and Jeremy Lee, the incumbent Head of Operations.

Jeremy's home was in the north-west. He spent his working week in Ipswich, returning back to his family at weekends. He was keen to return nearer home and had recently secured a post in Liverpool.

A lady from HMRC human resources was also present at the interview. My experience in investigation allowed me to answer questions on detection and surveillance techniques.

Fortunately, I recalled the right facts in the right order and in September 2006 I started the job as Deputy Director, Head of Operations for the uniformed Detection in the Central Region.

It had always been a rookie's ambition to join Uniformed Customs but, like many "Civil Services" of the time, it was almost always a wait for dead man's shoes.

Bob Skinner and I overlapped. He was a no-nonsense, ex-Army officer who had left the services to join Customs a few years before. Thankfully we got on really well.

Bob recognised that my continuing relations with ex-colleagues in Investigation helped both organisations to co-operate and share knowledge of events and personalities that otherwise would have been missed.

If interceptions of drugs were made at ports or airports the investigation teams adopted and progressed the case. It was then easy for me to persuade my former colleagues to take them on. Our region covered Felixstowe, Harwich, Holyhead, Fishguard, Stansted, East Midlands and Birmingham airports so there was no shortage of seizures.

The area I covered was large both in mileage and population.

In the first few weeks I made a point of visiting all the offices in the region. My journey time from home to Holyhead and Fishguard was about five hours so I had to stay over.

One of our inland depots handled parcels – the Coventry International Hub run by Parcel Force near Coventry Airport. This depot processed the majority of large parcels from overseas although some were checked at leading airports.

Parcels were examined for prohibited goods such as drugs, weapons tobacco and counterfeit medicines and ensured none escaped tax due. For example, if a mobile phone arrived from China, Excise Duty and a VAT charge would be imposed.

The building itself was vast, the size of a sports stadium with conveyer belts sending parcels to be scanned. Over fifty staff worked at CIH, the majority of whom were collecting payments due.

Customers who had bought goods online were often miffed at facing extra costs. Although an item can appear cheap on the internet by the time VAT and duty plus the postal charge it can prove to be a false economy.

The paperwork linked to importations was examined and if it was deemed suspicious it was set aside for opening. I could not believe the amount of tobacco, counterfeit and real, smuggled and diverted to the UK from other destinations. Millions of cigarettes arrived each day addressed to numerous private properties. Each importation was seized and Customs regulations meant a formal seizure notice had to be sent to the delivery address. Dozens were sent every week. This was sent to the recipient to give the opportunity for an appeal.

It was usually a waste of time waiting for a response that would admit knowledge or ownership of illegal goods. So, the parcels just sat there.

I attended a team meeting and the staff had the same gripe that the issue of the seizure notice was a complete waste of time. In the very unlikely event that somebody actually appealed against the seizure I suggested it would be more cost effective for them to purchase a replacement from Tescos.

Appeals were almost non-existent.

This scenario resulted in millions of unclaimed cigarettes from China seized and destroyed each week. They were taken to a local power station and incinerated thus ticking the environment box by generating electricity.

We couldn't understand the senders in China who were losing money as we were seizing so many packages and when you take into account the cost of packaging and postage. It didn't add up. A delegation of Chinese Postal officials visiting our office put us right. Not only were the cigarettes counterfeit but so were the postage stamps.

So, it cost them little to send parcels over and if a few got through they made their money.

Counterfeit medicines were a huge problem.

Viagra and other "recreational" drugs made up the bulk of entries which included tablets for heart problems and diabetes.

Ashley How, an ex-Met police officer, represented a group of pharmaceutical companies who were keen to identify the counterfeiters. Pfizer also sent staff to work with our uniformed officers to analyse shipments, list multiple offenders and pin-point those guilty of stealing intellectual property rights by packaging their goods in near identical design of genuine goods.

Consignments of cocaine and heroin were sent from South America and Pakistan. Seizures of drugs were offered to HMRC investigation teams and because I knew them, they often adopted the cases. If HMRC were not in a position to take the case on, it was offered to a local police force in the area that the parcel was addressed to.

It was often the case that because of historical acrimony between customs and police, the latter would respond with a heightened degree of scepticism. They were always resistant if the operation involved an informer. There would, they thought, be troublesome factors and that they were being asked to pick up cases the Customs wanted to wash their hands of. All the assurances that it was a straightforward seizure, nothing else, failed to allay their suspicions.

However, if they were convinced, they would come along, inspect and substitute the drugs, place a tracking device and carry out similar procedures that we used in Investigation.

At a staff team meeting at the Coventry International Hub I asked, 'Is there anything I can do to make life easier for us all?'

One of the officers, Mandy said, 'The trouble is we work above the machinery floor. It's hot in the winter, stifling in the summer. The conditions are not healthy.'

'I'll ask and see what I can do.'

Emboldened Mandy added. 'Senior managers have said that before but nothing's been done.'

It was a bit of a gauntlet for me.

In the ceiling, ducts had been installed ready for air-conditioning. So, I arranged for a meeting with the head of Parcel Force in his office which was air-conditioned next door to the ones that were not.

'I want to organise air conditioning for the Customs office next door,' I said. 'There are ducts already in place and there were some air conditioning cassettes already on the roof. Can we add additional units to service the Customs Office?'

The manager said he would look into it and two weeks later he confirmed there's no problem. 'Cassettes can be put in and run for you but it was going to cost £25,000 to do it'.

I rang the people who managed HMRC estates in London and was advised that we had to go through proper procedure. They were happy to do it and when I put the business case for the project it was agreed. But through the Civil Service channel it was going to cost £125,000 (£100,000 more than Parcel Force's estimate.) Parcel Force were also willing to include maintenance in their costing.

But no – we had to stick with civil service procedure who would pay the extra without blinking. As long as set procedure is adhered to it must be right. I didn't share that view. Civil Service contracts were costing the exchequer millions more than it needed to.

I recall my Investigation days when a works Vauxhall Cavalier car required four new tyres. There was no going down to the local fitter to get a change of tyre at £85 each – instead procurement procedure was put in place with a designated supplier at £120 per tyre.

'That's with discount,' I was told.

Eventually, at a premium cost, air-conditioning was installed in our Coventry office.

I often recall the Prime Minister, Mrs Thatcher saying, 'Someone has to add up the figures. Every business has to do it, every housewife has to do it, every Government should do it.'

I had Assistant Directors below me; Charlotte Mann, Sarah Wolstenhome, Bob Lyne and Caroline Stott. Thankfully, they were experienced and knew their jobs inside out. I was lucky to have Bill Form, a very experienced Senior Officer as my right-hand man. He kept me on track if I wandered off and used my investigation rather than detection "head". Although a "Geordie", Bill had spent nearly all of his career working in Felixstowe and was happy to be based in Ipswich with me.

We were still with HMRC, a tax collecting department that nevertheless were keen to exploit positive publicity when my teams had notable successes. Mandy and Jenny were on the media team.

In 2007 the BBC wanted to do a live broadcast from Felixstowe. Mark Murphy from Radio Suffolk was going to report on tobacco smuggling.

I was in Felixstowe a 5 o'clock in the morning when the broadcast started in the examination shed.

A scan of a container from China suggested there was a huge quantity of cigarettes inside. It had not yet been opened but the X-ray image was as conclusive as you can get. At 6 o'clock, radio microphone at the ready, the container was opened by uniformed customs officers. It was always a slow, meticulous process as any of the contents could reveal details that could be used as evidence. Crates were eased out of the container and as one was opened, I started my live commentary for the radio. My words would not go down in history as the contents were items of furniture. For some reason I opened a few top drawers to check for packages of cigarettes. There were none. An element of panic did set in but I held my nerve and continued with the commentary of the search. I was hoping and praying the scanner operative had got it right as a negative result would not be ideal for live radio. The team, lead by Higher Officer Kevin Sayer, persevered with a search of the bottom drawers that were crammed with packets of counterfeit Marlborough cigarettes. The writing and health warnings were in Spanish so we knew the cargo was not meant for the UK. I breathed a sigh of relief and carried on talking to Mark about Felixstowe, tobacco smuggling and the tax loss to the Treasury. I also provided him with information about drug smuggling. The live broadcast finished at 9.00.

A container full of young children's trainers arrived at Felixstowe. On initial inspection they appeared to be made by one of the leading sports brands. It is difficult for a customs officer to confirm 100% a trainer is counterfeit and the major sports companies, keen to protect their brand name, sent a technical expert along to verify they were indeed fake. These had to be destroyed as the materials used in Chinese sweat shops were often hazardous and therefore potentially dangerous.

I was often asked why we didn't send the counterfeit goods to less developed countries. The genuine manufacturers, eager to protect their brand, would not allow this. It was also thought arrogant for the western world to reject these goods but it was ok for kids in Africa. And there was also the question of safety as there was no way of knowing if all materials were non-toxic.

Suffolk Trading Standards or their colleagues in other parts of the UK often adopted the investigation if there was a possibility of a successful prosecution existed.

Cocaine weighing 20 kilos was concealed in a Dutch registered vehicle arriving at Harwich. Keven Birch from BBC's Look East covered the story and conducted the interview with me.

Very often the local newspapers would cover a case reporting the "scene" of the crime through to the Crown Court case in Ipswich and Chelmsford.

The High Sheriff of Suffolk, Diana Hunt asked to visit Felixstowe to see the work of Customs first hand. She was one of Suffolk's leading magistrates and in that position, she asked me to give a talk to a group of magistrates from all over the County. It took place in Ipswich Magistrate's Court. A reverse in roles saw me sitting on the magistrate's bench with them sitting in the well of the courtroom. It was a bit surreal but I had to admit I enjoyed being in that elevated position.

Some weeks later I escorted Jonathon Hunt, Diana's husband, on a tour of a Customs cutter moored at Ipswich dock. He was a maritime lawyer and was really keen to visit one of our coastal patrol cutters. I knew many of the maritime staff and as soon as one of the cutters visited Ipswich, I was able to facilitate the visit.

We had a seizure of cocaine in Coventry inserted in packets of dried prunes. The stones of the fruit had been removed and a small sachet of cocaine enclosed. The amount of drugs wasn't massive but the lengths taken to hide the cocaine was clever and unusual.

There was a Newspaper Report –

SMUGGLERS have tried to get £30,000 worth of cocaine through Coventry Airport - hidden inside prunes.

A total of 143 prunes had been split open, filled with 4.4 grammes of cocaine, placed back into packets and sent in the post.

The total weight of the cocaine was 629.2 grams, well over half a kilo, and it was 70 per cent pure.

Customs officers at the Coventry International Hub found the drug - wrapped in clear plastic - by prising open each individual dried fruit.

The consignment of four packets of prunes were found at the airport en-route from Guyana, West Africa, to Spain.

I was interviewed on National 5 live on which the interviewer said, 'The smugglers must have been stoned to get involved in this venture.'

'I've heard that one before,' I replied, followed by a groan and a shake of the head.

A suspect consignment arrived at Felixstowe from China and it was thought to contain smuggled tobacco as the delivery address had previously been used for smuggling. However, when examined the boxes were found to contain thousands of fake Viagra tablets. The consignment was formally seized and the pharmaceutical company that produced Viagra, informed by the uniformed staff at Felixstowe.

It attracted a lot of media interest. A reporter from the Sun rang my office and I gave him details of the case. He asked me if the pills worked.

My answer was short. 'I haven't a clue and how would I know.'

I could visualise him chuckling on the other end of the phone.

He persisted. 'Can I quote you that we need stiffer sentences for this offence?'

'Do you really think I'm going to respond to that question?' I thought it was a good line and it took all my willpower to stifle a laugh.

Located in Essex and the closest ferry port to London, the 92-acre Purfleet Thames Terminal handles trailers, containers and the annual import and export of 400,000 vehicles. It is a roll on/roll off ferry used to bring vehicles in from Zeebrugge on the coast of Belgium. Unaccompanied trailers are off loaded by a tractor unit and stored in Purfleet docks awaiting collection.

It was known that the soft sided containers were popular with clandestines (illegal immigrants).

On a drizzly day I went out with the officers examining the trailers. A detection machine was used that read the amount of carbon dioxide in the trailer. If the reading was high, it suggested humans were on board. This would be moved into a secure area and opened up.

The machine in one trailer and Pete, one of the officers, complained how unreliable the high reading was. 'It's far too high,' he said.

Nevertheless, the container was moved to the inspection area. To my utter amazement when the trailer was opened 28 Afghan nationals, primarily men, were found huddled together.

Very often these clandestines were finger printed and put back on the ferry to Zeebrugge particularly if it was a second attempt. Applications for asylum takes a lot of time.

I visited Coquelles, the French side of the Channel Tunnel and met with the French Immigration authority. It was part of the cross-channel co-operation on immigration and smuggling. We had UK border officials based in France as the French had officers in places like St Pancras Railway Station to assist in the examination of passports prior to journeys being undertaken.

There were so many news reports of people jumping on the back of lorries heading for the UK. Calais was the starting point and had a top end security system with plenty of staff. But as the security increased the activity went further afield. Lorries were targeted miles away from the departure point. The use of modern technology was becoming increasingly important and at Coquelles a machine that detected heart beats deployed in the vehicle channels. This system was developed to provide a unique and virtually unbeatable method of detection. By utilising extremely sensitive geophones (seismic sensors), and digital signalling software, it was found that the beat of a human heart could be detected through the walls of a container or trailer, whether empty or laden.

Officers would move away as the machine started operating and we remained as still and quiet as a grave.

Later in 2007 my Director, Bob Skinner, retired with John Whyte replacing him. John, a very experienced civil servant, had been working at Heathrow Airport. Thankfully, my personal rewarding rapport with Bob continued with John Whyte.

In late February 2008 John was taken into hospital for a major operation which meant he would be away from his office for several months.

As his Deputy I was temporarily promoted to the Senior Civil Service Grade 1A, one of the most senior positions in Customs.

So, I took on the role of Central Region Director attending many senior management meetings at HMRC headquarters in New Kings Beam House, Upper Ground, on the South Bank. It became clear the Uniformed Customs command didn't sit well in HMRC and following discussions at Cabinet level we were transferred almost overnight to the UK Border Agency. Our staff would combine with the Immigration offices at ports and airports and although we were part of UK Border Agency. Although I knew many of the staff, having met them during previous operations, it was different now I was managing them.

Much publicity followed the merged Customs and UKBA launch, so when, at 06.30 am, colleagues at Harwich intercepted a lorry carrying 30 kilos of cocaine in the cabin of the vehicle on the first morning of the merger, the powers that be wanted as much positive publicity as possible. The location of the holdall in the driver's cab meant that he must have known it was there and that it was illegal.

Our press office immediately contacted the national and local media. At 9am I was being interviewed by radio stations as this was the very first case under the new regime and it clearly demonstrated the officers on the ground professionally went about their business despite the organisational name changes.

On the 29th August 2008 I met with Liam Byrne, a British Labour Party politician and the Immigration Minister, at East Midlands Airport. He was on an official visit to the airport to "wave the flag" for the recent political measures.

A day or two earlier a seizure of horrendous knives was carried out by one of my teams in the cargo area. These had a serrated edge and doubled as knuckle-dusters. On hearing of this the Minister was astounded that it wasn't a one-off. I explained that for many gang members that latest piece of weaponry was a badge of honour. It could be a knife, a machete, a cross-bow or a firearm. Any weapon that was currently top of the range.

Liam Byrne was photographed holding the weapons.

I did say that I hope the magazine Private Eye magazine didn't pick this image up. The headlines would have been colourful.

I was at East Midlands Airport the day of the fluid ban on the air-side of airports due to a terrorist plan to detonate a liquid explosive aboard a transatlantic flight. Using hydrogen peroxide and other ingredients the explosive material would be constructed mid-flight before detonation.

The plot was discovered by British police during an extensive surveillance operation. As a result of the plot, unprecedented security measures were initially put in place at airports.

This also affected staff who were unable to obtain milk for their tea or coffee. They were not allowed to bring in a flask or cuppa-soup for their lunch. It caused a lot of angst for the Border Force as they were subject to thorough and, on occasions, body searches.

By September John Whyte had, thankfully, recovered from his illness and had returned to his post so I slipped back into my Deputy Director, Head of Operations role.

The parcel team based at Mount Pleasant, near Kings Cross station were looking to recruit casual Admin. Assistants, the lowest grade in the Civil Service, to help with the processing of small parcels sent from abroad. One of my sons, Alistair, was keen to get into Customs and Excise and he applied for the position. He was successful and to his credit he moved to stay with a family friend in Sutton, Surrey. He had to walk about half a mile to Sutton station and catch the first train into London. He worked really hard and he was asked by a senior manager to work at the larger Coventry International Postal Hub (CIH).

Staying in digs, he quickly settled into the work and when permanent Assistant Officer (the next grade up) roles were advertised he successfully secured a post. After a couple of years, he transferred to Felixstowe on the container search team. Whist on a "weapons make safe" course he was persuaded to apply to join the Maritime Branch, cutter crew. I asked him if he was sure as he had never been on a ship or yacht and he could spend months suffering from sea sickness. He became a crew member on the larger cutters and latterly on the five crew Coast Preventive Vessels (CPVs).

I had a call from HQ in Marsham Street London to say that Lord Carlile, the Labour Government's Advisor on terrorism wanted to see our operations at Felixstowe. It appeared that he was unhappy that we did not search every container arriving in the UK and it was obvious he did not comprehend the scale of the operations at Felixstowe.

I had met Lord Carlile before who, as a barrister, had defended Robin Thomson, a man we arrested in Anglesey onboard the yacht Eloise with a large quantity of cannabis from Morocco. We talked about this case over a coffee which helped smooth my meeting with this senior and influential member of the government. To demonstrate the security systems in place at Felixstowe I insisted that to gain entry into the docks he had to show his ID. His thumb and finger prints were taken and he was issued with a visitor's permit. My colleagues were amazed I didn't pull rank and ease him through procedures without normal restrictions.

I told them, 'It's pointless him only observing the system without knowing what everyone else goes through.'

The Lord did not complain.

Kevin Sayer drove us past row upon row of Mearsk, China Shipping, MEA and P&O containers and as we watched the giant cranes lifting them from over 50 metres.

As we paused, I asked him, 'Which, out of the hundreds of containers you've driven past, you would pick out for detailed inspection bearing in mind over 3 million containers go through these docks every year?'

He didn't answer that but he did bring up the question of searches up as we drunk coffee.

'Over seven thousand containers could be on one ship,' I said. 'Once you have selected one to scan, the containers would be moved by a stevedore who would get out before the x-ray takes place. Ten minutes for each container at best. If you decided to thoroughly search all containers on one ship it would take up to 15 years based on half a day for each container.'

The fact is that it is impossible to search every container arriving at a dock as it is impossible to search every passenger arriving at an airport. (Over 80 million people travel through Heathrow each year). Lord Carlile readily accepted that intelligence, target and selection was the key to identifying suspect containers rather than a blanket search for every consignment.

In September I had my first meeting at Luton Airport with Brodie Clark, the recently appointed Director General of Border Force. He had previously been employed in the prison service and had been a well-respected governor at some of the major prisons in the UK. He was a straight-talking Glaswegian and didn't do small talk, so I had to be completely focussed.

After the initial introductions he immediately asked, 'Is there anything you want to say?'

'I've heard you are not keen on Deputy Directors,' I replied.

'What do you think?'

'You make the big decisions, Brodie. They'll come thick and fast.'

Deputy Directors can play a key part. Give you the back-up you'll need when you need it.'

Thankfully it was agreed that the role of Deputy Director stayed.

In November 2009 Brodie and his team hosted a "Recognising the Best" Border Agency staff event at The National History Museum in London. George Alagiah OBE, a British newsreader, journalist and television news presenter was there. Under the giant dinosaur an award ceremony took place for those within the Agency who excelled throughout the year.

As a relative newcomer to the department, I was not surprised none of the former Customs staff were up for an award. Director John Whyte and I kept our cynicism to ourselves.

We left the Museum and hailed a taxi, noticing a number of press cameramen waiting outside.

It might have been a good idea for the event to take place in such illustrious surroundings but newspaper reports the next day were far from kind.

The Daily Mail's headline on 23 November read-

Border Agency's £140,000 beano (on the day it was revealed that 300,000 foreigners are wrongly let into the UK)

There were probably better ways of recognising endeavour.

2009 proved to be a difficult year with an alarming low level of seizures. Most of the former Customs staff were being trained up to enable them to man the Immigration desks at Primary Control Points at airports and ferry ports where new electronic passport readers had recently been installed. These suffered teething problems. The fallout resulted in long queues, a situation heavily criticised by airlines and the airport itself.

MPs were lobbied but problems continued. Complaints filtered down to our staff.

It was obvious to us all that villains knew what was happening and were sensing the change in our systems meant less vigilance on smuggling as we put greater emphasis on immigration.

As Head of Operations, it was my task to make sure they didn't take their eye off the ball.

The gaps and timing issues continued at airports. It may have been only six seconds more per passenger but multiply that by millions and bottlenecks occur. And one bottleneck leads to another.

For many budget airlines the window to move travellers in and out was a limited one so their staff had to be there on time, processing luggage, people and paperwork as quickly as possible. At the start of school holidays, the situation worsened.

At Stansted airport I hosted a staff forum of about 20 staff from all grades which ended with a Q and A session.

One of the officers said, 'We've been told not to look for drugs and concentrate on tobacco.'

'Who told you that?' I asked.

'A Senior Director level manager. We reached our find targets of cocaine and heroin so were told to concentrate on tobacco.'

'That's completely wrong.' I said, 'Drugs threaten people's lives. You've got to be looking for them more than anything else. Forget what senior management said. Take it from me you will continue to look out for drugs as well as tobacco.'

In January 2008 my freight team of four uniformed officers at Birmingham Airport had discovered a consignment of 25 carpets from Afghanistan.

It was thought at the time that because of the troubles in the area little would be exported from Afghanistan but in fact a sizeable amount was sent abroad. Main exports were carpets and rugs followed by dried fruits and medicinal plants. The country's legitimate trading partners were Pakistan, India and Russia. We also knew that the country was a source for heroin so special attention was paid to imports.

On weighing this consignment of carpets, the team concluded that they were much heavier than they should have been. A Scenes of Crime Officer from West Midlands Police inspected the carpets and discovered that sown into the weft and the weave were packets of cocaine, a highly sophisticated concealment.

The Midlands Serious and Organised Crime Agency in Birmingham were advised of this seizure by the uniformed team. They adopted the seizure and took over the investigation. A controlled delivery was made to the Leicester area and a number of arrests made in Birmingham.

In the *DAILY MIRROR* -29 MAY 2009
"Five men face long jail sentences after attempting to smuggle heroin worth s1.5 million into Britain by hiding it in hundreds of plastic straws woven into a consignment of Afghan rugs, a judge said today.
The gang admitted their roles in the foiled plot ahead of a four-week trial at Birmingham Crown Court, which concluded today.
Three men accused of being co-conspirators were cleared by a jury today of attempting to import class A drugs.
Judge Peter Carr said the five men will be sentenced next week at a date yet to be confirmed.
Customs officers at Birmingham Airport discovered almost 37lbs (16.7kilograms) of high-grade heroin stashed inside packages of hand-made rugs on January 30 last year.
Investigators found plastic straws had been stuffed full of the drug and carefully woven into the three bales of 25 rugs flown in from Afghanistan.
The find led to an undercover operation by officials at the Serious and Organised Crime Agency (SOCA) that led to the gang.
Investigators looked on as the rugs were delivered to a business centre on the outskirts of Leicester and then abandoned in a vehicle on a Birmingham street.
They identified the gang members by careful examination of mobile phone records and the paper trail created by the international delivery.
Mohammed Faisal Dad, 24, of Leam Crescent, Solihull, admitted his role in the plot. He was accused of overseeing the operation from start to finish.
The smuggler was finally captured several months after the arrest of his conspirators when police discovered him hiding in the false base of a divan bed.
Other gang members were Asif Khan, 23, of Evelyn Road, Sparkhill, Soyab Hansdot, 22, of Quorn Road, Leicester, and Ishmael Makda, 27, of Horston Road, Leicester.
All of the men admitted conspiracy to contravene the Customs and Excise Management Act."
 The case itself was featured on the BBC programme Crimewatch Case Re-Construction and I went along to the studio in London. They filmed me giving the Border Force side of the operation. I also saw this as an opportunity to praise the team at Birmingham airport who had identified and intercepted the carpets.

I arrived at the BBC Television Centre in Shepherd's Bush and taken through to the studio. It was very much open plan and whenever I watch the news on BBC and see the people in the background I think of this visit. The setup was very professional with police officers manning the desks and answering live telephone calls. Afterwards I had a drink with presenter, Rav Wilding who, being an ex-policeman, still had an enthusiastic appetite for crime related matters and was keen to know much more of the work that I and my department carried out.

In my few seconds of fame, I met Kirsty Young and Matthew Amroliwala.

In February 2010 a decision had been made to transfer all the HMRC investigators, dealing with non-tax investigations to UK Border Agency with a new command known as the Criminal and Financial Investigation. They were looking to appoint a Deputy Director, Head of Criminal and Financial Investigation for UK Border Agency. The position was advertised within the Home Office and much to my relief the post required the key skills and experience I had acquired throughout my career. It was an opportunity to return to Investigation and I relished the challenge.

Before I was called for an interview, I did my homework and read up a lot on the Border Force and wider Home Office activities. I didn't take anything for granted.

The interview panel consisted of the Head of Heathrow Airport, Philip Astle and Mark Fuchter, who was a former investigator in Customs and Excise. I was quietly confident on getting the post. The next day I received a call from Brodie Clark's office telling me I was successful with my application.

My new investigation teams were based primarily at ports and airports, with the Specialist Teams based in an Immigration office south of London Bridge. An agreement was in place that all seizures had to be offered to the Serious Organised Crime Agency but if rebuffed, it was our task to take the case on and identify the main players and prosecute them.

I had three Assistant Directors, Pete Avery, stationed at Staines, near Heathrow, who covered airports, Malcom Bragg was based in Dover. Malcom had been a drug Liaison Officer in Pakistan and Jamaica, covering maritime matters. Dave Fairclough headed our specialist teams that carried out covert activity such as the deployment of undercover officers and intercepts of communications, particularly in prisons.

Dave Pennant, a former Met and Surrey police officer, was the Agency's Head of Crime and managed the Immigration teams and was my immediate line manager.

Although under the spotlight from the Home Office Dave didn't interfere with the day to day running of my command. Immigration was Dave's priority but, as a police officer, he was very interested in drug trafficking. He was a clear-thinking man who understood investigation and we worked well together.

An initiative was to see how far we could exploit the drug seizures at the International Postal Hub in Coventry. Multi-kilo commercial quantities of drugs were regularly detected by uniform staff. If SOCA didn't adopt the case, we set about planning controlled deliveries, often dressed as postal workers going about their daily job. The parcels contained light sensitive alarms that alerted us when the parcels were opened. This provided us with proof of "guilty knowledge" and the recipient would be arrested.

When this "subterfuge" was mentioned at one of the monthly Home Office meetings someone said, 'What a great idea.'

I didn't have the heart to tell them we had a post parcel investigation team in Customs in the 70s that did exactly what we were doing nearly forty years later.

In April 2009 Rhino horns were intercepted at Manchester Airport on their way to China. The two horns were disguised as sculpture of a bird sitting on a log. Underneath the log camouflage was horn itself.

The Wildlife Crime team in Manchester who conducted DNA tests on the horn and discovered they were from a white Rhino called Simba that had died months before at Colchester Zoo.

The Rhino had died of natural causes and the body removed for disposal. The slaughter man in cahoots with an antiques dealer decided to cut off the horns and arranged the exportation.

It was estimated the horns were worth £60000 per kilo.

There was a BBC report 5th October 2010 -

"An antiques dealer who tried to smuggle rhino horns out of Manchester Airport has been jailed for 12 months.

Donald Allison, of Lancashire, hid the two horns in a sculpture as he tried to board a flight to China.

They were destined for the lucrative Chinese medicine market to be sold in powder form. Allison, 62, was sentenced at Manchester Crown Court.

Airport-based UK Border Agency (UKBA) officers foiled the plan on 30 June 2009 after intelligence reports suggested a plot to smuggle white rhino horns on to a flight from Manchester Airport to China via Amsterdam.

The two horns were discovered concealed in Allison's luggage.

Essex Police's Wildlife Crime Unit established that the rhino's entire head was stolen and sold for £400 after its body was sent to an abattoir for disposal."

It appeared to us that they were not career criminals but took a mercenary advantage of a tragic if slack procedure.

In July 2009 UK Border Force uniformed and Police Special Branch Officers were called to Mona Airfield in Anglesey, North Wales. It was a mile-long asphalt airstrip owned by the Ministry of Defence and used by the RAF and small aircraft.

A light aircraft had landed with a holdall carrying 14 kilos of cocaine. The pilot and a person standing near the light aircraft were arrested.

The aircraft had flown from Le Touquet, a small seaside town in northern France, had been tracked by French Customs who advised Jean Michell Manzoni, a senior Customs Attache, based at the French Embassy in London, who informed us of the aircraft's movements.

The unusual route, over England into Wales, had been chosen as they thought it unlikely to be suspect as it was on the western side of the UK, over two hundred miles from the near continent. Smugglers tend to take the shortest possible route if they are carrying drugs.

Crime Teams based in Manchester took on the investigation and arrested a pub landlord who was thought to be behind the importation and the person who arranged the shipment in France. He was been convicted of conspiring to smuggle cocaine worth £3.5m into the UK in a light aircraft.

Manchester Evening News 21st April 2011-
"The 14kg of the drug were smuggled into Mona airfield on Anglesey, north Wales, from Le Touquet, in northern France, in July 2009 in a private plane owned by David Watson, 54, from Prestwich.

Watson was found guilty of conspiring to smuggle class A drugs following a seven-week trial at Liverpool Crown Court.

The court heard that Watson conspired with others to smuggle the drug cache into the country by using his single-engine four-seater plane.

Co-accused Paul Roche, 55, from Prestwich, David Lloyd, 65, from Anglesey, and Richard McArthur, 45, from Carrickfergus, Northern Ireland, were all found not guilty of related charges.

The trial heard that the drugs were picked up in France by former soldier Mathew Lockwood, 29, from Prestwich, who pleaded guilty to conspiracy to smuggle class A drugs at an earlier hearing.

Michael Taylor, prosecuting, told the trial that when the smuggling took place Watson was in the US but that he 'was in control of the operation. When the plane touched down in France, Lockwood went to pick up the drugs from McArthur, the court heard.

However, the jury accepted that McArthur did not know the package contained cocaine.

David Watson got 20 years, his son, Andrew got 12, Richard McArthur got 6 years and Lockwood 6 years. Michael had pleaded guilty at a previous court hearing and was sentenced to 16 years."

It was a bonus for the Force. Picking up a light (four-seater Diamond)) aircraft that flew in unannounced was nigh on impossible and it did send a message to others contemplating this type of crime will be identified and detected.

I was asked to go to Liverpool airport where the seized light aircraft was stored. National TV and local press wanted to interview me regarding the detection and court result. I took one of the official vehicles and drove over five hours to Liverpool, did the press coverage and had a five- hour drive back home. My mind was still in motorway driving mode for a couple of hours when I got back home but a glass of Talisker whisky soon settled me down and my humour fully returned when the phone rang.

'I saw your dad on television last night.' joked Nick Baker.
We laughed about the lack of any make-up department when I do live interviews. I even suggested they could have supplied me with a wig.

In August 2010 reels of graphic paedophile film were found in a package at Coventry postal hub. These included, bestiality material.
 Details of the seizure was passed to the Child Protection Team that covered west London and a joint operation was instigated.
 The reels were addressed to Joseph Faul, a 48-year-old living in Beauliegh Place, Chiswick, in West London. Officers from my team arrested Faul and they were horrified when a vast amount of additional paedophile media was discovered stored in his flat. Electronic devices used to make copies of films and videos was also seized. A seven-ton lorry was needed to transport all the material and equipment away for examination.
 At the trial in 2012 Faul admitted 19 different charges including extreme paedophile and pornographic material.
 At Isleworth Crown Court he was sentenced to 12 months in prison and place on the Sex Offenders Register for 2 years.
 There were thoughts that Faul should be locked up and the key thrown away but he was given credit for pleading guilty and sparing a jury the traumatic experience of viewing the material he peddled.
 Using the money laundering "Proceeds of Crime Act," large seizures of cash, often running in to tens of thousands of pounds were uncovered at airports. If evidence of a link to criminality was found the money would be detained and taken through the courts. Fifty percent of cash seized through the courts would be returned to law enforcement to help fund money laundering investigations. Seized vehicles, jewellery and other trappings of crime could also be confiscated through the courts. The TV programme, "Ill Gotten Gains" often featured such cases.
 At Heathrow Airport, a Russian lady, heading for Moscow, was found to be carrying over nine hundred thousand euros. The money was seized and the Russian police were contacted via Interpol to ask them to identify the lady and if, as we suspected, was part of a money laundering scheme. Most of us travel with some cash but not 900,000 Euros.
 Eventually it was established that the money was destined for a construction project in Russia. Unfortunately, after discussions with the Crown Prosecution Service, we were told we would have to give back the cash, plus interest. This, like a few other similar cases, caused dismay among the officers. The phrase, "some you win and some you lose" never helped.
 Transactions in cash is the norm in most African countries and China. It is not an offence in the UK or indeed in Europe, to be in possession of large amounts of cash including when travelling on a plane. The passenger just has to provide paperwork proving the money has come from a legitimate source.

I received a phone call from SOCA in relation to a person flying from Zurich to Heathrow. It was known that this person was carrying three million US Dollars in cash.

'What's the background?' I asked.

'It's ransom money for a ship and its crew by Somali pirates.'

The person was observed landing at Heathrow, and was due to be driven to Luton Airport to board a private light aircraft heading for Djibouti in East Africa where he would hand over the cash to the Somali pirates.

This caused a few rumbles as the UK Government did not want to be seen to be playing any part in paying off ransom demands.

The pirates were thought to have close ties to terrorist groups but someone in authority decided to turn a blind eye to the matter. As the lead for Border Agency frontier crime, I had to give permission for the movement of this cash through UK borders.

Pete Avery had warned uniformed Customs staff at Heathrow and sent instructions that the courier was not to be stopped and searched.

The Director of Heathrow called me expressing his concern.

'The courier,' he said, 'looks nervous and twitchy when he arrived at Heathrow. I think we should seize the money as proceeds of crime.'

'You can't do that,' I said. 'He's got 3 million on him. He's got to be driven to Luton to fly to the horn of Africa and hand it over to ruthless Somali pirates. I'd be nervous, wouldn't you?'

'I'm not happy as this would be a major cash seizure for us and be good for our crime statistics.'

'I understand your concerns but I have to disagree. Serious Crime have agreed this cash transfer and if you seize the money the 14 crew members will be executed by the pirates.'

There was a deathly silence until he agreed he would not impede the courier's movements.

Sometime later I read that the ship and its crew had been released.

In April 2011 officers at Heathrow Airport arrested a Nigerian passenger who had travelled Business Class from Holland. Adegboyega Adeniji was a 48-year-old business man from Hemel Hempstead in Hertfordshire. In his suitcase officers discovered 31 kilos of cocaine, 5 kilos of heroin and 2 kilos of methamphetamine.

The case was offered to SOCA. They said no so Pete Avery's team at Heathrow investigated.

A search warrant was granted for the suspect's million-pound flat. In the bedrooms they found 23 suitcases and cash.

The drugs seized at Heathrow had a street value of £4 million. We estimated he had smuggled hundreds of kilos of class A drugs.

He always travelled business class carrying an array of documents on negotiations being carried out on oil fields and drilling operations in West Africa. His cover was very good. He looked like a genuine and successful businessman.

The suitcases in his flat contained traces of drugs. Airlines supplied details of his previous bookings. He travelled many times in a two-year period.

In March 2012 it went to trial at Isleworth Crown Court where he pleaded guilty to the one importation of drugs but pleaded innocent on all other accusations of conspiracy to import Class A drugs on previous flights. The jury found him guilty and he was sentenced to thirty years in prison, one of the longest prison terms ever given out.

Under the Proceeds of Crime Act a million pounds of assets were frozen including a house in Hemel Hempstead. There was a large amount of cash and also a property in Nigeria was discovered. The Nigerian security forces investigated money laundering offences.

The trial and sentencing attracted a lot of press attention.

The Home Office released a statement and I was quoted.

"Deputy Director Jim Jarvie, from the UK Border Agency's Criminal and Financial Investigation team, said: 'Adeniji was clearly a significant figure at the centre of an extensive criminal network. He was involved in the importation and distribution of class A drugs on a grand scale. Although the true amount of drugs he smuggled into the UK will never be known, it is probably safe to assume he has been responsible for the importation of tens - if not hundreds - of millions of pounds worth."

I went to the BBC in Millbank to answer questions on the case. I had great satisfaction talking about the professionalism of the investigators, the success of the court case and the 30-year prison sentence.

Behind me was a panoramic view that took in the Houses of Parliament. I didn't take this on board until Pete Avery sent me a message, 'Jim, please move. I can't see the time on Big Ben.'

At the beginning of 2012 I realised I was entering my last year heading for retirement after almost 40 years.

I did receive pressure to stay from my team members but after some soul-searching conversations with Pauline I decided to name my leaving date as my 60th birthday in November. I had no wish to be seen as an "old" investigator among the many young blades being sharpened with ultra- modern, technological based methods of operating. It would also leave a gap and a salary for one to progress as I did over 4 decades.

In the past I had discussions with colleagues about retirement believing it best not to leave at the last possible moment but to wind down over a few months.

I cannot say I took my own advice. There was too much going on.

The London Olympics was to take place 27 July- 12 August 2012. As a Senior Manager I was called in to various planning meetings to discuss how the UK could facilitate travel of participants and spectators from across the globe.

Tony Smith, a former Director of Border Force, Southern Region was appointed the Border Agency's lead for the Olympics.

The Government wanted the "border experience" for visitors to be as smooth as possible with little fuss and delay and no adverse publicity. All staff, including me, were trained or retrained to process passports.

I received my tutoring from the Immigration training teams based in Folkestone.

The Home Office then decided it would be a good flag waving exercise for staff manning the immigration desks to see senior managers taking on the role. I was asked to spend time on the actual passport desks so in April I went to Stanstead Airport.

Arriving at 6.30 for a 7am start on the immigration desk to process passports. To my horror the first queue of passengers contained a group of young men returning from a stag do in Prague. Bleary eyed, hungover they presented their passports all damp from a foam party the night before. I took hold of the first soaking passport and to my amazement it was successfully read by the passport scanner.

Passports are read by an E-reader that reads data off a biometric chip in the passport. The "reading" of the data takes 6 seconds. In that time, you have to compare the passport's image with the person standing in front of you.

If a person was of interest to any law enforcement agency or security services (Special Branch or MI5) a warning alert would come up on the computer screen.

Some countries such as Italy were allowed to travel on an Identity Card.

These cards, issued by the local town hall, cost 5 euros. There is a photo with a signature but there is no data. The officers then have to physically enter the passenger's details taking at least 60 seconds. As a result, queues ensued and quite rightly travellers who had paid £80 for a biometric passport were a bit miffed when they had to wait for up to an hour.

The first card presented to me looked badly printed so I asked for help from one of the experienced immigration officers who were watching over my shoulder.

'They're all like that,' he said.

On my third day a passenger in a full burka appeared at my desk. There was a photo in the passport but I couldn't see her face. I began to sweat until an experienced female officer took the passport from me and escorted the woman into a side office for identification.

As I commuted into Liverpool Street over a two- year period I watched the Olympic Park grow. The site covered parts of East London previously a mixture of greenfield and brownfield land and was transformed into a magnificent sporting complex. This extraordinary achievement was matched only by the Games themselves

In April 2012 a seizure was made from an Ethiopian passenger who was stopped in the "Nothing to Declare" channel at Heathrow Airport. She was to spend two days in London before flying to Washington. In her three suitcases she had 56 kilos of herbal cannabis. It turned out she was an Ethiopian diplomat accredited to Washington but not to the UK. Dealing with diplomats is another game altogether. Diplomatic immunity could be a whole minefield and we had to notify the Foreign and Commonwealth Office immediately.

Amelework Wondemagegne was arrested and questioned. After 2 hours Pete rang me to say he had heard from the UK Foreign Office asking what our intentions were. I rang the FO and spoke to a high ranking female official.

'We are concerned,' she said. 'You should be letting her go'.

'It seems,' I said, 'that she doesn't have diplomatic immunity in the UK.'

'Nevertheless, she is a diplomat. It will cause major ructions if she is charged and goes to court.'

I still thought I should stand my ground. 'She committed an offence at Customs Control and she was about to take drugs into the heart of the capital. She said she didn't know what was in the suitcase as she was carrying it for someone else. A common practice, she says, at Addis Ababa Bole International Airport.'

The FO official persisted. 'My recommendation is that you let her go'.

'That is not our position,' I said. 'She has blatantly broken UK laws and will face prosecution. I can only reconsider this if ordered by Theresa May, the Home Secretary.'

No order was forthcoming.

At her trial in August 2012 Amelework Wondemagegne defence was that she was entitled to diplomatic immunity. She should never have been arrested or charged. She was a mother of two and her family needed her with them.

The jury didn't accept her argument and found her guilty. She received a sentence of 33 months in prison.

In a report of *The Evening Standard* 2nd August 2012 –

"An Ethiopian embassy official who attempted to claim diplomatic immunity after trying to smuggle cannabis into the UK has been jailed. Mother-of-two Amelework Wondemagegne, a diplomat based in Washington DC, was stopped at Heathrow Airport carrying three suitcases containing 56 kilograms (123lb) of herbal cannabis with a street value of £160,000, Isleworth Crown Court in west London was told.

The 36-year-old initially said a man had given her the bags before she departed from Addis Ababa airport, and she then tried to claim diplomatic immunity.

But the court found she was not entitled to it and she was jailed for 33 months after admitting one count of drugs smuggling today.

Judge Richard McGregor-Johnson, the Recorder of Kensington and Chelsea, told her: "The fact that you smuggled these drugs in the expectation that you would not be prosecuted if you were caught because of your diplomatic status is a significant factor in this case."

The diplomat, who had worked in the visa section of the embassy since 2006, travelled into the UK on April 7 using an Ethiopian diplomatic passport and had a ticket to return to the US on April 17.

When her suitcases were opened by UK Border Agency officers at Heathrow's Terminal Three, they were found to be full of slabs of cannabis that had been sprinkled with chilli powder.

Wondemagegne had claimed she did not know what was in the suitcases, but that she believed it was meat and spices.

But photographs taken on her camera showed her with the bags. One depicted her wearing a necklace which was later found to be in a suitcase with the drugs.

Judge McGregor-Johnson said Wondemagegne had told "a pack of lies" and that she was caught with a "substantial quantity" of cannabis, in the second category of seriousness.

The judge described her as being "worldly wise", adding: "You knew perfectly well what you were doing and you knew perfectly well that drugs smuggling is illegally and seriously regarded."

Wondemagegne's two children, aged 10 and 17, live in Washington DC and are being cared for by Ethiopian Embassy staff there.

She has been their sole carer since her husband died of cancer in 2005.

Judge McGregor-Johnson said of that fact: "It makes it more extraordinary you should have committed this offence."

He told the court he was satisfied she had not been coerced into being a drugs courier and that she had played a "significant role" in the smuggling of the cannabis.

Wondemagegne, of Silver Spring, Maryland, will be deported from the UK after serving her sentence.

Peter Avery, of Border Force, said: "This was a significant amount of cannabis which could have ended up on the streets of the UK.

"It was the vigilance of Border Force officers which prevented this smuggling attempt from going ahead.

"Working with our law enforcement colleagues in the UK and around the world we are determined to do all we can to stop the international drugs trade. Wondemagegne was carrying so much cannabis that she had paid about £300 in excess baggage charges before boarding her flight to the UK.

She had a total of five suitcases with her, three of which contained the tape-wrapped packages."

The Serious Crime Agency had fallen into the trap of concentrating on known criminals referred to as "Core Nominals". My team was always on the lookout for "Clean Skins", criminal organisations we didn't know about and hadn't appeared on any law enforcement case notes.

We strongly believed that seizures at the border was the first step – from there a case can be progressed and unknown villains identified. Suppliers can be found, transporting, paperwork, couriers, receivers and distributors.

My specialist team led by Dave Fairclough was called upon by the "Immigration" to help on a major operation in St Leonards, near Hastings where Alex Brown, a local vicar, had officiated at over 400 weddings in 3 years whereas in the previous 2 years only 13 weddings took place.

His congregation averaged 15. The vicar was asked about these excessive numbers of people tying the knot.

Brown's response was that nothing unusual was taking place and that all the couples had fulfilled the church's requirements.

He admitted that most were people from outside Europe had married an EU citizen.

We were convinced they were sham marriages. The bride and groom had probably never met, didn't even speak the same language.

It was thought that few understood the vicar's words but had been schooled to utter an "I do" at the right time.

This ceremony didn't give the lawful status to stay in the UK or the EU which was the only purpose of this charade.

When they were raided in 2009. A Ukrainian, Vladimer Euchak and Michael Adelasoy, a Nigerian solicitor were arrested with the vicar.

At Lewes Crown Court July 2010 they were found guilty and all received a four-year sentence.

I did wonder how a rural vicar would cope behind bars.

On the 6th September the BBC reported the story –

"Sussex vicar Alex Brown jailed for sham marriages.

A vicar has been jailed for four years for carrying out hundreds of fake marriages to bypass immigration law.

The Reverend Alex Brown conducted 360 sham marriages during a four-year period at the Church of St Peter and St Paul in St Leonards, East Sussex.

Co-defendants Vladimir Buchak, 33, and solicitor and pastor Michael Adelasoye, 50, were also jailed for four years.

The Crown Prosecution Service said it was thought to be the largest sham marriage case yet brought to court.

The trio were found guilty at Lewes Crown Court in July of conspiring to facilitate the commission of breaches of immigration laws.

Judge Richard Hayward also handed Brown a five-month sentence for solemnizing a marriage without the banns being published.

The two sentences will run concurrently.

The court heard Brown presided over the marriages of hundreds of mainly African men to Eastern European women at his small parish church.

Buchak, of Anglesea Terrace, St Leonards, was responsible for paying women up to £3,000 to take part in marriages of convenience.

Adelasoye, of St Matthews Drive, St Leonards, used his knowledge of the law to help illegal immigrants with applications to the Home Office.

Earnings for the church rocketed from £1,000 before the hundreds of marriages occurred, to around £22,000 for the first six months of 2009.

The men had usually arrived lawfully in the UK but had exhausted the appeals process in applying to stay permanently.

Investigators from the UK Border Agency said Brown, Buchak and Adelasoye were "happy to exploit and take advantage of other people's desperation for their own ends".

During the trial, Brown insisted he only ever married couples he was sure were getting married for the right reasons.

"Without you this conspiracy would never have been able to come into effect," said Judge Richard Hayward.

The Prosecutors said Buchak was the principal organiser, Brown must have been aware that the majority of the weddings he was conducting were shams.

Throughout the trial Brown denied being manipulated or controlled by anybody or being involved in the scam for financial gain.

Buchak, a Ukrainian national, had been living illegally in the UK since 2004.

He was responsible for "cajoling and persuading" the Eastern Europeans into the marriages of convenience.

Documents found by investigators had been altered to show that most of the hundreds of people he had married appeared to live in the streets surrounding the parish with several brides and groom registered in the same property.

The Judge said, 'The couples involved beat a path to St Peter's because they all knew and you knew what was going on, and you were happy to play your part."

Outside the court, the Bishop of Lewes, Wallace Benn, said a review was being conducted into procedures within the diocese.'

Bogus Colleges were also of concern to Tony's team. We were surprised that anyone could set up a "college" or a language school. They offered fake degree certificates or misused the word 'university' which is a protected term under the 2006 Companies Act.

Advertisements were placed overseas to attract fee paying students keen to obtain a "degree".

A report said – "At their worst, these colleges offer degrees in return for nothing more than payment. Some expect students to go through the motions of submitting a minor amount of written work by post, but for the most part, essays are optional.

The motives of the students vary. Some believe that putting BA or MA after their name will help them find work or gain promotion. Others delude themselves that they are dealing with a genuine university that recognises their worth and has decided to award them the degree that they missed out on when they were young.

And for many from Third World countries, getting a letter of acceptance from a college that is really nothing more than a spare room over a corner shop is their ticket to acquiring a UK visa."

The adage "You should go out on a high" proved to be the case for me. Pauline and I were on holiday in Fuengirola, Spain.

Although it infuriated Pauline, I never turned my official phone off throughout the night and always took it on holiday.

One morning stretched out on a sunbed it rang. It was Malcom Bragg, my Assistant Director in Dover.

I walked to a remote part of the beach in case details were overheard.

'I've had a phone call from Jean- Michel Manzoni, the Customs attache based in the French Embassy in London,' said Malcom. 'A 65ft cabin cruiser is being transported on a cargo vessel, the Snoekgracht.

It had been in the Caribbean and a French Customs drugs dog based out there had gone crazy near one of the cabin cruisers called, The Louise'.

'What did French Customs do?' I asked.

'Nothing but the suspect cruiser vessel is destined for Southampton.'

For the rest of my holiday Malcom updated me with the progress of the ship.

The Snoekgracht had left Venezuela three months earlier and arrived in the UK early in July 2011. The cruiser, The Louise, was off-loaded ashore by a crane in the port of Southampton.

A specialist deep rummage search team was brought in to examine the luxury cabin cruiser.

The interior was immaculate and gleaming, not something you can approach with a sledge hammer or chain saw.

We also wanted to pick up forensic details, fingerprints, DNA. So, the search was done very methodically.

It took the officers six days to find the 1.2 tons of cocaine, cleverly hidden under the diving board at the stern of the vessel, access to which was through the engine room behind a false bulkhead.

When we seized the ship, we had no evidence so could not arrest the three crew members who had flown to Holland before the drugs were discovered.

The Dutch police asked for an urgent meeting in Southampton. A Dutch Prosecutor Gert Rip and Serious Crime attended the meeting. Although we continued to have the lead on the operation, we needed SOCA's help with surveillance and telephone interception if required.

I chaired the meeting which didn't start well. Without invitation Gert Rip the Prosecutor set out his demands as to how the case should proceed.

I let him finish before I spoke. 'Let me put my cards on the table. You will not dictate the operation. It is in UK territory and being so it is our case to progress.'

He knew that if the cruiser had arrived and departed from Southampton it would have headed straight for Holland. All of UK law enforcement would have been kept out of the loop.

'You had no intention of informing us,' I added. 'You were not going to cooperate with us. This is not how law enforcement agencies work together.'

Eventually, after he saw just how steadfast I was, he admitted that we were going to be kept in the dark.

'Okay,' I replied. 'We now have a job to do. All parties here will cooperate to find out who is behind this importation.'

The Dutch required time to investigate the Dutch connection having got details of the crew.

I resisted Brodie Clarke, the Director's suggestion, that we publicised the largest seizure of cocaine and recognised it would be a real positive media story for the Border Agency.

'We need to bide our time,' I said. 'We've got to give the Dutch space enough to track down the real villains. There will be ample opportunity to relish the success of the operation. You'll have to trust me on this.'

Ten days after we found drugs the skipper of the crew came back to Southampton to meet up with the port officials, one of whom was one of my undercover officers who had been in the role since the drugs were discovered.

The skipper wanted to sail the boat away immediately so various excuses were made. There were inconsistencies in the cruiser's Sea Worthy certificate as a number of holes had been drilled into the boat when being searched so we had some legitimate reasons to delay the cabin cruiser sailing to Zeebrugge in Belgium. This gave the Dutch police sufficient time to identify the principals and financiers behind the operation.

What we didn't expect was the delay would go on for two months which put pressure on our resources who were deployed in Southampton. I was also under pressure from Brodie's office to notify the press. Thankfully, again he trusted my judgement and called his press office 'hounds' off.

As the weeks went by the owner of The Louise threatened UKBA and me personally with legal action in the Hight Court suggesting we did not have grounds to further delay the cruiser.

Thankfully the Dutch had gathered enough evidence on the principle players including the money man behind it all.

Arrests were coordinated in Holland and Belgium so we could go public with the case.

Our press office went full steam ahead.

BBC News Report 22nd June 2012 –

"Gang behind Southampton £300m cocaine seizure jailed"

"UK border force officers found the drugs in a specially-built compartment. When the 65ft luxury motor yacht the Louise arrived in Southampton it had enough cocaine hidden on board to sustain a third of the annual UK market.

The gang behind the plot aimed to flood Europe with up to £300m of the Class A drug, the equivalent of about seven million street deals.

But the conspiracy was smashed after authorities, who had received a tip-off, intercepted gang members' telephone conversations with a wiretap and tracked the pleasure cruiser from the Caribbean to the UK.

Border force officers discovered one tonne of 90% pure cocaine, one of their biggest ever seizures, hidden in a deep compartment, during an almost week-long search of the yacht.

The haul accounted for almost half of the total cocaine seizures across the whole of the UK in 2010/11, which was 2.4 tonnes.

When the smugglers were arrested in a series of police raids across the Netherlands, officers recovered a loaded machine-gun, a handgun with silencer and 1.5m euros.

French authorities were first alerted that a shipment of cocaine had been loaded on to the Louise in May last year.

The Louise was tracked from the Caribbean to Southampton, where it arrived later that month, after being transported the British Virgin Islands on board a specially designed Dutch-registered ship, Snoekgracht, owned by Seven Stars Yacht Transport along with 30 others. It was coming to Europe to be refitted.

Border force officers, who spent six days searching the yacht with sniffer dogs, eventually discovered the cocaine bagged up in a deep compartment, specially designed for smuggling, beneath the diving platform.

Drugs being smuggled out of the Caribbean and South America on boats are usually hidden among tropical fruit, the border force said.

At the time of the discovery Brodie Clark, then head of the UK Border Agency, described the hiding place as "ingenious".

The cocaine, destined for the Netherlands, via England, was packed inside the boat while it was in Venezuela.

The haul was estimated to be worth about £50m wholesale and up to £300m on the streets.

The Dutch police tracked the gang to the Netherlands, which led to the Dutch defendants - referred to in court only as Klaas Lima, Mohamed Z and Robert Lima- being charged.

Klaas Lima, 61, owner of the Louise, and Mohamed Z, who handled all of the plot's finances, both headed up the gang, Dutch prosecutors confirmed. Both have former criminal convictions, but not for drug smuggling.

Klaas L, from the northeast of the Netherlands, was arrested, along with his son Robert L, 33, from the south of the country, following police raids.

When officers arrested Mohamed Z at his home in Amsterdam, they found 1.5m euros (£1.2m) and a loaded machine-gun. Two Harley Davidson motorcycles, a second firearm and a silencer were also seized. The gang had been waiting in the Netherlands for the drugs shipment to arrive."

It turned out to be a very good publicity for the Border Agency, the newly formed National Crime Agency and the Dutch police.

The Immigration Minister Damian Green said: "This was a significant drugs seizure which was made possible by the co-operation of our international partners. UK Border Agency staff have shown vigilance, dedication and determination to uncover this shipment."

As there were no UK citizens involved, the case went to the Dutch Courts. Their prison sentences ranged from 5 to 11 years.

The three crewman who had come to the UK to collect the Cruiser had no knowledge of the drugs aboard so were not charged.

By UK standards the sentencing was painfully lenient.

Although the lauded success was based on the amount of drugs seized it didn't result in a major gang being "smashed" in the UK so my "blaze of glory" before retirement was a little bit of a damp squib.

The cruiser, The Louise, was eventually sold at auction for £176,000 which was deposited into the government's coffers

A few weeks later Brodie, and Carol Upshall (Director South) and Graeme Kyle from Brodie's office were suspended for allegedly not ensuring the Governments dictum that all incoming passengers had their passports examined. School and pensioners bus trips were quite rightly not deemed a risk and as such were not given the 100% passport scrutiny as other passengers arriving in the UK.

In November Brodie resigned. I for one thought his treatment diabolical. He was a dedicated professional Civil Servant who deserved better. I was pleased to see sometime later he received a significant amount of compensation.

I was to retire on my 60th birthday November 2012 and I couldn't believe where the forty years of my career had gone.

In June of that yea,r I received a letter headed Buckingham Palace. I had been awarded an OBE in the Queen's Birthday Honours. I was delighted and proud. It was a secret that Pauline and I kept to ourselves. I did want to tell my mum who had been diagnosed with terminal cancer. Before her death in August I did tell her. Her smile overcame the ordeal she was going through.

As the leaving date got close, I tried to visit all the investigation offices throughout the UK to say my goodbyes to the staff who had done me so proud.

Suzanne Philpott and her support team organised my retirement party and Euan Stewart, my friend and former boss, was able to secure the Custom House in London for the event. I couldn't invite as many people as I wanted to as HMRC had put restrictions as to the number of people who could attend.

On the day two hundred former and serving colleagues arrived. Dave Fairclough and Pete Avery performed a skit about me and in particular how I got my nickname, "Trapper". David Wood, Head of Enforcement, made a speech and I was deeply touched when Terry Byrne and Nick Baker spoke about my early career when we all had experienced so much.

Pauline and my sons had travelled on the train from Suffolk and my dad and brother came down from Lincolnshire. This was on a Thursday, the day before I left for good,

The Friday, my birthday, I spent the morning organising a controlled delivery of drugs -so much for winding down gradually.

At 4pm I handed in my warrant card, my ID card and my Blackberry phone to Dave Fairclough and Susanne Philpott and walked across from Dave's office across London Bridge to Liverpool Street station to catch the train home. I glanced over to the Custom House as I crossed the bridge and the memories flooded in, right back to January 17th 1977, with a much-valued job title of Delta 8. Meeting my new bosses, Roy Brisley and Nick Baker and being locked in the back of a blue, unmarked, security van.

I had just said goodbye to 40 years career with an irreplaceable string of truly wonderful memories. I had now denuded myself of official validation. It was over and it felt very strange.

The personal phone I had just bought from Tesco rang.

It was Dave. 'Jim, are you okay?'

'I don't know'.

Over the next few days at home, I kept checking my phone convinced that the absence of calls was down to a technical malfunction.

There were no "updates" for there was nothing to update. The grey damp weather of November brightened when Pauline retired only a week later.

Our village hall held a charity Burns Night the next year and Rod, a bagpiper, played as guests arrived and piped the haggis in. My uncle Bobby was a great piper and had played at our wedding.

'I wish I had learned to play the pipes when I was younger' I confided in Rod.

'You are never too old to learn and I will give you lessons', he replied.

That conversation with him led Pauline buy me a practice chanter, a double-reed woodwind instrument.

Rod gave me a few lessons and after several few months I could play, "A Man's a Man, For All That." on the bagpipes. Surprisingly, with booming notes bouncing off our walls, I kept it from my neighbours and friends and when I piped in the haggis at our Burn's Night the following year, they could not believe it was me playing.

I count myself incredibly lucky to have worked for forty years with so many professional, dedicated and brave colleagues. I have experienced excitement, fear and fun with such great people and despite the sacrifices I made to my family life do not regret a day of it. Not many people can say that.

"Fair fa' your honest, sonsie face, Great chieftain o the puddin'-race! Aboon them a' ye tak your place……….."

Printed in Great Britain
by Amazon